Language
into Language

# Language into Language

## Cultural, Legal and Linguistic Issues for Interpreters and Translators

SAÚL SIBIRSKY *and*
MARTIN C. TAYLOR

McFarland & Company, Inc., Publishers
*Jefferson, North Carolina, and London*

Library of Congress Cataloguing-in-Publication Data

Sibirsky, Saúl, 1933–
Language into language : cultural, legal and linguistic
issues for interpreters and translators / Saúl Sibirsky and Martin C. Taylor.
p.    cm.
Includes bibliographical references and index.

ISBN 978-0-7864-4811-1
softcover: 50# alkaline paper ∞

1.  Translating and interpreting.    2.  Court interpreting and translating.
I.  Taylor, Martin C., 1932–    II.  Title.
P306.2.S66    2010
418'.02 — dc22        2010006955

British Library cataloguing data are available

Cover image ©2010 Shutterstock

Manufactured in the United States of America

*McFarland & Company, Inc., Publishers
Box 611, Jefferson, North Carolina 28640
www.mcfarlandpub.com*

The encouragement and support
of Anita and of loving sons
Stefan Sibirsky and Daniel Sibirsky
made this work possible

———————————

Martin C. Taylor expresses his appreciation to
his wife Beth for her care and perseverance;
to his son Edward, skilled in languages;
and to his parents and to all parents
who give children the gift of tongues

# Acknowledgments

The coauthors express their deepest appreciation singly and jointly to the relatives, friends, colleagues, authors, and personnel of institutions who have taken the time, energy, and interest to provide information and advice to make this work possible. Those consulted have been indispensable. They imprinted their ideas on our consciousness. We hope to have transformed their comments into clear and informed prose. Any discrepancies or errors that may arise from understanding and transcribing those ideas fall on the shoulders of the coauthors.

Appreciation goes out to Susan Madeo and Peggy Noonan of the Westport, Connecticut, Public Library, and in Broward County, Florida, to the personnel of the Southwest Regional Library and the W. C. Young Library. The staffs provided unfailing assistance in obtaining materials from interlibrary loan, in encouraging progress, and in making stylistic and substantive recommendations.

Innumerable judges, attorneys, court reporters, doctors, and social service agency personnel appear in profile in this manuscript. They are the anonymous muses in our quest for inspiration.

Thanks extend to the interpreters and translators who provided guidance and offered suggestions. We cite those who, in person, by phone, and by e-mail, lent support and information: Attorney/interpreter A. Samuel Adelo, Santa Fe, New Mexico; Russian interpreter Becky Blackley, at PTS Translations; Associate Professor Erik Camayd-Freixas, Florida International University; translator Fabio Cid, Rio de Janeiro; philosopher Thomas W. Clark, Somerville, Massachusetts; interpreter Dr. Bruce Downing, University of Minnesota; translator Steven M. Kahaner, New York; Russian interpreter Alla Kitova, Washington, DC, CEO of Bona Fide Translations, LLC; and French-English interpreter and writer Jennifer Mackintosh, England.

Two academics who reviewed the manuscript merit special appreciation. Dr. Virginia Benmaman, distinguished professor emerita of the College of Charleston, South Carolina, recommended changes that have clarified and shaped major themes. Professor Peter W. Krawutschke of Western Michigan University and former president of the American Translators Association, corrected some details, gave encouragement, and indicated the book's suitability for a college audience.

Two key figures stand out who ensured by their probity and perseverance that the work would continue. One is intellectual property attorney Frank Kubler, of Miramar, Florida, who volunteered his skills. The other is Daniel Sibirsky, the coauthor's son, who made this work feasible by providing unwavering support and cooperation during a stressful period.

Special recognition goes out to those who consented by telephone and e-mail to have their works quoted. Representatives of the American Translators Association, the Judicial Council of California (material "reprinted courtesy of the Administrative Office of the Courts"), and the Consortium of the National Center for State Courts. Their representatives, who wish to remain anonymous, permitted use of their online material. They and all others are referenced properly in the text, chapter notes, and bibliography.

Appreciation is extended to the following representatives of authors and publishing houses for signing Permission Request forms that allow quotations from their respective works. Their rights are reserved, and all are fully referenced in the text, end notes, and bibliography:

Bruce Downing, Translation and Interpretation Program, College of Continuing Education, University of Minnesota, for Laurie Swabey and Pam Sherwood-Gabrielson and their *Introduction to Interpretation: An Instructor's Manual.*

Coauthors Roseann Dueñas González, Victoria Vásquez, and Holly Mikkelson for authorized use of *Fundamentals of Court Interpretation: Theory, Policy, Practice,* published by Carolina Academic Press.

Estella Jap A Joe, rights and permissions manager for Springer Publications, for D. Gerver and H. Wallace Sinaiko and their *Language, Interpretation and Communication,* published by Plenum Press of New York and London and acquired by Springer.

Patrick S. P. Lafferty, director and owner of Pen and Booth, for the translation from French to English of Danica Seleskovitch's *Interpreting for International Conferences: Problems of Language and Communication.*

Marianne Lederer, executrix of Danica Seleskovitch and an editor of Editions Minard (Paris), for *L'Interprète dans les conferénces internationales: problèmes de langage et de communication.*

Patricia Leplae, rights and permissions representative, John Benjamins, B.V. (The Netherlands), for Alicia Betsy Edwards, author of *The Practice of Court Reporting.*

Theda Llewellyn, communications manager of RID Publications, for Nancy Frishberg, author of *Interpretation: An Introduction.*

Mordecai Schreiber, president of Schreiber Publishing (Baltimore), for Morry Sofer, author of *The Translator's Handbook.*

Julie Finnegan Stoner, permissions coordinator of Georgetown University Press, for Gerardo Vázquez-Ayora and his *Introducción a la Traductología.* Copyright 1977 by Georgetown University Press. From *Introducción a la Traductología* by Gerardo Vázquez-Ayora, a total of 14 lines from pp. 122, 257, 262, 358 and 362. Reprinted with permission. www.press.georgetown.edu.

Patricia Zline, rights and permissions assistant of the University Press of America, for Elena De Jongh and her *Introduction to Court Interpreting: Theory and Practice.*

# Table of Contents

### PART II: INTERPRETATION AND TRANSLATION IN CULTURAL, LEGAL, AND LINGUISTIC CONTEXTS

# A Note from the Authors

The authors would like to identify their joint and personal contributions to the statements and concepts. Together they leveraged their combined strengths in researching, writing about, and teaching the languages, histories, and cultures of Spain, Spanish-America, Portugal, Brazil, and France. Each author also possessed separate strengths.

Saúl Sibirsky's overarching contributions lie in transferring with passion and intelligence to the manuscript its guiding framework, that is, direct knowledge and experience as a court-certified and social agency interpreter and translator in Connecticut. The text coalesces around his personal and professional observations and the extensive research he performed to document these experiences. The hope is that the experiences in Connecticut will serve as a template to assist professionals in every state and venue.

Martin C. Taylor brought to bear strengths in researching and writing about interpreters and translators in military, political, diplomatic, literary, linguistic, bilingual, cultural, ethical, educational, legal, and economic situations. He also reorganized, rewrote, and edited the manuscript for coherence, clarity and style.

# Preface

Readers will discover herein the practices and ideas surrounding interpreters and translators who are involved with persons of limited English skills — principally Spanish-speaking individuals — in need of communication in U.S. courtrooms, social service agencies, international conferences, private corporations, and myriad other settings. Unique to this text are the abundant sources of information on educational sites, training facilities, and employment sources. The authors discuss and analyze numerous examples of bilingualism, the core of interpretation and translation, as it concerns culture, linguistics, science, legal issues, and sociopolitical matters.

English and Spanish are the vehicles of transmission with which the authors are most familiar. This language pair, English/Spanish, is important but incidental to the subject matter of this book. Interpreters and translators of any language pair, including American Sign Language, can benefit from the book's substantive material. Spanish, however, is the most widely used foreign language in the U.S., with more than 35 million speakers among 40 million immigrants and residents. Spanish speakers comprised "12.6 percent of the population," in 2007, according to the U.S. Census Bureau.[1] Although Spanish prevails, consider that in California 224 languages are in use; in South Florida more than 60 are spoken. A Babel of languages exists nationally. The crux is that interpreters and translators, whatever their language pair, are needed in the legal, social, health, and business settings of millions of immigrants and residents — about half of whom are individuals of limited English proficiency (LEP) — and for the commercial and security requirements of a complex and globalized nation.

The authors offer numerous illustrations of the broader intellectual framework with which translators and interpreters should become acquainted. A glance at the Table of Contents guides the reader to the extensive coverage of the practical and theoretical aspects of the interpreting act and the noble profession of translating. The authors promise an unvarnished look at both professions as they are practiced and conceived, their advantages and shortcomings.

The authors developed this book for several reasons and purposes. Reasons, which precede purposes, are the "whys" that explain an event by digging into motives. Inquiries into purposes for an event or action project forward. So, in English, the question, "Why did you write this book?" requires one to think for a moment. Is the questioner looking for motives or purposes? In Spanish, two similar interrogatives distinguish the difference: ¿por qué? — "why" — asks for reasons and motives; ¿para qué? — "why" in the sense of "for what" — asks about purposes. Both, however, can conflate into English as "why," unless the discriminating translator seeks out the proper nuance.

Before devoting the rest of the book to a serious, scholarly discussion, the authors use this section as a pretext for a playful piquing of the question: "Why this book?" The reason is that after years of serving as foreign-language and foreign-culture professionals and mavens, the authors wanted to bring forth a volume at the apex of their careers that represented their best and most current explorations of the practical and theoretical uses of English and Spanish, with flashes of French, Portuguese, Italian, and Arabic in the context of interpretation and translation. The authors honed these skills through advanced university training, teaching, and administration; research and publications; directing second-language and bilingual programs; and extensive travel.

What was the purpose in writing? At the back of our minds, after three years of research and writing, the authors might have projected a fanciful future of life-long lusting for limitless lucre. In their wildest dreams, the authors could project fugitive pursuits of a hefty advance, royalties, book signings at Borders and Barnes & Noble, and an appearance on BookTV-C-Span2. As realists, *hélas*, used to professorial budgets and frugality, we awakened from the dream and cast aside those vanities.

To the aforementioned *¿para qué?* one must add *¿para quiénes?*—"for whom?"—which determines the end users of the material. The authors intend to reach university students and professionals in all language and cultural specialties, but most of the illustrations will focus on the English and Spanish languages and their corresponding cultures.

Because American Sign Language is a vast topic and not the authors' specialty, the book touches lightly on sign language interpretation. Nevertheless, sign language interpreters will find in Chapter 12, section D, "Nonverbal Equivalencies," relevant information. Chapter 7, on "Training, Testing, and Certification," discusses programs where interpreters can get a degree (Gallaudet and the University of Arkansas) and explains how they can certify their training via the Registry of Interpreters for the Deaf. The book deals with the process that limited–English-proficient individuals have to follow to learn American Sign Language (ASL) through the English language (primary language > English language > ASL). Also benefiting from the material are the limited–English-proficient relatives and educators of the deaf clients of sign language interpreters, who need appropriate interpretation services within the same setting.

# Part I

# *Legal, Professional, Ethical, Educational, and Economic Issues*

# CHAPTER 1

# Introduction

## A. A Brief Overview

The **Preface** presents the reasons that gave rise to the text, the aspirations of the coauthors, and indicates some of the intended beneficiaries in the private and public sectors.

**Part I** covers **Chapters 1–8,** wherein historical, legal, professional, ethical, educational, and economic issues are discussed. Readers will find the quotations and statements documented by an abundance of source material in books, journals, newspaper and magazine articles, and on the Internet.

**Chapter 1,** "Introduction," presents the "whys," "whats," and "for whoms" that gave rise to the text and indicates the intended beneficiaries in the private and public sectors. The subject matter is especially appropriate for instructors and students at the college level. Professionals involved with the courts, social service agencies, and international organizations can benefit greatly from the variety of topics.

**Chapter 2, "Historical Perspectives from the New World,"** places into a cultural, historical, and linguistic context central themes of the book. Interpreters and translators have been employed since time immemorial in the affairs of businessmen, artists, and statesmen. But the military have been and still are (e.g., Iraq and Afghanistan) the prime employers of these professionals. Where invasion takes place "language usually follows the flag." The *conquistadores* Columbus and Cortés, via their interpreters and translators, ultimately imposed Spanish and crystallized a linguistic, legal, cultural, and sociopolitical model that persists until the present day. Pursuing this analogy, the book develops the idea that Spanish language and culture in the U.S. and the need for interpreters in a variety of activities have roots in the conquest and development of the Americas and prevails to the present time.

**Chapter 3, "Language and the Legal Systems,"** examines in detail the increased, heavy use of interpreters and translators in the U.S. as the result of rulings and decisions by Congress, the Judiciary, and the Executive Branch regarding the Constitution and the Bill of Rights. The chapter undertakes an examination of these questions, which led to, among others, the Civil Rights Act of 1964 and the Bilingual Education Act (1968). The preceding Acts and the Second Circuit Appellate Court decision, U.S. *ex rel.* Negrón *v.* NY 1970, paved the way for the Federal Court Interpreters Act (1978), the latter's Amendments (1988), and important Executive Orders. The legal support permitted millions of limited–English-proficient (LEPs) immigrants from hundreds of countries to have a right to due process, equal access, protection of the laws, and full disclosure in their native languages in all situations involving government agencies.

**Chapter 4, "Need for Adequate Interpretation and Translation,"** explains why competency is important and illustrates how anything less diminishes credibility, not only of the interpreter, but also of the profession. The federal legal determinations affect all people with limited English proficiency and cast in doubt the legal and administrative efforts by English-only advocates to curtail interpretation and translation in English-only states.

**Chapter 5, "Professional Standards,"** and **Chapter 6, "Professional Qualifications,"** taken as complementary units, describe and analyze the professional codes, standards, and ethical qualifications that affect all professionals in these fields. Meta-ethics defines the actions of one interpreter in condemning legal activities by federal agents against immigrant workers in Postville, Iowa.

**Chapter 7, "Training, Testing, and Certification,"** provides extensive, up-to-date information on institutions in the U.S. and abroad where training, exam preparation, and certification are available. The information and sources enable both the beginner and the veteran to find instruction or enhance performance.

**Chapter 8, "Economics, Jobs, Salaries,"** outlines the wide range of salaries and employment opportunities in the public and private sectors. The material assists salaried persons and the majority of professionals who serve as freelance, independent contractors. Note that the salaries mentioned are accurate up until the time of completing the research, that is, between 2007 and 2009. The safeguard is that names, addresses, directories, and websites are provided, so that readers can update the information to reflect changes over the course of time.

**Part II, Chapters 9–16,** provides in-depth knowledge and information on interpretation and translation in a variety of cultural, legal, and linguistic contexts. Special attention is paid to the courtroom, social service agencies, legal and medical venues, and international organizations. Useful illustrations derive from academic, literary, and working interpreters and translators, as well as from scientists and philosophers.

**Chapter 9, "Comparing Interpretation and Translation,"** captures the differences and similarities between the two facets of the same coin. The definitions explain why the term "interpretation" is preferred for oral communication and "translation" for written communication. Interpreters in modern fiction speak for themselves and differentiate themselves from translators. The chapter concludes with examples from classical and contemporary literature to illustrate how translators function with perseverance and courage to avoid meriting the Italian epithet of "translator, betrayer."

**Chapter 10, "Decoding and Encoding Multidimensional Language,"** analyzes the manifestations and applications of interpretation and translation as vehicles of communication in which linguistics and grammar play a significant role.

**Chapter 11, "Modes of Interpretation and Translation,"** delineates the major aspects of Summary, Simultaneous, Consecutive, and Conference interpreting, and Sight Translation. Diplomatic practitioners illustrate their craft and offer suggestions. A section explores how diplomatic and military practitioners are coveted as conveyors of nuanced policy or blamed and reviled as scapegoats when the policy fails or mistrust sets in.

**Chapter 12, "Verbal and Nonverbal Equivalencies in the Courtroom,"** includes the impact of the differences between the languages and the cultures of the limited-English-proficient (LEP) and the language-dominant groups. The chapter ends with a discussion of the language of nonverbal equivalencies, or gestures, which should interest practitioners of American Sign Language.

**Chapter 13, "Settings and Procedures in Legal and Social Venues,"** examines in minute detail the venues where the process takes place with their corresponding physical, logistical, and human aspects.

**Chapter 14, "Playacting and Power Relationships in the Courtroom,"** presents the interpreter as intervener and actor with visibility and the power of persuasion. Conversely, the chapter describes situations in which invisibility, humility, and discretion prevail.

**Chapter 15, "Implications of Bilingualism,"** restates the obvious, that bilingualism and biculturalism form the nucleus of the profession. The chapter reviews problematic issues in the linguistic, social, cultural, educational, political, psychological, and neuroscientific fields in learning and using a second language in the U.S.

**Chapter 16, "Cultures and Languages in Play,"** opens with a wide-ranging discussion of the complex and delicate facets of culture and language in which interpreters and translators have to operate. The chapter concludes with efforts to link the following areas to the profession: science, gene theory, the brain, nature *vs.* nurture, evolution, and ethics.

The **Chapter Notes, Authors and Works Cited,** and **Suggested Readings** reinforce the text, document the material, and point readers to relevant comments and sources.

## B. The Authors' Aspirations

While reading on and training in the field are absolutely necessary, neither one alone is sufficient to produce desirable and optimal results. Hands-on experience, buttressed by reading, training, and mentoring, comprise the key components that result in the best interpreters and translators. To this end, the authors present in summary form their goals:

Help interpreters and translators in their pursuit of employment as practicing professionals. The book has up-to-date information on educational sites, training materials, salaries, hiring entities, and employment hot-spots.
Show how interpreting and translating are actually performed to achieve a professional delivery of their performance.
Illustrate the numerous settings in which interpretation and translation take place.
Describe the realities and difficulties of the profession. By becoming aware of them, aspirants save time and money and avoid disappointment and false illusions.
Encourage the instructors to work harder to strengthen the skills of the aspirants. Or, show courage by discouraging those who have unrealistic expectations or insufficient interest to improve.
Commiserate with the veterans or laugh with them. They can take advantage of the tidbits, shortcuts, and suggestions to avoid the minefields.
Illustrate for the end-user clients — i.e., corporations, court and legal systems, and government agencies — how to identify the best-equipped interpreters and translators and how to help those in need of assistance.

And, finally, a word to the (administrative) judges, attorneys, health-care practitioners, social workers, physical therapists, and other professionals who are required to participate in and understand the interpretation and translation process. An invitation goes out to the personnel of the interpretation and translation companies. The book addresses the need to have the roles of the aforementioned clearly defined. Numerous passages and illustrations show how these professionals can become aware of how to help make interpretation and translation successful and, in so doing, assist their patients and clients. They will learn the following and more: how to engage and assess interpreters, the "rules of the game," and the flexibility they should apply to gain all the advantages possible from the event.

Our ideal will be achieved if our collective resources have put a clear, useful, and thoughtful book into the hands of aspiring and practicing interpreters, translators, linguists, students, teachers, researchers, and journalists, and those who surround them and depend on them in courts, attorneys' offices, social service agencies, medical settings, international conferences, global businesses, libraries, and classrooms.

# CHAPTER 2

# Historical Perspectives from the New World

## A. Communication and the Military

Translators and interpreters, according to the well-documented *Translators Through History*, have bridged the communication gap between and among different cultures since Pharaonic Egypt in the third millennium BCE. Consider, in a similar vein, the enormous communication requirements of Alexander the Great of Macedon (356–323 BCE), as he conquered Asia.[1] These are among the thousands of other scenarios where interpreters and translators have played major roles in creating understanding between nations, associations, and individuals and, conversely, in facilitating the transfer of military, social, and linguistic information and power between and among adversaries.

For centuries interpretation and translation have been the domain of diplomats, businessmen, religious, writers, public speakers, scientists, and statesmen. However, their most urgent and frequent users historically have been invading armies, whose logistics, reconnaissance, and intelligence officers have needed informants and/or spies. Before an operation they gather information on enemy positions and strengths; during an assault, they report progress of the tactics and strategies; and after an attack, they translate documents, advise on culture, and oversee prisoners, people, buildings, war booty, and conquered territories.

In war time, the persons gifted in tongues have never enjoyed an easy life. Disgruntled locals with linguistic skills pressed into service, or official interpreters and translators, have been subject to detention, torture, threats, distrust, and death for functioning either as collaborators or as spies. (The difficulties that interpreters in Iraq endure are taken up in Chapter 11, "Modes of Interpretation and Translation," section F, "Interpreters as Scapegoats.")

## B. The Americas: Language Follows the Flag

After a war, the interpreters and translators of the occupying forces collaborate in conditioning both victors and losers to a mutual understanding of the new rules of the road, where the winners write and rewrite history. This leads to the truism that "language follows the flag." This phenomenon occurs where, by dint of arms, invaders have imposed the victor's language and culture. Examples abound: English on India, Portuguese on Mozambique and Angola,

French on Algeria, and Incan Quechua on natives of past and present-day Ecuador and parts of Argentina and Bolivia. And nowhere is this more apropos for the Hispanic aspect of this book or better illustrated than in the conquest of the Americas.[4]

Christopher Columbus (1451–1506) set out for *las Indias* in 1492, at a critical juncture in peninsular Spain's history. By 1492, following eight centuries of battles with Muslims, a new order came to pass. The unifying sociopolitical force had crystallized in the marriage of the Catholic monarchs (1474–1504), Ferdinand of Aragon to Isabella of Castile. Militant Catholicism overpowered and undermined Islam and Judaism. Castilian, the politically correct language of the powerful central province, especially with its codification in Antonio de Nebrija's *Gramática de la lengua castellana* (1492, Grammar *of the Castilian Language*), overshadowed and supplanted the surrounding provincial languages. Thus, with the expulsion of the Moors, who spoke Arabic, and the Jews, who spoke Spanish but used Hebrew for religious ceremonies, Spain, in 1492, achieved political, military, religious, and linguistic cohesiveness. In this case, verily, language followed the flag.

Columbus, recognizing that a new route to the Indies for economic, political, and religious domination required an interpreter as well as troops, recruited to sail with him Don Luis de Torres, versed in Castilian, Latin, Arabic, Hebrew, Greek, and Armenian. Three ironies come to mind. The first is that Don Luis, a Jew and scholar, capitulated to the new power structure by becoming a *converso* (a convert) to save himself from experiencing expulsion, or worse yet, the Inquisition and burning at the stake via an *auto da fé* (act of the faith). As Columbus set sail from the port of Palos de Moguer, Luis de Torres would have witnessed from the deck of the *Santa María* boatloads of his coreligionists — those who refused conversion and repudiation of their other language — on their way as Sephardim to another diaspora that augured greater religious and social freedom in North Africa and Turkey. The second irony is that Luis de Torres's language skills would not avail him much rendering Taíno and other non–Indo-European, unwritten native languages during brief stays on the newly encountered islands of Guanahaní and Colba (re-named, respectively, Watlings or San Salvador, and Cuba). The third irony is that a Jew, who, it is presumed, converted to Catholicism to save himself, would be part of the militant Christian evangelization of the New World.

But one can't blame the messenger for messages gone awry. Columbus, later titled the Admiral of the Ocean Sea, did not end up in irons and ultimate imprisonment in a monastery because of the interpreter's shortcomings. Despite the Genoese's convictions, energies, heroism, and discoveries, he fell victim to political intrigue, greed, and excessive pride, from which neither the evangelizing of the natives nor his fervent Catholic piety could save him. Some scholars believe that Columbus covered up his own possible Jewish background with zealous, excessive prayer.

A different process and outcome awaited Hernán Cortés (1485–1547), who, with a comparatively small military force, conquered the Aztec Empire, in honor of which Charles V named him First Marquis of the Valley of Oaxaca. No small role in this outcome was played by Cortés's interpreters, the shipwrecked Spaniard Jerónimo de Aguilar and the enslaved princess Malintzín (or Malinalli in Mayan), Hispanicized to Malinche, and later upgraded to the respectable and politically correct Doña Marina. It happened this way. By sheer luck, Cortés came upon and recruited the abandoned Jerónimo de Aguilar who, for eight years, had learned Mayan during his enforced stay on Cozumel in the Yucatán. Once on the mainland, Cortés encountered Malinche among the Tlaxcalan Indians, the enslaved daughter of a deceased chief who knew Náhuatl, the language of the Aztecs, and that of the natives of coastal Tabasco, Mayan.[5] Working as "relay interpreters," Jerónimo and Malinche closed the language gap for the Spaniards. Having established mutual confidence, the two interpreters, operating in tandem, thwarted ambushes, overcame rivalries and hostile intentions, evangelized the natives, and mesmerized and weakened the Aztec leader Guatemotzín (Náhuatl for Cuauhtémoc). Doña Marina's contributions and other episodes inform the formidable and fertile memory of Bernal Díaz del Castillo, Cortés's loyal sergeant, who recorded the events in his *Historia Verdadera de la Conquista de la Nueva España*, written in 1575, fifty years after the conquest.[6]

Whereas Luis de Torres and Jerónimo de Aguilar passed unheralded into history, the opposite happened with Malinche. During and after the conquest, she learned Spanish, became a concubine, had a child with Cortés, married a Spaniard who rejected her, and earned the title of respect, Doña Marina. Despite her intellectual and social successes, because she aided the invaders and conquerors as interpreter, post-colonial Mexicans continue to revile this woman as a traitor, whore, and "mother of a bastard race of *mestizos*," according to *La Chicana: The Mexican-American Woman*.[7] Her reversal of misfortune took place, ironically, in the U.S. among the feminists of the sixties and seventies who enshrined her as a forbearing leader and martyr in a macho society. (In "Interpreters as Scapegoats" [Chapter 11, section F], Iraqi translators are similarly reviled.)

Luis de Torres, Jerónimo de Aguilar, and Malinche could never have known that their linguistic efforts changed the course of history, that they aided in the birth of a new empire, nor did they dream that their initial contributions would lead to the development of a legal and administrative system in Mexico that codified interpretation and translation in the "*Recopilación de leyes de Indias*" (1529–1630), or "Compendium of the Laws of the Indies." Following the pacification of the Aztecs, interpreters, called *lenguas* or "tongues," were prohibited from benefiting from their labors by accepting or receiving jewels, clothes, or food from Indians. However, by 1563, the colonial administration came to recognize and compensate fairly their hardworking *lenguas* who, like present-day professionals, were bound by ethical principles despite the prevalence of inequities.

Oral interpretation prevailed over translation of written histories for decades, because the military allied with the religious leaders sought pacification and conversion. The surest path to conversion, according to Bishop Juan de Zumárraga, in Mexico, was to obliterate traces of the written history of the Mayans and Aztecs. When the Spaniards' fears of revolt abated, Zumárraga relented in his zealotry and aided in the evangelization of the Indians by creating schools and by encouraging the scholarly labors of the Franciscan Bernardino de Sahagún (1499–1590). Sahagún, using native informants who worked with translators, took the initiative to preserve what was left of native culture by translating and preserving much of what remained of the pre–Cortesian history in his monumental twelve volumes titled, *Historia general de las cosas de la Nueva España* (*General History of the Things of New Spain*), which are known as the *Florentine Codices*. During and after the conquest, language skills, preservation of records, and defense of the natives were subordinate to the self-serving military and economic policies and religious edicts, respectively, of the Crown and the Church.

It might be a stretch to make this analogy, but imagine that these first Indians having their rights and duties explained from/to Spanish and Náhuatl/Mayan were the forerunners, the proto-ancestors, of the millions of Mexicans and other Latin Americans who are defended in today's courts and social agencies. This analogy proposes juxtaposing two different situations. Just as the original Indians of the post-conquest and colonial periods survived military, political, religious, and economic upheavals, so, too, have the millions who migrated — documented or undocumented — from the stressful civil, economic, and warring conditions of their native countries. The language pairs and the periods are different, but not the conditions. Have we come full circle? Is it true, as the French are fond of saying, that the more things change the more they remain the same?

Over the centuries, in war and peace, interpreters and translators have played pivotal roles — mostly behind the scenes, sometimes at great personal risk — in effecting changes, great and small, in the conduct of affairs of state between nations, peoples, and cultures. In the course of this text, readers will learn about some of the training, courage, dedication, wisdom — and shortcomings — of the practical happenings and theoretical underpinnings of these largely unsung professionals in modern times.

CHAPTER 3

# Language and the Legal Systems

## A. Federal Court Interpreters Act

It took the U.S. Congress fourteen years after passing the Civil Rights Act of 1964 to bring into existence the Federal Court Interpreters Act of 1978 (Title 18, §1827(d) 1–2). On 29 October 1978, President Carter signed Public Law 95–539 (92 Stat. 2040), which established legal standards to guarantee full disclosure and due process for all witnesses and defendants in judicial proceedings whose primary language was not English. The law mandated the use of qualified interpreters in criminal and civil actions brought forth by the *federal government* [emphasis added] in which a litigant or a witness "speaks only or primarily a language other than the English language [...] so as to inhibit such a party's comprehension of the proceedings or communication with counsel or the presiding judicial officer, or so as to inhibit such witness's comprehension of questions and the presentation of such testimony." The FCIA required court interpreters to assist persons with deficiencies in the use of English in legal matters in the judicial system. Accordingly, legal standards with teeth, funding, and regulations enable these laws to be carried out.

The Act and its Amendments, according to the "Report," required "the Director of the Administrative Office (AO) of the U.S. Courts to define criteria for certifying interpreters qualified to interpret in federal courts."[1] The important question of certification of interpreters — initiated in 1980 — will be dealt with at length in Chapter 7. The provision of interpretation has been recognized since its inception as a fundamental legal right of the non–English-speaking and the limited-English-proficient — or LEP persons — as mandated by the aforementioned Act and its Amendments.

But from what legal bases did the Civil Rights Act and the Federal Court Interpreters Act derive? The Bill of Rights to the Constitution — more specifically, the Fourth, Fifth, Sixth, Eighth, and Fourteenth Amendments — provides the framework of legal rights for all Americans and non-residents. These five Amendments supported the indirect legal justification and enforcement rights that enabled any person not proficient in English to benefit from the skills of an interpreter in order to comprehend the dominant language of the U.S. judicial system in its various modes:

> There is no explicit constitutional right to an interpreter; however, the Constitution specifically provides individual rights and liberties to all United States citizens, and for the Fourth, Fifth, Sixth, Eighth, and Fourteenth Amendments to have any legal meaning, provision of interpreter services must be offered to limited- and non–English speakers ["Report" 46].

What rationale did Congress use to infer from these Constitutional Amendments a mandate for interpretation services? As a preamble to discussing the following five Amendments, note that the role of the court interpreter does not include initiating a colloquy with defendants or witnesses nor in explaining them except as required by a judge or other authority. That does not relieve the court interpreter from understanding them nor from being able to explain them, if asked, in the required language.

A. The Fourth Amendment (1791) regulates the right by police officials to "search and seizure" using probable cause. A diligent court interpreter must understand the rights LEP persons enjoy in cases of illegal or legal scrutiny or confiscation of private property.
B. The Fifth Amendment (1791) calls for a fair trial and protection against self-incrimination and double jeopardy. On a practical level, "taking the Fifth" deals with when and when not to talk to the police or to the jury.
C. The Sixth Amendment (1791) recognizes the right to a speedy trial, to learn of the charges, to question witnesses for the prosecution, and to have an attorney provided without charge. It is obvious that an interpreter's service is a must for persons deficient in English who face a judge or jury.
D. The Eighth Amendment (1789) [1791] deals with excessive bail and cruel and unusual punishment, elements for which the LEP needs direct guidance in a primary language if he is to receive equal access to justice and a fair trial.
E. The Fourteenth Amendment (ratified 1868) provides for equal protection before the law and no deprivation of life, liberty, or property without due process, *sine qua non* for any accused person, but critical for an LEP person ignorant of U.S. law, language, and culture.

The Amendments to the Court Interpreters Act (Public Law No. 100–702, 102 Stat. 4654–4657 [1988]), add new dimensions to the FCIA:

• The Amendments make concerned and relevant persons acquainted with the professional definition of interpretation.
• They make evident the need for interpreters and their importance.
• They make clear how interpretation should be provided.
• They mandate the presence of the interpreter, as needed, in grand jury hearings.
• They require criteria for certification.

It is urgent to add that the use of interpreters not only protects the rights of the limited in English, but also serves justice in general. Justice to society at large is upheld when interpreters permit persons deficient in English to accuse or defend other language-impaired or unimpaired persons, who in turn can be adjudicated, sanctioned, or freed as the case may be. In her special comment for this text, Distinguished Professor Virginia Benmaman underscores the appropriate conclusion to these concepts: "It is the ultimate validation of our legal system and the judicial process."

## *Summarizing the Federal Court Interpreters Act:*

1. The use of interpretation services enables the limited in English to participate on an equal and fair basis and levels the playing field;
2. A uniform judicial process that is set up properly for the adequate provision of interpretation services also enables those representing the judicial system to interact with the limited in English proficiency; bridging the language and cultural gaps is critically important;
3. All court officers need to understand that the services must be provided and establishes how they should be provided;

4. The implementation of the Act in the federal judicial system has catalyzed similar standards at the state and municipal court levels nationally, as well as in administrative law agencies and quasi-judicial entities.

In short, the use of interpreters not only protects the rights of the LEP individuals, but also society as a whole. With the use of interpreters, the guilty LEP can be more readily found and sanctioned accordingly, doing justice to the non–LEP victim.

**FCIA IMPROVES EMPLOYMENT OPPORTUNITIES.** More than any other act of Congress, the FCIA increased exponentially the need for the professional services of interpreters and translators to interface with immigrants flooding into the U.S. The FCIA and its Amendments created a multiplier effect. The rulings extend their benefits and practice beyond the scope of the courts and the legal system to many other interpretation settings. The legislation increased the need for professional interpretation and translation services at every level of the legal, governmental, and private sector systems. The interpreter, since then, has become the almost indispensable "third person" to ensure that an accurate message is conveyed when communication would not be clear between speakers of two different languages and cultures. Opportunities also grew in the private sector owing to increased foreign trade. For most of these reasons, the U.S. Department of Labor's Bureau of Labor Statistics forecasts that, despite fierce internal competition for employment, "opportunities for interpreters and translators are expected to grow faster than the average through 2012."[2]

# B. Justice for the Limited-in-English Proficiency (LEP)

**WAIVERS AND THE LAW.** Some persons of limited-in-English proficiency, when asked by a judge whether they want a court interpreter, turn down this right. (See section D, following, for a full discussion of the acronym LEP.) Either through excessive pride, or because they think that they will obtain greater sympathy or a better reception in court if they show their English, however limited, some LEP individuals waive their rights to an interpreter or translator. Given the Civil Rights Act, judges currently stress to the LEP the importance of what they may be surrendering if they waive their right to an interpreter. First of all what is a waiver and what are its implications?

In *Black's Law Dictionary,* a "waiver" is defined as "the intentional or voluntary relinquishment of a *known* [emphasis added] right."[3]

If an accused LEP were properly counseled in his own language on the implications of relinquishing a legal right, benefit, or privilege, would he do so? A good court interpreter could explain, at the request of the judge or attorney, the meanings of the complexity of a "waiver," or *renuncia, abandono.* If so, the informed defendant might not blithely renounce the waiver. Consider the complexity and importance of the following eight waivers that an interpreter has to be acquainted with, taken from *West's Spanish/English Law Dictionary*[4]:

1. Express Waiver. *Renunciar explícitamente a un derecho o beneficio.*
2. Implied Waiver. *Renuncia implícita. Cuando el comportamiento de una persona permite creer que hay abandono de un derecho o beneficio.*
3. Waiver of Immunity. *Renuncia de inmunidad.*
4. Waiver of Jury. *Renuncia del derecho de juicio ante jurado.*
5. Waiver of Notice. *Renuncia de citación o de aviso.*

6. Waiver of Performance. *Renuncia de cumplimiento específico.*
7. Waiver of Rights. *Renuncia de derechos.*
8. Waiver of Tort. *Renuncia a daños por agravio.*

U.S. *EX REL.* NEGRÓN *V.* NEW YORK (434 F.2D 386 [2ND CIRCUIT 1970]). No Spanish-speaking certified court interpreter for the defense ever explained to Rogelio Nieves Negrón, a Spanish-speaking Puerto Rican with a sixth-grade education charged with homicide in a brawl, whether he understood the term "waiver" or wanted a waiver. His trial in Suffolk County, New York, continued despite being clear to all court authorities that Negrón neither spoke nor understood English. His lack of proficiency prohibited him from refuting adversarial testimony and adding mitigating circumstances. To him the proceedings were meaningless. Lloyd H. Baker, his attorney, who spoke no Spanish, never availed the defense of an interpreter, but depended on the prosecution's loan of an interpreter, Elizabeth Maggipinto, for "gratuitous" and infrequent translations for the benefit of the lawyer, the prosecutor, or the trial judge. In the course of a four-day trial, Maggipinto provided translation and summaries of proceedings during recesses to the accused and his lawyer for a maximum of twenty minutes. The jury convicted Negrón and sentenced him to twenty years to life.[5]

Prior to Negrón, according to Dueñas González, et al., in *Fundamentals of Court Interpretation,* "Many courts held that failure to request an interpreter constituted a waiver of that right, which in effect unfairly placed the burden of knowing the extent of one's legal rights upon the non–English-speaking defendant or his unknowing counsel."[6]

Irving R. Kaufman, the judge who spoke for the Second Circuit Appellate Court of New York (15 Nov. 1970), overturned the Suffolk County decision and affirmed the habeas corpus of U.S. District Court for the Eastern District. Kaufman held that "Spanish-speaking defendant [Negrón] in State homicide prosecution was entitled to services of translator, and failure to provide translator rendered trial constitutionally infirm, notwithstanding that interpreter employed on behalf of prosecutor from time to time supplied resumes of proceedings."

The Negrón decision set precedents, first by declaring null and void the thesis that the burden was on the LEP to request an interpreter. Second, on the question of an implicit waiver of rights, the Court held that they were illegal with regard to language-impaired persons in legal proceedings. Third, this chapter opened with the constitutional and statutory bases for the Federal Court Interpreters Act, but the Appellate Court's reasoning at the state level, in the Negrón case, according to Virginia Benmaman, had a greater impact on Congress and the Supreme Court and precipitated at the federal level the overriding and more encompassing FCIA.[7]

## C. English-Only Statutes, Challenges, and the LEP

Whether documented or undocumented, all immigrants require interpreters and translators to handle criminal and civil cases because of additional laws, such as the 1990 Americans with Disabilities Act, the 1973 Rehabilitation Act, and Title VI of the Civil Rights Act of 1964. The latter's Section 601 is categorical: "No person in the United States shall, on the grounds of race, color, or national origin, be excluded from participation in or, be denied the benefits of, or be subjected to discrimination under any program receiving Federal financial assistance."

On 11 August 2000, Section 601 of the Civil Rights Act was reinforced when William

Clinton signed Presidential Executive Order 13166, titled "Improving Access to Federal Services for Persons with Limited English Proficiency."[8] The Executive Order asserted that federal funds would be withdrawn from non-complying agencies at the federal and state levels. Although the laws require full access to the courts and the agencies of governments, possible evasions to providing language assistance may occur in English-only states at the risk of losing federal funding.

STATE "ENGLISH-ONLY LAWS" VS. FEDERAL LAWS. The U.S. Department of Labor's rosy picture for interpreters and translators based upon the increased cost of living, swelling immigrant populations, and the guarantees of the Civil Rights Act may be called into question by the palpable interest in twenty-six states and nationally by those who clamor for S. I. Hayakawa's (former California Senator) dream of an English-only amendment to the U.S. Constitution. (See Chapter 15, "Implications of Bilingualism.") These are definite threats, not only to those with limited use of English seeking aid in social service agencies, but also — beyond those threats already discussed — to employment opportunities of interpreters and translators. Consider carefully that state "English-only" laws impede access to assistance with English. One would think that the array of laws, starting with the Civil Rights Act, which protect and apply to LEP persons in the courtroom, would also provide full access and disclosure to those undergoing medical distress. Reflect on the strong language of Standards 1 and 4 from the U.S. Government's Office of Minority Health Standards:

> Health care organizations should ensure that patients receive from all staff members **effective, understandable, and respectful care** that is compatible with their cultural health beliefs and practices and preferred language.
>
> Health care organizations **must offer and provide language assistance services**, including bilingual staff and interpreter services, at no cost to each patient/consumer with limited English proficiency at all points of contact, in a timely manner during all hours of operation.

This may not be necessarily so. In its "Policy Brief 2" (Winter 2000, reprinted 2003), Georgetown University's Center for Child and Human Development, points to a basic loophole that vitiates the nondiscrimination clauses of the 1964 Civil Rights Act.[9] The "Brief" notes that "English-only statutes" in some states expressly prohibit funds for providing linguistic access. Although this matter is under litigation, "There is a perception that even federal funds can not be used for the provision of linguistic access services within English-only states." Should these state-wide rulings prevail, even the federal laws that specifically mandate language access in the health care field are brushed aside. Consider that poor immigrants — despite the laws prohibiting discrimination for national origin and creed — would not be able to avail themselves of hospital care under the Hospital Survey and Construction Act (i.e., Hill-Burton Act, 1946; amended and attached, 1975, to Title XVI, Public Health Service Act), Medicaid under the Health Care Financing Administration, the Medicare Program, and EMTALA (Emergency Medical Treatment and Active Labor Act). Not only are some states to blame for the erosion of the overarching legal protections, in addition "health care organizations have been slow to develop and implement policies and structures to guide the provision of interpretation and translation services." The "Policy Brief 2" concludes with the strong admonition that health care providers, even in "English-only" states, acting out of self-interest, would be advised to offer language access just to avoid malpractice suits for nonfeasance and/or malfeasance in the treatment of the immigrant sick. For additional information on these complex legal/linguistic issues contact the National Council on Interpretation in Health Care, in Seattle, WA, at *www.xculture.org*.

Let it suffice here that when interpretation is carried out in settings other than those related to the judicial system, the same equal need for services is required to ensure fairness and appropriate care for the rights of the LEP persons. Two examples, among the many other settings, include medical or mental health clinics for treatment, assessment, and physical rehabilitation evaluations, and the Office of Hearings and Appeals of the Social Security Administration for administrative reviews of disability claims. Yet, despite those assurances and President Clinton's Executive Order 13116, states which have passed English-only laws call into question whether the federal courts will allow those states to prohibit the services of interpreters for LEP persons requiring medical, health, and financial assistance.

ENGLISH-ONLY STATUTES: ORIGINS AND DIFFUSION. English as the official language of the thirteen colonies and subsequently of the newly forming nation might have taken root in 1780 at the Continental Congress. John Adams was the first to plant the English-only seed. In a burst of newly minted national pride and chauvinism, Adams recommended that an official academy of the language be established to enshrine and control English in order to "purify, develop, and dictate usage of" the national tongue as had occurred in Spain and France in that Age of the Enlightenment. Adams did not prevail. The other delegates rejected his concept as undemocratic and a threat to individual liberty. Support for this subject can be found at several websites, among them, that of *U.S. News and World Reports* (www.lect law.com), the American Civil Liberties Union of Florida (www.aclufl.org) and James Crawford (www.languagepolicy.net/archive/Adams.htm).

Unfortunately, the theories of democracy and freedom of expression conceived by the Founding Fathers have not persuaded present-day state legislators. Twenty-six state legislatures, increasingly apprehensive that "foreigners" with strange languages would overwhelm schools, dilute national pride and energy, and eventually control elections, imposed English-only requirements. Either by statute or constitutional amendment, there presently exist — or once existed — English-only requirements where interpreting and translation programs reside. The states in alphabetic order: Alabama, Alaska (ruled unconstitutional), Arizona (enacted, but overturned), Arkansas, California, Colorado, Florida, Georgia, Hawaii, Iowa, Illinois, Indiana, Kentucky, Mississippi, Missouri, Montana, Nebraska, New Hampshire, North Carolina, North Dakota, South Carolina, South Dakota, Tennessee, Utah, Virginia, and Wyoming. Does it seem anomalous and anachronistic to have English-only laws in the U.S., when, as indicated earlier, in California people communicate in 224 tongues, and in South Florida more than 60 languages are spoken?

Although Tennessee forms part of the aforesaid list, Nashville, the home of country music, international corporations (Nissan, Bridgestone, and Caterpillar Financial), and 11,000 Kurds, repudiated the state legislature. Some 41,752 voters, or 57 percent, opposed the referendum of 22 January 2009, "to make English the official language [...] and prohibit government services from being offered in any other language." Nashville's mayor, Karl Dean, summed up the symbolic issues: "To me and to the diverse coalition of community members who joined together to defeat these measures, the election sends a clear message about our city — Nashville is a welcoming and friendly place that values diversity[...]." (Go to *www.nashville.gov/mayor* to read Dean's complete statement.) The symbolism of diversity was not the only thing at stake. If a majority of the 73,896 voters had prevailed, Nashville would have put at risk its legal, financial, social, and economic well-being.

In support of the unsuccessful minority in Nashville was the Federation for American Immigration Reform (FAIR), which posed as the ProEnglish group of Arlington, VA, having been founded as English Language Advocates (1994). At this point, it would be useful to point out other associations with similar agendas. The oldest is Hayakawa's U.S. English (1983), followed by Linda Chavez's Center for Equal Opportunity (1995), and Ronald Unz's English for the Children (1997).

LEGAL, JOB, AND SECURITY RISKS. The state laws and their amendments and any proposed English Language Amendment to the U.S. Constitution affect a range of issues. At risk is the Equal Protection Clause of the Fourteenth Amendment, which evolved to permit those with limited proficiency in English, such as in the Negrón case, to benefit from access to many systems and agencies. Without a doubt, strict enforcement of English-only statutes can only have a deleterious effect on the civil rights of LEPs and on the jobs of interpreters and translators. Where English-only statutes may only cause partial crippling of the rights of LEPs and impede access to basic services, imagine the effect of a proposed English Language Amendment to the U.S. Constitution in the context of a fenced-in America on the southern border and strict homeland security measures at every frontier and portal. Some of these concepts resurface in Chapter 15, "Implications of Bilingualism," sections F and G. Readers who wish for more information on these complex legal themes will benefit from the extensive writings of James Crawford.[10]

## D. The "LEP" Controversy

A brief aside is in order to explore an important controversy that exists with regard to the term "limited-English-proficient" and its acronym "LEP." In some intellectual and social quarters both the term and the acronym are considered defaming since they seem not to recognize the speakers' intelligence in their native language or culture and cast them in an unequal power struggle with the language-dominant class. But many linguists employ the full term and the acronym — including Stanford University expert on bilingual education Kenji Hakuta. Both are used steadily and purposely in this book without any trace in mind of racism or denigration of native abilities. The authors consider that the terms are reasonable descriptors for the witnesses, plaintiffs, and claimants who present themselves before the courts and social services agencies for interpretation or translation assistance. The fact is that the recently arrived immigrants have a recognizable limited ability in English. "LEP" describes the language deficit, not any shortcoming of personality or intelligence. "LEP," used in common parlance, does not detract, in our mind, from the immigrants' hard work, honesty, and efforts to care for themselves and their families under trying circumstances.

The term "LEP" is not usually applied across the board and equally to diplomats or businessmen who require assistance in English in the course of their affairs. Take, for example, the persons of limited English proficiency at the United Nations. Those individuals cannot be equated socially, financially, legally, politically, or intellectually with an LEP in a civil, criminal, or administrative hearing in a downtown courtroom or social services agency. The LEP at the UN has been sent in an official capacity, typically, from the elite class, trained at quality universities at home and abroad where he or she learned at least two foreign languages, among them probably English and French. Applied to that person, "LEP" can be a misnomer. Chances are that a representative at an international conference knows one of the official languages, but speaks publicly in a native tongue to underscore personal and national pride in that international setting. He or she employs the native tongue in correct grammar to go on the record and to achieve a precise cultural dimension. The listeners of the many native languages at the UN use earphones to hear the translation in the official languages delivered in a clear, precise, and often elegant manner, but not because they are illiterate or deficient in tongues, especially English. Nor do these so-called LEPs need an interpreter or lawyer to safeguard their rights, because they probably have diplomatic immunity in legal matters, ranging from parking infractions to more serious affairs. Perhaps this dichotomy between social classes accounts for the LEP controversy.[11]

CHAPTER 4

# Need for Adequate Interpretation and Translation

## A. Are Interpreters Interlopers?

*INTERLOPER: a person who becomes involved in a place or situation where they are not wanted or are considered not to belong*

INTERPRETERS AS INTERLOPERS. Do courtroom interpreters provide an important service, or are they nuisances who prolong an event, say a trial or deposition? Do they make serious mistakes, as some judges, attorneys, and court reporters seem to feel? It is obvious that when one interprets for the first time at a trial in a courthouse, at a deposition in an attorney's office, or in other places and on other occasions, one may or may not be recognized as an "adequate" interpreter. But mistakes are not relegated to beginners; even more experienced court interpreters are prone to mistakes. The court interpreter who performs well and has the confidence of the other participants will hear, as coauthor Sibirsky has heard, horror stories that have befallen previous attorneys, court reporters, judges, social workers, and others. Sibirsky reports that some interpreter-originated distortions and confusions resulted in useless deposition transcripts that prevented the reaching of agreement, precipitating a trial by jury. For these and other similar reasons, an interpreter, however well prepared, whether blameful or blameless, will be confronting at times a hostile or certainly apprehensive attitude from other service providers.

Hostility towards immigrants and toward interpreters may also arise from prejudicial attitudes, according to Sibirsky, who witnessed the following incidents in his experience as an interpreter in courtrooms and in social services agencies. Some prosecutors, court clerks, and other personnel voice complaints, to wit, that that there should be no need for interpreters, because "after all, everyone should learn English." He reports having heard that some prosecutors impose harsher fines and penalties on undocumented (i.e., illegal) immigrants than on legal residents or citizens. The reverse idea also makes the rounds, that is, that immigrants without full command of English are given an unfair advantage by the provision of an interpreter. This attitude, Sibirsky avers, is noticeable especially in the body language of some staff in doctors' offices who, at times, treat the patient and the interpreter with a certain haughtiness, irritability, and patronizing attitude that reflect the message "we wish you were not here." And still more demeaning on a personal level is the attitude of those who will hint — sometimes with a smirk or a snide remark — that the interpreter, owing to his bilingual ability, has found a profitable "cow to milk."

Despite these difficulties, flawed human nature is perfectible. Negative behaviors transpire in every professional environment because of stress, striving for perfection, and competing personalities. It is in the nature of the job of translators, but especially interpreters, to confront difficulties, mollify critics, and provide competence, so that others may also discover the virtues of language professionals and praise them. Then the whole profession benefits, and persons who at times label interpreters interlopers will be in the minority.

## B. Language Mistakes

ERRORS AND INADEQUACIES. It would be remiss not to mention that interpreters and translators do commit errors. To err is human. Yet some interpreters pretend to have high skills when they do not possess mastery of two languages; thus error and deficient ethical behavior derive from arrogance and ignorance. Let us be fair and truthful. Not all interpreters possess true bilingualism, competent interpreting skills, and master sufficiently a specified vocabulary for a specific assignment. In these instances, further study, training, and experience are required.

Many types of errors or inadequacies prevail. Just a few are mentioned here, leaving for other chapters a more complete presentation. (See Chapter 9, "Comparing Interpretation and Translation.") With regard to an agile memory — a critical skill in consecutive interpreting — the span of focus or attention cannot be too short or information will be omitted and/or the process will be unduly interrupted.

Another shortcoming in a poorly trained interpreter is a tendency to transpose false cognates from Spanish, for example, the source language (SL), to English, the target language (TL). English and Spanish have a common base of Latin and Greek, so many borrowings between both languages exist, often resulting in overlaps and confusions. Even in the best interpreters, but more probable in a less-trained person, false translations occur. Two examples, among many, come to mind. The Spanish *suceso* and *éxito* look, respectively, like the English "success" and "exit," yet they really refer to "event" and "success." It is incumbent upon an interpreter or translator to identify a problem of false cognates. Further examples of deceptive cognates appear in Chapter 9, subsection "Two translation gaffes." In the chapter note that corresponds to this paragraph and in "Authors and Works Cited," the readers will find useful dictionaries by Bernard Hamel, Marcial Prado, and Rose Nash regarding false cognates in Spanish and English.[1]

## C. Ad Hoc or Stand-In Interpreters

"BILINGUAL" ATTORNEYS, DOCTORS, AND RELATIVES. Cases exist of attorneys and others who are bilingual, or consider themselves to be so and are not, and who either do not really master the SL and TL other than English, or if they master both languages, also have to perform simultaneously their role as attorney, which precludes being able to interpret appropriately because very different simultaneous skills are required by the two functions. Secretaries, relatives, friends or others, whether in the legal system, medical settings, or elsewhere, can do a lot of damage by misrepresenting questions or answers, because they are most probably not sufficiently competent in one or both of the languages, nor are they trained to perform in a professional manner.

Inadequate interpretation occurs frequently in medical offices when relatives intervene. Coauthor Sibirsky notes that this happened on several occasions. Having arrived on schedule to doctors' offices — but not before the patients who had arrived even earlier and been taken in right away — upon entering the consultation rooms, he found relatives interpreting. On some occasions, they were obviously ill themselves and in pain and therefore not able to concentrate. On others, they were bilingual, but actually of low fluency in both languages. At other times, undereducated relatives were trying to help the patients to fill out the basic data forms in the waiting room, but were obviously unable to get all the pertinent information out of the forgetful patient. In short, well-meaning but unprepared relatives lacked fluency, training, and questioning techniques to extract the information on all the ailments of the patients as well as the corresponding symptoms and medications.

Certified interpreters will encounter doctors and their staffs who bypass them and attempt to communicate directly with patients and, with less than a basic Spanish vocabulary, try to elicit answers from their LEP patients. This leads to misunderstanding and the omission of critical information about the patient's condition, or simply a lack of input from the patient, with the same potentially disastrous result. A study of psychopathological evaluations by Luis Marcos revealed the following:

1. Treating the psychiatrist's evaluation and comments subjectively and distorting the psychiatrist's statements:

> The psychiatrists emphasized distortions stemming from the interpreter's attitude toward either the patient or the clinician (e.g., an interpreter's over identification with the patient leading him or her to challenge the clinician's suggestions to the patient).[2]

2. Feeling uncomfortable about the malady of the patient who is close to them emotionally, and/or the responsibility to interpret on their shoulders:

> Most of the interpreters agreed that they often felt embarrassed or anxious about some of the clinician's questions to the patient. [...] All of the interpreters felt overwhelmed by the responsibility of serving as translators [Marcos 172].

3. Lacking the knowledge and skills required to interpret the affective, non-formal aspect of interpretation:

> Also, certain ambivalent attitudes on the part of the patient were difficult to evaluate through interpreters. Part of the problem appeared to be that untranslatable paralinguistic and vocal cues were not available to the clinician. [...] Although, in general, the interpreters were proficient in the source and target languages, various types of clinically relevant errors of translation were detected [Marcos 172–3].

The dialogue below illustrates typical errors by stand-in or ad hoc interpreters:

> *Clinician to Chinese-speaking patient:* "What kind of moods have you been in recently?"
> *Ad-hoc interpreter to patient:* "How have you been feeling?"
> *Patient's response:* "No, I don't have any more pain, my stomach is now fine, and I can eat much better since I take the medication."
> *Ad-hoc interpreter to clinician:* "He says that he feels fine, no problems" [Marcos 173].

Often the children of the LEP are asked to interpret, adds author Nancy Frishberg, which should be shunned for several reasons:

> The child's role as dependent and subordinate to the parents potentially conflicts with the child's function as interpreter for the parents.... The child [...] may be uncomfortable expressing culturally appropriate expressions from the source language, if they are inappropriate in the target language.[3]

It is particularly onerous for children and other relatives of patients or claimants (or other relatives) to be asked to interpret for their parents.

4. Offering an answer without eliciting one from the LEP individual or refusing to pose the requested question prompts Haffner's example followed by that of Marcos:

> The physician tells the family that the mother is dying and needs radical surgery, but he emphasizes that the surgery would prolong her life only a little. The physician wants to tell the patient and to ask for her consent to the operation. The daughters are very upset and against saying anything to their mother.[4]
>
> Another common observation was that relatives serving as interpreters answered the clinician's questions to the patient without actually asking the patient. For instance, the son of a patient was asked to inquire about his father's possible suicidal ideation. Without asking his father, he insisted on a negative answer [Marcos 173].

5. Refusal by the LEP individual to use a child or relative as an ad hoc interpreter:

> As we learn, the poor woman has a fistula in her rectum. In her previous visits, she could not bring herself to reveal her symptoms in the presence of, and therefore to, her son as he interprets for her. She tells me that she has been so embarrassed about her condition that she has invented other symptoms to justify her visit to the physician [Haffner 256].

These are not isolated cases. On 30 October 2005, *The New York Times* (Section 1, 22, for all quotes following) reported that public hearings were to be held in California, in November 2005, about draft regulations that would "prevent children from interpreting at private hospitals, physicians' offices or clinics. The rules would not apply in emergencies." The piece asserts that "the use of children as medical interpreters is common in states like California with high immigrant populations. Yet studies have illustrated the potentially lethal consequences of faulty translations. [...] California would be the first state to pass such a wide-ranging prohibition." Therefore, despite the advances made, ad hoc interpreters still abound, with potentially harmful results: "Experts say children lack the vocabulary and the emotional maturity to serve as effective interpreters. And two of every three mistranslations have clinical consequences, according to a 2003 study." As a consequence of the hearings, the State of California passed a law prohibiting children from interpreting for parents and adults.

The judicial setting has been more demanding in requiring a professional interpreter than the social service agencies. But under certain conditions, such as time constraints, judicial discretion — especially in the case of an uncommon language — may allow somebody other than a professional interpreter to serve. An anonymous report has come to our attention of language and legal distortion in a courtroom. In this case an insistent public defender with some knowledge of Portuguese persuaded the judge to allow him to "speak" to potential and then actual clients in what he considered understandable Spanish. But the language that came forth was really a distortion of inadequate Portuguese, leaving the client mystified and too often not comprehending or misunderstanding. The judge who permitted this displayed a lack of knowledge of the role that language plays in the courtroom.

Greater flexibility occurs in hearings for disability claims in the Office of Hearings and Appeals of the Social Security Administration. If a claimant appears to have adequate use of the English language and is sufficiently comfortable using it, some administrative judges will allow the claimant to use English, with the understanding that if the claimant does not understand a question or finds it difficult to answer it in English, that person can call on the interpreter (who is usually present in the hearing room sitting next to the claimant). In other circumstances, an interpreter can assist an LEP person who knows enough basic English to handle many social interactions sufficiently well, but who cannot understand the intricate English used, for example, in the various proceedings of the Social Security Administration, the State Commission on Human Rights and Opportunities, and the National Labor Relations Board. One indirect advantage of the LEP using English in these setting is that it makes it easier for an administrative judge to determine the types of jobs for which the claimants may be qualified based on their level of English proficiency. The reader is referred to Chapter 13, "Settings and Procedures in Legal and Social Venues," for a more detailed review of language possibilities in dozens of settings. Also in Chapter 13 is a discussion of the controversial statement that in some settings it may be appropriate for the interpreter to offer professional advice, or preferably an opinion, on these matters.

## D. Interpreters Bridge the Gaps

It is clear, then, that adequate interpreting and translation depend on a high level of professionalism. *Language into Language* will illustrate the characteristics deemed best and attainable from the writings and practices of the most distinguished members of the profession and from the authors' experiences. Negative experiences—and everybody has had them—ought not to discourage the determined individual to become an accurate interpreter and translator. Interpreters in a courtroom scenario or assisting in a social service agency, over time and with training, will perform a critical positive bridging role in helping limited-English-proficient persons overcome their language gap and—to the extent possible—the cultural gap. A conscientious court interpreter can thus remediate the negative impressions about the actual abilities of their cohorts and gain the appreciation and gratitude of the LEP persons and of the other participants involved, including (administrative) judges, attorneys, court reporters, medical doctors, and social workers. And a good interpreter can help the LEP learn of available resources, of the importance of having an attorney, how to respond appropriately to a doctor's queries and so on, depending on whether the particular characteristics, guidelines and requirements of the setting permit one to go beyond the act of interpreting.

The interpreter can be a channel for communication for and with the LEP person to achieve the following objectives:

1. Help deliver a fair and equal administration of justice;
2. Ensure the rights of due process and achieve the equitable participation of the LEP in the judicial system;
3. Enable the accused to understand the charges and ensure their right to be informed of those charges;
4. Enable the LEP to gain an understanding of court procedures and instructions to a jury;
5. Allow a plaintiff and/or a defendant to comprehend the testimony;
6. Permit the LEP persons to communicate with their attorney and participate in their own defense;
7. Protect the rights of the LEP to a fair trial or hearing, whatever the outcome. If the accused LEP should be found guilty, then society has been served also.
8. Explain and clarify to the LEP fee schedules for professional services.

## E. Consequences of a Lack of Interpreters

The need for professional interpretation services has been increasing because of the large number of immigration flows from countries afflicted by economic and political strife. Their presence represents a large potential economic market which requires language services in work areas, such as supermarkets, banks, airports, real estate offices, as well as in the allied health and social services areas. Unfortunately, potential large U.S. government agencies that employ individuals with a capacity in languages not common to the U.S. cannot find enough of them or qualify them.

With respect to legal, diplomatic, and security matters, the FBI and the U.S. Department of State have few personnel in proportion to the need and the demand. The FBI — which, in 2008, only employed ten Arabic speakers out of 12,000 employees for critical areas — is scouring Middle-Eastern communities in the U.S. for interpreters of Arabic. The CIA and the National Security Agency compete with the FBI and State in their quest for a limited pool of qualified speakers of Middle and Far Eastern languages. In a parallel but more dangerous situation, the U.S. State Department, in 2007, employed ten Arabic speakers among 1,000 personnel for its huge embassy in Iraq. According to *Time*, about "190,000 [...] U.S. military contractors [reside] in Iraq and neighboring countries,"[5] about 38,700 of whom are U.S. citizens. In "Interpreters as Scapegoats" (Chapter 11, section F), the sorts of threats that await interpreters are described, especially those in Iraq, not only from al Qaeda and other anti–American elements, but also from the employers of interpreters.

On the domestic front, in the area of health services, other downsides occur that are not usually contemplated when interpretation services are lacking or inadequate, such as misdiagnoses that result in confinement in mental health institutions owing to interpreters' errors or absences. If interpretation is not provided, serious repercussions flow with regard to health and other issues for the LEPs and the general population. Both abroad and at home, negative, unintended consequences in the areas of national security, health, and commerce flow from the limited use or absence of interpretation services.

The need for adequate professional interpretation services is clear. The following comment of Nancy Frishberg hits the mark. The most obvious need, in concluding this chapter, is the provision of a two-way communication vehicle:

> The interpreter-as-window metaphor again emphasizes the clarity and fidelity of the interpretation. The interpreter-as-bridge and interpreter-as-phone connection likewise point to the distances or barriers between the participants who do not share the same language or communication system [*Interpretation* 60].

This chapter has reviewed the various multiple reasons why there is a dire need — and legal right — for interpreters who possess the required skills. This will be discussed further in Chapter 6, "Professional Qualifications," regarding the requirements for becoming a capable interpreter and translator.

# CHAPTER 5

# Professional Standards

## A. *Ethical Conduct*

People of most nations regard with esteem His Holiness, the Fourteenth Dalai Lama, whose Tibetan name is Tenzin Gyatso, recipient of the Nobel Peace Prize (December 1989). He held in his acceptance address and in additional writings that persons of goodwill should be able to encompass an ecumenical ethical attitude and values that are compatible with all of humanity. In an article, "Our Faith in Science," in *The New York Times* (12 Nov. 2005), he wrote:

> I believe that we must find a way to bring ethical considerations to bear upon the direction of scientific development, especially in the life sciences. By invoking fundamental ethical principles, I am not advocating a fusion of religious ethics and scientific inquiry. Rather, I am speaking of what I call "secular ethics," which embrace the principles we share as human beings: compassion, tolerance, consideration of others, the responsible use of knowledge and power. These principles transcend the barriers between religious believers and non-believers; they belong not to one faith but to all faiths.

The Dalai Lama's principles might properly serve as an introduction to the official oath administered to an interpreter and bear witness to the ethical standards required of the profession.

Professional standards and ethical conduct loom large among those who write about and practice the rendering of one language into another. This discussion starts with the perspective that ethical conduct is a subset of professional standards, but not necessarily linked to it. One example: Professional standards require a male interpreter to wear a jacket and tie at a court appearance. The absence of proper attire is not a breach of ethics but a lack of norms of propriety, common sense, and good taste. Ethics transcend good taste and proper attire. The key rhetorical question: Why are professional standards incumbent upon interpreters and translators? A brief answer that should surprise nobody is that at stake at a local level are legal, physical, and mental health issues, and other matters, such as reputations, money, deportation, and jail time. Interpretation and translation at national and high socioeconomic levels require professional standards because they involve serious matters, such as international contracts, sales of equipment, transfers of funds, treaty obligations, and security relations between countries.

A central thesis, which will be dwelt upon at greater length in Chapter 14, "Playacting and Power Relationships in the Courtroom," is that the interpreter—despite needing to be modest, discreet, and unassuming—plays a pivotal role and wields power beyond what the

professional title suggests. The interpreter is usually the only person during the interpretation act who understands in depth both of the languages and cultures involved. The ethical
aspect of professional standards are violated if the interpreter fumbles, omits something,
invents a translation or realizes that there is a misunderstanding caused by different — and
even seriously differing — cultural ways. Unfortunately, the courtroom interpreter is prohibited from explaining the misunderstanding, even if he, in effect, is dictating, narrowing, and
even distorting the possible outcomes. In a courtroom situation, for example, at least two or
more persons, in addition to the interpreter, get involved every time: administrative judge
and claimant, doctor and patient, an attorney for the accused and for the defendant. The ethical aspect of professional standards becomes perverted when the interpreter, poised between
two parties, skews an event. This action shows that the interpreter's ethical responsibility for
clarity, accuracy, and objectivity looms larger than his power over control of the event.

Other ethical or moral perspectives come into play in rendering statements from one foreign language to another. Whether the rendering takes place in a library, in a courtroom, or
at a diplomatic conference, professionals have to adhere to standards. The translator who confounds an important written word or phrase bears, for the most part, a burden of private
embarrassment when the glitch is finally revealed. In contrast, the courtroom interpreter who
commits a gaffe that is made public suffers embarrassment. The courtroom interpreter adheres
to standards when he has transmitted a correct version of a patient's symptoms, health status, and subsequent treatment. The correct version results in a fair and just implementation
of the laws. On a diplomatic assignment, the interpreter who furthers tension between foreign ministers when not rendering faithfully the cultural content of a phrase can be held as
the scapegoat. (The theme is dealt with in Chapter 11, "Modes of Interpretation and Translation," section F, "Interpreters as Scapegoats.") The diplomatic interpreter can feel content
when a fair rendering avoids frayed relations or, at worst, armed conflict. Although both the
interpreter and the translator are "bridges," they cannot divest themselves from responsibility. Ethics becomes the silent, internal lamp that illuminates the conduct of both professionals when they act out responsibly their respective duties. A sense of ethics through training
will ensure, more than any academic diploma, impartiality and will also earn the respect of
the other participants. While payment and tangible rewards flow from unimpeachable performances, the unheralded, silent reward of personal satisfaction is greater because it benefits
the individual and enhances the profession.

## INTERPRETING: AN "ACT OF TRUST"

The other protagonists rely on the professionalism and ethical behavior of the interpreter because they cannot verify directly the adequacy of the interpreter's performance, as
Nancy Frishberg aptly phrases it: "When the decision is made to involve an interpreter, the
clients enter into an act of trust. They trust that the interpreter [...] will not become emotionally involved in the issues to the detriment of the interpretation. They trust that the
interpreter will be discreet about the knowledge acquired during the interpretation or as a
result of the interpreting situation."[1]

On going over the definitions of "profession" and "professional" in the next chapter,
"Professional Qualifications," keep in mind that the interpreter must train to be a highly

qualified person to avoid interpreter errors which lead, for example, to unjust decisions in court and in mental health institutions. Complying with the written standards is one thing; it is quite another having the brains, personality, and integrity to do so. Take as an example the capacity for impartiality and detachment. It is critically important that the courtroom interpreter not embellish or in other ways try to make the witness's testimony more credible or sympathetic. Consider the unlikelihood — because it is outrageous — of the opposite, that is, that an interpreter might disparage a witness because of a lack of education or poor attire. The ethical principles and the Codes of Ethics, as well as the foundation for the ethical standpoint, treated at length below, establish a framework for setting standards. Other vital aspects are proper training, maturity, and a utilization of good sense.

# B. Expectations of Professionals

A discussion of standards for professional interpreters and translators can start with a personal distillation of the "don'ts" and "do's" derived from practical field experience. While the negatives and positives adhere to professional guidelines, they go beyond the objective and limited lists of the associations and delve into practices and details that will forestall personal grief and embarrassment.

## The "don'ts" of interpreting or, where applicable, translating

- Do not consciously omit, alter, or add to court testimony in interpreting. In translating don't omit or add to the text elements that violate the author's sense and sensibility.
- Do not guess when interpreting or translating. An interpreter in doubt can ask for a timeout to consult a dictionary. Translators, with the benefit of time, should consult dictionaries, a thesaurus, and outside experts.
- Do not express your emotional reactions, only those of the witness in the courtroom. A translator should not prettify or reject "dirty" words or phrases that seem obscene or blasphemous in a text.
- Do not reflect the posture, facial expressions and gestures of the witness while interpreting in court, despite being the personal and cultural patterns that accompany the utterances.
- Do not give declarations to media representatives on a case nor divulge at any time to anyone confidential or contractual matters for the purpose of self-aggrandizement. (On this delicate matter, see the section below "Ethics, Meta-ethics, and Postville," regarding an interpreter whose revelations made national headlines.)
- Do not take attorney referrals nor ask for special favors.
- Do not posture while before a judge or attorney.
- Avoid proximity (labeled proxemics) with relation to a witness or claimant.
- Do not provide legal advice to anybody.
- Do not act as an expert in the field of culture in the courtroom, even if asked by a judge or attorney to explain a facet of a foreign culture. A translator, on the other hand, has to immerse himself in a foreign culture to penetrate a text.
- Do not get lunch for a judge. Translators should not pander to an editor by inviting that person to lunch.
- Do not make false statements nor misrepresent facts or ideas.
- Recusal is the only option if not qualified to interpret or translate in a particular field.

### The "do's" that one should or even must adhere to

- Request repetition and/or clarification whenever necessary. Query the author or an expert if a text gets involved in unknown areas.
- Remain impartial and detached and retain objectivity at all times. The same applies to a translator of material that he repudiates or is not in agreement with.
- Provide, if required by a court authority, explanations of words and terms as a language specialist outside the courtroom, but not as an official interpreter in the courtroom. Translators can add footnotes to clarify arcane words or ideas.
- Only perform those duties directly related to interpreting and translating.
- Be unobtrusive in every way possible (posture, gestures, proximity, facial expressions, grooming, etc.). The translator of texts, in contrast, does not have a physical presence, except on the printed page, in negotiations, or in giving a lecture on the subject treated.
- Report any type of connection to another participant that may affect your impartiality or proper compliance, or may give that appearance.
- Keep current on languages, culture, and training techniques.

## C. NAJIT's and SDNY's Codes

The National Association of Judiciary Interpreters and Translators' (NAJIT) Code of Ethics and the Southern District of New York's (SDNY) Code of Professional Responsibility (CPR) propose eight principles. NAJIT's eight points run parallel to the eight points of the CPR, the latter subtitled "Federal Court Interpreter Ethics and Protocol," issued by the Interpreter's Office of the U.S. District Court of New York. The latter concludes with the pledge:

> I hereby swear, affirm, or promise that I shall accurately and faithfully interpret during any and all proceedings before the court to the best of my knowledge and ability.

What follows is, first, a listing of NAJIT's and SDNY's eight points, followed by a review and gloss of them. Some of the ideas and examples have already been discussed above in one form or another:

1. Accuracy
2. Impartiality
3. Confidentiality
4. Limitations of practice
5. Protocol and demeanor
6. Maintenance and improvement of knowledge
7. Accurate representation and credentials
8. Impediments to compliance

     **1. ACCURACY.** It is the responsibility of the interpreter to reflect the message in the source language into the target language as accurately as possible. The interpreter is the medium for other human beings: claimants, defenders, accusers, parents at risk of losing custody of their children, patients, judges, attorneys, social workers, and psychiatrists. The Code of Professional Responsibility requires proactive efforts to correct errors: "Interpreters have the duty to correct any material error in the interpretation of testimony." The interpreter must take action to correct a perceived or actual error. In the case of a challenge to an interpretation, say by an opposing attorney, a judge has to decide whether a correction should be made to modify the target language for greater accuracy.

## A DISPASSIONATE MESSENGER

According to Danica Seleskovitch, "Unlike the speaker, who takes his listener more or less consciously into account, and adjusts his speech accordingly, the interpreter is a messenger. He does not solicit a direct response and does not have to respond to the reaction elicited by the message he transmits. Consequently, he scarcely needs to take a professional interest in the personalities of the people whom he interprets, except to represent them accurately through their message."[2]

2. **IMPARTIALITY.** The interpreter needs to mask and compartmentalize emotions. Even when an obvious injustice is observed, the interpreter must not take sides or show a preference. Interference violates the interpreter's role, a fact which must be accepted. The court interpreter cannot favor any player: the accused, witness, judge, attorney, or public defender. This impartiality applies even when a contracting attorney requires a deposition, or a medical insurance company contracts one for a home investigation or a medical evaluation. The role stays the same, to be impartial — which is accomplished by performing accurately and objectively. To ensure impartiality the Code of Professional Responsibility affirms that "court interpreters are forbidden from accepting any gift, gratuity or valuable consideration in excess of their authorized or contracted compensation."

3. **CONFIDENTIALITY.** Confidentiality is also of the utmost importance. For that matter, at the Connecticut State Department of Children and Families (DCF) and other official sites, the person for whom one interprets has to give permission to perform for certain procedural activities, such as an Administrative Case Review (ACR), because of the confidential nature of the case. To avoid unpleasant surprises, do not mention a confidential matter to an outsider, however interesting the case or friendly the person, because that person may mention it to somebody else, and it can get to the wrong ears and harm the interpreter.

4. **LIMITATIONS OF PRACTICE.** Interpreters need to restrict themselves to interpreting. A claimant or witness unhappy with the attorney and impressed by the interpreter may try to hire the interpreter, or ask that person to recommend an attorney, or how to seek counsel and other recommendations. It is not proper to provide legal advice, and the interpreter must reject — courteously and with an explanation — any attempts by others to gain counsel from the interpreter or from any other person. It turns out that some interpreters have solicited direct assistance from attorneys and/or institutions and agencies while at the place of service under subcontract from an interpretation company. This is unethical conduct according to their contract with the interpretation company. It is also a breach of standards to provide one's personal or professional card while representing an interpretation company. To avoid uncomfortable moments, if the interpreter is asked to leave his personal references and/or card for legitimate reasons, the interpreter should ask to be contacted through the interpretation company and subsequently seek the interpretation company's permission to contact the person directly.

5. **PROTOCOL AND DEMEANOR.** The practices and protocols followed in the courts and other settings in which the interpreter provides services are described in detail in Chapter 13, "Settings and Procedures in Legal and Social Venues." Three points need to be emphasized here. The first is that every setting is idiosyncratic and different. The interpreter should

be aware of the setting beforehand. Or if not — which is usually the case — the interpreter must take the responsibility of asking a contracting agency about the particular setting's protocols and personalities before serving there. The second is that the interpreter must respond by standing when a judge or jury enters or departs a courtroom; sit when permitted or asked. The third, interpreters need to remember that they play only a discreet, if albeit important, role, which is as a medium of communication, and should therefore abstain from interfering with activities that do not pertain to that role. A modest image and a professional appearance are expected.

6. **MAINTENANCE AND IMPROVEMENT OF KNOWLEDGE.** Languages change. Vocabulary is endless. The interpreter should make it an imperative to review the (bilingual) glossaries and add to them. A bilingual dictionary at hand is *de rigueur*. Technology and customs continually modify and amplify vocabulary. The interpreter should be working on improving a store of knowledge related to the profession. This, of course, brings improved performance and therefore also greater satisfaction with the profession.

7. **ACCURATE REPRESENTATION AND CREDENTIALS.** The interpreter must be totally honest in the presentation of a professional résumé and background related to the position. Many books emphasize the importance of honesty in recording one's own skill level and qualifications when applying for a job.

8. **IMPEDIMENTS TO COMPLIANCE.** The interpreters must relay any particular problems that prevent, or can prevent, compliance with the conditions surrounding appropriate interpreting. Naturally, in order to detect noncompliance, including an inadvertent one, interpreters need to absorb the protocols, proceedings, procedures, and rules of every setting.

**CODE OF STANDARDS FOR NONJUDICIAL SETTINGS.** The "Six Ethical Standards [...]" listed below refer to the health and social services agencies, but do not differ greatly, or at all, from the canons applied to all settings, especially the judicial system. The Ethical Standards derive from "Bridging the Language Gap: How to Meet the Need for Interpreters in Minnesota. Interpreter Standards Advisory Committee, University of Minnesota, November 1998."

*"Six Ethical Standards for Interpreters in Community and Health Care Settings" require an ethical interpreter to...*

1. Maintain confidentiality.
2. Interpret accurately and completely.
3. Maintain impartiality.
4. Maintain professional distance.
5. Know one's own limits.
6. Demonstrate professionalism.[3]

# D. The Interpreter's Role in Unfair Situations

Although some of the situations described below have been discussed earlier, they are particularly apposite at this juncture. Interpreters may find that some medical doctors reach mistaken medical conclusions, which may be based on mercenary self-interest, bad diagnoses, or negative attitudes. For example, some doctors may state that a client whom they have been asked to evaluate has a "low threshold for pain," when it appears to the interpreter that this is not the case. The interpreter may or may not be right but, nonetheless, the only thing to do is to stick to a professional responsibility of interpreting adequately. Without going into specific details, one of several unpleasant experiences comes to mind. An investigator for an insurance company asked an interpreter to sit in the waiting room to eavesdrop on future interviewees and to relay the comments to him. This interpreter politely demurred and indicated to him that the request did not fit within the duties and ethics of an interpreter. He accepted the refusal sheepishly and simply said, "I understand."

Other situations are certainly problematic for the interpreter. In the following, who is at fault? Who is responsible? In one instance a doctor may point out that a patient being examined for a state or federal agency to ascertain the extent of an injury or illness is holding a cane in the wrong hand. This may lead to the assumption, true or false, that the patient is "putting on a show," as the doctors commonly say. This behavior will influence the doctor's opinion, leading to a distrust of the patient regarding the level of pain experienced by the patient. What can the interpreter do? It may be that the patient is dissembling in order to obtain a greater benefit. On the other hand, to give the patient the benefit of the doubt, it may also turn out that the patient never received proper instructions, or misunderstood them, or did not remember them accurately, or the cane was not prescribed by a doctor, but lent by a helpful acquaintance, leaving the patient unaware of the negative impression being created. Personal experience shows that several LEP persons did not use a cane properly because of ignorance. An interpreter can do very little lacking proof, or even with it, regarding a patient's misfeasance. Nor is it the interpreter's role to weigh in. However, if the doctors were friendly and confidentiality prevailed, then, still balancing the risks, it is possible to indicate to them that there might be dissembling, but that also several other possibilities existed and describe them.

The interpreter who believes himself the target of an unfair act should usually voice the feeling off the record and out of hearing range of the witness or patient to a responsible official. In one case, an inexperienced female attorney shouted at an interpreter, "You *will* do that, won't you?" It turns out she had complained bitterly to a female court reporter before a deposition started about sex bias against female attorneys. She subsequently, in an authoritarian manner, told the interpreter in front of opposing counsel, the LEP witness, and the court reporter that it was she who was in charge of the deposition; she rejected the interpreter's suggestion about explaining beforehand to the witness the regulations regarding depositions. Her ignorance of the protocols that applied to deposing LEP litigants were obvious to most everyone present. Although her brusque attitude was very difficult to accept, the interpreter decided not to take the attorney seriously and not force the other participants to postpone the deposition by departing. So the interpreter, instead of leaving in a huff, swallowed his pride, preserved his integrity and that of the deposition, and acquiesced to the lawyer's demands. Afterwards, the interpretation company was made aware of the transgression. Thankfully, that attorney never appeared again. If no satisfaction is achieved in an egregious situation, a complaint can be lodged at a different forum or level, but before anything else, the interpretation service should be carried out.

A lack of objectivity is noticeable, often, among attorneys taking depositions and court reporters transcribing dialog. Perhaps they have their reasons or sad experiences. As described earlier, there are grounds for lawyers' misapprehensions, but the interpreter must display detachment and objectivity and do the job for which he was hired. It is not possible to take to task the attorneys for lack of objectivity and bias and not criticize the same traits in the interpreter. It is critically important that the interpreter not embellish or in other ways try to make the witness's testimony more credible or sympathetic, or the opposite, i.e., to disparage a witness because of lack of education or poor attire. The long-term, desirable outcome for the interpreter who remains objective is that the lawyers will come around, be grateful, and show appreciation. And so will the witness, who is immensely relieved to be readily understood by the interpreter to the attorneys. A high ethical sense on the part of the interpreter will avoid or reduce errors that have led to unjust decisions in court and in mental health institutions. Complying with the standards and having the personality and integrity to do so are requirements for any professional interpreter.

## E. Ethics, Meta-Ethics, and Postville

PRECURSORS OF THE CODES OF ETHICS. The aforementioned codes of professional conduct and responsibility for interpreters and translators derive from hundreds of philosophers' writings about appropriate human behavior in civilized Western society to ensure group survival and fair treatment among individuals. Taylor, in writing this section, realizes that the limitations of space can only allude to the most pertinent philosophers. The ideas in the codes find support in Aristotle's ethics, which entail acts in accordance with man's nature to realize his full potential so that he will do good and be content. Aristotle's ideas prepared the groundwork for an ethicist like Immanuel Kant (1724–1804), whose philosophy undergirds the codes. This professor from provincial Konigsberg developed a universal *Critique of Practical Reason*, which holds as its core that man should be treated as an end in himself, not as a means to an end. In line with this argument, a shabbily dressed, undocumented LEP should be considered a human being, worthy of humane treatment under the law, not as a means or instrument in the grip of a zealous prosecutor desirous of greater office or reputation by inflicting punishment.

A contemporary of Kant, the Scot Adam Smith (1723–1790), in the *Wealth of Nations* stressed that man, acting in his "enlightened self-interest," would seek the highest good for himself, his family, and his nation with the least amount of pain. To this end, it cannot be overlooked that self-interest ties in to the LEPs' plight. The penurious Latinos cross the southern border in their self-interest, whatever the risk, to seek jobs that pay dollars, in part to cover personal expenses, but the remainder to transmit as remittances—amounting collectively to roughly $69 billion in 2008—via Western Union for families at home.[4]

Philosophers Jeremy Bentham (1748–1832) and his fellow Utilitarians, James Mill and son John Stuart Mill, transformed a Manichean pain/pleasure concept into the aphorism the "greatest good for the greatest number," which was reduced "to the greatest happiness." The Mills' concept of the "greatest good" and its development into "consequential ethics" have great impact on Latin America and Latin Americans. For centuries the "greatest good" has remained confined to the ruling minority, in charge of arms, government, education, jobs, property, and ideology. Not finding the "greatest good" at home, millions of desperate Latin Americans, consequently, have turned to the U.S. for the "greatest happiness," a chance to make a living wage denied to them in their native lands. Note the following examples.

Millions, labeled "wetbacks," crossed the Río Bravo under cover of darkness for subsistence survival on farms, in restaurants, and tending gardens. The Marielitas traversed the choppy Straits of Florida on rafts from Fidel Castro's Cuba to take advantage of the "wet foot/dry foot" political philosophy to create new lives in south Florida. Thousands sought political exile status; they fled military dictatorships, such as Augusto Pinochet's (Chile, 1973–1990), and Jorge Rafael Videla's (Argentina, 1976–1981), for welcoming refuge in the U.S., Canada, Europe, Australia, and other Latin American countries. Finally, the semi-privileged class: Nurses, doctors, mathematicians, and engineers by the hundreds of thousands came from Latin America — as well as from Asia and Europe — to America with H-1B non-immigration visas and job possibilities in hospitals, universities, and corporations.

In short, many of the ethical principles elaborated in the varied and complex philosophies of Aristotle, Kant, Smith, Bentham, and the Mills, among others, form the basis for the ethical codes that have shaped the conduct of interpreters and translators in their dealings with themselves, with immigrant LEPs, and with legal, governmental, and corporate systems.

META-ETHICS. It is not the job of the courtroom interpreter to make or carry out the law on murder, nor is it the obligation of the diplomatic interpreter/translator to formulate national policy on war and aggression. Yet, both from their respective positions are entitled to think about rightness or wrongness, i.e., the ethical questions that underlie the decisions held by judges, diplomats, and the military in their respective fields. Court interpreters are wise to display tact and prudence when faced with discrimination by doctors, wise in not questioning judges' and attorneys' arbitrary opinions and methods during a trial, and wise to refrain from explaining unusual cultural issues to officials, even if asked discreetly after a proceeding. This process of thinking about moral values, without participating in them or acting upon them, is termed "meta-ethics."[5] When employed discreetly, for example, thinking about the implications of abortion for the woman and the family, meta-ethics implies sensitivity to people and society. A grey area occurs for interpreters (and for judges, lawyers, physicians, and teachers, etc.) when in the exercise of Constitutional guarantees of freedom of assembly, speech, and the press, they act in favor of or against issues by distributing leaflets, or marching in demonstrations, or writing about it.

The negative aspect of meta-ethics, or "going above and beyond ethics" as its definition suggests, consists of crossing over into unethical conduct when the complex situations of abortion, murder, or immigration compel courtroom interpreters to refuse to perform their duties, to lash out at the judges or attorneys, or to disrupt a proceeding. In the course of this text, readers have witnessed the opposite, that is, numerous examples of a courtroom interpreter using discretion, maintaining confidentiality, and behaving impartially. Legal, not ethical, transgression arises when interpreters as well as others take action to bomb clinics, maim doctors, kill judges and attorneys, or harbor illegal persons. It follows from the preceding that interpreters and translators, in carrying out their professional functions, despite their personal beliefs about abortion, homicide, and undocumented aliens, must remain within the bounds of their codes and not trespass into illegal behavior in the name of a higher ethics. Or if they do, they face the consequences.

POSTVILLE, CONFIDENTIALITY, AND COURAGE. Erik Camayd-Freixas, associate professor and director of the Translating and Interpreting Program at Florida International University, a certified interpreter with 23 years of experience, tested the Codes of Ethics to the fullest after federal government law enforcement agents raided the kosher meatpacking plant, Agriprocessors, Inc., in Postville, Iowa, on 12 May 2008. After Immigration and Customs Enforcement agents (I.C.E.) rounded up, arrested, and charged 297 non–English-speaking

Guatemalan workers for bearing false Social Security cards and numbers given to them by their supervisors or bought from smugglers, a mass trial took place in which Camayd-Freixas and 25 interpreters intervened. During the proceedings, he reports, his team followed the codes of impartiality, neutrality, completeness, nonintervention, and confidentiality to the letter.

Things changed following the hearings, acceptance of guilty pleas, verdicts, and five-month sentences given to 262 workers. Camayd-Freixas denounced the roundups, detentions, hearings, judgments, and sentences in a fourteen-page article to *The New York Times* (13 June 2008), subtitled "A Personal Account: The Largest ICE Raid in History."[6] Further details from the author and commentaries pro and con by interpreters, political figures, and reporters is available online. The controversy, for the purposes of this section on meta-ethics, is whether impartiality, confidentiality, and nonintervention were bent or broken. Camayd-Freixas sincerely believes in and documents his appropriate action, first and foremost while interpreting and supervising, after the hearings as a citizen in expressing his strong views publicly against a powerful government agency that arrested illiterate migrant Guatemalans who *unknowingly* were carrying false documents and breaking the law. In line with the definitions of meta-ethics presented, Camayd-Freixas contends that no code infraction occurred because his public claim took place after all legal matters were settled and he was no longer under contract nor obligation to remain silent and indifferent to the legal, but not humane or legitimate, jailing of illiterate migrant workers who could not read nor recognize their misdeed.

Two schools of thought exist. Prominent French–English interpreter Chris Durban, citing anonymous informants for her *ATA Chronicle* article, writes that "there is no doubt that Camayd-Freixas violated the letter if not the spirit of the code — interpreters cannot morph into investigative journalists midway into an assignment. [...] He should have disqualified himself." Durban, to balance the argument, cites others in her article. She reports that "[...] no consensus is in sight. If anything, a professional interpreter's sober account of justice as administered is a timely reminder that this language business is not black and white but grey. And definitely, passionately human." While no leader of ATA or NAJIT has weighed in publicly (up until December 2008) with opinions on this incident, Congresswoman Zoe Lofgren was concerned enough about the human rights issues to call a hearing on the matter.

Camayd-Freixas appears to have acted within NAJIT's Code of Ethics in the face of improprieties by the legal and judicial systems. He did not disrupt proceedings or violate confidentialities while contracted to perform his duties. His writings and speeches after his contractual obligation expired characterize a use of meta-ethics, which permit the use of public documents and personal interviews as a citizen to call attention to what Durban labels "a miscarriage of justice." While some have labeled it a violation of confidentiality, many others might consider opposing the government an act of righteous courage.

The public position that Camayd-Freixas single-handedly espoused against the harsh actions of I.C.E. and the Department of Justice was vindicated by the U.S. Supreme Court's ruling (05 May 2009) in another case (Flores-Figueroa *v.* U.S., No. 08–108).[7] The Court's unanimous decision held that the authorities had selectively parsed the law and misapplied it to immigrant groups. The ruling came too late to protect the imprisoned and deported Guatemalans, but the outrage at Postville resonated in the Court's decision, thus preventing federal authorities from misapplying the law in future cases. A visible and verbal interpreter who risks everything to speak up for a just cause at the proper time, place, and manner put into motion meta-ethics.

# F. The Judicial System and Science

THE INTERPRETER, SCIENCE, AND THE LEGAL SYSTEM. As a court interpreter, Sibirsky has been concerned with the philosophical and intellectual bases of decisions and positions taken by jurists and attorneys. As a believer in the advantages that science can bring to these decisions, Sibirsky has researched answers to these questions in the writings of leading criminologists and neuroscientists. The questions that may be answered in this brief section are: How do the theories of evolutionary biology, the gene, the brain, and neuroethics have implications for the translator and interpreter *vis-à-vis* the legal and judicial systems? These modern scientific theories could constitute the foundations of human behavior. Despite their applicability, they have not yet been fully utilized, unfortunately, to the workings and philosophy of the legal and judicial systems. This concept may appear esoteric and too far removed from the actual interpretation process, but consider that U.S. judicial systems have not caught up sufficiently with what science has learned with the implications of this for the understanding of justice and its achievement.

Sibirsky's colleague, Thomas W. Clark, founder and director of the Center for Naturalism, on whose board of directors Daniel Dennett serves, finds that an outmoded criminal justice system based on supernatural traditions that seek retribution and punishment instead of a humanitarian attempt to rehabilitate is inadequate because it fails to account properly for the injuries caused by the various members of society who have created conditions that lead to immoral and destructive behaviors and inner biological determinants:

> Support for retribution stems at least partially from a supernaturalist conception of the criminal, who, it is commonly thought, could have chosen *not* to commit the crime whatever his internal and external circumstances might have been. [...] But the reasons they become offenders in the first place lie in the conditions that created them, so we must hold *society* responsible — ourselves, our families, schools and communities, as well as offenders — in our quest for a safe, flourishing culture.[8]

As the imprint of the findings by neuroscientists grows larger, national and international judicial systems will need to confront the importance of causal factors on behavior. The legal precepts that are dictated by traditional moral interpretations incrusted in laws can lead to injustice by giving precedence to probably outmoded legal strictures rather than unavoidable behaviors explained by causal factors unraveled by science.

On this question, cognitive neuroscientist Michael Gazzaniga asks, "Did the defendant carry out the horrible crime freely and by choice, or was it inevitable because of the nature of his brain and his past experiences? [...] Some day the issue will dominate the entire legal system [affecting] those old chestnuts — free will and personal responsibility."[9] Gazzaniga, thus, constructs a dichotomy: The brain is automatic, not yet fully understood and operates to a great degree nonconsciously, blindly, and automatically. It is this automaticity that obviates responsibility, and yet the human being in whose body the brain is housed and who is affected by it carries "personal responsibility" in the interactions of a so-called social world. Gazzaniga brings this crucial matter regarding the inner and social reality to the interpreters' environment to show how the legal system interprets how and why humans act from the perspective of the outer, social construct, without looking at our inner (brain) world, at how our behaviors are dictated from within by causal factors. First among these is the law's perspective: "At the crux of the problem is the legal system's view of human behavior. It assumes that Harry is a 'practical reasoner,' a person who acts because he has freely chosen to act. This simple but powerful assumption in the law drives the entire legal system" (Gazzaniga 100). The neuroscientific perspective: "We are all part of a deterministic system that some day, in theory, we will completely understand. Yet the idea of responsibility, a social construct that exists in the rules of a society, does not exist in the neuronal structures of the brain" (Gazzaniga 101–102). (For a further discussion of language and the brain, see Chapter 15, "Implications of Bilingualism.")

MEMORY, TESTIMONY, AND ETHICS. Not only have the judicial systems not taken sufficiently into account the motivators (i.e., the triggers of behavior), in contrast, they also give too much credence to witness testimony, which is such a crucial component for the achievement of justice. Memory is by nature flawed, occasioning partial details of what a witness thinks or believes and what really happened. It is sad that "truth" too often falls between the cracks: "The day is approaching when the failure to handle such testimony as by nature flawed will be considered unethical. [...] Once we recognize this, the way testimony is used in a courtroom may change forever. Furthermore, once the variations on how memory betrays us are understood, new techniques for acquiring testimony should be used" (Gazzaniga 124).

CONCLUSIONS ON PROFESSIONAL STANDARDS. Interpreters ought to take to heart reflecting on their professional standards. This book has pointed out repeatedly the importance of interpreting adequately for the benefit, not only of the LEPs with their limited economic and political resources, but also for the sake of honesty in the judicial system. This is why a code of professional standards that reinforces ethical behavior is of great importance for interpreters in all the settings in which they provide their services. It is important for interpreters to uphold ethics; doing so provides a range of standpoints from an intellectual, philosophic, religious and scientific perspective. The material should be useful to interpreters and translators and to those associated with them professionally as they interweave their own personality with external reality. It is important, in this regard, to absorb professional standards and play a part in preserving an honest and just legal system. What could be more important in a democracy?

Sibirsky concludes with a personal reflection: If there were a mantra for the interpreter, it might be that "I am important to the clients because I am their bridge [...] in all the settings, not only in courtrooms and related, but everywhere else as well. It is, then, my ethical responsibility to be the best I can be."

# CHAPTER 6

# Professional Qualifications

## A. Interpreting Day by Day

The reader has by now seen that a professional interpreter requires high-level qualifications and ethics to be able to cope with the tasks — which range from routine, easy, and subtle to difficult and confrontational — that occur in the normal course of business. To underscore these points, the authors will present a realistic picture of a typical day in the life of interpreter Sibirsky to illustrate the need for fairly demanding qualifications.

Before passing to describe the experiences of Sibirsky, consider the following quotation from Elena De Jongh, who cites Nancy Festinger's view of a busy schedule in court interpreting:

> Festinger points out some of the demands connected with court interpreting: "[...] we perform mental gymnastics, jumping from an attorney's constitutional argument in a motion to suppress, to a drug addict's slurred explanation, to a witness's deliberately elusive answer, to the socio-psychological jargon of a probation report, to the small print of a statute, to a judge's syntactically convoluted charge to the jury — often, all in the space of a few hours."[1]

Sibirsky's events in a typical week substantiate the complexity of interpreting. He interprets all over the small state of Connecticut in various venues: courthouses, attorneys' and doctors' offices for depositions and consultations, warrens of the various branches of the State Department of Children and Families, the Commission on Human Rights and Opportunities, and the Social Security Administration's Office of Disability and Adjudication and Review. Home visits with social workers and insurance investigators are part of the job.

The personal and professional itinerary of a freelance interpreter working for an agency requires extensive travel in order to take advantage of employment opportunities. Two visits to two sites or towns per day are normal. The hours always vary. In accessible Connecticut one can start in a town one and a half hours from home at 9:00 A.M., interpret for about two hours, and then have to interpret again, perhaps at 3:30 P.M., in another town one hour away from home (and not always in a straight line). Often, in "spare time," one supplements income from interpreting assignments by translating documents.

When serving as an independent or freelance interpreter for the courts or private companies, the working professional needs to be in a constant state of readiness to travel and to perform in often unexpected and, indeed, extremely varied settings, often the same day. All aspirants need to be ready for trials, home investigations by an insurance company, home visits with a State Department of Children and Families investigator, and actions in a shelter for homeless and troubled adolescents. An interpreter on assignment by an agency does not usually know in advance what specialized vocabulary may be required. These are some of the trials and tribulations of independent contractors, the working stiffs in the workaday interpretation field at the local and state level. As promised, readers get an unadorned and unembellished view of the vicissitudes of the field, where most translators and interpreters labor.

## B. Journal of an Itinerant Interpreter

From the following diary of a week's activities, the reader will capture the interpretation event and the human, political, psychological, and linguistic processes involved in the episodes. They deal with the life of a working, itinerant interpreter. The readers will find instructive the hectic, fascinating, terribly sad, and exhilarating events that occur while acting on several stages that vary in plots and actors, and yet had one unifying element, i.e., that the interpreter would never know how the play turned out for the actors involved. Most often, interpreters do not find out the results of cases, having been long gone from the event. Occasionally a piece of gossip informs of a handicapped person awarded benefits or children returned to a rehabilitated mother. Lamentably, and this thread runs through the book, the cases too often deal with excruciating chronic pain that often eventually leads to severe depression and homicidal and suicidal ideas, often caused originally by work or automobile accidents.

Not infrequently, field interpreters are involved with family matters: parents whose children are removed from them because of their substance abuse and/or domestic violence; parents whose children are taken away because they do not know how to manage and control their children's behavior; children with attention deficit disorder (ADD) and hyperactivity, also accompanied by asthma. A high percentage of the limited-English-proficient are woefully undereducated, with very poorly developed cognitive skills and a very limited vocabulary, which exacerbates interpreting accurately for them. Join in this journey, and let us get underway.

I rose early that Monday morning from my home in Westport to face a full load of weekly interpreting assignments. The first took place in another town at the State Department of Children and Families (DCF), where I attended an Administrative Case Review (ACR in DCF jargon). It turned out to involve a 27-year-old, single Hispanic mother of three, whose ages ranged from 4 to 9 years. Mental health issues induced by stress from the children had prompted her to ask for assistance. All three children displayed serious behavioral problems. For example, the 9-year-old had cut off the ears of a neighbor's cat; the boy, aged 7, had tried to drown a dog in a toilet. That difficult scenario is among many similar ones that the freelance interpreter gets involved with.

But the central point of the story concerns the earnest Hispanic social worker and his supervisor who attended the aforesaid meeting. To my surprise, the social worker violated the "rules of the road." He spoke to the client in Spanish, knowing that that was the interpreter's responsibility, in front of the attending supervisor who did not speak Spanish. I interrupted the social worker and diplomatically suggested that he speak in parts so that I could translate what he was saying into English. Then I added tartly, "for the benefit of your supervisor." He captured my not so subtle message and said that he would only speak in English, from which point the meeting proceeded smoothly. The delicate issue here was to operate inferentially, if possible, so as not to belittle the social worker, who, at best, tried to be helpful, but at worst tried to upstage the interpreter.

When the meeting was over and everybody had left, the supervisor congratulated me for a job well done. He went out of his way to explain that he understood my obligations, but that he had undergone a very sad experience with a previous interpreter during a case with serious charges involved. He related that the female interpreter had shown up "with her boobs practically hanging out," was not able to express herself well in Spanish, to the extent that the client complained of not being able to understand her. Additionally, the interpreter did not re-create what the speaker said by providing an equivalent translation, but rather "explained" what the social worker was saying, and even made mistakes while using the third person. The incident reflected poorly on the profession, and with reason the supervisor was skeptical of interpreters. This situation cast into disrepute the hiring agency, which, perhaps despairing of losing a client, did not screen the interpreter for competence or for appropriate behavior.

Following that conversation, I traveled to three different towns and three different doctors' offices for Workers' Compensation cases over the next few days. The individuals in the three cases had in common physical therapy for serious chronic pain that would be permanent for two of them. I requested and received permission from the doctors to explain to the patients that they had to describe fully their symptoms. I made them understand — disabusing them of their cultural heritage — that it was wrong to assume that doctors knew everything from knowledge and experience and thus did not need to be told — and might be offended if they did so — that one felt pain and where it was located. Despite that, they held fast to their strongly-held, culturally-based beliefs, even though the doctors who were examining them asked specifically about the source and location of the pain. The turning point came when I clarified that the doctor was not looking at faces, but rather at the spot being touched and therefore could not notice pain in the patients' expressions. Patients and doctors benefited from the advice and assistance. The patients relaxed greatly owing to my personal ministrations and felt less lonely and desperate. The doctors, who were at first apprehensive about using interpreters, also relaxed and learned to take full advantage of and benefit from the interpretation services.

Later that same week, in still another town, I attended a six-and-a-half-hour meeting at the Commission on Human Rights and Opportunities (CHRO). Two fired Puerto Rican workers had accused their former employer of discriminating against them because of their national origin. One of the workers, who had already migrated to another state, was interviewed via a telephone conference call. The two Hispanic workers were obviously competent according to their excellent record of performance. Their lack of English, inadequate formal education, and unfamiliarity with the laws probably were key factors in not checking out carefully the areas in which CHRO could get involved. They were also incapable of giving "yes or no" answers and just could not be responsive to the questions asked. This possibly had its origins in their alienation from the English language and the dominant mainland culture, and, in my estimation, also to what I denominate "the culture of the undereducated," by just rambling on and changing the subject when the CHRO investigator confronted them about a *non sequitur*. To compound the difficulties of communication, the investigator was blind; this being so, I could not send her adequate visual or body language messages. However, I overcame this handicap by raising my voice after not interrupting the interpretation process during the claimants' long-winded explanations. She smiled, however, thus signaling to me that she had captured my subtle message. I did not find out about the outcome of the claim, but I was proud to have discovered a strategy to interpret for exaggerating or lying claimants with English deficiencies and a handicapped claims officer as objectively as possible. In my opinion, which ethically I could not voice, they had probably been mistreated in different ways and by several people, but they were wrong to claim that kind of discrimination when about 80% of their co-workers were Hispanic, including their immediate supervisor.

During that same week, I was involved in a deposition that lasted only 35 minutes regarding an undereducated LEP person who, accidentally, had crashed his car into a person on a bicycle. The defendant was deposed by the state's attorney, a male, an extremely experienced professional. The defendant's attorney, a female, was assertive and objected very well several times, forcing her adversary to change his line of questions. The undereducated, but very mature and sincere, defendant admitted to his linguistic and cultural inadequacies several times to explain why he did not understand certain official matters, and took an extremely long time to answer questions and examine photographs. My only question to myself was why the state's attorney took a mere 35 minutes for the deposition? But it was not my place to question that.

When a witness to the accident took the stand, I had to alert both attorneys to the "rules of the game" on a notepad. The problem was that after being sworn in, the deposing attorney proceeded to ask him questions before going over the rules of a deposition that involves an interpreter. Both attorneys acceded to my highly visible alert scribbled on the notepad, which prompted them to tell the witness to slow down and wait for my interpretation to be completed before responding even if he understood the question in English.

As a personal and concluding sideline to the interpreting matters of that week, I must add that I had asked the court reporter before the preceding deposition began to "affirm me" under the law when she administered the interpreter's oath to me. When I asked her if she knew how to do it, she said yes. Typically enough, she administered the oath with, "Do you solemnly affirm [...]" and ended with "[...] under God?" I was forced then to partially disavow by saying, "I do affirm, not under a God, but rather under the penalty of perjury." This rectification was and is very important to me and perhaps to others. If an interpreter's philosophy does not include a personal God, or believes that the law, not a deity, should be the dominant force in a sworn public oath, or believes, furthermore, that it is being hypocritical to swear on a Bible or any other text, then it is ethical and legal to make that known. This could be controversial in some venues and may result in being rejected as the interpreter, as once happened to me. But any professional who strongly adheres to this belief has the right to address this issue discreetly but firmly with the official charged with the swearing-in procedure.

The bottom-bottom line regarding these lived mini-dramas is that the interpreter on center stage has one short and irreversible shot at correct communication and clarification with all the actors while the play is in progress. No understudy, no repeat, no "one more take," no "I'll rehearse and do better tomorrow night." The interpreter, like a stage actor, prevails or fails "in the moment" and can neither return to the scene nor influence the outcome once the players exit left. More often than not the fate and fortune of persons who do not understand English hang on the interpreter doing a good job presenting their story, their claim, their complaint, and their remedy. Chapter 14, "Playacting and Power Relationships in the Courtroom," will examine in detail the interpretation act as theater and the interpreter as one of the actors.

## C. Neutrality and Decorum vis-à-vis Misfortunes

It is pertinent to present here two more aspects of an interpreter's experience, this time related to sensitivity and control over it. The point is to paint a true image of the world in which most freelance interpreters act and interact. The following descriptions attempt to introduce topics that alert the interpreter to realistic events without covering up what really affects performance. An interpreter who works with courts and the social service agencies has to develop a thick skin. Without that carapace, that protective shell, he or she could not be of adequate service in assisting victims of bad luck or victims of perpetrators of criminal action. It is important not to put oneself in denial about the sad circumstances so many humans have to endure in life. It is critical to avoid pessimism or cynicism despite working in environments that are depressing.

MAINTAIN IMPARTIALITY. Practically every day, one witnesses very sad experiences during interpretation services: crippled lives, tragic happenings, and sad memories. In most settings, the interpreter will face sad and tragic events: The witness may be in excruciating pain, relate misfortunes galore, and tell of hallucinations and homicidal and suicidal thoughts. This can culminate in the witness breaking into tears. Other witnesses and spectators can empathize with what is taking place and therefore further exacerbate the situation.

The interpreter affected with this intensity and drama who tears up and hesitates to perform his obligations does nobody favors. Any interpreter greatly affected by this human drama should wait out the emotional experience and resume duties when able to function again. Another recommendation is to step back, recognizing and accepting that these misfortunes are part of reality. An interpreter has to protect his own well-being by not internalizing others' misfortunes. This also occurs with medical doctors and police officers who have to steel themselves from illness, accidents, and death. It goes against the Codes of Ethics to lose impartiality by injecting personal judgments and personal biases and emotions. One can sum up by saying "impartiality" yes, "indifference" no.

MEDICAL AND LEGAL INDIFFERENCE. An interpreter who performs before seemingly heartless professionals "just doing their jobs" for maximum personal profit and few ethical scruples needs to remain composed. Behold a few personal experiences. Some doctors conclude with little evidence that a patient has a low threshold for pain. This medical diagnosis may be a way of pandering to those who contracted them, that is, to evaluate a claimant adversely in order to continue getting "business" sent their way.

On the other hand, some medical specialists demand exhaustive medical evidence, whether pertinent or not, in order to be able to recommend against the LEP's claim. This can occur when the reports are, as the specialist is aware, from doctors who are overworked in clinics for the poor and simply do not have the extra time that private practitioners may have. The specialists may also be rotated, requiring a case conference of several practitioners in order to compile an even more exhaustive and perfectly put together report.

Civil and criminal trials involve adversarial tactics by attorneys; by their training and disposition, lawyers strive to best one another for the sake of their clients and reputations. In so doing, some carry their tactics to extremes, becoming sadistic in an attempt to upset the witnesses emotionally and cloud their thinking and then use apparently contradictory or false statements in court to minimize or eliminate their credibility before the judge or the jury. In other situations, some attorneys and court reporters joke and laugh about unrelated matters, displaying indifference or callousness to the claimants' difficulties.

INDIFFERENCE TO THE INTERPRETER. Some attorneys, court reporters, doctors, and their staff do not greet the interpreter nor say goodbye, perhaps because the interpreter is obligated to remain impartial and not get involved with jokes at the clients' or witnesses' expense. Other professionals act boorishly and need to exert their authority over interpreters, presuming intellectual deficiency, or assuming that they will overburden or complicate their jobs. Why do some act this way? One can give them the benefit of the doubt and say they may also be fatigued or overburdened. Or with less benefit, one can blame it on personality quirks. Still other reasons are possible. In a written comment to a draft of the manuscript, Virginia Benmaman adds that "most have absolutely no understanding of the skills required for an interpreter." She continues that "translation and interpretation are not considered a profession and garner little prestige and respect." In the face of these challenges, the interpreter must be firm and stoic, and continue to provide quality services.

## D. *Physical and Emotional Conditioning*

How can the typical or atypical interpreter prepare for the arduous day-in and day-out stresses of physical travel and emotional and intellectual stresses that beset this profession?

The following statement may sound bathetic, but it should be given high consideration: In order for the interpretation performance by the interpreter to have a greater assurance of success, it is advisable that the interpreter be at peace with the world and devoid of anxieties. Daniel Goleman, in *Social Intelligence,* follows Antonio Damasio, the eminent neuroscientist from the University of Southern California, in the contention that inner peace has been found to be helpful for persons in general and for professionals in the pursuit of their tasks. Our moments of greatest exultation are a result of total attentiveness, strong interest, and an emotional immersion. When this takes place, all persons can perform optimally.[2]

This state of preparation does not come naturally or easily. The interpreter has to train for this profession, as would an athlete, by exercising, maintaining a good diet, and getting sufficient rest. The Latin maxim applies: *mens sana in corpore sano* (a healthy mind in a healthy body). Total concentration to the nuances is essential for a successful interpreter. To achieve that focus, body and brain-mind must work in harmony and blend speed with confidence.

Similarly, the interpreter is required to process as objectively as possible the experience the LEP individual is undergoing and not let the latter's stress impede one's ability to perform with concentration. It would be foolish to underestimate the stress of the LEP and its effect on the interpreter. The mere fact of being interrogated in court or in a deposition — in addition to being in an English-dominant setting — can create anxiety in the LEP witnesses. The individual being questioned who feels that her or his value as a member of society is at stake, which can lead to a drop in self-esteem, is able, directly or indirectly, to transmit that anxiety to the interpreter. This can lead to diminished concentration and performance.

The libraries and bookstores contain abundant material on how to achieve good condition and also relaxation techniques. Both are critically important to confront the routine life of an interpreter, interrupted abruptly and often by unpredictable happenings and challenges. Following is an example of useful tips that are attributed to attorney/interpreter A. Samuel Adelo, of Santa Fe, New Mexico:

• Proper breathing is the first step to reduce tension and to be able to articulate properly.
• Now, for some ways to relieve tension when you are under pressure. Tighten the muscles, then relax them. Sometimes, we do not realize how much our muscles of the head, neck, and upper torso have tightened.[3]

The importance of voice in the interpretation act and how to train that instrument for maximum effectiveness cannot be underestimated. Practical experience dictates that proper breathing and inhaling deeply with the shoulders lowered takes away tension from the vocal area. One has to practice expressing oneself with the exhaled air. Projection of the sounds takes a special effort. Even the use of a microphone will not rescue the interpreter who mouths and swallows the sounds and uses a breathy voice; these sounds will be lost. Acoustics affect projection. Look around the room to see if it is heavily draped, has marble floors or has tall ceilings. These elements absorb sounds and thus call for greater projection.

Proper phrasing and rhythm contribute to clarity and interest. The interpreter who does not learn to phrase properly the words and sentences will not capture the listeners' attention. It is important to establish a rhythm to carry the phrases to completion.

In addition to mastering control of one's voice quality, the throat has to be protected with hydration, i.e., drink soothing fluids that are not too warm or cold. To guard against a dry mouth or a hoarse throat, determine in advance where the water fountain is and inquire about coffee or tea, often available upon request. To guard against laryngitis, take to the event throat lozenges or a spray.

The interpreter who, to remain alert, relies on quick fixes like caffeine in coffee or stimulants in pills, or even worse, controlled substances, may succeed in the short run, but long-term use jeopardizes the body and the job. Excessive use of alcohol — a depressant rather than a stimulant — to gain courage ends up as slurred speech and transmits an odor that breath mints cannot fully disguise. Other elements of careless habits that undermine one's reputation include a heavy meal prior to going on the job, which results in sluggishness, or a lack of sleep, which leads to confusion and mistakes.

All forms of prolonged interpretation result in fatigue. There is no question that the interpreter must take care of his physical condition to have stamina and to remain alert, clear, and focused. This could mean, as discussed above, a regimen of exercise, dietary control, and even meditation. In conclusion, only those who train like athletes for a long-term marathon, rather than for a sprint, have a chance of enduring.

## E. Professional Qualifications Defined

The mere description of a typical day in the life of an interpreter makes vivid that interpreting requires appropriate and multiple qualifications to achieve adequate and repeated performances. What are the achievable and doable goals that should prevail? The answer depends in part on personal aspirations. Does one want to be a "run-of-the-mill" interpreter, or does one aspire to become one of the rare, highly specialized and knowledgeable interpreters? To answer this, let us proceed in parts. First, what is a professional in a profession, and then what is a professional interpreter?

*Black's Law Dictionary* defines "profession" and "professional" as follows:

A vocation requiring advanced education and training; esp. one of the three traditional learned professions — law, medicine, and the ministry.
"Learned professions are characterized by the need of unusual learning, the existence of confidential relations, and the adherence to a standard of ethics higher than that of the market place, and in a profession like that of medicine by intimate and delicate personal ministration.... Commonwealth *vs.* Brown, 20 N>E2d 478, 481 (Mass. 1939)" (1246).[4]

*Black's* sums up "professional" as "a person who belongs to a learned profession or whose occupation requires a high level of training and proficiency."

The following nuances on "profession" and "professional" derive from *Merriam-Webster's Collegiate Dictionary*:

**profession 4 a:** a calling requiring specialized knowledge and often long and intensive academic preparation
  **b:** a principal calling, vocation or employment
  **c:** the whole body of persons engaged in a calling
  **professional c** (1): characterized by or conforming to the technical or ethical standards of a profession
  (2): exhibiting a courteous, conscientious, and generally businesslike manner in the workplace.

The New Jersey Supreme Court Task Force on Interpreter and Translation Services (1984) provided the following additional recommendations, which are reported by Roseann Dueñas González and her colleagues Victoria Vásquez and Holly Mikkelson:

professionals are individuals who not only possess specialized knowledge, but also adhere to a code of ethics, demonstrate their mastery of skills through a licensing or certification process, and serve the public interest in the performance of their services.[5]

Elena De Jongh has one of the most convincing and comprehensive statements on what a profession encompasses and how interpretation matches up to it. Her conclusion is that interpretation has met the conditions associated with the characteristics of a full-fledged profession:

> the essential criterion of a "cognitive base of empirical, scientific and theoretical knowledge" has been met. [...] "It is an attitude towards work which views it as an end in itself, performed with affinity primarily for personal satisfaction and not monetary gains, and requiring total personal involvement" [*Introduction* 119–20].

De Jongh aptly adds that professional interpreters now need to persevere in the accomplishment, not only of quality performances, but also in improvements in all the dimensions in which all professionals (inter)act in all the specialized fields.

Indeed, strides have been made. Although the federal judicial system has led the way, many state judicial systems have followed suit with the following opportunities:

• Training programs and publications are available. (Chapter 7 discusses training programs.)
• Full-time and part-time interpreter positions exist. Although many are not at the most desirable level, they can be remunerative. (Chapter 8 deals with salary scales and job opportunities.)
• Minimum standards for interpreters exist.

If this book can point the way to greater professionalism, job satisfaction, and employment opportunities, it will have achieved some major goals.

## F. Minimal and Desirable Characteristics

By this time, readers sense that interpreters are a special breed. Some would say that the characteristics for a skilled interpreter are inbred and not acquired. Others might add that, to the requisite inborn personal traits, training can widen and deepen the untested to create adepts. Indeed, neuroscientists are discovering that practice can help perfect skills:

> Neuroscientists use the term "neural scaffolding" to describe how once a brain circuit has been laid out, its connections become strengthened with repeated use — like a scaffold being erected at a building site. Neural scaffolding explains why a behavioral pattern, once it is established, requires effort to change. But with new opportunities — or perhaps just with effort and awareness — we can lay down and strengthen a new track [Goleman, *Social Intelligence*, 161].

What are the characteristics that are more desirable in an interpreter? Some of the more salient characteristics are the following:

• Appreciating the appearance of real-life situations developing as on a stage, or the stimulus received when experiencing this;
• Enjoying participating in events involving many persons, including spectators;
• Playing a neutral role dictated by others (e.g., attorneys, medical examiners) and enjoying the theatrical exercise;
• Adjusting to constant changes, travel, and unexpected events.

Alicia B. Edwards puts it this way:

Interpreters need to be assertive, and tend to be more outgoing, lively, and noisy than translators. [...] Thus, the profession of court interpreter is not for the shy or retiring, not for the person who likes peace, calm, or routine. It requires your full attention and devotion.... No schedule is sacred, and one needs to be able to jump fast both mentally and physically.[6]

Chapter 8, "Economics, Jobs, Salaries," reviews in great detail the knowledge, skills, and abilities officially required of interpreters and translators, but the following description by Maurice Gravier (University of Paris [Sorbonne]) of the personality, skills, and other qualifications for conference interpreters anticipates that review and gives an excellent summary that applies to all interpreters in all the interpretation modes and settings. Note the distinction between what they "must be able to do" and what they "must have":

They must be able to move rapidly from one sphere of knowledge or human activity to another: from economics to physics, from politics to textiles or to the leather trade. [...] These aspiring interpreters must be versatile and [...] be fast thinkers and [...] must have an inborn curiosity, and must have the ability to take an interest in each and every area of human activity, [...] have nerves of steel, great self-control and acute and sustained powers of concentration.[7]

The following list summarizes the most significant characteristics. They are treated in greater detail following the list:

- self-control, "cool under fire";
- assertiveness;
- self-awareness about biases and attitudes;
- physical and cognitive speeds commensurate with the speed of the interpretation events;
- a commitment to ethics;
- command of communication skills;
- an ample knowledge base undergirded by interest and curiosity;
- language expertise and mastery of every aspect of language;
- understanding of the interplay between language and culture, and the expression of culture through nonverbal language;
- advanced reasoning skills, including awareness of the importance of analytical skills;
- awareness of the image projected when one is interpreting;
- being prepared to learn about the various settings in which interpreting takes place;
- and sensitivity to being a language and cultural bridge.

ACADEMIC QUALIFICATIONS. Various recommendations regarding academic qualifications and certification requirements that should be required to become a professional interpreter have been made. Before treating the specific requirements for interpretation, everybody agrees, at minimum, that a mastery of English and one other language must take place first. A typical statement follows:

The creators of the federal certification exam for Spanish court interpreting [...] say that one needs at least 14 years of schooling in English to understand the English used in court. Competent interpreting requires a solid liberal arts foundation, a foundation best acquired at a university here or abroad. I recommend at least a B.A. or B.S. degree, while an M.A. or a Ph.D. in the language, literature, history, or art of an area can be helpful [Edwards 4].

# G. Defending Professional Standards

COMBATING DUPLICITOUS AND AGGRESSIVE BEHAVIOR. The interpreter often finds it necessary to educate the clients about the responsibilities and limits of the interpreter's role.

This will be treated also in subsequent chapters, but the stress here is that one will run into attorneys who will try to find fault with the interpreter — although blameless — in depositions. Two examples come to mind. A lawyer finds that the deposition is not going favorably and decides to blame the interpreter in order to begin to prepare a case for an eventual appeal. Another comes up when a lawyer who has studied Spanish in high school, college, or abroad tries to correct the language. The interpreter will have to learn how, with assertiveness and tact, to control one's attitude and try to "put the attorney in his or her place" and simultaneously not allow the behavior to affect the quality of the interpreter's work.

SELF-CRITICISM IN ADJUSTING TO BIASES. As in any other endeavor, knowing personal limitations is crucial to being able to behave in accordance with the professional standards for interpreters. Every one of us has erected social prejudices in response to our surroundings. In response to our genes, we even possess genetically built-in biases and particular attitudes. These biases interfere with our ability to judge objectively, with our ability to hear and listen accurately and fully what is being said to us or asked that we interpret. It does behoove us, then, to delve into ourselves, suggests Carl Weaver, and try to examine those biases and attitudes in order to be able to develop the skills that can free us — to the extent possible — from undermining subjectivity:

> Your own inner states make it difficult to hear anything above the level of the simplest messages. You will have to become more aware of your biases and do what you can to control them in order to become a better listener.[8]

BIASES AND THE ROLE OF CULTURE. The causal factors for the biases and pre-developed attitudes, according to Weaver, serve to introduce the reader to the important roles played by culture and the self (treated in greater detail in Chapters 15 and 16):

> Most of your biases, if not all of them, are based on the norms of the culture. A society builds a set of requirements and taboos. [...] Thus close relatives do not marry, sex deviants are segregated, family structure is preserved, people wear clothing. [...] Even small behaviors are thus prescribed: the way you cut your hair, the kind of clothing you wear under various conditions, the ways you talk to people, the kinds of games you play, the way you blow your nose, and thousands of others [Weaver 93–4].

CAN CLOTHING AND COSMETICS OVERCOME INCOMPETENCE? To make the work easier and more effective, a professional appearance and attitude is a requirement. For one thing, proper image, say Alicia Edwards, helps the interpreters be accepted on an equal footing with other colleagues:

> Image is important because it will be taken for the reality. Thus, for example, we should not put on a face of disgust at having to sit next to a man accused of an especially obnoxious crime. [...] The interpreter should dress soberly. [...] The image the interpreter wishes to project is that of someone serious, who has interpreting and only interpreting on her mind, and who has taken the care to come in looking neat and well-groomed [Edwards 71].

These words are not simply space fillers. Who has not personally witnessed a new, inexperienced interpreter who thought that fashionable, tight-fitting clothes and heavy makeup would compensate for inadequate training and preparation? In one case, an interpreter from Latin American parents who spoke Spanish — although English was the dominant language at home — and who was facing personal and financial problems, believed that her profession provided "a cow to milk." After applying to an uncritical agency for part-time employment as interpreter, she was sent out without any pre-testing of English and Spanish proficiency and without any training on consecutive interpretation and proper grooming. Her background, dress, and lack of training worked against her. Her discrepancies were obvious, and her lack of mastery of Spanish vocabulary in the divorce and legal fields made for agonizing moments in the procedure.

INFORMATION, CURIOSITY, AND REASONING. Because interpreting encompasses global information, one has to be current with what is going on in the world. Information increases exponentially with each passing month. An interpreter needs to maintain interest and curiosity and must have the ability to cope with it all. Nonetheless, specialization is not the answer or a panacea; an adequate knowledge base, nurtured by constant reading accompanied by well-developed reasoning skills, will suffice to perform the interpretation act adequately. More space will be devoted to the high level of reasoning skills a professional interpreter should have. Let us state here, and stress once again, two aspects: first, the importance of the acquisition of excellent analytical skills; and second, the need to learn "everything possible about everything." To process accurately during the interpretation act in our complex, technological, media-dominated and ever-changing world, we need to understand everything. The conundrum consists of determining from one interpretation assignment to another the future linguistic and cultural demands.

THE KNOWLEDGE BASE: LANGUAGES AND CULTURES. In addition to keeping abreast of constant changes in the technical and intellectual fields, the skilled interpreter needs to anticipate the demands in language and culture. Mastery of English and one other language are givens and must be verified before an interpreter can be deemed qualified. Just being bilingual does not guarantee success, because "[interpretation] is an activity of bilingual processing that can only be performed by bilinguals who process the two languages in such a way that the message remains intact while the code is changed" (De Jongh 63–4). (Chapter 15, "Implications of Bilingualism," delves into this theme.) Yet, it is difficult to attain this mastery.

"*Knowing a language also means knowing its structure*," argues Danica Seleskovitch, who goes on to say "that a language is not only the sum total of its words, it also represents a frame of mind, a way of looking at the world. Knowing a language means having a feel for its structure, so that it is possible to understand a message by following its internal logic, even when a specific word has been missed" (*Interpreting* 79–80).

As the quotation below states, hardly anyone has equal, native-like, complete mastery of two languages. Even so the interpreter has to strive for those goals:

Ideally, an interpreter should fit [Christopher] Thiery's description of the so-called true bilingual, that is, someone who is "taken to be one of them by the members of two different linguistic communities, at roughly the same social and cultural level." However [...] those who [...] have reached an equivalent competence in those languages and can pass as monolinguals in each language are rare [Seleskovitch, *Interpreting*, 73].

MASTERING EVERY ASPECT OF A LANGUAGE. As will be seen later, mastery and proficiency in the two languages includes the knowledge of the abstract, grammar-and-convention-based language and the various languages that are actually used, called dialects, idiolects, argot, and jargon, and other terms. And that includes the non-formal variants of paralanguages and the gestures governed by personhood and cultures.

COMMUNICATION SKILLS. If the interpreter wants to perfect speaking skills, a course in communication skills would be most appropriate, one which included "voice control and unobtrusive behavior. [...] Eye contact and body language. [...] People with an abrasive voice or distracting mannerisms will have difficulty" (De Jongh 38).

**REASONING SKILLS *VS.* THE SPEED OF SPEECH.** Fortunately, the interpreter need not master the actual fields of specialized knowledge. It is proper for the interpreter, though, to hone the analytical and other reasoning skills to be able to handle the source language [SL] material in an orderly and sense-making manner and transmit it appropriately in the target language [TL]. Seleskovitch wisely notes that the interpreter's "power of reasoning, rather than his command of the facts [...] must be on a par with that of the speaker" (*Interpreting* 63). And the interpreter must accomplish the processing of the data and its comprehension at a rate of speed that matches the utterances in SL, estimated to vary between 120 and 150 words per minute, but may increase to 220 words per minute. Some time will be given over later to the cognitive aspects, from the functioning of the brain to memory and prediction, and schemas and scripts. The curiosity about the makeup of the human being will go far both to help the potential interpreter to qualify and to develop as a top-notch professional.

**AVOID ASSUMING SETTINGS AND COURT PROCEDURES.** The interpretation settings, as detailed in Chapter 13, "Settings and Procedures in Legal and Social Venues," outline the conduct and logistics of many interpretation events. The interpreter who studies and learns them will avoid a lot of guesswork and embarrassment. The alert interpreter will study closely the judicial and nonjudicial proceedings, procedures, rules, and protocols in order to be effective. In this vein, it is also vital that the interpreter ask for information and clarification whenever necessary; this is preferable to assuming things, stumbling into surprises, and risking errors.

**"MY IMPORTANCE AS A BRIDGE."** The interpreter bridges the gap between two or more linguistic and cultural entities. To do this, communication skills are essential. And interpreters are therefore obliged — obligated really — to recognize the LEP individual as a person with a particular need. The interpreter has the unique moral obligation to serve the LEP and others also involved, including attorneys, judges, doctors, social workers, or psychologists. The interpreter should always keep in mind that in courtrooms and elsewhere, "I am important to them because I am their bridge." It is, then, the interpreter's ethical responsibility to perform in the most accurate and professional manner possible.

# CHAPTER 7

# Training, Testing, and Certification

## A. Colleges/Universities: U.S., Canada, and Other Areas

This chapter summarizes many training, testing, and certification resources available to novice and veteran interpreters and translators. With regard to training, some beginning and veteran professionals have alluded to the paucity of training programs and the inadequacy of some of those encountered. The ample material in this chapter should dispel any doubts about availability as it points to programs nationally and internationally at universities, colleges, community colleges, and private institutes that purport to offer competent training. The chapter concludes with a debate on the necessity and sufficiency of training.

AMERICAN TRANSLATORS ASSOCIATION. One of the chapter's missions is to identify and organize new training programs. In the late 1980s, the American Translators Association sponsored *Park's Guide*, which reviewed 41 institutions. Unfortunately, the guide is no longer in print and will not be revised and updated until resources are available. A debt of gratitude is extended to one of the directors of ATA for sending a photocopy of some key pages of his only copy of *Park's Guide* and for encouraging this book's mission of updating current resources.

*THE COLLEGE BLUE BOOK* AND THE INTERNET. If not *Park's Guide*, then other more recent sources are available. Interested parties can find in the library the comprehensive six-volume *The College Blue Book*.[1] The section "Translation and Interpretation" in volume 3 lists 15 schools. Unfortunately, the symbols that refer to the institutions' programs (O for other or certificate, M for masters, D for doctorate) are inaccurate, perhaps outdated.

Additional shortcomings of the *Blue Book*:

a. It records 9 certificate programs, but 8 is the correct number.
b. It does not cite an A.A. degree, but one exists at the University of Arkansas.
c. It omits bachelor degrees, but 3 exist, at Arkansas, Gallaudet, and Kent State.
d. It cites 9 master degrees (M), rather than 5 in operation.
e. Finally, *The Blue Book* indicates 1 doctorate (D), but 5 exist, according to a recount.

The authors salute the noble and encyclopedic *Blue Book,* which has the herculean task of dealing with more than 3,000 universities and classifying many thousands of programs. The purpose of scrutinizing and calling attention to its material is to ensure that the readers of this book, where this subject is paramount, have more reliable information.

Fortunately, the technology exists today to identify and update translation and interpretation programs in academic and commercial venues. Seekers can benefit from Google's referrals to "Translation and interpreting courses in the U.S.A," where it introduces, among others, "Lexicool," an important website started by Sebastian Abbo of Paris, in 2000, which purports to have 5000 links. Lexicool.com refers the reader to 24 schools, among which six are also mentioned by *The College Blue Book*. Moving between these two sources, the reader can peruse 22 non-overlapping schools for certificates and degree programs. In the following subsection, the material in the previous sources and in others is enfolded to come up with 26 U.S. listings. Later in the chapter, dozens of additional schools in California, Arizona, South Carolina, Florida, and the District of Columbia are discussed at greater length. In this fashion, perhaps, *Language into Language* can compensate for *Park's Guide*'s absence and *The College Blue Book*'s inaccuracies with useful current material. A note of caution, however: changes in programs, personnel, and factual material occur frequently. The reader is advised to double-check prior to making decisions.

**U.S. TRAINING PROGRAMS.** The following section identifies briefly 26 universities, colleges, and institutes that teach translation and interpretation. The information, based on the schools' websites and other sources, is as current as possible until December 2009.

**American University**, District of Columbia: Fifteen hours of course work for certification in undergraduate and graduate translation programs. Undergraduate languages: Russian, Spanish, French, and German. Graduate languages: Russian, Spanish, and French.

**Bellevue Community College**, Bellevue, WA: The well-staffed Translation and Interpretation Institute presents two 24-credit-hour Certificates of Accomplishment. The specialties are in Spanish, French, and Japanese.

**Columbia University**, New York City, enjoys a renowned M.A. in Russian and Slavic Languages and Cultures; translation forms a part of the program.

**George Mason University**, Fairfax, Virginia: The Department of Modern & Classical Languages offers a graduate certificate in Spanish and French that requires 12 credits for the core courses.

**Georgetown University**, Washington, DC, offers a course or two in its School of Continuing and Professional Studies.

**Georgia State University**, Atlanta, offers translation and interpretation certificate programs in French, German, and Spanish.

**Indiana University's and Purdue's**, Indianapolis: joint undergraduate certificate programs in Spanish, French and German require 27 credit hours. Arabic, Chinese, and Italian may be available.

**Kent State University**, Kent, Ohio: The Institute for Applied Linguistics presents comprehensive 60-credit-hour programs. Degree programs in translation: a four-year B.S. and a two-year M.A. in French, German, Russian, Spanish, and Japanese. The Ph.D. is in Translation Studies and Informatics.

**Marygrove College**, Detroit: The Modern Languages Department offers certificates in translation for Arabic, French, and Spanish.

**New York University**'s School of Continuing and Professional Studies presents a multilayered and comprehensive program that involves seven languages (e.g., Arabic, French, German, Spanish, and Portuguese, etc.) in legal, medical, commercial, computer-assisted, financial, diplomatic, localization, and literary translation.

**Rose-Hulman Institute of Technology**, Terre–Haute, Indiana: The Department of Humanities & Social Sciences offers engineers and scientists a Certificate of Proficiency in German translation.

**Rutgers University** at New Brunswick, NJ: The Department of Spanish & Portuguese offers an M.A. with a Translation option (12 credits); a certificate requires 3 courses in English/Spanish interpreting and translation.

**S.U.N.Y. at Albany:** The certificate program seems doubtful; the program includes one translation course in Spanish and one in French.

**S.U.N.Y. at Binghamton:** TRIP (Translation, Research & Instruction Program) offers a graduate-level certificate in translation and a Ph.D. in Translation Studies.

**University of Denver:** The School of Professional and Continuing Studies offers graduate-level certificate programs online and on campus in Translation and Advanced Study in Community Interpretation; each requires 4 core courses and 5 electives totaling 36 quarter hours.

**University of Florida,** Gainesville, has a Translation Studies Certificate Program.

**University of Hawaii,** Manoa: The comprehensive Center for Interpretation and Translation Studies (CITS) displays 17 courses, with strengths in Mandarin, Japanese, and Korean.

**University of Illinois,** Urbana-Champaign, and the Dalkey Archive Press have set up, under the supervision of Elizabeth Lowe, a Center for Translation Studies dedicated to translate major literary works.

**University of Iowa,** Iowa City: At the undergraduate level, certificate-bearing courses and workshops in literary translation are given. Iowa offers an M.F.A in Translation and a postgraduate program in Translational Bio-medicine.

**University of Massachusetts,** Amherst: The Translation Center presents an online Medical Interpreting Certificate and a one-year M.A. in Translation Studies (33 credit hours).

**University of Minnesota,** Minneapolis: The Program in Translation and Interpreting offers two interpreting certificates with specializations in health care and in legal matters. The Program sponsors two texts: see Swabey et al. and Newington et al. in, respectively, "Authors and Works Cited" and "Suggested Readings."

**University of North Carolina,** Charlotte: Languages and Culture Studies Department offers two certificate programs; each requires four courses: undergraduate (French, German); graduate (Spanish).

**University of Puerto Rico** at Río Piedras offers a certificate program and a masters degree in interpretation and translation.

**University of Texas,** Brownsville, sponsors a Translation Studies Program specializing in Spanish and English. (See www.utb.edu.)

**University of Wisconsin,** Milwaukee: An M.A. in Translation is available in French, Spanish, or German flexible enough to match the students' goals in industry or academia.

**Wake Forest University,** Winston-Salem, NC: Certificate programs in the Department of Romance Languages include Spanish Interpreting (6 hours) and Spanish Translation/Localization (12 hours).

CANADA. The following four universities offer students comprehensive programs in French/English translation and interpretation:

- **University of Ottawa,** Ontario, bachelor, master, and doctorate;
- **York University,** Ontario, a master;
- **Concordia University,** Quebec, a certificate program;
- **Université Laval,** Quebec, a master and doctorate.

EUROPE, AUSTRALIA, AFRICA, THE MIDDLE EAST, AND TAIWAN. A brief mention is in order of the Ecole Supérieure d'Interprètes et de Traducteurs (ESIT), part of the Sorbonne, which has excellent professors, such as Marianne Lederer. For certification, consult the Association Internationale d'Interprètes de Conférence (AIIC), with 2823 members who deal with 48 languages and live in 265 cities in 96 countries (www.aiic.net). For detailed material on training programs in these areas, consult Mary Phelan's *The Interpreter's Resource.*[2] Although Phelan's book is outdated (2001), it contains useful reference material that will guide the reader to many sites and persons of interest outside the United States and Canada. Her material can be supplemented in updated websites, i.e., www.lexicool.com and www.betrans-lated.com.

## B. California

THE JUDICIAL COUNCIL OF CALIFORNIA. The Administrative Office of the Courts, a division of the Judicial Council of California, in its splendid thirty-nine-page "Report" (revised September, November 2006 [www.courtinfo.ca.gov]) asks, perhaps rhetorically, the key question: "Is special training recommended to become a court interpreter?" The question begs the only positive response, which has been the constant theme of *Language into Language*. Let the Judicial Council speak for itself and on behalf of organizations that justify their special training programs:

> The level of expertise for this profession is far greater than that required for everyday bilingual conversation. The interpreter must be able to handle the widest range of language terms that might be presented in the courts, everything from specialized legal and technical terminology to street slang. Most people do not have full command of all registers of both English and the foreign language and, therefore, require special training to acquire it.[3]

UNIVERSITIES AND SCHOOLS. In California, where 224 languages are spoken, the Judicial Council has taken a proactive policy in providing information on training, testing, and certification in its comprehensive report. Among the "Report's" highlights is an outline of the educational institutions in-state and out-of-state where interpreters and translators can receive adequate training. The "Report" identifies the University of California system and the parallel, but separate, State University of California branches. They provide one- to two-year courses and certificate programs in Spanish-English interpretation and translation in their Continuing Education and Extension divisions. UCLA Extension is unique in also offering a Mandarin-English Legal Translation and Interpretation Program. For more information, direct inquiries to the corresponding Extension Divisions at UCLA, UC Riverside, UC San Diego, and UC Santa Barbara. Include in the inquiry the Extension Divisions of California State University at Fresno, Long Beach, Los Angeles, Northridge, Stanislaus, and San Francisco. Three California community colleges offer certificate programs: American River College in Sign Language, East Los Angeles, and Southwestern College. The Judicial Council, although a state agency, wisely includes private schools: College of the Sequoias, Del Sol Academy of Interpretation, National Hispanic University, the Southern California School of Interpretation, and the Monterey Institute of International Studies. It is beyond our scope to cover the whole gamut, but the last two merit further consideration.

SOUTHERN CALIFORNIA SCHOOL OF INTERPRETATION (SCSI). The Southern California School of Interpretation's six-month program deserves further attention because of its flexibility, modularity, and popularity. Heralding its own qualities, this proprietary school, founded in 1993 by Néstor Wagner, MSAA, proclaims in its pamphlet that approximately "70%–80% of those [800 Certified Spanish Court Interpreters] are graduates" of its own schools. Although this sounds like hyperbole, it is believable because — in addition to programs at its headquarters in Santa Fe Springs, CA — SCSI consists of two other branches in California (San Diego and Corona), and one in Las Vegas, Nevada. In Santa Fe Springs, SCSI offers the three training programs approved by the state for certification: Court Interpreter, Medical

Interpreter, and Administrative Hearings Interpreter. The courses, given in three academic sessions called quarters, are oriented toward passing the exams. For example, for the Court Interpreter Program, the courses are Interpreting Criminal Proceedings I, Interpreting Criminal Proceedings II, Preparation for Written Exam — English I & II, Preparation for Written Exam — Spanish I & II, Sight Translation for Court Interpreters, and Interpreting Criminal Proceedings in Municipal and Superior Courts. A separate series is aimed at preparation for state and federal certification. The Continuing Education Program, which consists of 14 courses, is open to certified interpreters or those working as interpreters. The seven instructors, whose education and degrees are not provided, are "State certified Court, Administrative Hearings, and Medical Interpreters, except written exam instructors." The school boasts of fifteen "Free Services" to participants, among them are "unlimited access to onsite and online language labs," "mock exams," "job referrals," and "Certificate of Completion." In Santa Fe Springs, interested parties can contact the administrator at 10012 Norwalk Boulevard; phone (562) 906-9787. In Nevada, the campus is at 4055 South Spencer St., Las Vegas, NV 89101; phone (702) 932-2038. The e-mail is info@interpreting.com; the website is http://www.interpreting.com.

**MONTEREY'S GRADUATE SCHOOL OF TRANSLATION AND INTERPRETATION (GSTI).** Of overriding national and international eminence in breathtaking Big Sur sits the Monterey Institute of International Studies' International Interpretation Resource Center, located at 460 Pierce Street, Monterey, CA 93940 (Phone/FAX: 831-647-4100). More than 200 students are enrolled in one of the GSTI's four two-year Masters of Arts degrees in Translation, Translation, and Interpretation, Translation/Localization Management, and Conference Interpretation. Each requires 60 credits of varying units. This affiliate of Middlebury College also offers short-term courses and seminars. Among its 41 renowned faculty with advanced degrees are Chuanyun Bao and Holly Mikkelson. At last count, the Institute boasted of 20 long-standing faculty, 13 visiting professors, and 8 adjuncts, versed in English, Spanish, French, German, Russian, Chinese, Japanese, and Korean. The Institute's depth, breadth, and quality merited a contract, in 2007, to train U.N. interpreters and translators.

**GSTI'S MASTERS OF TRANSLATION/LOCALIZATION MANAGEMENT.** Especially unique are GSTI's degree courses on localization translation, which feature advanced studies on the use of computerized telecommunications to convert, convey, and apply translated information to the international business community. While localization is a comparatively new field, it gains importance in the computerized age because it "involves the complete adaptation of a product for use in a different language and culture," via "Internet sites and products in manufacturing and other business sites," according to the *Occupational Outlook Handbook* of the U.S. Department of Labor's Bureau of Labor Statistics. Furthermore, "the goal of these specialists is [to make] the product [...] appear as if it were originally manufactured in the country where it will be sold and supported."[4] GSTI provides more direct information on its website: www.miis.edu/gsti-progs-short.html.

## C. Arizona and South Carolina

**UNIVERSITY OF ARIZONA, TUCSON.** The University of Arizona's National Center for Interpretation embraces testing, research, policy, and education. The National Center sponsors the Agnese Haury Institute for Interpretation. In existence for 25 years, the Institute is "the longest running intensive Spanish/English interpreter training program in the United States." On its Arizona campus, the Institute offers year-round courses; it also runs three-week seminars in July for practitioners and trainers. For 2009, thirteen two-day preparatory workshops on the Federal Court Interpreter Certification Oral Exam (FCICE) are listed. Three seminars take place on its Tucson, Arizona, campus; the other cities in the order in which the seminars are given: El Paso, Nashville, Miami/Orlando, Las Vegas, Washington, DC, Los Angeles, Houston, Chicago, Boston, and Omaha. Among its distinguished faculty are the director, Roseann Dueñas González, and other degreed court interpreters, including Linda E. Haughton, Ph.D., Joyce García, M.A., and Ramón Del Villar, J.D. Those who wish to apply for scholarships and tuition assistance can obtain further information from the website http://www.nci.arizona.edu, by phoning (520) 621-3615, or by writing the University of Arizona, National Center for Interpretation, P.O. Box 210432, Tucson, AZ 85721-0432.

COLLEGE OF CHARLESTON, SOUTH CAROLINA. A four-course certificate program exists alongside an unlinked 18-months-long Master of Arts in Bilingual Legal Interpreting at the Graduate School of the College of Charleston, in South Carolina. Admission requirements for the Spanish/English certificate program are an A.B. and/or "concurrent enrollment in a related graduate field." A candidate must pass a General Test of Interpreting Aptitude. The College's centerpiece, however, is the comprehensive master's program that emphasizes Spanish/English, supported by the state and originally funded in part by the State Justice Institute and in part by a law firm whose generous contribution made possible a state-of-the-art digital interpreting facility. An announcement proclaims boldly that this "graduate program continues to be the only [one] in the U.S. that offers students the opportunity to receive the education and training of a professional degree-holding legal interpreter." According to its announcement of March 2007, in the streamlined program a student completes thirteen courses in this order: Fundamentals of Interpreting, Fundamentals of Translation, Legal Processes and Procedures in the U.S. Legal System, Practicum I, Consecutive Interpreting I, Language and Culture or Spanish in the U.S., Law and the Legal System of the U.S., Practicum II in Legal Settings, Legal Language, Consecutive Interpreting II, Simultaneous Interpreting I, Sight Translation, Simultaneous Interpreting II, and the capstone Internship in Legal Interpreting. Further course and admissions information can be gotten from Bilingual Legal Interpreting, c/o Office of Graduate Studies, Randolph Hall, 66 George St., Charleston, SC 29424-0001, phone (843) 953-5670, 953-5718. The website is www.cs.cofc.edu/~legalint/. Appreciation goes out to Virginia Benmaman for providing the preceding details.

## D. Medical Interpreting in English-Only States

To comply with the Federal Court Interpreters Act and its Amendments, more than sixty training programs have been established in the United States, mostly to respond to legal needs, but many others exist in response to the need for interpretation in other fields, especially in the allied health professions:

> The Massachusetts Medical Interpreters Association (MMIA) [...] sponsored the first National Conference on Medical Interpreting on May 17, 1997 [...]. Hospitals in the Boston and Seattle areas, along with several in the Twin Cities of Minneapolis and St. Paul and in various parts of California, have been leaders in the employment of full-time and increasingly professionalized interpreting staffs.[5]

The College of Charleston, for example, in its Graduate Programs in Bilingual Interpreting, initiated a Certificate Program in Medical and Health Care Interpreting. In starting this Certificate Program, Charleston became a serious academic contender in this field of study. One of the sections in this book covers the many useful functions that trained interpreters and translators — as distinct from friends and relatives — play in helping patients communicate accurately with doctors, nurses, and other medical staff. The reader will also note the need for cultural awareness and sensitivity in dealing with medical issues. In anticipation of these comments, Holly Mikkelson explains these points in her lucid review of the interpreter's role in a medical setting.[6] But do Charleston and other universities and institutes with medical interpreting programs become victims of their own entrepreneurial eagerness in the face of the English-only state laws and the clamor for an English-only amendment to the Constitution? It appears not, despite political obstacles, since the universities have not shut down their medical interpreting and translation programs.

Supported by legal pronouncements from the U.S. Government's Office of Minority Health Standards that health providers "must offer and provide [free] language assistance services" (Standard 4), the University of Arizona's National Center for Interpretation charged ahead, in 2008, with its 7th Medical Interpreter Training Institute, consisting of basic techniques of interpretation, plus seminars on major diseases, ethics, terminology, and multicultural awareness, offered on-campus and off-campus in Orlando, FL, and Sacramento, CA. Despite the statutes and amendments, Charleston and Arizona join the University of Minnesota, Florida International University, the Southern California School of Interpretation, and others — all in English-only states — with medical interpretation programs. This matter of English-only laws and their effect on jobs was discussed at great length in Chapter 3, "Language and the Legal Systems."

## E. Florida

FLORIDA INTERNATIONAL UNIVERSITY. In South Florida, particularly Miami and Hialeah, where Spanish-speaking residents outnumber English-speaking citizens, abundant banking, commerce, and litigation require translators and interpreters. Florida International University's Department of Modern Languages hosts a long-standing evening and weekend Certificate Program in Translation Studies and/or Legal Translation/Court Interpreting for "bilingual students as well as for professional translators and interpreters." Prior to full admission, students take pre-requisites either in Spanish or English grammar and writing. The required program for the Translation Studies Certificate features translation practica in the legal, business, technical, and medical areas, plus a judicial internship. The Legal Translation/Court Interpreting Certificate embraces the same overlapping practica and includes the courses Oral Skills for Interpreters and the Interpreter and Languages. Two additional courses are required in allied subjects. F.I.U. recently announced an analogous program in Portuguese. Erik Camayd-Freixas, a Ph.D. from Harvard, who is a federally certified interpreter, directs a team of degreed professionals certified by the American Translators Association. The director can be reached at (305) 348-6222, at camayde@fiu.edu, and at the website www.flu.edu/translation.

## F. Sign Language: D.C. and Arkansas

GALLAUDET UNIVERSITY IN D.C. Although the book concentrates mainly on oral interpretation and written translation, it would be useful to glance at academic programs in interpretation for the deaf and blind at Gallaudet and Arkansas. Gallaudet describes itself "as the only university in the world that offers both an undergraduate and a graduate degree in ASL-English Interpretation, centered around [...] a unique opportunity for interpretation majors to live, study, and interact with Deaf people." Gallaudet's B.A. major, to begin with, involves 12 courses in a 33-credit basic program, plus six required courses at 18 hours. "The M.A. in Interpretation is designed to prepare and educate deaf, hard of hearing, and hearing persons in working as interpreters in deaf and hearing communities." The rigorous two-year M.A. consists of 23 courses in four semesters and one semester in an internship, for a total of 59 credit hours, which merits recognition and approval by the Conference of Interpreter Trainers. The M.A. in Deaf Studies can qualify students to enter a Gallaudet Ph.D. in linguistics, at a savings of time and money, "since as many as 25 [...] M.A. credits may be credited toward the Ph.D." Judging from the careful organization of the program, the quality of the instructors, and the dedication of the students, those who succeed in graduating do not have to feel handicapped or incapable of landing a job. For ample information, consult the website at http://interpretation.gallaudet.edu. See the section "Certification," below, for a discussion on ATA, the Registry of Interpreters for the Deaf (RID), and the role of the Office of Court Interpreting Services in aiding the hearing disadvantaged.

UNIVERSITY OF ARKANSAS, LITTLE ROCK. The school offers two comprehensive, accredited degree programs in American Sign Language and Interpreting for the Deaf and the Deaf-Blind at the A.A. (63 credit hours) and B.A. (124–25 credit hours) levels. It also offers an M.F.A. in [Literary] Translation (3 years: 12 hours of workshops; 24 hours in literature). For more information, see the website www.universityofarkansas.edu. As with Gallaudet, see the section "Certification," below, for a discussion of certification via the Registry of Interpreters for the Deaf (RID).

## G. Tests and Testing

DETERMINING APTITUDE. It is a given that demand exceeds supply for interpreters/translators, and by "supply" we mean "qualified supply." Given, also, that the exigencies of law, time, money, and the welfare of immigrants is uppermost, action is required to fill the gap for interpreters. University and local training programs, long- and short-term ones, staffed with doctorates or with capable trainers, therefore, are essential. Although no national form of obligatory training for certification of proficiency currently exists, translators and interpreters can voluntarily subject themselves to tests before, during, or after training and education. Why take a test before undergoing training? The answer is twofold. The potential interpreter/translator needs to test whether he or she possesses an aptitude for this field of study before spending additional time, money, and energy on pursuing this goal. From a school's perspective, aptitude tests are administered prior to admission to find out whether a student is capable of understanding and applying the basic "rules of the road" of English and of a foreign language, i.e., grammar, syntax, vocabulary, sentence structure, logic, and metaphor. All of the previously mentioned schools require passing a test of interpreting and translating to determine aptitude prior to official enrollment. Unfortunately, most of the schools could not or would not provide a copy of a test, even an old one, to analyze and discuss. The exception is the GSTI.

**PRE-TESTING AT THE GSTI.** Prior to admission at most graduate schools, a standardized test is required, usually the GRE (Graduate Record Exam) for the humanities, or the GMAT (Graduate Management Aptitude Test) for business and the social sciences. In the absence of a national standardized test for this specialty, the renowned Monterey Institute's GSTI faculty designed their own Early Diagnostic Test (EDT) to pre-determine capability and eligibility for admission to its desirable and demanding programs. Fortunately, the EDT, although proprietary, is not secret and accompanies the marketing packet mailed out to interested parties. It will become clear after reading the information that follows about GSTI's self-administered Written and Oral Tests that they serve several purposes. First, in order to attract the best applicants, especially from abroad, a test of this type is essential for a private institution that seeks selective students with financial means. The many applicants for the few openings — whether residing in the U.S. or abroad — cannot be expected to travel to GSTI for a diagnostic test that may not gain them admission. To overcome this obstacle, GSTI's representatives travel each year to graduate school recruiting fairs in the United States, South America, the Middle East, Europe, Asia, Africa, and Canada to seek out the best and to administer exams. The GSTI test avoids fill-ins and short-answer questions. Successful candidates paint a varied and complex written and oral picture of linguistic competence to a committee of professionals. Of course, the applicants also present backup documentation: transcripts, grade point averages, letters of recommendation, a *C.V.* listing achievements, and unusual language skills that the school desires to cultivate.[7]

As a point of comparison, consider the Education Testing Service's nonselective, proctored TOEFL (Test of English as a Foreign Language) Exam, a mainly fill-in type that tests English competence, which is given to more than 350,000 students per year in the U.S. and via U.S. consulates and cooperating schools in different countries. To its credit, the TOEFL Exam also offers an alternate that requires essays.

**GSTI's EDT WRITTEN TESTS.** The twelve-page test form, including instructions, attempts to determine written and oral skills of the applicant in the Native Language (A Language, or that of greatest comfort), the First Foreign Language (B Language), and Second Foreign Language (C language, if applicable). In Section 1— Essays, the candidate writes an essay of 300–500 words on pre-determined themes in the A, B, and, if required, the C language — which are, for purposes of the exam, English, French, German, or Spanish. In Sections 2a and 2b — Translations, the candidate first, in 2A, translates a given, long paragraph from English into an A or B language, then, in 2B, a passage in Spanish into an A or B language. GSTI requires the "style and tone" to be "consistent with those of the original text, and the grammatical conventions of the target language should be observed." It adds, rather sternly: "There should be no spelling or punctuation errors," the more so since the applicant is unobserved and can use dictionaries and seek assistance. Section 3—Abstract, requires a summary in 100 words in the native language, in no more than 60 minutes, of a 500-word passage called, in 2007, "All Creatures Great and Dying."

**GSTI's EDT ORAL TESTS.** The quality of the Written Tests determines whether the required three-part Oral Test will be graded. The caveat is that the applicant's "written skills indicate (readiness) to enter the GSTI program." The candidate must submit a 45–60-minute audio tape that covers the three given parts. Part One: Pronunciation Skills involves reading long passages in English and in Spanish. Part Two: Abstract Thinking Skills/Extemporaneous Speech requires the candidate, in the B and C (if applicable) languages, to speak naturally, off-the-cuff for five minutes on a given topic. Part Three: Self-Assessment/Extemporaneous Speech, as with Part Two, precludes a prepared text. In the two sections, the candidate answers each of the prepared questions in five minutes using the A and B languages.

FLORIDA'S COURT INTERPRETER'S APTITUDE WORKSHOPS. To ensure that potential court interpreters are capable of serving the public, the Supreme Court of the State of Florida had the Court Interpreter's Program provide two-day Orientation Workshops conducted in English, which are open to all foreign language and sign language interpreters. Attendance is a prerequisite to sit for the Written Exam and Oral Qualifications Exam. The workshops immerse candidates in a sixteen-hour overview of the profession, discuss ideas, role play, examine the Code of Professional Responsibility for Interpreters in the Judiciary, and practice the three modes of interpreting. The skills assessment part deals superficially with improving language and memory proficiency and offers options for further training.

FLORIDA'S WRITTEN AND ORAL EXAMS. After attending the orientation workshops, candidates who have been assessed positively, or who feel themselves capable of success in this line of endeavor, can go on to the written exam and the oral qualifications exam. To cover the languages prevalent in the state courts, oral exams are available in Spanish (4 versions), Haitian Creole (2 versions), Russian (2 versions), Polish, Korean, Laotian, Vietnamese (2 versions), Hmong, Cantonese, Mandarin, and Arabic. As an indication of the seriousness and scope of the emphasis on aptitude in anticipation of testing for capability, from July 2008 to August 2009, orientation workshops, written exams, and oral language exams were scheduled for Orlando, Miami, Tampa, and Fort Lauderdale. More information can be obtained from the Court Operations Consultant, Office of the State Courts Administrator, Supreme Court Building, 500 South Duval Street, Tallahassee, FL, 32399-1900. Call 850-922-5107, and consult http://www.flcourts.org/gen_public/interpret/faq.shmtl.

AMERICAN TRANSLATOR ASSOCIATION'S LANGUAGES AND TESTS. The American Translators Association, an affiliate of the Fédération Internationale des Traducteurs (FIT) and the leading organization of its kind in the U.S., offers an optional and voluntary "Practice Test for ATA Certification Exam" at a cost of $40.00 per language pair. One language pair involves translating any one of thirteen foreign languages into English. The languages are Arabic, Croatian, Danish, Dutch, French, German, Hungarian, Italian, Japanese, Polish, Portuguese, Russian, and Spanish. Fourteen target languages are offered for translating from English into the foreign language. All but two (Arabic and Danish) of the previous languages are offered; three are added: Chinese, Finnish, and Ukrainian. The Practice Test, taken at home, is available to Active, Corresponding, and Associate members.

To join the ATA, call 1-703-683-6100 or contact it at ata@atanet.org. The address is: ATA, 225 Reinekers Lane, Suite 590, Alexandria, VA, 22314. All professionals are encouraged to join the ATA, attend its frequent seminars and national conferences, read the *ATA Chronicle*, and get on the approved list of world-wide translators. The website is http://www.atanet.org.

# *H. Certification*

**ATA CERTIFICATION EXAM.** Consult *The ATA Chronicle* and its home office for updated information on sites for the official ATA Certification Exam. From 2007 to 2009, it was given in at least 16 U.S. and 3 foreign cities. Among them: San Diego and San Francisco, CA; Chicago, IL; Lawrence, KA; Portland, OR; Philadelphia, PA; Irving, TX; Salt Lake City, UT; Seattle, WA; Orlando, FL; Minneapolis, MN; and Buenos Aires. The exam usually consists of the same previously mentioned languages. The Certification Exam, which costs $160, is taken under strict, proctored conditions: one exam per sitting; exam must be returned intact; no revelation of contents; the appeal process is final and irreversible. A passing grade permits an Associate member to rise to Active member status. It is a difficult exam in which only 20 percent of the candidates are expected to pass.

***ATA CHRONICLE* CLARIFIES "CERTIFICATE"/"CERTIFICATION."** Few national organizations have been as diligent as ATA in collecting, organizing, and promulgating information about certification. In 2003, according to *The ATA Chronicle*, ATA's president-elect compiled 24 of the journal's articles about the subject with the purpose of "helping professionals and the public at large to obtain information regarding current certification programs."[8] Nataly Kelly reviewed extensively the progress that certification has made since 2003 in the following fields: medical, health care, legal, educational, financial, training, and sign language. She asserts that "certificate" and "certification" do not mean the same thing, and defines the elusive terms from the academic and association perspectives. Kelly shows that for-profit schools and not-for-profit institutions with Extension Divisions issue "certificates" of attendance or completion, rather than diplomas, to students who finish their courses on related subject matter. This is apparent with regard to the universities in California with interpretation and translation studies, mentioned earlier by the Judicial Council, that do not incorporate the interpretation/translation courses into academic departments, but relegate them to the Extension Divisions as work training or continuing education certificate programs. This contrasts, for example, with the Graduate School of the College of Charleston and the Monterey Institute of International Studies, diploma-granting institutions, which elevate their interpretation programs to master's status. On the other hand, "certification," according to Kelly's article, stems from additional testing and approval by professional associations, such as ATA and NAJIT, and individual states, like Colorado and California — the latter via the Judicial Council — and groups of states through the National Center for State Court's Consortium. (See below for a discussion of the Consortium.)

**ATA, RID'S CERTIFICATIONS, AND UNITY OF ASSOCIATIONS.** Except for American Sign Language, overseen by the Registry of Interpreters for the Deaf (RID), this book has covered prominent diploma and certificate programs and most of the certification entities. Although the authors' training and experience do not involve what RID offers to its clients, we focus briefly on RID, which has gone through decades of inventing and discarding certification practices, trainings, and tests. Currently, according to Nataly Kelly's article, RID's website lists seven general tests: Oral Transliteration Certificate (OTC), Certified Deaf Interpreter (CDI), Certificate of Interpretation (CI), Certificate of Transliteration (CT), and the combined CI and CT. RID also has two industry-specific tests: the Conditional Legal Interpreting Permit-Relay and the Specialist Certificate, Legal. The five general tests have had more relevance and immediacy than the two specialized ones required by the legal profession.

Indeed, candidates must pass one of the seven general tests before proceeding to one of the two specialties. Ironically, this procedure goes against the national trend in the interpretation field, that is, specialization produces more impact and even more monetary advantage than being a generalist. For greater depth and more information, go to RID's website at www.rid.org.; phone 703-838-0030; or e-mail membership@rid.org. To sum up, Nataly Kelly's excellent article, which supports ATA's philosophy of inclusion and cooperation, proposes that RID and the other associations that believe in quality professionalism and protecting their membership combine efforts for sharing intellectual resources. As a footnote to the preceding commentary, it is worth mentioning that in the District of Columbia, the Office of Court Interpreting Services (OCIS) provides assistance to the deaf or hearing impaired, as well as for LEPs.

**NATIONAL CENTER FOR STATE COURTS: THE CONSORTIUM.** Indispensable for future court interpreters is the website of the National Center for State Courts, founded 1971, whose Consortium for State Court Interpreter Certification is the administrative arm for state and federal court interpreter examinations (www.ncsconline.org). The National Center's Consortium, located at 300 Newport Ave., in Williamsburg, VA (800-616-6109), was founded in July 1995 by Minnesota, New Jersey, Oregon, and Washington "to coordinate test development efforts and investments on a national scale," with the purpose of creating common standards and of achieving economies of scale in the development process. The 18 language tests available to the 40 member states as of February 2009 are Arabic (Modern, Egyptian, Levantine), Chinese (Cantonese, Mandarin), French, Haitian Creole, Hmong, Ilocano, Korean, Laotian, Portuguese, Russian, Slavic (Bosnian, Serbian, Croatian), Somali, Spanish, Turkish, and Vietnamese. A senior Consortium representative who prefers anonymity, in a telephone call placed to her on 12 March 2007, most graciously permitted quotation and reproduction of its copyrighted material for the purposes of this book, for which the authors are grateful.

**THE CONSORTIUM'S WORKSHOPS AND TESTS.** The Consortium organizes and publishes an annual "Schedule" of Orientation/Skills Building Workshops, Written Tests, and Oral Tests given by its thirty-two member states. Its Research Division Office (research@ncsc.dni.us) also provides a complete directory of "Contact Persons for State and Federal Interpreter Programs." The actual tests for each language are privileged information, but the Consortium offers a Practice Examination Kit for Spanish, which can be purchased online for $39.95. The kit includes an instruction manual, a CD with audio files, and hard copies of the test scripts. The Consortium also presents gratis a very short sample test, taken online, which will give the aspiring interpreter a feeling for the real test, and, once scored, a probable outcome in the actual test. Included among the useful material on the website are a series of eight "Manuals" that provide detailed insight into the nature of the exams and the criteria used for preparing and scoring them. Needless to say, an applicant who faces a difficult, unknown test that can determine the course of his career would do well to take advantage of the Consortium's practice exams, kits, and manuals.

**CONSORTIUM'S FCICE.** At the federal level, the Consortium currently organizes and administers the Federal Court Interpreter Certification Examination Program (FCICE) in Spanish, Haitian Creole, and Navajo. In the past, the University of Arizona held the contract for creating and administering the federal exam, but currently offers preparatory seminars for the FCICE. As with the state exams, the Research Division provides practice materials for the written and oral parts. In the practice exam, the oral part follows the written part; in the real test, an applicant must pass the written before proceeding to the oral. The practice test sequence emulates the actual test, which goes as follows:

Part 1: English to Spanish Sight Translation;
Part 2: Spanish to English Sight Translation;
Part 3: Simultaneous Monologue;
Part 4: Consecutive;
Part 5: Simultaneous Witness Examination.

**AN FCICE SAMPLER FROM THE CONSORTIUM.** To obtain a sense of the flavor and difficulty of the exam, consider the first sentence of the Practice Sight Translation English to Spanish, which must be rendered quickly:

> Your Honor, if it please the court, the Government would establish that Mr. Juan Domínguez was a citizen of the Dominican Republic, having been born there, and initially entered the United States legally with his parents and siblings on a visa in 1985.

The Practice Sight Translation from Spanish to English requires bilingual agility and knowledge of the terminology. Native English speakers with a good knowledge of Spanish would benefit from testing their skills against the following fragment:

> Expediente: D 220124. María del Carmen Pérez de López, de generales conocidas en autos que cito al margen superior derecho, ante usted señor juez, respetuosamente comparezco y expongo [...].

This could be a linguistic minefield for the unwary and unprepared. An English-speaking person with a general background in Spanish might be stymied by the Spanish "*expediente*," perhaps translating the cognate falsely as "expedient," instead of "document"; or be tempted to translate "*generales conocidas*" as "known female generals," instead of "well-known personal data" or "whose background is familiar"; or think "*autos*" were "cars," instead of "proceedings" or "judicial decrees." Furthermore, even the most ardent grammarian would strain when the legal jargon distorts traditional word order. The verbs dizzy the reader with swings from one direction and one person in third-person singular, apparently to another person in first-person singular, whereas both verbs refer to one and the same person. Judging from these terms, it becomes clear that both parts of the exam are difficult and require extensive involvement in encoding and decoding two languages quickly and correctly in legal terminology, grammar, syntax, vocabulary, false cognates, nuances, sentence structure, and logic. The typical bilingual person whose native language is Spanish or English — however well trained at a university English or Spanish department — cannot jump into this multilevel language labyrinth without prior study and practice. And even the training will not be sufficient if the individual, once on the job, does not possess additional capabilities in memorization, energy, curiosity, and intellectual ability.

**"REPORT," FEDERAL INTERPRETER CERTIFICATION PROGRAM, WASHINGTON, D.C.** The Office of Human Rights of the Government of the District Columbia, via its Language Access Program, published a provisional "Report," June 2005, which reviews laws relevant to the rights of individuals entitled to interpreters in court proceedings and when appearing before federally funded agencies.[9] Following the Court Interpreters Act (28 U.S.C. § 1827), the "Report" (p. 4) specifies that the director of the Administrative Office (AO) of the U.S. Courts is required to "define criteria for certifying interpreters qualified to interpret in federal courts." The AO's certifying exam is not detailed in the "Report," except to say that it is written and oral, "administered in two phases," and measures "a candidate's ability to accurately perform simultaneous interpretation, consecutive interpretation, and sight translation." Three categories of interpreters fall under its aegis: "Certified" for Spanish, Navajo, and Haitian-Creole; "Professionally Qualified" for other languages; and "Language Skilled." The selection process for "Professionally Qualified" involves serving as a conference interpreter with a U.S. agency or the UN, and one of two further requirements: the first, "successfully passing an interpreter examination"; the second, "being a member in good standing in a professional interpreter association that requires a minimum of 50 hours of conference interpreting and the sponsorship of three active members of that association" who will attest to the candidate's qualifications. The third category, "Language Skilled," refers to candidates who can demonstrate to the court's satisfaction their capabilities in a foreign language and English in court proceedings. For more detailed and direct information on freelance employment, see online the "Contract Court Interpreter Services and Conditions."

**"REPORT" AND THE DEPARTMENT OF STATE'S EXAMS.** The "Report" reviews the Department of State's increasingly difficult three examination levels for "contracting," but not — oddly enough — "certifying," interpreters:

Escort Level: Consecutive interpretation ability required.
Seminar Level: Consecutive and Simultaneous interpretation abilities required.
Conference Level: Consecutive and Simultaneous interpretation abilities required.

For permanent, in-house, bilingual employees, the State Department uses a similar three-tiered testing model. "Additionally, the State Department administers a general bilingual assessment test for bilingual employees as part of their day-to-day work. This examination tests both spoken and written language capacity, but does not specifically test an individual's ability to translate or interpret" ("Report" 5). With regard to translators, the State Department offers to both "contractual" candidates and in-house personnel an exam that consists of three passages, minimum, requiring skills from source to target language and vice versa. Although the State Department does not certify directly, the private and public sectors recognize the difficulty of these interpretation and translation exams and cedes to any successful examinee with State's imprimatur high consideration for placement in a position.

**PREPARATION FOR FCICE AT NAJIT AND ACEBO.** Just as the Consortium provides its readers with sound information on preparing for the FCICE, so, too, does the National Association of Judiciary Interpreters and Translators (NAJIT), via its affiliate, the Society for the Study of Translation and Interpretation (SSTI). With the cooperation of Portland State University, SSTI runs Test Preparation Workshops in Korean, Russian, Spanish, and Vietnamese. NAJIT also makes available a Spanish Practice Test by contacting www.najit.org.

Holly Mikkelson, a founder of ACEBO, developed a six-page essay, "Tips for Taking the Federal Oral Exam," which is available on its website, www.acebo.com.

Mikkelson's information extends beyond the usual linguistic information techniques and delves into the psychological and emotional aspects that the test taker must bear in mind. Having passed the exam and having served as a Federal Court Interpreter, she offers ten paragraphs of sage advice on a personal level to anxious test takers. From the ten tips, consider the following four:

Tip 1: "Don't worry when the examiners begin writing. They have to take notes to evaluate you, and they are not writing down all your mistakes; they are merely keeping score."

Tip 3 is deceitfully calming: "You do not have to be perfect to pass an interpreter certification exam—you just have to be excellent. If you make a mistake, don't let it get to you, just keep going."

Tip 8, regarding nervousness, belies the human condition: "Don't let your nerves get the best of you."

Tip 10, an appeal to logic and good sense, says: "Use your common sense, just as you do when you interpret in real life."

No person who expects to do well in these trying tests can afford to overlook these two additional sources of assistance. The assistance, however sound and merited, makes the most sense to very gifted people.

**JUDICIAL COUNCIL OF CALIFORNIA'S CERTIFICATIONS.** In California, the previously cited online "Report" of the Judicial Council's Administrative Office of the Courts admits that "although there are no minimum requirements that must be met in order to apply to take the state certification test, applicants are encouraged to complete formal, college-level course work and training in both languages (Spanish and English) to acquire it." The Court carefully distinguishes between certified and registered interpreters. To qualify as Certified, interpreters have to pass the Court Interpreter Certification Examination in one of twelve designated languages: Arabic, Eastern Armenian, Western Armenian, Cantonese, Japanese, Korean, Mandarin, Portuguese, Russian, Spanish, Tagalog, and Vietnamese. One can be titled a Registered Interpreter when no state certifying exam exists in their foreign language specialty; the only requirement is to pass the English Fluency Examination. Certified and Registered interpreters must also fulfill additional requirements, such as registering with the Council, paying dues, attending workshops on orientation and ethics, and completing 30 hours of continuing education every two years. Sign Language Interpreters must be certified by the Registry of Interpreters for the Deaf. An important point is that a court interpreter does not need U.S. citizenship for employment; however, he or she must prove eligibility to work in this country. The Judicial Council is located at 455 Golden Gate Ave., San Francisco, CA, 94102-3688. Its website: www.courtinfo.ca.gov.

**JUDICIAL COUNCIL'S AND PROMETRIC'S TESTS.** The Judicial Council's Administrative Office of the Courts contracted with the very experienced Thomson-Prometric Corporation to prepare and administer the Court's copyrighted Court Interpreter's English/Spanish Written and Oral Examinations. If the practice test of November 2006, available at www.prometric.com/california/cacourtint, is any indicator, future successful candidates will be few and far between, because that exam requires a very knowledgeable and sophisticated person to respond to the nuances of both languages in quick order. For the bilingual Written Exam, applicants have four hours and fifteen minutes to answer nine sections containing 155 bubble-in or short answer questions that involve: English ↔ Spanish Vocabulary, English ↔ Spanish Grammar and Word Usage, English ↔ Spanish Reading Comprehension, English to Spanish/Spanish to English Vocabulary, and finally Spanish Sentence Translation. As if that were not enough, the "Sample Court Interpreter Oral Examination" includes the three aspects: Consecutive Interpretation, Sight Translations, and the Simultaneous Component. The authors encourage potential court interpreters and—for its complexity in two languages—Spanish/English translators and instructors to test their mettle against the rigors of these exams. The instructions allege that the questions are not "tricky"; that is an understatement. For its part, the Court needs to assure itself that only the most prepared in a large pool of bilingual individuals bear the seal of Court Certified to handle an array of complex assignments, many unexpected, as this book has pointed out in the preceding chapters. To its merit, an individual who can pass California's tests is eligible for certification in Colorado and other states.

**JUDICIAL COUNCIL'S "SKILLS-ENHANCING EXERCISES."** In the preface to its ten-page summary of "Exercises for Interpreters of all Languages," at the beginning of California's Judicial Council's thirty-nine-page "Report," the authors justify the inclusion of the "Exercises" with the lament that "so few interpreter-training classes [are] available [that] it is often difficult to obtain feedback on interpreting performance." This belies the large number of programs, schools, and institutes in California that the Judicial Council lists where just such training and feedback can be obtained. In this ongoing discussion of practice exercises, it might prove useful to list the titles of the sections and subsections of the Judicial Council's "Report"; the curious reader can download it in its entirety. The "Report" offers techniques about Effective Listening and Memorization Techniques for Consecutive Training. In the long section, "Exercises for Sight Translation," the "Report" covers Exercises in Public Speaking, Reading Ahead in Text, and Analytical Skills. With regard to the section "Simultaneous Interpreting Skills," the exercises "are based on experiences gained in the training of both conference and court interpreters" (p. 15), which embrace Dual-Tasking Exercises and Analysis Exercises. Recognizing its own limitations and eager to help, the Judicial Council refers readers who want more complete exercises to the classic *Fundamentals of Court Interpreting: Theory, Policy, and Practice*, by Roseann Dueñas González, Victoria Vásquez, and Holly Mikkelson. The authors also recommend *Fundamentals* and summarize its findings and offerings below.

# I. Self-Directed Competency

*FUNDAMENTALS OF COURT INTERPRETING.* If, in your state, no standardized test exists to measure competency, seek out respectable ways to measure language and cultural proficiency through criterion-referenced tests and try to develop experience as an interpreter in varying interpretation settings. *Fundamentals* has excellent suggestions, which include a four-level interview that takes the candidate from A to D:

a. Basic résumé-type data.
b. Questions about travel and serious matters that call for advanced vocabulary.
c. Actions the candidate would take as an interpreter if confronted with certain happenings in a courtroom.
d. A discussion on the American judicial system.[10]

This, in effect, is a criterion-referenced type of oral test to measure English language proficiency and sophistication, and possibly the proficiency in the second language. When there is no one available to measure the proficiency in the second language, at least that of the English language is measured, and one can develop a profile of the cultural and intellectual background of the individual in lieu of the criterion-referenced test in the second language.

Similarly, *Fundamentals* also recommends a biographical sketch:

> The interviewer provides the candidate with a sheet of paper and asks the candidate to write a first-person narrative on personal background. This exercise requires no preparation or special

knowledge on the part of the applicant, and deals with a subject on which everyone is an expert. This exercise provides the interviewer with insight into the candidate's sophistication in English by evaluating the variety of the vocabulary and syntactic structures employed. It also yields more information about the candidate's personal background [Dueñas González et al. 193–4].

Both tests add, then, at the very least, the written component, let alone reading and the interpretation modes.

This section is not about training. Nonetheless, similar techniques can be used to assess candidates. We have studied the importance of memory in the interpretation process, in particular the consecutive mode, and in this case, then, short-term memory (STM). According to Elena De Jongh, for example, "Memory exercises initiate consecutive interpretation training. In the beginning, students practice with rather simple material. The length and difficulty of the exercises is gradually increased. These first exercises involve retention and subsequent repetition of utterances in the same language without taking notes."[11]

Interpretation companies can develop memory tests with the help of experienced interpreters who have been in training programs. See the excellent suggestions in *Fundamentals*:

A simple device to test for short-term memory is to read a question as it might be posed by an attorney and to ask the interpreter candidate to repeat as much of the question as possible. This exercise is a monolingual exercise and requires no interpretation. The only problem facing the candidate is to retain the content of the utterance long enough to deliver it back verbatim in the same language. This is in essence the consecutive interpretation counterpart to shadowing [Dueñas González et al. 195].

A similar technique, called *shadowing*, can be followed to assess the ability for simultaneous interpretation, realizing, of course, that the results may predict the need to undergo training, which could be an excellent motivator for the applicant. According to De Jongh, "Prior to [...] interpreting in the simultaneous mode, beginners should practice shadowing, [i.e., repeating] everything they hear word-for-word, simultaneously and in the same language (De Jongh 130).

The interviewer places the candidate in a situation that utilizes a tape recorder, headphones, and a pre-recorded monologue. This might be one or two minutes of an opening or closing argument recorded at a moderate speed, 120 to 140 words per minute.... [The interviewer] asks the candidate to listen to the monologue and simply to shadow the content of the tape, that is, to repeat the narrative simultaneously [...] [Dueñas González et al. 194].

Jerry A. Fodor believes that there is a scientific, experimental basis for using the shadowing technique to exercise, to wit:

In particular, appreciable numbers of subjects can "shadow" continuous speech with a quarter-second latency (shadowing is repeating what you hear as you hear it).[...] Since shadowing requires *repeating* what one is hearing, the 250 msec. of lag between stimulus and response includes not only the time required for the perceptual analysis of the message, but also the time required for the subject's integration of his verbalization.[12]

Consider the following technique, described in *Fundamentals*, that can be used to check proficiency in the other language and the ability to interpret, called the back-translation technique: "The test administrator can check the accuracy of the candidate's interpreting performance by not only requiring a candidate to interpret into the language, but also by requiring the candidate to interpret her own rendition back into English" (Dueñas González et al. 196).

**ACEBO AND OTHER SELF-STUDY PROGRAMS.** Not everybody has the time or money to attend a school to learn the trade or to sharpen existing skills. For those with limitations, but no lack of desire, self-study/independent-study programs are available for Spanish, Cantonese, Korean, Mandarin, Russian, Polish, Japanese, Portuguese, and Vietnamese. A pioneer in this field is ACEBO, at P.O. Box 7485, Spreckels, CA, 93962; phone (831) 455-1507, or contact at www.acebo.com. ACEBO, led by Holly Mikkelson and her partner/husband Jim Willins, has dedicated itself to publishing an excellent series of do-it-yourself books, audiocassettes, and audio-CDs. Professionals who are organized and who can schedule their time and energies can benefit from the self-study packages that accompany Mikkelson's series called *The Interpreter's Edge: Generic Edition,* which is designed for moving from English to languages other than Spanish.[13] It features an Introduction to Sight Interpretation (20 lessons), Consecutive Interpretation (6 memory and 9 interpreting lessons), and Sight Translation (12 lessons). ACEBO also produces, of course, a comprehensive Spanish-English series called *Edge 21.* The website is a source of useful material on Mikkelson's pertinent writings and on dictionaries and other works of reference; it also contains excellent suggestions on what to expect on the Federal Oral Exam. Altogether, ACEBO works diligently for the professional.

Alexander Rainof ([310] 828-4950, [562] 985-1599), a professor at California State University, Long Beach, who has distinguished himself with many books on interpretation and translation on a variety of themes, has also produced tapes for simultaneous practice.

Another extensive source of video training materials is Kenneth Gaer, at Bristol Productions Limited, 2401 Bristol Court S.W., Olympia, WA, 98502. Phone him at 360-754-4260; E-mail him at ken@bristolproductions.com. Gaer's website is www.bristolproductions.com.

Tapes are also available from Alicia Ernand Productions, in Santa Clarita, CA (661-296-4682), and from the Bryan School of Court Reporting, in Los Angeles, CA (213-484-8850).

The University of Arizona's National Center for Interpretation offers five sets of self-study materials: Two separate sets of *Interpretapes* for Spanish/English practice cover the legal and medical fields. The legal set costs $99.00, and includes eight CDs and three manuals to improve terminology. The *Interpretapes Medical Edition* costs $95 and involves three CDs and five manuals. *The Essentials Medical Edition* costs $80 and covers Consecutive, Simultaneous, and Sight Translation, for which 3 CDs and 26 Practice Scripts are provided. The remaining two sets of materials are dedicated to test-taking: The *Spanish Talking Manual* has 136 pages and 2 CDs for a price of $80 to cover the Oral Federal Court Interpreter Certification Exam. The FCICE written part is dealt with in three "FCICE Sample Written Examinations," for a cost of $195. The NCI's phone is (520) 621-3615; its e-mail: ncitrp@u. arizona.edu.

**ON-THE-JOB TRAINING (OJT).** Academic training is essential but not sufficient to allow an interpreter to perform well on the job. (On this matter, see section K, below, for a full discussion.) There is no replacement or substitution for direct trial-and-error OJT. And, Alicia A. Edwards adds helpfully, if in your geographical area inadequate and scarce training opportunities occur, OJT may be the only way out:

> Much of your learning will be on the job, because the best way to learn is to do, and because so many local variations of practice affect our work. [...] To learn on the job means you have to ask a lot of questions and observe a variety of cases. Once you have begun work, your observations will be more valuable because you will have a better idea of what you are seeing and what you need to concentrate on. [...] With some few exceptions, the general lack of in-house training and supervision for court interpreters means that the burden falls on us to seek and create our own training.[14]

# J. Additional Research Resources

INTERNET. The Information Super Highway, through searches via Google, provides computer-literate persons with overwhelming material on all phases of languages, institutions, and materials. The Google search leads to hypertext links (Hypertext Markup Language, or HTML) that connect to pertinent websites of individuals and institutions and their e-mail addresses. Information is "virtual," that is, with the ubiquitous laptop computer the interpreter can find this information on the road or in a courtroom. While traveling on research business, needed information from a foreign news stand, bookstore, or university library may not be handy. Enter the Internet. Its global reach provides practical and esoteric offerings, permitting the language specialist to whet his appetite on domestic and international happenings and learn new vocabulary. The computer offers an array of technologies for translators and interpreters, in that it has embedded English and foreign-language dictionaries, a thesaurus, and recommendations for using correct grammar and style. Translators will find the website called www.Baby lon.com very helpful. Especially useful for Spanish/English sources on translation, grammar, and bilingual dictionaries is the University of Illinois at Urbana-Champaign's website: www.library.uiuc.edu. The authors refer the reader below to other websites and e-mail addresses of major organizations, persons, and materials pertinent to this profession.

BOOKSTORES AT HOME, ABROAD, AND ONLINE. Citizens of Connecticut are fortunate to have nearby the World Language Center, a part of the renowned Yale Bookstore, now a branch of Barnes and Noble, where one can buy specialized bilingual dictionaries and books on interpreting and translating. Of course, the shelves of local and university libraries, and bookstores such as Barnes and Noble, Brentano's, and Borders in major cities harbor relevant texts or can locate them via interlibrary loan. Used or second-hand bookstores contain incredible surprises and values in dictionaries, journals, and texts. Check the super-extensive "Dictionary" section of Morry Sofer's *The Translator's Handbook.*[15]

Online bookstore websites, like barnesandnoble.com, Amazon.com, BookFinder.com, and Ebay.com, are open 24/7 via the computer for reviewing thousands of books, tapes, and cassettes at competitive prices. The procedure is simple: After registering with a user ID, a password, and a valid credit card, selected materials are mailed to the purchaser's address. Among the bountiful material relating to court interpreters is the Judicial Council of California's online document, which gives sections on dictionaries and unique bookstores: www.courtinfo. ca.gov. In its document, the Judicial Council refers to thirteen bookstores in the United States, England, Germany, and France (23–24). In the U.S., five are worth mentioning:

**Rizzoli International Book Store**
712 Fifth Ave.
New York, NY, 10019
(212) 397-3700

**International Learning Center**
1715 Connecticut Avenue, N.W.
Washington, DC, 20009
(202) 232-4111

**InTrans Book Service**
P.O. Box 467
Kinderhook, NY 12106
(518) 758-1755

**Modern Language Book Store, Inc.**
3150 "O" Street
Washington, DC, 20007
(202) 338-8963

**World Language Center**
Yale University Bookstore/Barnes & Noble
77 Broadway
New Haven, CT, 06511
(888) 730-YALE. FAX: (203) 772-2146
worldlanguagecenter@snet.net

**BOOK PUBLISHERS.** Among the hundreds of book publishers, three abroad — one in Holland and two in England — specialize in topics that abet the profession. Among the most prestigious for serious researchers is the family-owned John Benjamins Publishing Company, with headquarters in Amsterdam (P.O. Box 36244, 1020 ME, The Netherlands) and an office in Philadelphia, PA (P.O. Box 27519, 19118-0519). Books and monographs flow out each year. For example, in 2007, according to its website, the Translation Library had published 130 new titles. Authors derive from, among other countries, Canada, Czechoslovakia, France, Denmark, Germany, Israel, Spain, and the United States. To get a taste of J.B.'s esoteric and practical interests, consider the title of its first publication in 1994: *Language Engineering and Translation.* Ten years later, continuing with its tradition of encouraging excellence and complexity, J.B. published Ebru Diriker's *De-/Re-Contextualizing Conference Interpreting: Interpreters in the Ivory Tower.* In that same year, it brought out David B. Sawyer's *Fundamental Aspects of Interpreter Education: Curriculum and Assessment* (2004), referred to in Chapter 7, endnote 7. In 2001, J.B. launched the academic journal *Gesture,* edited by Adam Kendon, with the input of the University of Pennsylvania, which is discussed in Chapter 12, section D, "Nonverbal Equivalencies or Gestures." Consult its website: http://johnbenjamins.com.

Also dedicated to interpretation and translation is Multilingual Matters Ltd., out of Clevedon, England, with offices in Tonawanda, NY, and Ontario, Canada. For greater details, see http://www.multilingual-matters.com. Among its twenty-plus useful publications are Leo Hickey's *The Pragmatics of Translation,* the fourth edition of Geoffrey Samuelsson-Brown's *Practical Guide for Translators,* and James Nolan's excellent volume for students and teachers, *Interpretation: Techniques and Exercises,* quoted in Chapter 11, section C, "Consecutive Interpreting (CI)."

St. Jerome Publishing of Manchester, England (www.stjerome.co.uk), directed by prolific author Mona Baker since 1995, has produced a remarkably varied series of books, journals, and monographs on multiple aspects of translation and interpreting that benefit academics as well as practitioners. The initial publication was the journal *The Translator* (1995). Very useful for researchers is *Translation Studies Abstract* (1998). The company's first series consists of *Translation Theories Exploded* and *Translation Practices Explained.* The second is called *Encounters,* whose contributors include Holly Mikkelson (*Introduction to Court Interpreting*), Ian Mason (*Dialogue Interpreting*), and Roderick Jones (*Conference Interpreting Explained*).

Culling through keywords on www.Amazon.com and www.BarnesandNoble.com, one finds a few academic and commercial presses in the U.S. — in contrast to the singular commitment of the three aforesaid European presses — that have published books on the profession, among them are Carolina Academic Press (Roseann Dueñas González, et al., *Fundamentals of Court Interpretation*), Taylor and Francis (Mona Baker's excellent *Routledge Encyclopedia of Translation Studies*), A-Lexis Publications (Alexander Rainof's books), and St. Martin's Press (L.G. Kelly, *The True Interpreter*).

Publishing-house personnel in the U.S. and Canada turn to the two-volume, encyclopedic *Literary Market Place (LMP 2009)* for accurate information on a wide-range of issues. Especially apposite is volume 2 of *LMP 2009,* which organizes "Translators and Interpreters" by source language (65), target language (66), and by the names and addresses of companies and individuals that offer these services.[16]

**SOURCES OF REFERENCE MATERIAL.** The interpreter and translator adept in combining bilingual dictionaries with a thesaurus in the source language and target language to locate the closest nuance will avoid embarrassment and avoid false cognates. Morry Sofer's *The Translator's Handbook* is a first-class guide to dozens of English/foreign monolingual and bilingual technical, legal, medical, chemical, architectural, engineering, and pharmaceutical dictionaries. Again, in addition to Sofer's lists, consult the Judicial Council of California's online document on interpreters for specialized bookstores that carry dictionaries on the Romance languages, Near Eastern languages, Chinese, Korean, Russian, Czech, Slovak, Scandinavian languages, and Hungarian (Sofer 25–29). Indispensable for the advanced professional and academic is Mona Baker's and Gabriela Saldanha's *Routledge Encyclopedia of Translation Studies* (1998, and 2nd ed. revised 2009). They contain dozens of articles, country histories, and an extensive bibliography.

BILINGUAL GLOSSARIES. Translators and interpreters would do well to develop their own bilingual glossary, which will then store their personal and professional accumulated vocabulary developed over time based on actual use. This should prove invaluable because it will contain an individual's most frequently used vocabulary as well as low-frequency words. However difficult, it is important to maintain a personal bilingual glossary by jotting down the new terms as soon as possible in a notebook, on index cards, or on a hand-held or laptop computer. For those who need to amplify their glossaries, consult the compilations in the books of two leaders in the interpretation field, i.e., Holly Mikkelson, who authored *The Interpreter's Companion*, and the prolific and assiduous Alexander Rainof. The latter has compiled glossaries on finance, real estate, automobiles, fingerprints, firearms, weapons other than firearms, ballistics, insults and invectives, false cognates, medicine, and penology.

This chapter has reviewed many states with large populations of foreigners in which private and public sector institutions, universities, colleges, extension divisions, academies, and schools have put into place degree and non-degree certificate programs that offer preparation, testing, courses, and seminars in interpretation and translation. Some programs are designed for high-level practitioners, teachers, and researchers; others, the majority, have as their target audience the generalist eager to qualify as a part-time or full-time professional. Sufficient information enables the beginner to find a program and for the veteran to sharpen his skills. The sources listed permit interested persons to scan the industry for official places to take exams and to qualify for certification in the interpretation and translation fields with the purpose of finding gainful employment. Employment requires knowledge, skills, and abilities. In anticipation of the following chapter on jobs and salaries, the present chapter is helpful in locating prime sources for improving opportunities for jobs by pointing to the Internet, libraries, publishers, and bookstores with relevant material. Our purpose is realized if we have "taken the horse to water."

# *K. A Debate: Ortega and the Necessity and Sufficiency of Training*

After having offered myriad sources for training and education, it may seem strange to contemplate a debate about training and the methodology and journey to achieve success in becoming an interpreter and translator. The objective of this line of questioning is not to undermine our strong belief in education and training, but rather to open new lines of thought and to involve in the debate concepts from the Spanish philosopher José Ortega y Gasset.

Can performing as an interpreter or translator be learned by oneself with tapes, or at a technical institute, or even completing a series of extension division courses? The training is definitely *necessary* but not always *sufficient*. The training courses taken surely sharpen skills, increase interpretation speed, familiarize the individual with terminology in two languages, emulate courtroom or diplomatic procedures and protocols, and channel the memory and mindset of the students towards the details of the workplace. Those and other elements are necessary. But taken alone the insufficiency is stark.

Doesn't the future interpreter and/or translator need to develop his mind before attending technical schools and extension courses through a liberal arts education at a college or university where the student comes in contact with professors who, for four to six years, test performance in logic, ethics, history, political science, biology, chemistry, physics, mathematics, writing, reading, speech, literature, culture, English and foreign languages? Doesn't the future interpreter and/or translator need to display a tested knowledge of his native language first and then that, at minimum, of a second language?

As one example, it may appear absurd and out of place to question the ability of native speakers of Spanish who stand for exams about their knowledge of the details of their language and culture. But the University of Arizona's qualifying tests to thousands of Latin Americans who aspire to acquire Federal Court certification revealed a pass rate of 17 percent. With regard to translators, the ATA certification exams reveal that only 20 percent pass. Will the Latin Americans who at first fail the language exam be better prepared to defend LEPs after going through the courses of a commercial training institute or extension division? Tapes, training institutes, and extension division courses do sharpen basic skills and prepare candidates for pragmatic courtroom procedures. But by themselves are they sufficient — that word again — to enable the interpreter to transmit the deeper cultural and linguistic values?

The situation brings to mind concepts from José Ortega y Gasset (1883–1955), known for, among many other works, *The Revolt of the Masses* (1930) and *The Dehumanization of Art* (1925). Ortega criticized modern man, especially Spaniards, using the euphemism *sabio-ignorantes*. Modern society, according to Ortega, develops individuals "wise" (*sabio*) to the tricks of their particular trade, but blissfully "unaware" (*ignorantes*) of the deeper meanings to life, language, and culture. In opposition to the tradition of inward-looking and self-sufficient Spain ["*¡Que inventen ellos!*," proclaimed Miguel de Unamuno. ("Let {the foreigners} invent!")], Ortega had included translations of European philosophers in his journal, the *Revista de Occidente* (1923). Opposed to Franco's dictatorship, Ortega sought safety and unfettered creativity via exile in Argentina (1936). In Buenos Aires, Ortega had the freedom to continue his critique of the Civil War (1936–39) and modern man, and to delve into the value of translations as an instrument of revitalization. In 1937, he wrote essays for the newspaper *La Nación* of Buenos Aires, translated as "Misery and Splendour of Translation." In them, he "called for a revitalization of Spain based on individualism and elitism [...] and saw the translator as an idealist who should enable the reader to experience the strangeness of foreign works."[17] These concepts tie in with Ortega's condemnation of mass culture and provincialism, and also provide a pertinent lesson for interpreters and translators.

Following Ortega's reasoning, can interpreters — on whose nuances depend life-and-death matters of state and potential gains or losses of money, security, and health — justify themselves and feel completely satisfied falling into the category of *sabio-ignorantes*, that is, taking focused and specialized training courses that improve speed and terminology without penetrating the more profound university subjects talked about previously? Surely, a deeper and wider appreciation of the profession is required. Indeed, this book points to and attempts to offer the deeper intellectual and ethical sensibilities which lie at the heart of interpretation and translation through readings and inquiries into ethics, philosophy, and science, in addition to naming the places and means of acquiring those skills and then describing them in detail.

# CHAPTER 8

# Economics, Jobs, Salaries

## A. Skills vs. Economic Worth

However much an interpreter and translator, whether new to the job or a veteran, may enjoy the personal satisfaction of implementing difficult-to-acquire professional skills by helping indigent LEPs, by conveying nuanced speeches of ambassadors for the U.S. Secretary of State, or by transliterating an Egyptian papyrus or a Mayan glyph, such a gifted professional requiring uncommon knowledge, skills, and abilities needs adequate financial support in a high-maintenance economy to eat, to afford comfortable shelter, to pay for insurance, and to send the kids to college. It is common knowledge that the profession, overall — however much needed, wanted, and legally required — is not as well remunerated as others where analogous participants require years of university education, foreign travel, personal diplomacy, verbal skills, a keen memory, and an innate flavor for the nuances of words and culture in a native language and a target language.

Aspiring interpreters often feel disappointed because being fully qualified to be a full-time professional requires many and very advanced skills, continuous preparation, and upgrading of knowledge. Despite the time-consuming preparation, salaries are not commensurate for full-time employees and part-time hires. One has to make difficult choices, and the choice becomes self-identifying and self-validating, if one believes in Jean-Paul Sartre's existentialist expression: *Il faut choisir, et en choisissant, on se choisit* (Loosely translated: [As a human being] one must choose, and in choosing you choose [i.e., identify or validate] yourself.) Some have particular circumstances that impel the choice, that make the profession more palatable. For example, a retired person with a pension who needs to supplement his income, structure his time and space, and desires to lend a hand to society, can find translation very desirable. Again, mothers with small children may be attentive to interpretation because they may want to work only a few hours per week. Part-time qualified interpreters are in demand and can generate a satisfactory supplemental income, especially so if they are capable, willing, and eager to accompany interpretation with translation services. A newcomer in a costly college program needs to know that the knowledge being sought after will be compensated eventually, that the training is worth the opportunity costs.

ECONOMIC WORTH *VS.* KNOWLEDGE, SKILLS, AND ABILITIES (KSAs). A rational person might think that one's economic worth in the marketplace is congruent with supply and demand for service as well as with the knowledge, skills, and abilities (KSAs) needed for a demanding job. Most professionals in this field would be astonished, first, to examine the official KSAs for this profession and then, second, gauge them against the prevailing wage scales in the public and private sectors.

If the readers are willing, kindly follow along in an examination of this hypothesis, and then play a game of "What am I really worth?" To begin, pore over the tediously long and densely worded list of **"Knowledge Definitions," "Skills Definitions," "Abilities Definitions," "Work Activities Definitions,"** and **"Work Context Definitions,"** attributed to and required of "Interpreters and Translators," according to the online version of the *Dictionary of Occupational Titles.*[1]

Now if the reader would follow along and review the first ten categories presented below (all of them can be viewed online). Please add to or fill in your personal definitions of the **KSAs:**

**"Knowledge Definitions"** refer to thirty-one categories of competencies. We sample only the first ten. Readers are free to infer from personal experience the meanings of the categories: Foreign Language, English Language, Communications and Media, Customer and Personal Service, Computers and Electronics, Geography, Clerical, Education and Training, Administration and Management, and Psychology, and so on.

**"Skills Definitions"** contain thirty-four categories. What do the first ten mean to you?: Active Listening, Speaking, Reading Comprehension, Writing, Service Orientation, Active Learning, Learning Strategies, Coordination, Instruction, and Complex Problem Solving.

**"Abilities Definitions"** talk about fifty-two categories pertinent to this occupation. The absent forty-two are as relevant as the first ten: Oral Comprehension, Oral Expression, Written Comprehension, Speech Recognition, Written Expression, Speech Clarity, Memorization, Selective Attention, Near Vision, and Auditory Attention.

**"Work Activities Definitions"** consider the effort that must go into the job to make it viable. Again, enter your own comments, judging from the first ten of the forty-one listed: Interpreting the Meaning of Others, Getting Information, Identifying Objects, Actions, and Events, Processing Information, Documenting/Recording Information, Updating and Using Relevant Knowledge, Communicating with Persons Outside Organization, Thinking Creatively, Establishing and Maintaining Interpersonal Relationships, and Monitor Processes, Materials, or Surroundings.

**"Work Context Definitions"** is the last section that concerns us. Here the interpreter and/or translator supplies statements to the following ten categories among the thirty-eight presented according to one's personality and energy level: Importance of Being Exact or Accurate, Contact with Others, Indoors — Environmentally Controlled, Spend Time Sitting, Deal with External Customers, Outdoors — Exposed to Weather, Spend Time Making Repetitive Motions, Consequence of Error, and Coordinate or Lead Others.

To sum up, determine from the complexity inherent in the aforementioned KSAs — even with the definitions omitted, absent the remaining categories — whether you or your colleagues can measure up to the challenges. Then figure out whether you are underpaid, properly paid, or overpaid in this profession.

**THE PROFESSION NEEDS YOU.** The authors — sensitive to the economic vagaries of the profession — would like to share in the course of this chapter additional personal information and factual data with potential, recent, and seasoned colleagues on some economic and business factors. The intent is not to dissuade persons considering the profession to reject it, nor to persuade veterans to try another. The authors hope to be directing these pragmatic comments to professionals — future and ongoing — who are possessed of an innate drive, an inalienable pride and zeal to find a comfortable and satisfying niche in this business, despite the vicissitudes and pecuniary meagerness, because gifted people — and that is precisely what interpreters and translators deserve to be called — want to and have to utilize skills that few others possess. It is worth emphasizing again that salary scales described herein are accurate at the moment of writing, change often, and fluctuate according to many budgetary, political, and economic variables.

## B. Government Agencies

UNITED NATIONS. The U.N. employs a large number of translators and interpreters. After long and specialized training at the University of Geneva's School of Translation and Interpretation (http://www.unige.ch/eti/en), the most capable are hired. Over the years, the U.N. has also contracted alumni of the Graduate School of Translation and Interpretation, at Monterey, CA (discussed at length in Chapter 7). Indeed, the relationship of confidence established between the two resulted, in 2007, in the U.N. contracting with GSTI to train its personnel.

U.N. STAFF SALARY SCALES. U.N. interpreters and translators receive remuneration commensurate with their special skills, the rarity of the foreign languages, length of service, and quality of performance. Figures based on 1 January 2007, data, derived from the U.N.'s "Common System of Salaries, Allowances and Benefits," lists the ascending salary scale for these positions:

### Table 1: U.N. Position Titles for Interpreters and Translators

P1. Beginner/Trainee
P2. Journeyman
P3. Master
P4. Supervisor
P5. Chief (difficult to attain)

The spreadsheet's horizontal lines indicate the flow of the increasing gross salaries, from Step I to Step XV, but salaries for translators and interpreters may or may not reach Step XV. Thus, for the sake of practicality and convenience of comparison, we stop at Step X:

### Table 2: U.N. Salary Scale for Position Titles of Interpreters and Translators

P1. Step I, $44,614; Step X, $55,488
P2. Step I, $57,153; Step X, $72,106
P3. Step I, $70,222; Step X, $86, 938
P4. Step I, $85,974; Step X, $104,266
P5. Step I, $104,600; Step X, $124,415

SHORT-TERM SALARIES FOR U.N. FREELANCERS. Two charts came out on 1 January 2007, one titled "Salaries for Short-Term Interpreters," the other, "Salaries for Short-Term Translators and Revisers." They have in common gross daily and gross monthly payments in dollars for both categories of personnel. A short-term interpreter (60 or fewer days) at the U.N. in New York could expect daily gross pay to be $492.50 for Grade I and $321.50 for Grade II. The gross monthly pay for Grade I would be $13,245, and for Grade II, $8,665. The chart for short-term translators and revisers contains thirty categories and greater complexities. It shows gross daily pay (60 days or less) and gross monthly pay (over 60 days), with add-ons or inclusions for local recruitment *versus* non-local recruitment, post adjustments, cost-of-living supplements, and special negotiated entitlements. To illustrate in a simple way translators' wages at the U.N., look at the gross daily rates of local recruits:

### Table 3: U.N. Salary Scales for Freelance Interpreters and Translators

Translator I, $272.52
Translator II, $332.19
Translator III/Reviser I, $392.26
Translator IV/Reviser II, $440.35
Reviser III, $488.42

Consult the "Common System" online at www.icsc.org for more complete details on benefits, dependents, locality pay, hazard pay, relocation pay, and travel allowances. Our appreciation goes to the director in charge of salaries and allowances for posting the data online.

**U.S. GOVERNMENT'S GS-SCHEDULE.** The GS-Schedule applies to U.S. citizens who qualify for employment with the agencies that have a high demand for translators and interpreters, i.e., FBI, CIA, and the National Security Agency. The NSA, for example, "has a critical need for [...] Arabic, Dari, Farsi, Kurdish Sorani, Pashto, Punjab, Sub-Saharan African, and Urdu," among others, detailed at www.NSA.gov/Careers. All applicants can benefit from the objective, general outline presented in the excellent chapter "Interpreters and Translators" of the *Encyclopedia of Careers and Vocational Guidance.* While the text in general is very useful, the salary figures from 2004 merely serve as a point of departure for current salaries. The *Encyclopedia* estimates that the annual salary range is from "$24,075 to $40,000 to $80,000."[2]

Compare the *Encyclopedia*'s figures with the updated January 2007 numbers from the U.S. Government's Office of Personnel Management. Excluding locality pay, trainee interpreters and translators who start the climb up the GS-Schedule ladder at the GS-5 rating can earn from $25,623, at Step 1, to $33,309, at Step 10. For those with a college degree and experience, the salary range starts at $31,704 (GS-7 level), and goes to $41,262, at Step 10. For those with an advanced degree, the Step 1 through 10 salary ranges are:

### Table 4: GS-Salary Schedule for U.S. Government Employees

GS-9: $38,824 to $50,470
GS-10: $42,755 to $55,580
GS-11: $46,974 to $61,086

According to data in the chapter "Interpreters and Translators" of the U.S. Department of Labor's *Occupational Outlook Handbook,* language specialists with a command of exotic dialects pertinent to national security issues can earn more than $75,000 annually at the GS-11 level.[3]

**U.S. DEPARTMENT OF DEFENSE.** A word of caution is in order. From April 2007 through December 2009, the DoD abandoned the GS-Schedule and implemented its own performance-based National Security Paybanding System (NSPS). In 2010, the DoD reinstated the GS-Schedule and is re-evaluating all civilian payroll and performance systems. Potential and ongoing interpreters and translators for the DoD should consider whether the following alterations that took place under NSPS still apply.

1. Under NSPS, starting and ongoing salaries derived from a pool of money whose shares were controlled and dispensed by committees of unit supervisors that determined excellence, needs, and performance.
2. Tenure, under NSPS, despite a trial period of successful employment, was no longer assured. Starting 2010, it would be prudent to determine whether tenure is restored.
3. Starting 2010, check whether salaries correspond to NSPS or to the GS-Schedule.
4. Check whether the lockstep GS-Schedule ladder of advancement and promotions for time and service still applies.

## C. Federal and State Courts

**SOUTHERN DISTRICT OF NEW YORK (SDNY) SALARIES AND WAGES.** Freelance federal court interpreters, according to New York federal court interpreter David Mintz, writing on the National Association of Judiciary Interpreters and Translators' (NAJIT) website, could expect, in 2000, $305 daily. The year 2000 salaries serve as a point of departure and comparison for the remuneration on or after 2 January 2008, offered by the Federal Court of SDNY. While SDNY employs five Spanish interpreters full-time at salaries ranging from $30,000 to $80,000, the Court offers numerous contracts to freelancers on an as-needed basis. For example, to cover the 33,310 legal actions from June 2001 to February 2007, SDNY contracted interpreters of fifty-six languages. The Federal Court Administrator establishes rates for all contracted interpreters and separates them in two major categories, i.e., an hourly and a daily wage structure. Salaries continue to rise, but at the time of writing this, in the category of Certified and Professionally Qualified Interpreters, the scale is the following: For a full-day assignment, the Court pays $364; for a half-day, $197. Overtime pay consists of $51 per hour or part of an hour. In the category of Language Skilled (Non-Certified) Interpreter, SDNY pays $181 for a full day and $100 for a half-day appearance. Overtime pay comes to $31 per hour or part thereof. While overtime in both categories applies to courtroom activities in excess of eight hours per day, the pay is not applicable to travel time. SDNY added the following clarification to avoid paying extra for overlapping daily assignments: "A contract interpreter cannot charge different court units half-day or full-day for which he or she is already receiving payment from another court unit."

**SDNY'S LANGUAGE POOL.** On an individual level, the wages and salaries may seem paltry, but the overall economic upside is that remuneration in the U.S. is on the rise to keep up with the cost of living and the increased number of translation and interpretation opportunities. This is due in no small measure to the huge increase over the past three decades in immigrants from Central and South America, from the Middle and Far East, and from the former Soviet Union. SDNY contracted interpreters for fifty-six languages from June 2001 to February 2007, which is quite a departure from the traditional "PFIGS," that is, Portuguese,

French, Italian, German, and Spanish. In that six-year period, the ten languages most called for were the following:

## Table 5: Descending Order of Foreign Language Cases in SDNY (2001–2007)

Spanish (26,632, or almost 80 percent of legal actions)
Chinese (Mandarin [1,241], Foochow/Fuzhou [1072], Cantonese [636])
Arabic (833)
Russian (515)
Punjabi (267)
Urdu (253)
French (239)
Korean (155)

SDNY's calendar also included the languages of Afghanistan (Pashto, 110 cases) and Iran (Farsi, 54 cases), even more prominent because of international turbulence. The complete list of languages and their frequency, along with other valuable information, is available on SDNY's website: http://www.sdnyinterpreters.org.

FEDERAL COURT JOB APPLICATIONS. SDNY asks persons seeking positions to fill out a standard application available on-line at its website: http://www.sdnyinterpreters.org/faq. php. Prospective candidates in other court districts can benefit by SDNY's examples and guidelines as they apply for positions to districts nearer their homes by accessing key words on the computer, such as "Salaries Interpreters Federal District Court Los Angeles," for example.

SCHEDULING/WORK ASSIGNMENTS IN STATE COURTS. Depending on the size and complexity of the state court system, on the case loads, and on the number of professionals available, interpreters may be assigned to one courthouse or serve on a contingent or rotating basis as an itinerant interpreter. In the large districts, the supervisor of the command center of the court system makes these assignments once or twice a day as needed. The interpreter, whether assigned to one court or traveling among several, should be prepared to serve gladly and should be willing to take on other assignments, such as record keeping, filing, updating archives, answering the phone, writing reports, and making coffee.

CONSORTIUM: STATE COURT SALARY SURVEYS. The Consortium for State Court Interpreter Certification, founded July 1995 — a subdivision of the National Center for State Courts — published, in 2002, on its website (http://www.ncsc.online.org), two national surveys of salaries, one for freelance and the second for contracted state court interpreters. The Consortium's ample and detailed survey covers 32 states. It was modified 12 April 2006, but even at that time was not guaranteed to be accurate or up to date. The Consortium advises that more accurate information "can be viewed on the following PDF page: http://www.ncsonline.org/WC/Publications/Res_CtInte_StateFedContactsPub.pdf.

The survey lists the 32 responding states in alphabetical order and groups the headings for each one in the following way: Location (i.e., State, Major Metro, County, Other Typical, and 13th Judicial District in Palm Beach, FL); Per-Hour wage with subdivisions of High, Low, and Minimum Number of Hours; Per-Half-Day wage with High and Low subdivisions; Per-Day wage with High and Low designations; Travel; and, finally, Comments. The high or low per-hour wage for Connecticut, to take a simple example, is $15.93 for a minimum of four hours.

Notably absent from the survey are eighteen states: Alabama, Arizona, Iowa, Kansas, Louisiana, Maine, Mississippi, Montana, New Hampshire, New York, North Dakota, Oklahoma, Rhode Island, South Carolina, South Dakota, Vermont, West Virginia, and Wyoming. The omission of New York can be explained by saying that its court systems and wage scales are too complex to be encapsulated in a single survey. Even so, the reader can view above the salaries of the Southern District Court of New York to get an idea of state court salaries.

CALIFORNIA: COURTS, SALARIES, AND LANGUAGES. The scant information in the Consortium compensation survey regarding California reveals only that salaried employees, who receive a low of $30,000 and a high of $66,000, are hired at the county level. Greater information comes, oddly enough, from the marketing pamphlet of the Southern California School of Interpretation, discussed at length in Chapter 7: "State court interpreters earn $265.00/day; Federal interpreters earn $355.00/day." And sufficient reasons abound for these high salaries. Consider the numbers. According to the pamphlet, "California has 11.6 million legal immigrants and an estimated 2.4 million illegal immigrants," the majority from Spanish-speaking countries. It adds that California "spends $82.7 million a year on court interpreters and has 1,316 Certified Interpreters in 13 languages. Approximately 800 are Certified Spanish Court Interpreters, and of those, 500 work in Los Angeles County." According to the Commission on Access to Justice, "an estimated 40 court proceedings are continued (i.e., postponed) every day in Los Angeles County Superior Court due to a lack of a Certified Interpreter, resulting in some 10,000 delayed proceedings." There is no shortage of jobs in California. See Chapter 7 for a list of California schools that offer job placement, training and testing. Persons interested in greater details can contact the Judicial Council of California's Administrative Office of the Courts and inquire about the Court Interpreters Program at its toll-free telephone (866) 310-0689, or at its e-mail, CourtInterpreters@jud.ca.gov.

CONSORTIUM'S SURVEYS. Other states in the Consortium's survey, such as Florida, Georgia, Michigan, Nevada, and Pennsylvania, present a more varied and complex wage structure. In Florida, for example, interpreters and translators are in great demand—as they are in California—to service a large population of documented and undocumented immigrants from, among other areas, Central and South America and the Caribbean nations. Under the aegis of the State Supreme Court, the Office of the State Courts Administrator created the Court Interpreters Program. The Program helps interpreters and translators obtain recognition and employment by displaying on its website the names, addresses, telephone numbers, e-mail numbers, and foreign language credentials of all federal and state court interpreters who have successfully completed a series of orientation sessions, written exams, and skill-building workshops. Applicants who are successful in the written exams can proceed to take the Oral Language Proficiency Examination for specific languages, such as Spanish, Haitian Creole, Portuguese, and Russian. State court administrators can, thus, pick from a large number of qualified professionals. As an added benefit, the persons who make the list can tout their qualifications to private-sector hiring sources.

PAY SCALES: FL *vs.* CA, CO, NV, AND PA. With regard to Florida's salaries and wages, the supervisor of the Broward County, FL, court interpretation system indicated (2008), that state wages generally fall below those of other states with similar case loads. Florida's lower compensation scales are borne out on the two surveys by the Consortium for State Court Interpreter Certification. At the state level, there are no salaried personnel. Salaried personnel exist at the county level, where the annual take-home pay runs from $22,400 to a high of $42,000. In comparison, look at the annual lows and highs of four other states at the county level:

### Table 6: Comparison of Salary Scales at County Level in Four States

CA, $30,000 to $66,000
CO, $37,176 to $64,000
NV (Clark County), $37,467 to $58,069
PA, $36,326 to $44,985

For independents or freelancers, the per-hour, per-half-day, and per-day stipends depend on whether the interpretation takes place in a lower pay Major Metro area (*i.e.*, Miami, Fort Lauderdale, Tampa, Jacksonville), or in the upscale 13th Judicial Circuit of Palm Beach County. The Major Metro hourly for a two-hour block is $25/hour; Haitian Creole warrants $30–$35/hour. In contrast, the 13th Judicial Circuit pays $60/hour for a two-hour block involving interpreting in Spanish; $15 per additional hourly block. There are no per-half-day or per-day wages in the Major Metro areas. On the other hand, for Spanish, the 13th Judicial Circuit again pays better, e.g., for a half-day a low of $75 and a high of $90. Once again, for Spanish, the 13th Judicial Circuit's full-day compensation is a low of $125 and a high of $150. The 13th Judicial District also remunerates for travel expenses at the rate of $0.29/mile. Supply and demand, as well as longer travel distances, play a large role in the differences between the pay in the Major Metro areas, with their surfeit of eager interpreters, and that of the 13th Judicial Circuit. The pay, for sure, is not as high in Florida as it is in the four states mentioned previously, but the volume of work is high and constant for ambitious interpreters.

COLORADO: SALARIES FOR MINIMUM QUALIFICATIONS. What minimum education and work experience must a candidate possess to be considered for a single vacancy as court interpreter in the City/County of Denver, CO, and merit a salary ranging between $43,452 and $63,396? Based upon an actual listing for a vacancy, dated 23 January 2007, consider the requirements: The candidate must "interpret from English to Spanish and from Spanish to English in the criminal courtrooms, and in the jail. The position involves interpreting in the simultaneous, consecutive, and sight translation modes." But the responsibilities do not begin and end in the courtrooms and jail. For that salary, the successful candidate "will assist in administrative duties, such as answering the phone, gathering and maintaining statistics, keeping up interpreting equipment, filing, organizing reference materials, and other duties as required." One might think that a bachelor's degree, even a master's, would be required to deserve that munificent salary for handling complex multitasking legal, personal, and administrative activities. The following is a direct quote of the minimum, formal educational qualifications: "High School diploma or possession of a GED (General Education Diploma) and have two years of experience working in a professional capacity as an interpreter working with English to Spanish or Spanish to English speaking persons. A combination of appropriate education and experience may be substituted for the minimum education and experience requirement." Can one be prepared for the complexities and protocols required of an interpreter on the basis of a GED, which requires minimum exposure to a high school environment, or through on-the-job training? The qualifications continue, but get progressively more difficult, and one again wonders how an individual with a GED can also acquire, "possess, and maintain a Colorado Certified Interpreter Credential," or a certificate from "the Consortium," or, if an out-of-state candidate, a certificate from "NAJIT or California"? A Supplemental Questionnaire to the application underscores clearly the complexities and pressures of the job: "Are you willing to work in a high volume 150 clients per day environment such as in-court proceedings, arraignments, trials, plea bargains, or hearings?"

COLORADO: LAW VS. REALITY AND GOOD SENSE. While no doubt exists that the appointee, with either the minimum salary or the maximum, will be subject to demanding work, one wonders whether the administrators of the Colorado Court Interpreter Program had calibrated accurately the appropriate educational qualifications to the job requirements and salary range. Denver officials informed us by phone that a law, which had watered down the qualifications from a bachelor's degree to a GED, obligated the supervisor of the Denver City/County Interpreter's Program to post qualifications according to the law, rather than permitting good sense and pragmatism to prevail. Did this happen because the lawmakers recognized the level of candidate it wished to attract or was locally available, or did it mean that the legislators were not apprised of the complexities that the interpreters face? Fortunately, degreed and experienced candidates from out of state appeared, undaunted by the announcement, who felt that a serious and realistic evaluation process would be based on merit. They decided to pony up willingly the travel expenses to compete for a difficult, but well-compensated position in a state that also offered skiing and scenic beauty. Fortunately, the profession in general had reason for optimism when the selection committee evaluated candidates on merit and, bypassing the minimum requirements, sought to hire a quick-thinking individual with a university degree who had the skills plus experience to protect LEPs in difficult court proceedings. The authors are indebted to the court's administrators of interpreters for their professionalism and frankness in discussing these problems. Further information on public sector positions in the Denver, CO, area is available through two websites: http://www.courts.state.co.us; http://agency.governmentjobs.com/denver.

COLORADO VS. NEW JERSEY. Contrast with those of Colorado the positions, salary ranges, and qualifications of potential job openings posted on 11 January 2007, for the Superior Court of New Jersey, Hudson Vicinage. The first difference is that Colorado had one specific opening. New Jersey, with larger operations and a greater turnover of personnel, collected résumés for "positions that may be filled over the next six months." Salary ranges at three levels of competence were given, with a relevant asterisk after each one. The salary range at the highest level, or "Court Interpreter — Master Level 3 — Master," was $55,141.20-$83,232.00. The general job description expected "Employees [...] [to] interpret complex legal proceedings and translate forms, letters and other court-related documents." For "Court Interpreter 1— Journey Level 2 — Journey," the range was $52,020.00 to $73,868.40. The candidate at this level interpreted "legal proceedings and translated forms, letters, and other court-related documents. At the lowest level, "Court Interpreter 1— Conditionally Approved/Trainee Level 1— Conditionally Approved Trainee," the potential employee's salary can vary between $44,264.03 and $73,868.40, for which that "Employee [...] interpreted proceedings of limited legal significance or limited linguistic complexity and prepared translations of forms, letters, and other court-related documents." The aforementioned asterisks pointed to pertinent information, to wit:

For newly hired individuals, the starting salary will normally be at the minimum of the salary range or up to 15% above the minimum salary based on education and experience, however, a higher salary may be approved based upon the particular qualifications of the selected individuals or the difficulty of the recruitment. In no case may the employee be paid more than the maximum salary for the title.

A close reading of the announcement reveals that similar waivers and exceptions apply to ongoing employees. Other posted positions in New Jersey proposed similar salary ranges, qualifications, and benefits. Jersey's well-paying jobs remain accessible to persons living in New York or Pennsylvania. Individuals interested in the Hudson Vicinage or the neighboring Cumberland/Gloucester/Salem Vicinage can direct inquiries via an e-mail to hudsoncareers.mailbox.@judiciary.state.nj.us, or to the website www.judiciary.state.nj.us/interpreters/intro.htm.

COLORADO, NEW JERSEY: SEVEN EMPLOYMENT LESSONS. The job openings in Colorado and New Jersey produce seven lessons:

1. Most obvious is that computer skills are indispensable for locating, competing for, and obtaining a position locally and nationally.
2. Decent salaries do exist, but the competition can be fierce.
3. A serious applicant must be willing to relocate.
4. Education and experience are givens, but all things being equal, the hiring committee will favor an interpreter who adapts quickly and discreetly to changing circumstances, displays people skills in addressing colleagues, lawyers, and judges, and maintains toughness and calm in the face of suspected and convicted felons.
5. No officially prescribed credentialing exists. Despite that, the great leveler of the applicants resides in presenting an approved "good housekeeping seal of approval," in the case of Denver, a Colorado Certified Interpreter Credential. For other states, it is important to display analogous certificates, and/or a Certificate from the Consortium, the Administrative Office of the U.S. Court (Federal), NAJIT, or California. Possession of a certificate will not guarantee employment, but absent one, a job offer is doubtful. All vacancies are supposed to adhere to the guidelines of the Equal Employment Opportunity Act.
6. Trumping the law and job descriptions, in many instances, is the sixth, but certainly not the least, factor for landing a job, i.e., possession of a competitive edge. That edge could be discreet personal influence, insider knowledge, charming personality, being fortuitously available, an emergency hire, and even a job description tailored to favor an individual.
7. And when all is said and done, a bit of luck always helps.

# D. Private Sector Opportunities

In addition to the sources of employment detailed above for the U.N., the U.S. government, and the state and federal courts, where opportunities are steady and frequent, but hard to qualify for, interpreters can find positions via private, for-profit, interpretation and translation companies. Some hospitals, both public and private, hire full-time interpreters. Interpreters with an entrepreneurial spirit can develop their own company, but be warned that it is a difficult, time-consuming and risk-laden task. Freelancers can seek their own opportunities and work, as well, for the private interpretation and translation companies. Some freelancers only work with federal courts.

The Yellow Pages of every city, and the *Business to Business Directory* in every state, under the heading of "Translators" and/or "Interpreters," identify local, state, and national companies. Now and then one can find ads in big-city newspapers. In Connecticut, for example, *The Hartford Courant* lists openings. Availabilities can also be found with the State Employment Offices, and more directly with each of the State Judicial Systems. One can call the Interpreters Central Office or visit them on the Internet. Among the best books with extensive information and directories on locating private and public sector companies hiring interpreters and translators is Morry Sofer's *The Translator's Handbook*, available in libraries or via bookstores and www.Amazon.com. A long list of companies appears in volume 2 of the *Literary Market Place (LMP 2009)*, section "Translators and Interpreters."

The Internet harbors a mountain of information on availabilities at companies in the U.S. and abroad via the popular employment websites www.Monster.com and www.careerbuilder.com. The website www.TranslationDirectory.com reported, in October 2008, access to 4,702 agencies nationally and internationally. Among the services TD offers, two are very useful: A professional can either inquire about a position or post a résumé on its bulletin board. Some positions may be located far away, but today's technology enables translators to complete an application, sign a contract, get an assignment, and compose and submit documents without getting into the car, i.e., electronically, via e-mail attachments, faxes, compact disks, and flash drives.

JOBS IN NEW YORK AND WASHINGTON, D.C. The concentration of international companies doing business in banking, foreign trade, diplomacy, and government work in New York City and Washington, D.C., means that a large number of interpreters and translators find work there. Again, the previously mentioned *Translator's Handbook* by Morry Sofer and *The Encyclopedia of Careers and Vocational Guidance* point to the national panorama of "publishing houses, schools, bilingual newspapers, radio and television stations, airlines, shipping companies, law firms, and scientific and medical operations" (*Encyclopedia* 802). All things considered, pay scales may not always be lucrative, work schedules may be uncomfortable, and jobs may be sporadic and part time, but sufficient opportunities exist to make the capable, energetic, and well-organized professional continue the quest.

## E. Journals with Jobs

All professionals who seek positions in the U.S. should join, at minimum, the American Translators Association (ATA), with more than 10,000 members in 70 countries, and the National Association of Judiciary Interpreters and Translators (NAJIT), with 1,000 members. NAJIT publishes *Proteus*, a trade journal that lists vacancies and opportunities. *The ATA Chronicle*, published eleven times a year, starting in 2008, offers in its pages and online a job bank. To get an idea of the opportunities available, *The Chronicle* of January 2007 listed three translators who offer their services to clients in translation design and the Indian languages of Urdu, Hindi, and Punjabi. Alongside were two job vacancies from Middle America: a Tarboro, NC, corporation sought a "Customer Relations/Translation Manager" with two years' experience in Japanese. Another company in Oak Park, IL, also required Japanese. Both organizations post members' names, specialties, and e-mails on their directories, which interpretation companies and corporations can consult to locate a professional. *The Chronicle* of Nov.-Dec. 2008 posted an opening for an Assistant Professor of Spanish and listed two ads for translators offering services in Korean and Indonesian. Full addresses for NAJIT, ATA, and other professional organizations can be found in another part of this chapter. For positions abroad, consult the website of the International Association of Conference Interpreters (AIIC in French): http://www.aiic.net. AIIC's address: 10, Avenue de Sécheron, CH-1202, Geneva, Switzerland.

## F. Networking at Conferences at Home and Abroad

PROFESSIONAL ASSOCIATIONS. This profession not only offers opportunities to network at home and abroad for employment, it also provides intellectually stimulating encounters at its annual and regional seminars and conferences. The November-December 2008 issue of *The ATA Chronicle* lists ten national and two international meetings for 2009. At its conferences, ATA features key speakers, special seminars, mentoring forums, job interviews, publishers looking for manuscripts, and networking. For those who need language certification, an exam session is scheduled. The offshore sites for 2009 include cities of great cultural and historic relevance: Haifa, Amsterdam, and Buenos Aires. The main point of listing these conferences is that the associations work actively and continually to reach out with continuing education and networking opportunities.

INTERNATIONAL TRAVEL. Translators and interpreters do not have to work cloistered at home, in the office, or in the library. They are not chained for sole company to a laptop or desktop. Imagined sounds do not only emanate from tapes, exotic dictionaries, and musty texts. Instead, professionals can translate on the road, laptops in tow. Who can argue that foreign language sounds are sweeter *in situ* instead of on tapes? Questions asked directly — U.S. visitor to citizen abroad and vice versa — resonate with greater clarity. In the company of professional cohorts roaming through towns and cities in reach of *trattorias*, Plazas Mayores, Great Walls, and *librerías de segunda*, learning becomes personal and fun. Through these travels and people-encounters, friendships are formed that can lead to jobs, personal refreshment, and an understanding of other cultures.

NETWORKING PROS AND CONS. Networking one-to-one and at regional and national conferences expands the chances of finding opportunities. Some caution and wariness are in order to be able to discern whether a "sharing collaborator" is not a fair-weather friend trolling for openings, or one who views another professional as a competitor in a zero-sum game. One caveat is to verify that interpreters who share information behave ethically and are not contravening the contracts with the interpretation companies. If an exchange of leads and information takes place carefully, one may be able to get good tips, and, over the long haul, make professional relations that are mutually enhancing.

## G. Private Employment Agencies

Private interpretation agencies seek out individuals who do competent work, have a great interest and skill, and are willing to travel for specific assignments and special schedules. The individual who fits this mold can work for several of the companies on an ongoing basis.

Because of personal circumstances, some persons prefer few assignments, do not like to drive far or at all, and choose only assignments in their hometown.

Provided that the résumé results in a successful phone or in-person interview, each particular company will ask the candidate to sign a contract that requires the appropriate confidentiality and — a very important matter to each company — not to use one's work as an interpreter for the company to solicit direct work and to not make available a personal telephone number and address. Cases have arisen in which interpreters acted unethically by not complying with the signed agreement, and when discovered, were denied future contracts and/or were discharged from state government.

The interpreter working as an independent contractor can expect phone calls from the companies to ascertain availability for a specific assignment, be it in divorce court, a state agency, doctor's office, insurance home investigation. Depending on assignment and availability, the following takes place: some companies will send a contract by fax or by e-mail attachment for each specific assignment. In this contract, the details of the assignment are stipulated. Under these circumstances, the designee is legally an independent contractor, not an employee, who has to report the income to the Internal Revenue Service on or before April 15, from a 1099 form previously supplied by the agency by January 31 of each year. In effect, the interpretation company is contracted to subcontract the interpretation assignment to a qualified person. The contacted interpreter responds by faxing or e-mailing the agreement, signed or unsigned, to indicate acceptance or refusal. Once a contract is signed, and the interpreter proves to be competent and reliable, most companies will simply give out the pertinent details over the phone. These include date (including day and hour of start), address, phone number, and contracting party. Other important information include the name of the contact person and the name and title of the person for whom you will be interpreting, i.e., attorney, social worker, medical doctor, or other data identifying the case.

Experience dictates attention to the following details to save time and frustration. Always ask the interpretation agency representative for driving directions; ask whether parking is available. In all probability, the interpretation company will not have bothered to get this driving information. While MAP-QUEST on the computer will most often give good driving directions, it does not reveal parking availability nor the cost of private parking, which will be borne by the interpreter unless prior arrangements are made. Time is money, goes the refrain, and punctuality to the job assures the client that he is getting what he paid for. For these and other reasons, it is important to allow extra driving time. Anticipate the probability of traffic accidents, road work, detours, a blowout, and the time to take on gas.

The standard rate per hour, with two hours as a minimum, will apply. Some of the out-of-state interpretation agencies pay higher hourly rates and may even have three hours as the minimum interpretation time that they will pay. It does not hurt to request a higher hourly rate after working for a company for a period of time. However, the possibility of getting the higher rate is uncertain and depends on many factors. There is a higher fee for simultaneous interpretation; some agencies have a fixed rate, and with others it is negotiable.

Agencies differ with regard to travel time and mileage. One agency may pay for both, using the federal mileage rate to reimburse for the number of miles traveled. Most agencies pay for the duration of travel on the basis of 60 minutes of travel time at half the interpretation rate per hour. It is based on "portal to portal." Another company may be flexible and allow one to choose whether to be paid for travel time or mileage. The mileage, when not covered by a company, can be deducted from federal taxes. Regarding taxes, it is advisable to consult a tax advisor for other possible business-related deductions, for example, on diction-aries, travel to conferences, and registration for seminars that maintain and upgrade profes-sional skills.

If the client company requires an invoice for professional expenses, ask for date-stamped receipts for services and products bought by credit card/cash/check for the assignment (i.e., videotapes, audiotapes, and compact disks). Use a salesman's notebook or an electronic device to keep track of relevant and agreed-upon travel and transportation expenses, which could include tolls, mileage, gasoline, oil changes, and parking. Time is always a factor in interpre-tation assignments. Most short-term jobs pay a pre-arranged hourly rate or a flat rate for a two-hour minimum travel/assignment period. According to the arrangements, document one-way or roundtrip travel time, arrival time, interpretation time, and departure time. Calcu-late, if required, to the quarter-hour prorated expenses for less or greater travel and interpretation time. Some agencies require completed timesheets; an authorized staff person may need to sign and verify them. Others do not use timesheets and just expect an invoice to be sent. Policy can vary according to the company. Some require a mailed invoice for each assignment; others require an attachment to an e-mail; still others require mailing the timesheet, writing your invoice on it.

Interpreters, in their own best interest, should demand a contract and read it thoroughly. Especially important, to avoid disputes and deceitful practices, are the sections that pertain to cancellations. Be aware that some agencies use unscrupulous practices. Some will lie about or dispute the moment in time of cancellation to shortchange the interpreter, to benefit the agency, or to remain in the good graces of the hiring unit. Common practice of interpreta-tion agencies is to require that those requesting interpretation services cancel the contract 24 hours before the scheduled delivery of the service in order to avoid a charge. If the cancella-tion is within the 24-hour period, the agencies charge for the service; in this case the inter-preter gets paid the two-hour minimum interpretation charge for the "late cancellation" only. This occurs unless the interpreter found out about the cancellation when she or he arrived to perform the service, in which case the interpreter gets the other charge(s) covered as well, e.g., travel time, and parking expense if any, and for at least one company the mileage charge as well.

It is extremely useful for the interpreter to organize a log listing each assignment, by date, and all the other information pertinent to each assignment, so that comparisons can be made with the agencies' timesheets. The agencies customarily enter the information on invoices or timesheets and send checks, usually on a monthly basis, for the sum total owed or frac-tion. One agency requires one monthly invoice detailing charges and pertinent information (e.g., travel duration and its cost) per assignment. There will be times during the calendar year when mistakes are made, either by the interpreter or a staff person in the interpretation agency. The interpreter's log will be very helpful in clearing up differences. Of course, copies of invoices and timesheets should also be kept. The detailed log will also make it easier to calculate the number of miles driven and other information at other times, as needed, for example, to include the non-reimbursed mileage in your IRS deductions. If one interprets for several agencies, errors are bound to arise. The daily log will help determine what the mis-take is and how to rectify it.

Finally, it bears reiterating that, as with state agencies, it is highly unethical to try to solicit direct customers while representing an interpretation company and, for the same rea-son, to give out a personal (or business) telephone number(s) and e-mail, and other addresses.

Some interpretation companies offer their business cards, and others even include the interpreter's name on them. If somebody needs to contact you for a special reason, instruct them to do so through the interpretation company.

OVERCOMING LACK OF SPECIFICITY. Seldom does an interpretation agency provide specialized information for an assignment. One can save time, energy, and embarrassment by asking for more specific information to pre-determine the specialized terminology. For a doctor's appointment, agencies tend to overlook or omit the part of the body involved. With regard to a matter that involves a state or police investigation, more often than not the agency will not have obtained information about whether it is a trial, a plea, motions, a home investigation by a social worker, a psychological evaluation, or a physical examination. Specialized language for translation is needed for car accidents or for a work-related injury involving unusual equipment. Or will it be for a doctor's examination of an injured worker for the Worker's Compensation office or a medical insurance company, in which even the parts of the body will have to be translated? Once the type of case is determined, more specific information about it is necessary to prepare in advance for the specialized technical terminology. Inquire about the name of a pertinent contact person, corresponding telephone number, and/or e-mail address to obtain the needed information and for follow-up questions. Some experienced interpreters take a cynical view about the scarcity of important information from an agency, believing that the agency does not want the interpreter to know an abundance of information so as to gain personal advantage, i.e., may be seeking to establish an agency of their own, or may try to lure customers away.

PROFILES OF LANGUAGE AGENCIES. Translators and interpreters who seek a position or contract can Google the many hundreds of language agencies nationally and internationally to make the necessary inquiries. In preparation for this subsection, Taylor originally contacted two national and two local agencies to profile them in the text free of charge, without any endorsement, to be more useful for the readers. All tries were in vain. The few representatives who returned a call did not grant an interview. The repeated, quick claim was that they were attending to deadlines for Fortune 500 companies, leaving the inference that they were either busy competing for contracts or did not want to answer questions.

So instead of highlighting any, it might be useful to point to possible positions offered at two large agencies. A very large one in Atlanta, formed in 1998, employs, according to its website, six full-time project managers, uses 274 independent contractor linguists, and completed "1,936 projects in 2000." Professionals who meet their criteria can qualify for positions as language trainers, evaluators, materials developers, translators, interpreters, editors, proofreaders, programmers, network and communication people, and localization project managers. A second large agency, based in Salt Lake City and formed in 1993, claims on its website to provide assistance to companies worldwide in 120 languages via 1,400 certified translators and/or interpreters. Professionals in areas populated by residents from foreign countries — for example, South Florida — ought not to worry about the reticence of agencies to be forthcoming. South Floridians can avail themselves of many agencies engaged in business with banks, international organizations, newspapers, legal systems, and public sector entities that utilize foreign languages.

It is worthwhile restating that if a contract as a freelancer is desired, either with a local or national agency, it would be advisable to understand the terms of the agreement and heed the advice given in this book regarding pay, schedules, cancellations, benefits, deadlines, overtime, travel, parking, and responsibility for the oversight of the quality of the translation or interpretation.

SALARIED *VS.* FREELANCERS. With full-time salaried employment limited in both the public and private sectors, freelance or self-employed contractors face a different, perhaps harsher, perspective. According to the U.S. Department of Labor's Bureau of Labor Statistics, of the 31,000 persons who, for IRS purposes, earn money as interpreters or translators, some 15 percent of them, or 4,650, work part time or sporadically. What makes matters worse is that the unsalaried do not qualify for the fringe benefits of a retirement pension and health and life insurance. With luck and pluck, the freelancers make a living at the behest of private employment agencies and public-sector human resource offices who subcontract for hourly, daily, weekly, or longer assignments of interpretation or translation. The independent contractor might negotiate a flat fee for a short translation, say, one page, for the kingly sum of $25, notwithstanding the importance of the document. Then, again, the offer may be a "paid-by-the-word" arrangement. The fee per word can range from a low of $0.07 to $0.19 or more, perhaps, depending on the variables of language rarity, document length and complexity, availability of translators, urgency, region, and other negotiable arrangements. The downside, of course, is that the contracting employment agency, to gain a competitive edge over fierce rivals, may have to negotiate less than a top rate; half of the fee, at most, goes to the translator. The custom in the industry is that freelance interpreters can expect to be paid for a minimum of two hours of travel and/or service, even though the job is shorter or canceled without sufficient advance warning.

## ON AGENCY RESPONSIBILITY IN SUPERVISING INTERPRETERS

Interpretation agencies expect a profit and therefore control costs to make their quotas and budgets. But hiring poor interpreters and translators at the expense of quality control and assurance is penny wise and pound foolish. To ensure long-term success, rather than short-term profits, it is important for them to monitor the quality of the interpreters they subcontract.

Three suggestions:

1. Urge their clients to fill out and return confidential evaluation forms.

2. Provide on-site monitoring by trained office staff or by the most trusted interpreters. The procedure is to accompany new or untested interpreters with the best ones to various settings as observers who provide feedback to the agency and to the recently hired.

3. Urge the company to share its collection of glossaries and publications on interpreting — if it has them — and in that same fashion urge all the experienced interpreters to share their materials.

## H. Salary Surveys and ATA's Role

Below is an ATA Salary Survey comparison of 2005 with 2003 for translation dollars per word for median full-time independent contractors for some common foreign-language-into-English pairs. It might be useful to chart them so as to illuminate the preceding and following observations.

## Table 7: Comparing Translators' Cents/Word Earnings — Foreign Language to English

|            | 2005   | 2003   |
|------------|--------|--------|
| Chinese    | $0.19  | $0.19  |
| French     | $0.19  | $0.12  |
| German     | $0.12  | $0.12  |
| Italian    | $0.12  | $0.12  |
| Portuguese | $0.14  | $0.12  |
| Spanish    | $0.12  | $0.12  |

The two-year comparison reveals a low-level stagnancy in every category but one, Portuguese to English, where a 14 percent decline occurred.

From an unsolicited e-mail on 13 September 2007, by a member of ATA who prefers anonymity, the authors learned of this salary inadequacy. The sender, with a certain amount of resentment, revealed that in the past fifteen years of professional translation he has increased rates 20 percent; in comparison, the Consumer Price Index, in that period, went up 40 percent. Because of his undocumented claim that agencies in collusion with the ATA control per-word rates, he was/is forced to charge rates below those of the current ATA Survey, $0.12/word for Spanish and Portuguese. He vented his frustration at the ATA for not "working toward" making "ATA certification mean something in the market in the way a CPA designation does." In order to "save about $5000.00 a year," and to "not work [himself] to death to make ends meet," he plans to drop ATA membership "next year," not attend "continuing education and overpriced conferences," and let his certification "lapse."

Is he justified, shortsighted, or unduly harsh? Although one can sympathize with this professional translator's plight, it is hard to accept the allegation that ATA colludes with agencies to hold down rates. More to the point is that market forces, such as supply and demand for rare and common languages, personal and professional factors, globalization and virtualization of the industry, and competition among agencies, rather than conspiracies, have more to do with the rates that providers charge and users are willing to pay. Yet this translator's cry in the wilderness for more money is understandable. Who wouldn't want more in the face of inflation and stagnant terms? One can turn his claim into a question, rather than an accusation.

With ATA's moral and professional suasion and outreach, it takes action to help members find jobs and increase their earning power and morale. First, ATA instituted a Job Bank program, in 2008, via its *Chronicle* and online database. Second, ATA provides on its website a Translator Earnings Calculator to determine wages: www.atanet.org/business_practices/earnings_calculator.php. Third, at its regional and national conferences, ATA dedicates a room for interviews and tables for résumés. Fourth, these conferences permit members to network, learn new ideas, and to take the certification exam. These are among the many activities that indicate ATA's concern for its members' well-being.

SUMMARY: MEDIAN SALARIES AND WAGES. A pertinent, additional viewpoint is found in the previously mentioned chapter "Interpreters and Translators" of the *Occupational Outlook Handbook*. In the section "Earnings" (269), the authoritative *Handbook* carefully nuances the bottom line with the caveat, "Earnings depend on language, subject matter, skill, experience, education, certification, and type of employer, and salaries of interpreters can vary widely." Taking all variables into consideration, the *Handbook* provides the following extrapolated data: "Salaried interpreters and translators had median hourly earnings of $16.24 in May 2004. Add ten percent to arrive at Year 2010. The middle 50 percent earned between $12.40 and $21.09 per hour. The lowest 10 percent earned less than $9.67, and the highest 10 percent earned more than $27.45." The *Handbook* adds that the more fortunate and skilled can earn, for high-level, full-time conference interpreting, salaries at the $100,000 mark.

# Part II

## *Interpretation and Translation in Cultural, Legal, and Linguistic Contexts*

# CHAPTER 9

# Comparing Interpretation and Translation

## A. *Formal Definitions*

DICTIONARY DEFINITIONS. For those comfortable with the question, "What does Webster's say?" dictionary definitions can be a point of departure. From there, the definitions will proceed to more profound meanings of interpretation/interpreting and translation based upon personal experiences and on those of writers on the subject and practitioners in the profession.[1]

But let us start off with Webster's.

**Interpret: a. Transitive verb:** "To explain or tell the meaning of: to present in understandable terms"; "To conceive in the light of individual belief, judgment, or circumstance." **b. Intransitive verb:** "To act as an interpreter between speakers of different languages."

**Interpreter: Noun:** "One that interprets, as one who translates orally for parties conversing in different languages."

**Interpretation: Noun:** "The act or the result of interpreting."

**Interpreting:** This verbal noun does not appear nor is it defined in the dictionary, although it will be differentiated from interpretation in the following discussion, The act [...] of interpreting.

Webster's does not define directly "interpreting." This verbal noun or gerund contrasts, in the mind of professional interpreters, with "interpretation," a concept that will be reviewed under "Operational Definitions."

Turning to the corresponding "to translate," the dictionary offers, among its various meanings of this Latin-derived, Middle English verb, the following pertaining to language:

**Translate: Transitive:** a. "to turn into one's own or another language"; b. "to transfer or turn from one set of symbols to another."

**Translate: Intransitive:** a. "to practice translation or make a translation."

**Translation: Noun.** "Translation" dates from the 14th century. a. "an act, process, or instance of translating"; b. "a rendering from one language into another; also, the product of such a rendering."

**Translating:** As with "interpreting," this verbal noun does not appear in the list of dictionary definitions. Despite that, it means "The act [...] of translating."

While useful in a preliminary way, the dictionary has almost nothing to say about the doer or actor, i.e., the translator, nor the difficulties of the processes involved. The reader will discover a variety of activities in this book regarding the actions and actors concerned with the verbs and nouns.

## B. Operational Definitions

Laurie Swabey and Pam Sherwood-Gabrielson offer two preliminary definitions of "interpreter" which merit further explanation in the course of the book. They list and describe critical components of the interpreter's qualifications and actions: "An individual with appropriate education and experience that demonstrates the linguistic and cultural competence to interpret accurately; understands and follows ethical principles for interpreters." The professors add: "The interpreter manages the flow of communication. The interpreter will ask for clarification and pauses as needed in order to fully understand, process, and convey the message."[2]

It is important to emphasize that interpreting goes on during the process of living. Persons constantly and unremittingly assess their senses and ascribe meaning to them, an "interpretation" which permits anticipating how to handle experience. This "interpretation act" includes the apparent meaning the event appears to represent as well as a possible dissimulated intent.

The interpretation we create in all experiences represents a coming together not only of words, but also of other linguistic factors as well as cultural and personal ones. The crosscurrents affect the interpretative interaction between speaker and listener, and the interpretation of the event within each one of them.

It is worthwhile revisiting here some definitions that arose in Part I. In general terms, to interpret is to translate. Why, then, the preference for calling the oral act and process of translating "interpreting"? The ample definition of "translation" is that it is the equivalent transmittal of something either written or expressed verbally, which goes in one direction only, from source language to target language (SL to TL). In both cases — interpretation and translation — the person who transfers ideas from SL to TL represents a "bridge" or "vehicle" between those uttering in SL and the recipients needing to understand in the TL. On the other hand, in the courts "interpreting" denotes the ***oral*** transmission of another language. Danica Seleskovitch concurs in that "translation," even though it includes in its meaning the oral as well as the written action, is usually reserved for the ***written*** version:

> Yet, although the terms "translator" and "interpreter" are often used interchangeably, they do represent two rather different professions [....] Translation converts a written text into another written text, while interpretation converts an oral message into another oral message.[3]

Academics writing about and practicing the profession, with regard to the act of interpretation, point out an important distinction not mentioned by the dictionary. They prefer the verbal noun "interpreting" to the more general noun "interpretation" when it is a question of defining the "act" in progress or the "mode" in use in the courtroom. In keeping with this distinction, the coauthors refer to the act in progress as "interpreting" rather than "interpretation."

## C. Philosophical Definitions

"Logical thinking" can lead one astray when the premises are wrong. Some users of interpretation services object even to the use of the word "interpretation" itself. It implies to them that the presentation in the TL is not objective, it "interprets" the SL content, which to them then means that it "distorts." They therefore prefer that the word "translation" be the only one used. The critics are usually not familiar with the field of professional interpretation and therefore "interpret" the issue with limited information at hand. For that matter, the act of translating — orally and in writing — also forces the translator to "interpret," because languages cannot be transmitted equivalently, directly or verbatim, meaning literally, from one to the other.

Languages employ words that are used figuratively and literally. By introducing the word "interpretation," one is able to differentiate between the two modes and therefore demark their distinguishing characteristics and differences. Yes, this brings up the possible amphibology, i.e., that if in both acts we interpret, why restrict the use of "interpretation" to one of them? In the end, one has to admit it is basically a practical determination, a pragmatic way to distinguish. We simply need to accept that. Some try to justify this convention and possible solipsism by arguing that there is "more interpretation" when you interpret, which is not a logical argument because it is a matter of fact and not of quantity.

## D. Guide to Classified Definitions

DISTINCTIONS SET OUT IN PARALLEL COLUMNS. The distinct differences between the two acts and the participants are laid out in succinct language and style in the following 27 classifications prepared by Sibirsky. The chart compares and contrasts the most distinguishing and differentiating aspects between interpretation/interpreter and translation/translator.

1. Attitudes toward speech and writing.
2. Clarifications and sense.
3. Clarifications and source availability.
4. Contrasts between spoken and written alphabets.
5. Contrasts between spoken and written forms.
6. Different evolutionary stages.
7. Editing, polishing, correcting.
8. Explanation of roles and behaviors.
9. Forms of expression in spoken and written language.
10. Grooming and etiquette.
11. Interpersonal interactions and emotions.
12. Interpersonal interactions and deciphering meaning at speed.
13. Language dominance, fatigue, and stress.
14. Mistakes and corrections.
15. Nonverbal language.
16. Omissions.
17. On-the-spot consultation.
18. Personality and language orientation.
19. Personality required.
20. Public speaking skills.
21. Register, prosody, and intent.
22. Register, style, and intention.
23. Register and style.
24. "Speak in parts."
25. Time and correctness.
26. Time factor.
27. Time factor, pace, and *personae.*

CHARACTERISTICS IN PARALLEL COLUMNS. There are distinct differences between the two acts, which should be known to the interpreters because they may wish to expand their services to the translation field, and also because at times they are asked to translate a document during the interpretation service. The themes below, in alphabetical order, compare and contrast the most distinguishing and differentiating characteristics between interpretation/interpreter and translation/translator.

---

*Interpretation—Interpreter*                          *Translation—Translator*

### 1. Attitudes toward Writing and Speech

Spoken language, says David Crystal, was considered until the twentieth century as lacking in rules and was in disrepute. It is now understood that speech is thousands of years older than written language, develops spontaneously in children and is the mode used by most humans on earth (many languages even lack a written system).[4]

Traditionally, writing was the preeminent skill and the marker of linguistic standards. This only changed in the twentieth century. It is now understood that speaking and writing are two co-equal and very different systems of communication.

According to M. A. Halliday, writing emerges "so that new registers could be created," different from those of the spoken language, resulting in a "new range of functional variation, which lead to the emergence of configurations of semantic and lexico-grammatical patterns that then come to be recognized as characteristics of writing."[5] Lexically more dense than spoken language, writing favors an organized clause structure that features hypotaxis and parataxis, organizational elements found in the construction of prose in general and technical material.

### 2. Clarifications and Sense

When the witness slurs or speaks in too low a voice or uses an utterance totally unfamiliar to the interpreter, she or he has to so indicate, interrupting the flow of the interpretation event.

When the text does not render clearly or simply does not make sense, the translator can write "illegible" or "unintelligible" and go on, or sometimes find alternative solutions.

### 3. Clarifications and Source Availability

The interpreter has all the protagonists at hand to get immediate clarification.

If a document in question was written ages ago, no living person could consult on it. There are times when an equivalent translation in reading level may not be desired because of the characteristics (e.g., under education) of the TL audience or other reasons, but if this is not communicated to the

*Interpretation — Interpreter*

*Translation — Translator*

translator beforehand because there is no contact person a serious problem may develop. The clients who contracted the translation company may not understand the responsibility that the translator has of providing an equivalent translation. If a different reading level is desired, the condition needs to be placed when the assignment is given; otherwise, a serious ethical and professional conflict may arise.

## 4. Contrasts between Spoken and Written Alphabets

The speaker of English, based upon the International Phonetic Alphabet (IPA), must master 17 vowel sounds and 24 consonant sounds. "It is this discrepancy, of course, which underlies the complexity of English spelling" (Crystal 57). "Children learning the sounds of speech have quite a mountain to climb. In English, for example, they have over forty vowels and consonants to learn [...] some 300 ways in which these combine to produce syllables [...] and several dozen patterns of stress and tones of voice" [...] (Crystal 79).

The translator only has to deal with the permutations and combinations of 26 letters of the English alphabet.

## 5. Contrasts between Spoken and Written Forms

"Speech uses *phonic substance*, typically in the form of air-pressure movements. [...] Speech is time-bound, dynamic, transient — part of an interaction in which, typically, both participants are present, and the speaker has a specific addressee (or group of addressees) in mind [...,] the spontaneity and rapidity of speech minimizes the chance of complex preplanning, and promotes features that assist speakers to 'think standing up'— looser construction, repetition, rephrasing, filler phrases (such as *you know, you see*), and the use of intonation and pause to divide utterances into manageable chunks" (Crystal 149–50).

"Writing uses *graphic substance*, typically in the form of marks on a surface.

[...] Writing is space-bound, static, permanent — the result of a situation in which, typically, the producer is distant from the recipient, and, often, may not even know who the recipient is. [...] The permanence of writing allows repeated reading and close analysis. It promotes the development of careful organization and more compact, intricately structured expression" (Crystal 149). "Written language displays several unique features, such as punctuation, capitalization, spatial organization, colour, and other graphic effects [....] [The] majority of graphic features present a system of contrasts that has no spoken-language equivalent. As a result, there are many genres of written language whose structures cannot in any way be con-

*Interpretation — Interpreter*

*Translation — Translator*

veyed by reading aloud, such as timetables, graphs, and complex formulae" (Crystal 150).

## 6. Different Evolutionary Stages

"The parts of the body used in the production of speech are called the vocal organs, and there are more of them than we might expect [...] the *lungs*, the *throat*, the *mouth* and the *nose* [...] the *lips*, the *tongue*, the *teeth*, the roof of the mouth (or *palate*), and the small fleshy appendage hanging down at the very back of the palate (the *uvula*) [...] *pharynx* [...] *larynx* [...] *vocal folds* [...] the *glottis* (Halliday 18–20).

"Written language, only some 10,000 years old [...] is too recent a development in human history. As a consequence, research into the way we write devotes little time to the structure and function of the eyes and hands, focusing instead on the way the brain works when it processes written language" (Halliday 121).

## 7. Editing, Polishing, Correcting

The interpreter must be faithful to the original expression and cannot polish, correct, edit, or make it more understandable or aesthetic, and yet must maintain, adds Maurice Gravier, "the sparkle which makes ideas come alive."[6]

The translator can usually review carefully, thus "improve on the original," by polishing, correcting, editing, and making it more understandable or aesthetic.

## 8. Explanation of Role and Behaviors

The interpreter often needs to make other protagonists aware of their actual role and of how the interpretation process needs to function.

The translator may need to defend the translation or parts of it (even differences in punctuation between languages), but not as an immediate and quickly moving process.

## 9. Forms of Expression in Spoken and Written Language

We speak by using our vocal apparatus, to which we can add body language. It is "[...] difficult to identify sentences in speech, [...] where the units of rhythm and intonation often do not coincide with the places where full stops would occur in writing. In informal speech, in particular, constructions can lack the careful organization we associate with the written language. [...] It is not that conversation lacks grammar: it is just that grammar is of a rather different kind, with sentences being particularly difficult to demarcate" (Crystal 248).

In the written form, the translator encounters various forms of graphic expression in addition to words. Other specialists may need to be involved for complex graphic representations.

"People [...] often disagree about the best way to punctuate a text. In some manuals of style, it is recommended that we should not end a sentence before a coordinating conjunction (*and, or, but*). But there are often cases where an author might feel it necessary — for reasons of emphasis, perhaps — to do the opposite" (Crystal 248).

*Interpretation — Interpreter*  *Translation —Translator*

## 10. Grooming and Etiquette

Proper grooming, etiquette, and professional demeanor are important requirements for the interpreter.

The translator, working in seclusion, normally does not have any grooming and etiquette "constraints." It is important, however, to be presentable in public and maintain good rapport with the hiring client and, when available, with a counterpart for direct consultation on the document in question.

## 11. Interpersonal Interactions and Emotions

The interpreter faces the person requiring this service. This adds an interpersonal interaction that can be highly gratifying or the opposite, and stressful emotionally, especially when the person being interpreted breaks into sobs, expressions of strong pain, or irrational behavior, and displays characteristics of major depression.

In general, the translator works with the text and avoids contacts with outside persons. Kenneth S. Goodman and Frederick V. Gollasch note the obvious, that the translator "is most often unseen and unknown."[7] However, the translator may possibly interact with the author, editor, publisher, and proofreader. These contacts may engender questioning and criticism, but not usually strong emotions.

## 12. Interpersonal Interactions and Deciphering Meaning at Speed

The interpreter works, often simultaneously, with many and varying protagonists during the interpretation act (e.g., judges, prosecutors, public defenders, attorneys, court reporters, medical doctors, nurses, clerks, social security disability administrative judges or hearing officers and corresponding monitors, and insurance company investigators doing home interviews. Danica Seleskovitch observes that the interpreter has to constantly decipher meaning to render it in the TL, and at a speed estimated to be, for example in conference interpreting, thirty times greater than that of the translator (*Interpreting* 2).

The translator's target audience may be a single person or hundreds of thousands, depending on the document being translated, but the translator can work on deciphering meaning alone with the text in the immediate working environment without having to worry about extracting meaning at excessive speed.

## 13. Language Dominance, Fatigue, and Stress

Very few individuals are equally proficient in two languages. According to Stanislav Dornic, studies have shown that in cases of high fatigue and stress, the more powerful language becomes more dominant.[8]

Seldom does the translator have to face the stress and fatigue that interpreters do; and the translator usually has the opportunity to interrupt the translating and reduce the levels of fatigue and stress. Therefore, the impact of

*Interpretation — Interpreter*

*Translation — Translator*

language dominance on fatigue and stress usually does not occur.

## 14. Mistakes and Corrections

At times, the interpreter gets corrected on the spot, for varying reasons, and at times wrongly. As a result, the interpreter can experience high stress.

If a client thinks that a mistake has been made, the translator has much more time to make a correction or prepare a rebuttal, and there usually is a much lower stress level as a result.

## 15. Nonverbal Language

M. A. Halliday et al., in *The Linguistic Sciences and Language Teaching*, add that in addition to interpreting connotative and denotative language, a full message may require kinesics, or nonverbal components.[9] Nonverbal equivalencies are discussed in Chapter 12, section D.

The translator is not usually concerned with nonverbal components, unless translating a movie or theater script. Goodman and Gollasch stress that there is an "absence of supportive situational context" (257), which can make it more difficult at times to understand the intent and stresses of the communication.

## 16. Omissions

The courtroom interpreter must interpret everything, even redundancies. The U.N. and business interpreters have greater flexibility in editing for clarity, style, and emphasis.

The general and literary translator have general flexibility and can often omit useless redundancies.

## 17. On-the-Spot Consultation

The interpreter can consult directly with dictionaries, colleagues, witnesses, employers, and clients.

The translator can consult source books directly and colleagues by phone, fax, or the computer for information, but does not usually have a contact person for on-the-spot consultation. The translator should have in mind a specialist to consult if needed.

## 18. Personality and Language Orientation

The interpreter's personality leans more toward the use of oral language and its interplay with nonverbal expression.

The literary and general translator often has to penetrate and absorb the unheard sounds of the text and delve into complex meanings or technical terms. A line from John Keats's "Ode on a Grecian Urn," comes to mind: "Heard melodies are sweet, but unheard ones are sweeter."

*Interpretation — Interpreter*          *Translation —Translator*

## 19. Personality Required

Interpreters require a personality that can accept change, unexpected circumstances, and resistance. Freelance interpreters need to be on call, travel to the job, and interpret in settings which have varying expectations. It is very important that they be assertive to ensure independence and objectivity.

Full-time translators, by their nature, tend to be less aggressive than interpreters. Their work is physically more sedentary. They need to do research and work assiduously at a computer for long hours to meet deadlines, and often, to translate difficult technical work.

## 20. Public-Speaking Skills

An interpreter needs to have acceptable public-speaking skills to accommodate the multiple and diverse clients and target audiences.

Only if the work product is significant — e.g., a new translation of the Qumran — will the translator give lectures at universities and at other public forums. Generally, this professional does not require public-speaking tasks.

## 21. Register and Intent

"When you say a simple word like 'really,' you can inflect, modulate, resonate in countless ways, which causes the word to convey almost any meaning you wish, from question to affirmation, from sorrow to derision. Writing is incapable of doing this," declares Morry Sofer.[10] This is an example of prosody.

Sofer explains, praising the spoken word over the written word: "[...] the written word is, after all, a record of the spoken word. It is a set of combined symbols, namely, letters and characters, or, in some languages, ideograms, put together to produce syllables and words and phrases, which invariably fail to convey most of the nuances of the spoken word" (Sofer 52).

## 22. Register, Effort, and Style

The interpreter needs to follow the rhythm of the occasion, speak rapidly or haltingly like those for whom he or she is interpreting. In other words, the interpreter needs to maintain the SL's register and style, at times for several hours.

The translator cannot account for mode of presentation, paralinguistic factors, or emotion (the register) outside the verbal content.

## 23. Register and Style

The interpreter has to be faithful to the SL utterance, rendering it in the TL with the register and tone of the SL. Depending on the setting, and based on an understanding with the clients, the interpreter can make the

The translator, when aware of the target audience for the document being translated, can most often use a style geared toward this TL audience. The translator is often more interested in "for whom" the translation is

*Interpretation — Interpreter*

version in the TL more in consonance with the style of the TL protagonist. However, the interpreter must make certain that the person whose message being interpreted into the TL knows fully well what the actual register and style of the SL are. This is vital when the witness is highly undereducated and has poor cognitive skills development.

*Translation — Translator*

intended. "This means, add Eugene A. Nida and Charles R. Taber, that several different levels of translation, in terms of vocabulary and grammatical structures, are required, if all people are to have essentially equal opportunities to understand the message."[11]

## 24. "Speak in Parts"

The interpreter often has to get the witness or claimant to "speak in parts" instead of several sentences at a time or "run on" forever.

The translator usually works in a setting of personal preference and does not need to interact with anyone else while performing the act of translating.

## 25. Time and Correctness

There is no time to prepare once the interpretation process begins; the TL response must be created at high speed, with no chance to review for correctness. "The content of the message must be understood at the very moment it is uttered; if not, it will vanish without trace — it will be as if it had never been uttered" (Seleskovitch, *Interpreting* 14).

The original material can be reviewed many times to find an appropriate rendering. It is unchanging, fixed, on a page. In Halliday's words, "Good or bad, this text is static, immutable in its form and fixed in time" (*Spoken* [...] *Language* 2).

## 26. Time Factor

The interpreter has to find an immediate equivalent in the TL that is in consonance with the characteristics of the TL language, and immediately go on to the next utterance (Halliday, *Spoken* [...] *Language* 131).

The translator has much more time to find equivalents, etc. (how much time depends on the requirements of the particular translation job). The translator can overcome deadlines.

## 27. Time Factor, Personae, and Pace

The interpreter "impersonates" the speaker and the listener, as well as then the listener converted to speaker and the speaker converted to listener. In addition, the interpreter has to concentrate totally to understand what is being said, in its context, extract its meaning, and reproduce it in another language, all of it at high speed. This can produce great fatigue and thirst; in addition, the fatigue

The act of translation is demanding and tiring. For example, the translator has to become involved with the language and feelings of the multiple [*personae*] in a novel, or a poem. Nevertheless, it is not immediate, and the translators can usually pace themselves.

*Interpretation — Interpreter*          *Translation — Translator*

and the thirst can lead to distraction, loss of
content and so on (Dornic 267).

---

# E. Desirable Characteristics in Interpreters

The following material augments the detailed section on "Knowledge, Skills, and Abilities" regarding professionals in Chapter 8, "Economics, Jobs, Salaries." During that presentation, the reader could check off the array of classified traits of professional interpreters and translators and judge whether the requirements merited the salary being earned. Here the characteristics are presented in a different, easier-to-read format. But the reader can continue checking them off to measure his personal KSAs against the ideal.

## Perceptions of Interpreters

**Actor in real-life situations:** Appreciates and enjoys the real-life situations developing in interpretation events as if on a stage.
**Multiple masks:** Enjoys participating in events involving several persons.
**Bridge:** A communication channel for the words of other players.
**Image projection:** Sensitive to the image projected when interpreting.

## Personal Attributes

**Code of Ethics:** Adheres to a Code of Ethics — for example, that of the National Association of Judiciary Interpreters and Translators (NAJIT) — and upholds a personal honor code.
**Time factors:** Aware how rapid speech obscures time boundaries and causes fatigue.
**Cognitive skills:** Enjoys and uses advanced memorization, concentration, reasoning, and analytical skills.
**Agility:** Knows that swiftness of mind and speech are keys to adjusting to constant changes.
**Neutrality and self-control:** Believes that self-control while in possession of power allows for playing a neutral role.
**Communication skills:** Displays strong communication skills that permit confronting and combating duplicitous and aggressive behaviors. They permit, also, rendering a clear message.
**Sociability:** Requires a person who is sociable, outgoing, and not shy.
**Appearance and etiquette:** Is aware that appropriate professional grooming and etiquette are indispensable.

## Perception of Others

**Biases and prejudices:** Sensitive to attitudes of others. Has self-awareness about biases and attitudes and exercises self-criticism to adjust to them.

## Knowledge/Cultural Base

**Knowledge base:** Includes mastery of languages and the varieties in languages.
**Cultural base:** Understands the following: that culture expresses itself through verbal and non-

verbal language; that culture is also an emotional reinforcement; and that interplay exists between language and culture.

**Multiple interests:** Has the studiousness, curiosity, and imagination that allow the interpreter to switch from one area of interest to another with ease.

**Organizing information:** Knows how to organize information at hand and in memory, rather than the impossible task of having a command of all types of knowledge. The interpreter, given enough forewarning, can organize information on a variety of subjects.

**Settings:** Is prepared to become familiar with the various settings.

**Bilingualism:** Understands the interplay of bilingualism.

## F. Traits of Successful Translators

Morry Sofer, in his *Handbook*, describes in succinct fashion traits and competencies to be expected of professional translators (33–37). With interpreters, translators share a need for high academic and intellectual skills. The important exceptions are that the translator does not require skills in interpersonal relationships and the ability to think quickly on his feet. But the translator, and to a lesser extent the interpreter, requires excellent research and writing skills. A ten-point summary will be helpful:

1. A mastery of two languages.
2. A thorough knowledge of at least two cultures.
3. An awareness of the constant changes in both languages.
4. A talent for writing concisely, clearly, and to the point in the target language, whether it is a native language or not.
5. A flexible writing style that allows for staying close to the source language in tone and content and to improve on content if called for.
6. Sufficient training and curiosity to cover many fields of knowledge.
7. Ability to translate fairly rapidly if translating to earn a living.
8. Talent and patience to do research, develop a good personal library, and constantly expand lists of reference sources.
9. Mastery of ever-increasing technological tools, such as computers, scanners, and printers.
10. Match language expertise with the geographical demand for the language(s).

The previously presented parallel columns and paragraphs that detail skills, abilities, and temperaments of interpreters and translators give the impression that the two professional tracks do not cross over. Parallel lines do not converge in Euclidean geometry, but in real life one finds interpreters translating all the time, mostly on the spot for a specific purpose, less often for a living. In reverse, one finds fewer dedicated professional translators prepared to interpret as a living. Despite cases of overlapping talents and reinforcing training, jealousies and rivalries crop up. They shall be pointed out in section H below.

## G. Machine Translators vs. Human Translators

Human translators expend great efforts to produce quality material, at reasonable cost, in the shortest amount of time to satisfy a variety of users. But since the first Russian-English IBM translation project of 7 January 1954, reports Joel Garreau, technology has raced human capabilities and advanced to the point where computer-based devices using artificial intelligence and the World Wide Web have — at nanosecond speed, with no boredom or fatigue, low cost, and little regard for the cultural nuances of the target language — "statistically [expressed] the probability that words in one language line up together in a fashion comparable to another set of words in another language."[12] Google's "Translate" is capable of handling forty language pairs, which makes it the leader in the field. Alon Lavie, the president of the Association for Machine Translation in the Americas (AMTA), has measured Google "Translate's" success rate. With the aid of AMTA's "Meteor," using a scale of 1 to 100, "Translate" scored 50 in a rendering from Arabic to English, thus "far better than gist." The end game of the assiduous proponents of the machine translator, such as the American Association of Artificial Intelligence (AAAI), is not retiring or modest in competing with human translators. Its mission comes down "to design computers and software that smash language barriers and create a borderless global marketplace."

Garreau hits the mark in his article that machine translators will prevail where one is "willing to settle for blazingly fast, cheap, good-enough translations. Especially those aimed at languages spoken by the rich, multitudinous, or dangerous." With regard to those latter three — the moneyed, the many, or the dangerous — Garreau points out that the Department of Defense's DARPA (Defense Advanced Research Projects Agency) has already field-tested portable, voice-actuated and implemented Arabic ↔ English interpreting machines to replace diminishing and uncertain human interpreters. In certain tasks, human interpreters and translators will lose jobs and give way to machines. The best that can be hoped for is that humans and machines can operate side by side, each in its own sphere of influence and capability, with the humans polishing and perfecting the imperfect results of the machine translators.

The thinking behind AMTA's and AAAI's scientists and technicians may be reduced to a linguistic/geometric triangle. The discussion (Chapter 10, section B, "Triangular and Multidimensional Interpretation") describes and discards the triangular theory with regard to interpreting as inadequate and oversimplified. On the other hand, the triangle metaphor has more validity with translation, especially performed by machines, because the process is devoid of human intervention and not carried out in a multidimensional environment, but rather

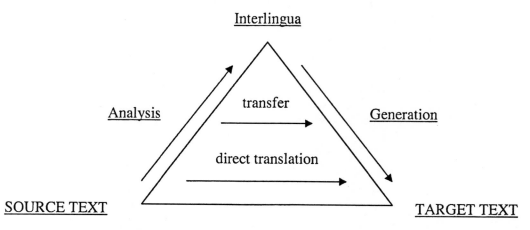

Fig. 1. **Harold Somers's Configuration of Interlingua Machine Translation. "The pyramid diagram, probably first used by [Bernard] Vaubois (1968): The deeper the analysis the less transfer is needed, the ideal case being the interlingua approach where there is no transfer at all."**

confines itself to transposing electronically analogous lexical/syntactic units of the source language into the target language. Harold Somers diagrams machine translation via the "interlingua" process in the triangle (Fig. 1). To cap his argument, Somers adds, "Source text is transformed into the target text indirectly via an intermediate representation." In this case, the intermediary is a machine.[13]

As a counterweight to the preceding mechanistic approach to translation, consider briefly Jean Delisle's intellectual/cognitive approach. The Canadian scholar believes in the interlingual transfer of communication and stresses the nonverbal stage of conceptualization. In "Interpretive Approach," Delisle views translation as a heuristic process of intelligent discourse analysis involving three complex stages: Comprehension, Reformulation, and Verification.[14] Humans, obviously, not machines, are best able to employ these complex stages.

## H. Translators and Interpreters in/of Literary Texts

The reader may better capture the rivalries between the jobs of interpreters and translators through the boasts of arrogant interpreter-supreme Bruno Salvador, the protagonist of John le Carré's novel *The Mission Song*, as he touts his intellectual and physical prowess in rendering five languages orally — two European (English and French) and three African (Swahili, Shi, and Kinyarwanda) — at the expense of bookworm translators:

> Never mistake, please, your mere translator for your top interpreter. An interpreter is a translator, true, but not the other way round. A translator can be anyone with half a language skill and a dictionary and a desk to sit at while he burns the midnight oil: pensioned-off Polish cavalry officers, underpaid overseas students, minicab drivers, part-time waiters and supply teachers, and anyone else who is prepared to sell his soul for seventy quid a thousand. He has nothing in common with the simultaneous interpreter sweating it out through six hours of complex negotiations. Your top interpreter has to think as fast as a numbers boy in a coloured jacket buying financial futures. Better sometimes if he doesn't think at all, but orders the spinning cogs on both sides of his head to mesh together, then sits back and waits to see what pours out of his mouth.[15]

Taylor has ferreted out an analog of Salvador Bruno in another novel. The interpreter Osiris appears in Robert Ludlum's *The Ambler Warning*. Like Bruno, Osiris dominated African languages. In Osiris's case, they were Igbo, Hausa, and Yoruba. With regard to European dialects, Osiris "knew whether a German came from Dresden or Leipzig, Hessen or Thüringen; he could tell the vowels of one Hanseatic province from another." As for the Middle East, he "could differentiate thirty strains of 'street' Arabic."[16] Osiris, as egocentric as Bruno about his craft, was not above poking fun, like Salvador, at scholarly and bureaucratic interpreters: "He could listen to recordings that would cause experts at the State Department's Africa Desk to throw up their hands or ask for a three-month study period, and provide an instantaneous rendition of the rapid-fire palaver."

However much one enjoys the divine hubris of the interpreters Bruno Salvador (whose name translates as the "brown savior") and Osiris (after the Egyptian god of the underworld), one cannot fail to see that translators, too, can be inspired by a heavenly muse as they labor over the perfect word and phrase. Perhaps one can balance off the two fictional interpreters' self-serving opinions with Sofer's earlier kudos about clever translators.

**LITERARY TRANSLATORS.** Translators of literature fall into a separate and smaller category than the most respectable majority of them who labor on a daily basis rendering unintelligible reports, speeches, contracts, engineering plans, birth certificates, menus, and advertising on cereal boxes into intelligible, useful foreign languages in as short a time as possible for employers who count pennies per word or dollars per hour. The latter form the special cadres of the American Translators Association, while the American Literary Translators Association, or ALTA, housed at the University of Texas, Austin, would pride itself on serving, as the name suggests, professionals who work for a commission or stipend on classical and modern texts that require a lot of time and diligence.

**TRANSLATORS: RE-CREATORS NOT TRAITORS.** Haunting professional translators, Taylor believes, in their attempts to find equivalency in words linked to the culture and the psyche of the author is the disparaging epithet in Italian, *traduttore, traditore* ("translator as traitor or betrayer"), or even other debasing metaphors, such as "servility, bastardization, or usurpation."[17] Many Italians, not all, might be mollified by the fact that one of their greatest works, Dante's *Divina Commedia* (1308–1321), defied the previous metaphors after being translated by the distinguished American poet Henry Wadsworth Longfellow into graceful rhythms and unexpected concepts. Listen to the first tercet, "Nel mezzo del cammin [...]," and compare it with Longfellow's rendition:

> Nel mezzo del cammin di nostra vita
> mi ritrovai per una selva oscura,
> ché la diritta via era smarrita.
>
> Midway upon the journey of our life
> I found myself within a forest dark
> For the straight forward path had been lost.[18]

Longfellow, first of all, confronting 14,000 verses of rhyming (aba, cbc) hendecasyllables (11 syllables), rejected as unattainable rhyming the first and third lines ("vita/smarrita") of 4,666 tercets. He sought, instead, poetic vision, linguistic precision, and smooth cadences. In Longfellow's quest, he avoided transforming the grammatically correct Italian "selva oscura" (noun + adjective) into the grammatically obvious "dark forest" (adjective + noun). Instead, he avoided a prosaic, expected rendering and created the poetic "forest dark." For Dante's unobstructed *"diritta via,"* Longfellow imagines a "straight *forward* path" for the sake of rhythm and impetus. "Cammin," a simple road, redeems itself as the allegorical "journey." The linguistic and poetic challenge that Dante's Italian imposed forced the American poet to create adequate language to find a way around the hurdle of rhyming the first and third verse of every tercet composed of hendecasyllables.

**TWO TRANSLATION GAFFES.** Given the variety of ways in which a translator can render a given text (Dante's is one example) and still remain faithful to the grammar and syntax, at what point does a translation become unfaithful? Everybody would agree that a definition that "traduces" and does not "translate" the original text would not qualify as faithful. Note in the following two examples provided by Taylor that two different translators — whatever their reasons — traduced and did not translate:

A humorous mistake appeared in the excellent movie titled *My Name Is David*. In it, the English-to-Spanish translator, in reference to David, the wandering, homeless, dirty-looking boy, rendering in the caption the spoken English for "urchin" as *erizo* (literally a sea urchin and a seafood delicacy in Chile) instead of *pilluelo* or *granuja*. The translator did not catch that single mistranslated word out of thousands of well-translated ones in a compelling script. What was at stake in this humorous glitch that few caught? No money, life, treaty, or oil equipment was at risk. This was the innocuous glitch that did not change the world nor attract much attention.

In the process of editing a manuscript on the Chilean Nobel Laureate Gabriela Mistral (1889–1957), Taylor came across a translation in one of her poems as "Russian mountain."[19] Since neither Mistral nor the poem had any connection to Russia, further research revealed that the original "*montaña rusa*" was not a "Russian mountain," but Spanish for "roller coaster," indeed a metaphor for a volatile personal situation that beset the poet. This text has stressed that it is better not to assume when faced with a cognate. Any error regarding a false cognate is deplorable. Is the error more excusable in an interpreter who must produce foreign language text rapidly, and less so in a translator who enjoys the benefits of time and dictionaries, but lacks curiosity and aesthetic sensitivity?

CERVANTES AND HIS TRANSLATORS. ALTA's advocates might consider the aforesaid disparaging epithet in Italian as damning with praise. What might ALTA's scholars say regarding the iterations of Miguel de Cervantes's *Don Quixote* (Part I, 1610; Part II, 1615)? A dozen English and American writers, starting with Cervantes's contemporary, the Englishman Thomas Shelton, have attempted this novel of chivalry with varying results (Part I translated 1612, and Part II, 1620). Although many translations to English exist, the three I would point out are those of Samuel Putnam (1949), Burton Raffel (1999), and Edith Grossman (2005), each with great strengths and limited shortcomings, depending on who is judging. Would ALTA's directors share the cautious remarks, similar to those of the Italians, of an anonymous critic that "for in truth there can be no thoroughly satisfactory translation of 'Don Quixote' into English or any other language?" He continues that it is not the words, "but rather the terseness to which the book owes its flavour [which] is peculiar to Spanish, and can at best be only distantly imitated in any other tongue." Another anonymous critic recommends that untying the Gordian knot of a translation of the classics can be done only in parts.

And what ultimate objective resides in resurrecting, via a translation, a past work of literature? Perhaps the illustrious Walter Benjamin has posed the reply with great sensitivity: "Their translation marks their stage of continued life [...] all purposeful manifestation of life [...] in the final analysis have their end not in life but [...] in the representation of their significance."[20] Can one make the argument that however close to perfection the original work, it was still written by an imperfect human being?

Consider very briefly Cervantes's overall courage in overcoming failure with his early writings and personal misfortune. Eugenio Florit, retired professor from Barnard College, reports that Cervantes lost the use of his left hand in the Battle of Lepanto, earning the derisive sobriquet *el manco de Lepanto*.[21] After the battle, while returning from Naples to Spain in 1575, Barbary pirates enslaved him for five years until his family and friends paid the ransom (1580). To survive in Spain, he took a menial job as tax collector, but was imprisoned for misusing funds. Was it while in prison that Cervantes, harnessing his imagination, conceived *El ingenioso hidalgo Don Quixote de la Mancha*, about the adventures and quest of a delusional knight-errant and his faithful squire Sancho Panza? The tales, based on humorous adventures, captured the imaginings of Spaniards, the Englishman Shelton, and other translators over the centuries. The result has been, as Benjamin suggests, that less than perfect translators have paid the imperfect Cervantes homage by attempting to approximate and re-vivify for their respective audiences a metaphorical medieval landscape and inscape where a knight tilts at windmills that look to him like dragons. Could that have been a metaphor, not only for the mutilated author — who died a year after Part II debuted and never got to enjoy his belated fame — but for all frail humans who seek an ideal, imaginary world?

In addition to some very clever re-creators of Dante and Cervantes, a contemporary writer, like the Colombian Gabriel García Márquez (*One Hundred Years of Solitude*), has found his re-creator into graceful English in the hands of Columbia University's Gregory Rabassa. The worthwhile goal of the translators of classical writers has been to employ enormous amounts of creative energy and diligence to find equivalencies of someone else's language, ideas, and culture that would be relevant to their contemporaries. It is fortunate that readers can find thousands of dedicated translators in every language who have expended time and creative energy into rendering classical writers.

It is definitely clear from the contrasting perspectives that interpreting and translating are two facets of the same coin, apparent equivalents of the process of transmitting one foreign language into another, but practiced in different ways, for different purposes, for different audiences by types of individuals with differing personalities. Once one penetrates, however, into the nature of their separate operating systems and practitioners, interpreting and translating converge only superficially in their definitions and elaborations. Lucky and very talented is the individual who can handle both skills with confidence and clarity.

# CHAPTER 10

# Decoding and Encoding
# Multidimensional Language

## A. *Interpretation as Communication*

Three outstanding specialists in language and communication — Danica Seleskovitch, Elena De Jongh, and David Crystal — concur in that the interpretation act is an illustration of the communication process. The uniqueness of interpretation, Seleskovitch argues, lies only in the fact that, before formulating "his" thought, the interpreter appropriates the thought of another person. We might say that interpreting is a process of speech-thought-speech, in which the words of the speaker become the thought of the interpreter and are then reconverted into speech by him.[1] Interpretation and communication fuse, according to David Crystal, because interpretation is the most studied communicative act.[2] In order to understand the linguists' collective observations more fully, it would be useful to situate their thoughts in a courtroom context to scrutinize their versions of communication in action. The three writers on this subject — for example, Elena De Jongh — usually indicate that the interpretive communication act includes three individuals:

1. an interrogator,
2. the limited-English-proficient (LEP) individual, and
3. the interpreter/intervener as the bridge.[3]

What is usually left out is that the interpreter has to communicate with the witness or client to interpret the comments among some twenty or more officials, participants, or observers. In a trial, an interpreter may have to convey the judge's questions and directions to six to twelve jury members, prosecutors, attorneys, witnesses, and court attendants, such as marshals, court clerks, court reporters, hearing monitors, and receptionists. If a matter of public notoriety should ever reach an open federal courtroom, such as the trial of a Guantá-namo detainee who requires an Arabic interpreter (in 2010), the latter, along with the judge and attorneys, might play to a televised national and international audience in order to ensure impartiality.

And the combinations and permutations become even more pronounced as the situation becomes more complicated. Take the case involving three police officers before a Police Commission accused of improper treatment of five Mexican immigrants. The accused, supported by three attorneys from the Police Benevolent Association, dart intimidating looks at the accusers being deposed. Are they thinking that their unsubtle behavior is not being noticed and that their uniforms will shield them from the judge and jury? The interpreter, in carrying out the job impartially, is caught in a delicate situation of multi-level, tense communication with the three officers and their respective lawyers parrying off the diverse allegations of five accusers and their Mexican-American Legal Defense Fund (MALDEF) legal team.

Even in the three mundane court proceedings that follow, court interpreting involves more than three persons. In a divorce regarding an immigrant couple, an interpreter renders the dialog among a judge, at least two attorneys who represent separately the contending spouses, and their children. In a case regarding Workmen's Compensation, additional persons in communication are usually a doctor, a health assistant, representatives of insurance companies, and officials of compensation-related agencies. In the third, very clear illustration, several attorneys present in a deposition absorb every word of testimony and also try to determine whether the interpreter omitted something in every single question being asked of witnesses. Each attorney awaits his chance to ask questions of the same witness.

The thing speaks for itself. Court interpreting involves more than three individuals. All of the players have an impact, whether orally, nonverbally, in writing, transcribing, distracting by producing noise and objections, and so on. In Chapter 14, "Playacting and Power Relationships in the Courtroom," the roles of the principal and ancillary protagonists who communicate with each other will be examined in greater detail vis-à-vis the interpreter and/or translator.

THE COMMUNICATIVE PROCESS. The title *Language into Language* symbolizes the essence of oral interpreting and written translation as acts of communication. Oral interpretation involves the transmission of a communication by an interpreter (apparently verbal only, but in reality a combined, interacting, nonverbal + verbal message) from one language, usually called the source language (SL) to a different one, usually called the target language (TL) or the receptor language (RL). To illustrate, during a deposition in an attorney's office, a lawyer asks a question in English (i.e., = source language [SL]), which the interpreter converts into a Spanish equivalent (i.e., = target or receptor language [TL/RL]). The interpreter transmits the question in Spanish (TL) to the witness. In turn, the interpreter then converts the witness's Spanish-language response (new SL) into an English equivalent (new TL) and, in turn, transmits the response to the original interrogator, now a listener. To all appearances, it is a simple linear process:

$$SL \rightarrow Interpreter \rightarrow TL \rightarrow New\ SL \rightarrow Interpreter \rightarrow New\ TL$$

INTERPRETATION IS NOT LITERAL. In language in use, a sequence of words does not lend itself to easy comprehension because the words (termed "lexemes") are not to be taken literally (i.e., denotatively), but figuratively (i.e., connotatively), when one transfers context from one language to another because cultural differences are involved. Consider the following four apparently simple and common English and Spanish expressions. The exercise here involves translating Versions 1 and 2 from English to Spanish, and Versions 3 and 4 from Spanish to English. In so doing, the goal is to capture their literal and figurative meanings in both languages and to glimpse, hopefully not "through a glass darkly," the linguistic and cultural complexities involved:

Version 1: How are you doing, man?

*¿Cómo estás haciendo, hombre?*
*"How are you doing* or *making, man?"*

Version 2: How are you doing today?

*¿Cómo estás haciendo hoy?*
*"How are you making today?"*

Possible explanation of Versions 1 and 2: The literal translation to Spanish creates errors and confusions. "How" (*Cómo*) usually refers to process, but no process is implied. The progressive verb "doing" (*haciendo*) emphasizes ongoingness, but no action is in progress, except possibly "living." If one translates "doing" using *hacer,* then it is valid to infer an alternate rendition of *hacer,* i.e., "making," which lends further confusion.

Version 3: ¿Cómo estás, [her] mano?

*"How are you, 'hand'?"*

How are you doing, bro?

Version 4: ¿Cómo le va hoy?

*"How is it going to you today?"*

How are you today?

Possible explanation of Versions 3 and 4: Here the progressive "doing" of Versions 1 and 2 is eliminated, but two other verbs (*estar* and *ir*) come into play. In Version 3, a figurative translation recognizes the cultural cognate *mano,* an abbreviation of *hermano,* as a metaphor for "man" or "brother" and disregards the literal *mano* for "hand." In Version 4, the first translation follows doggedly the awkward grammatical sense (indirect object *le* "to you"), but is pursued and rescued by the more common and fluid expression recognized in English.

In another illustration of the weakness of literal translation, one goes from Spanish to English and distorts by using the wrong rendition of *tirarse,* which is redeemed by another rendition, i.e., "kept on going."

> Example:
> *No paró y se tiró.*
> Literally or denotatively:
> *He did not stop and threw himself.*
> Figuratively or connotatively:
> *He did not stop and kept on going.*

These examples demonstrate how the languages in use are not composed exclusively of the formal, verb-based, abstract and grammar-driven structures called "standard English," often overly stressed in school environments with the future world of work in mind. In truth, several dimensions of reality come into play simultaneously in the interpretation process, among them, language variations, cultural factors, and personal idiosyncrasies. If nothing else, those simple examples of current English and Spanish attest to the challenges that the interpreter and translator face trying to communicate appropriately.

## B. Triangular and Multidimensional Interpretation

The interpretation act is not static, unchanging, and absolute; it is a living event that evolves through time and in space. Many factors intervene simultaneously and sequentially. While some call interpretation a linear process, others envision interpretation as a "triangular process." Does supporting the triangular theory of interpretation create an inherent contradiction? Does not "triangular" refer to three interconnected lines joined at three points? It seems that "triangular" used in this linguistic context refers metaphorically to a flat, Euclidian geometric design of three individuals expressing meaningful sounds to one another from three intertwined points. The interpretation act, reduced to a linguistic diagram, is triangular in its barest Euclidian sense. The Viennese scholar Franz Pöchhacker, adapting concepts

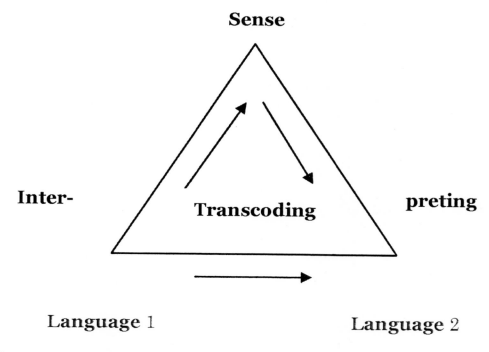

**Fig. 2. Franz Pöchhacker's version of a triangular depiction of interpreting. Borrowed from Danica Seleskovitch and Marianne Lederer.**

from Danica Seleskovitch and Marianne Lederer, illustrates the constituents of the triadic process, "whether [they be] linguistic units or mental constructs (Fig. 2)." Pöchhacker posits the triangular process as a point of departure and cleverly builds on this initial design to proceed to describe and illustrate the interpreting process through even more complex multidimensional linguistic/geometric constructs.[4] One has to coincide with this scholar in that the process is neither triadic nor one-dimensional, but much more complex. Although respect and admiration go out for Pöchhacker's more advanced linguistic/geometric constructs, which the readers are urged to peruse, one must demur insofar as accepting linear designs to describe a multidimensional activity.

In the following paragraphs, other concepts besides Pöchhacker's complex linear projections will be illustrated. In so doing, bear in mind the unavoidable, overarching human, spatial, temporal, and physical dimensions which make the interpretation event both multidimensional—human, mental, physiological, linguistic, cultural—and four dimensional, since the process is an activity in time and multidimensional space, where people with voices and gestures sitting on chairs and leaning on tables, or standing and moving, are asking for water, reaching for documents, and interrupting each other. One cannot help noting that the preceding verbs (sitting, leaning, standing, and moving) involve the gerund to symbolize that it is better to focus on humans—less on linear designs—who use language, display vitality, and show emotions to best capture the interpretation act.

This is also why it is preferable to represent the interpretation act realistically, as it is lived, as a circle within which many things happen at the same time around the critical event. Only at its barest, referring back to De Jongh, does it concern the interrogator, the LEP, and the interpreter who bridges the gap.

## C. The Speech-Chain Bridge and Diagram

### Questioner BRIDGE: INTERPRETER LEP Person

**INTERPRETER BRIDGES THE ENTIRE MESSAGE.** The interpreter does serve as an intermediary who bridges the cultural and linguistic gap between two or more transmitters and receivers of information in two or more different languages.

The interpreter needs to transmit the entire meaning of an utterance, all the various components that combined convey a special meaning. In deconstructed form, the act follows this sequence:

1. Translate (i.e., "interpret") the contextual meaning of the utterances.
2. Avoid a literal translation of words which will not render an equivalent rendition.
3. Transmit the complete message.
4. Omit nothing, neither (a) the verbal component, *NOR* (b) the emotional content of the meaning, which may be (c) that part of the message conveyed by nonverbal signals (if necessary and possible).

Interpretation requires, then, the simultaneous interplay of several components as well as several actors.

The Speech-Chain Bridge and Diagram is usually replicated with variations in writings about the interpretation process. It is part of a lengthy description of the interpreting event. The illustration below from Etilvia Arjona underscores and reiterates the essential components of the act and the roles and interrelations of the participants.

**THE INTERPRETER [...]**

a. receives the incoming message (SL-to-TL bridge) through cultural and linguistic filters for intelligibility; then
b. the interpreter processes the information, which encompasses the analysis of what the speaker infers, and, finally,
c. as "inter-cultural communicator (analyst/processor/executor)," sends the communication in the TL, with the appropriate verbal and nonverbal symbols and codes that match to the extent possible the sender's message and the receiver's cultural experiences without adding or deducting from the message.[5]

**INTERPRETER'S THIRTEEN STEPS.** It is helpful to disaggregate the stages in the process:

1. The SL utters a message in language A.
2. The interpreter (INT) hears the message.
3. INT listens to the message.
4. INT uses previous knowledge to anticipate and predict the message.
5. INT decodes the message.
6. INT tries to "memorize" (i.e., internalize) the entire message (linguistic, paralinguistic, intent, and meaning).
7. INT converts the message into an abstract form.
8. INT remembers both the abstract and the pragmatic forms.
9. INT translates the message into language B.
10. INT checks the accuracy of that version in the TL.
11. INT makes changes or corrections, if necessary.
12. INT adds the paralinguistic, nonverbal part, to maintain the register of the SL.
13. INT delivers an equivalent interpretation in the TL.

INITIAL ANALYSIS, PREDICTION, AND SENSE. The interpreter's foremost task consists of analyzing what he hears and chooses to hear. In that analysis, the interpreter has to ponder at superspeed the results of the assessment of the inter-relatedness of the message from SL, as well as what knowledge the interpreter brings to the event to forecast the message's meaning (Seleskovitch, *Interpreting,* 51). The initial and immediate forecast is too rapid to be conscious. The prediction is based on either a sense of the *meaning* of the SL message at the beginning itself of the reception of the SL message, or a prediction of the *language* the interpreter will receive in the SL based on the initial words. As indicated earlier, the interpretation act involves a complex process. It is important to stress at this point the very beginning of it, in which anticipation and prediction, according to Marianne Lederer, play a large role in the rapid formulation of the units of meaning, the "sense expectation" and the "language prediction."[6]

## D. Memory in Storing and Decoding "Units of Meaning"

Further analysis transforms words and phrases into "units of meaning" or "chunks of sense" stored in short-term memory (STM) or working memory. The interpreter plays a complex mental game. The game in simultaneous interpretation is for the interpreter to find and store new and ongoing cognitive "units of meaning" in short-term memory. The interpreter then seeks to find meaning in the words, or "chunks of sense," until, as a result of this analytical process, sense is found either immediately — after a few obvious words have been translated while the interpreter continues to fish for meaning — or after a very slight pause. The process ends at this point. If the analysis is successful, the result is that the interpreter has found the verbal and nonverbal meaning. He completes the SL in its TL version of this small portion of the action. The interpreter gets ready mentally, if needed, for consecutive translation. All utterances in the SL are entered into short-term memory to prepare for the new SL utterances (Lederer 330).

In order to render an equivalent TL version of the SL speaker, the interpreter must bear in mind intent, style, and register. Two processes are running at the same time. One process requires recording in memory the verbal and nonverbal parts of the SL communication for later equivalent reproduction. At the same time, one must transform the language of the utterance into an abstract conceptual form to analyze the communication and decipher its intent and meaning. A successful synthesis of the two processes would revert the original SL message stored in memory to its equivalent TL version joined by the concomitant verbal and nonverbal components.

CAPACITY TO RETAIN INFORMATION DEPENDS ON TIME, SPEED, AND MEMORY. Time and speed are of the essence when interpreting. The brain-mind cannot consciously keep up with the speed at which data penetrate and suffuse the individual. The interpreter needs to decide immediately, without pondering, nonconsciously, what the equivalency is in the TL, despite the fact that usually 120 to 150 words are uttered per minute. Faster speaking individuals — and there is no shortage of them — even utter up to 220 words per minute. In addition, short-term memory (STM) loses new information within 15 to 20 seconds. STM is, therefore, very limited in duration, but it can store about 7 bits of information, or chunks, quite consistently. A trained interpreter can use this to his or her advantage. In contrast, the capacity of long-term memory (LTM) is without bounds, virtually limitless.

**REHEARSING OVERCOMES MEMORY LIMITATION.** Interpreters in training, as well as those in the profession, can deploy strategies to counterattack the capacity limitation of memory. Rehearsal is a critical concept to assisting short- and long-term memory. By using chunking, messages can be broken down into memorizable units. The first thing is to organize what is heard in order to understand its meaning. Once completed, the analytical process starts without carryover of language units from the previous segment: According to Peter Milner, "Another example of immediate memory is the storing of words that you are performing at this moment in order to extract some meaning from this sentence. At the end of the sentence some clearing process takes place; the parts of speech of one sentence do not leak through to the next, as a rule." Milner provides an illustration of the sequence one can follow in rehearsing to help memorize chunks of ever greater complexity:

> If we want to retain a complex input for a longer time, we "rehearse" it. Once a number has been put into a long-term store and tagged as someone's telephone number, for example, it can be recalled as a unit, even after much interpolated activity, and each time that it is recalled the trace seems to be further strengthened. [...] Chunks can then become the elements for more complex memories still.[7]

One demonstrates the importance of rehearsing, i.e., of learning to retain in short-term memory — as indicated earlier when discussing memory and the relationship between speed of entry of speech into our brain and the nonconscious state — by the limited time in which we retain information without rehearsing. Camille Wortman, Elizabeth F. Loftus, and Mary E. Marshall ask and answer: "How long can new information stay in short-term memory without rehearsal? Studies yield figures less than twenty seconds."[8] In conclusion, to increase the nonconscious listening skills in the face of an inability to process myriad bits of data being transmitted, one can study and perform exercises described elsewhere in this book. In turn, these efforts help this enlarged capacity to also benefit from becoming nonconscious and routine.

**COMPREHENSION OUTWEIGHS MEMORIZATION.** Appearances can be deceiving. The interpreter does not need to memorize what is heard; rather the interpreter looks for and stores meaning in STM by using substantive memorization. De Jongh once again uses a felicitous expression, this time to emphasize the overriding of memorization by the more pressing need of comprehension: "[...] a message which is not understood cannot be retained" (De Jongh 31–32). Nonetheless, the interpreter does have to recall the nonverbal aspect to be able to complement, if necessary, the meaning expressed verbally when rendering the TL version.

**ATTENTION, MEMORY, AND HEARING VS. LISTENING.** The trained skill of concentrated listening is critical to perform the interpretation process successfully and to achieve equivalency. Understanding encompasses hearing and listening. The interpreter needs to understand what is being heard, add David and Margaret Bowen, and must be aware of what falls under the category of listening.[9] If one is distracted for whatever reason, comments Loftus, it is not possible to place the information in active memory. The result is that the incoming information is lost within seconds.[10] The interpreter needs to identify quickly what is important, and also what is more difficult to understand and remember, by applying the interpreter's analytical and memorization skills; memory aids such as a notepad will also be valuable tools. To perform this role, the interpreter must be fully attentive. It is not enough to listen merely to the superficial aspect of a communication. According to Wortman et al. (158), "[...] processing that is shallow, inattentive, and concerned only with superficial features — is undoubtedly the cause of many common memory lapses. Why, for instance, do you sometimes forget a person's name just seconds or minutes after you've been introduced?" Attentiveness also entails not letting intervening events interfere with the recording of an original event, e.g., extraneous sounds and even what causes them if they are not a part of the interpretation process. Quickly place the irrelevant in memory while consciously repeating to oneself the original event that must be remembered. In effect, stresses Loftus, block out the interference.[10] The inattentive interpreter will forget (at least in part) what needs to be interpreted, including register and tone.

DECODING AND RE-ENCODING SIGNS AND SYMBOLS. Signs and what they stand for (the area of semiotics) are part of the art of decoding languages. Signs, however, become more complex when they are used as symbols. It is a neat skill to be able to understand a language and its culture, hear and process a message in it to understanding (decoding), and then automatically know how to render the same message in a different language (re-encoding). Utterance by utterance, cultural factors in them are often more associated with language we know natively than with the one we learned later or as a second or foreign language. It is important to learn what is better expressed in which language, find equivalent ways to express it in the other language and, most of all, develop sophistication, experience, knowledge, and language and cultural fluency by observing, studying, and experiencing. It helps to learn about the conformation, salient features, and driving patterns of an LEP person's culture and those of the dominant culture in the U.S. when the interpreter is forced to seek equivalency in utterances that are not similarly developed and influential within their own cultures. This is why, in Christopher Thiery's well-documented view, any aspirant to the interpreter's profession needs to be as fluent as possible in at least two languages and their accompanying, respective cultures prior to learning the specialized interpretation knowledge and skills.[11] The interpreter's mediating act of speech is a complex system of decoding and re-encoding that involves semantic, syntactic, and pragmatic operations.

# CHAPTER 11

# Modes of Interpretation and Translation

## A. Overview of the Modes

Following the previous discussions of the interpretation process — the act and analysis of the multiple dimensions involved in the simultaneous and consecutive modes — this chapter goes on to complete the discussion, and then goes on to an internal review of the modes and services. Several modes exist, depending on the nature of the settings in which they take place, to provide the services. (See illustrations in Chapter 13, "Settings and Procedures in Legal and Social Venues.") This chapter covers, following, the three most employed modes of interpreting and one variant from another perspective (1–4), although five modes are possible, according to author Mary Phelan who discusses them in great detail.[1]

1. Summary Interpreting (SummI)
2. Consecutive Interpreting (CI)
3. Simultaneous Interpreting (SI).
4. Conference Interpreting (ConfI): a variant of SI

In both CI and SI, the same nonlinear interpretation process takes place. Because the differences, if any, consist more of procedures, practically everything referring to CI and SI to this point applies to both modes. At this juncture, it will be useful to add two elements and mention one:

a. Add, for emphasis, important reminders to material already treated.
b. Add information on the distinguishing characteristics among the modes.
c. Mention useful particular strategies for successful deliveries.

Translation plays a role prior to, during, and after an interpretation event. Three types of translation may be required:

1. Sight Translation (ST)
2. Document Translation (DT)
3. Tape Transcription (TT)

The three types of translation will be reviewed toward the end of this chapter.

# B. *The Summary Interpretation Mode (SummI)*

SummI, as the name implies, consists of offering an abridged version of what is being said. Summaries, whenever legally allowed and used, enable the limited-English-proficient person(s) to learn or clarify what "other actors" are saying. This summary mode is seldom used in the courts anymore, because the Federal Court Interpreters Act of 1978, and the subsequent Amendments of 1988 (18 U.S.C.), restricted the modes to be used to CI and SI (Subsection [k] of Public Law 100-702, # 709), to ensure that the LEPs obtain complete information and full disclosure. For example, a judge may order, albeit rarely, the interpreter to use the summary mode to highlight what is taking place and being said. Or an administrative judge in a hearing at the Social Security's Office of Hearing and Appeals may instruct the interpreter to provide a summary in the interests of saving time in order to keep the claimant informed of salient statements. Even though the interpreter may feel that by rights the claimant should have everything interpreted, the court's instruction overrules that. It is ironic that, despite affording a complete interpretation or paraphrase of the source language to the LEP claimant or witness, that person probably will not understand lengthy legal language or will find the terms confusing. Alas, the interpreter has to be aware of the limitations and realities of the job and that the process revolves around more people and issues than one individual.

Why is the summary mode used at times in settings other than the courts? Despite the fact that SummI may curtail or deprive the LEP of some of his legal rights under the letter of the law, it is used and useful where practical matters of expediency, such as maintaining the flow of information, simplifying language for the LEP by giving the gist, saving time by not having the interpreter work in tandem with informants, and accelerating a proceeding that has slowed down. SummI also finds favor most often where one individual is the sole decider in a setting of indeterminacy, such as where one person decides how procedures are to be implemented, and where attorneys and other actors may not be able to speak directly to the LEP, and one in which the interpreter and the LEP individual sit at a distance from the other participants.

The summary mode becomes a lifesaver, a device of last resort — even in the courts — to the interpreter who falls behind, when, in the worst case scenario, one cannot keep up with the fast flow, or the level of noise impedes understanding the witness. Flexibility, calm, and courage are the key components in admitting the problem and seeking a solution. A wise interpreter in difficult straits calls out humbly, "Your honor, the interpreter respectfully requests [...]," and states the need for slowing down. The request is almost always granted. The idea is to translate and summarize the most important highlights. Knowledge, experience, ability to predict, and capacity for concentrated listening are critical elements in avoiding this dilemma. Once in it, the interpreter must do his/her best to show a professional approach in a delicate situation.

# C. *Consecutive Interpreting (CI)*

It would be useful at the outset to underline the following distinction between the use of CI and SI, especially in the courtroom. For the witnesses, the **consecutive** mode usually comes into play. For the litigants the **simultaneous** mode is used.

Consecutive interpreting, according to James Nolan, was "the standard method" until it was found that simultaneous interpreting could be used "on a large scale." Nolan defines CI in this succinct way:

> A consecutive interpreter listens to the speaker, takes notes, and then reproduces the speech in the target language. Depending on the length of the speech, this may be done all at one go or in several segments. The consecutive interpreter relies mainly on memory, but good note-taking technique is an essential aid.[2]

Nolan's perspective is useful, and it would be worthwhile to build on it. It supports the authors' previous analysis of this complex process and shows that the interpreter needs to take into special consideration the following four details:

a. The actual sequence followed.
b. The fact that before speaking every listener has to wait his turn.
c. The intervals between the utterances of the conveyors of SL and TL.
d. The interpreter's role as the bridge.

The interpreter needs time to process what is heard, and then the listener needs time, also, to process the utterance. Some experienced interpreters have found that CI is more difficult to perform than SI because more effort is required. This is debatable. Before arriving at a more lengthy explanation of SI in the next section, glimpse the differences between CI and SI in an abbreviated, parallel presentation:

1. (a) In CI, the register (i.e., level of language) has to be as representative as possible, which may include a linking of verbal and nonverbal communication. (b) In SI, in contrast, most often it is impossible to accomplish this because time does not permit it.
2. (a) In CI, if the register is not as representative as possible (linkage), the message of the LEP individual can become distorted and misunderstood. (b) In SI, in contrast, the verbal aspect is most important.
3. (a) In CI, the utterances by any and all the three participants cannot go on for too long to enable the interpreter to provide an equivalent rendition (what some erroneously call a "verbatim" rendition). (b) This is unlike SI, in which you can listen and respond by interpreting (seemingly) simultaneously for a relatively extended period of time. Some estimate that in conference interpreting—a form of SI—a speaker can possibly perform for 20 minutes.

**CI SETTINGS.** CI takes place on most of the occasions when interpretation services are needed and where expensive equipment is not available. It is used in one-on-one interviews, such as most court and related proceedings, including trials, depositions, pre- and post-trial events and medical consultations, meetings and home visits of social workers with clients. Elena De Jongh reports that CI is preferred "in diplomatic interpreting or high-level talks, welcoming addresses, speeches for banquets or similar occasions, press conferences, and two-language negotiations for industry or business."[3] CI comes into play via on-call guides or escorts for tourist groups; the protocol offices of the U.N. in New York and the U.S. Department of State in Washington, for example, utilize CI to attend to official delegations from foreign countries. Regarding the use of CI for domestic social issues, see Chapter 13, "Settings and Procedures in Legal and Social Venues," for a long listing and detailed description of the multiple CI (and SI) locations or sites.

**GUARDING AGAINST CI BARRIERS.** The characteristics and qualifications which interpreters must meet have been reviewed. Here it is important to stress that CI can last several hours and be tedious, terribly repetitious, often boring, and inconsequential to the interpreter but not to the surrounding actors.

**IN CI, THE INTERPRETER AS CYNOSURE.** CI can take a long time in the courtroom. This produces two problems. The first is that this mode can be fatiguing as the interpreter has to rely on memory skills and note-taking. Second, CI can also be nerve-racking because the attending officials and family members are listening attentively to the interpreter. Despite linguistic insufficiencies, some officers of the court may have studied Spanish in college; family members of the Spanish-speaking witness are present who cling to every word translated. As a result, the attendees pay careful attention to whether the entire message is transmitted. Those present want to know that if the defendant says that he was arrested *ayer,* the interpreter included "yesterday." Upon a detail such as the correct or incorrect day in the legal proceeding may hinge an alibi or defense, and with it a loss or gain of fortune, freedom, and reputation.

This puts the interpreter at the center of attention; he can neither hide nor remain "invisible." Judges claim that the interpreter's job requires "invisibility." But "visibility" comes with a cost. The interpreter has to take public scrutiny and possibly notoriety as part of an occupational hazard. (Invisibility and visibility are studied at length in Chapter 14, "Playacting and Power Relationships in the Courtroom.")

**DESIRABLE SKILLS IN CI.** In addition to the skills mentioned in other sections, the focus, at this juncture, is on summarizing targeted skills and strategies:

a. **Public speaking:** An interpreter who has studied and practiced public speaking will be able to transmit by his mellow and modulated voice the message of the LEP.
b. **Minimizing mannerisms:** The CI interpreter should not have mannerisms or tics, or any other any patterns of behavior that will distract the listeners, or that can be misinterpreted as an LEP individual's traits which the interpreter may imitate.
c. **Focused listening/speaking time:** Carl H. Weaver says that "people in general spend about 45 percent of their communicative time in listening as opposed to about 25 percent in talking."[4] These percentages contrast sharply with the concentrated efforts of interpreters. Research by Barbara Mercer-Moser indicates that in SI the interpreter is listening and/or speaking from 60 percent to 75 percent of the time, which makes it very exacting and tiring.[5] Studies and training, in general, have given priority to speaking skills. In interpreting, visual and audial alertness and skills are critical to avoid missing details. If needed, it is important to be able to impart communication visually.
d. **Seek "relevant meaning":** Look for meaning instead of attempting to retain each word. Danica Seleskovitch urges trying to grasp the intent and sense of what is coming through the sensory act of hearing as you listen in a most concentrated manner.[6] During the analysis of what you are hearing/listening to, adds De Jongh, filter out the unimportant:

> Another element to consider is the nature of the input (coherence, density, speed of delivery, and so on). Baddeley (1976) notes that the storage of information in STM [short-term memory] seems to rely on acoustic encoding (remembering the sound of words), while storage in LTM [long-term memory] relies on semantic encoding (analysis of meaning) [De Jongh 383].

e. **Memorization by chunks:** To begin with, practice exercises to increase retention capacity and then look for the chunks, i.e., the units of syntactic meaning. In other words, organize what is coming in by segmentation.
f. **Schemas use prior knowledge:** Apply schemas based on memorized experiences. Use them to predict and understand what is being said. Use memorization skills and attach the nonverbal component when uttering the TL message:

[...] the interpreter stores the SL message in memory and processes the message for comprehension by activating the relevant modules and schemata. These schemata contain the meanings associated with the SL terms in the message, and probably the appropriate TL terms as well [...] inserting the paralinguistic elements where appropriate [De Jongh 383].

To amplify and clarify the definition of "schemas" as used in interpreting, it might be useful to cite the two ways in which Webster's defines them: (1) "a diagrammatic presentation"; "a structured framework or plan." (2) "a mental codification of experience that includes a particular organized way of perceiving cognitively and responding to a complex situation or set of stimuli."

g. **Anticipate key words, grammar, and repetition:** Key words, emphasizes Gerry Abbott, will facilitate predicting and detecting the grammatical and sense units:

> If we *know* what is coming we have, in a sense, already understood it before we hear it. This ability to predict is invaluable in listening. [...] Many words and phrases used to link sentences and clauses lead us to expect that the next thing we hear or read will be a reason (*because*), a contrasting statement (*but, however*), a result (*so, therefore*), an addition (*also, not only that*), a rephrasing (*in other words, that is to say*), or an example (*for instance*).[7]

Two additional practical strategies that can prove very useful in CI (and in SI) depend on the use of instinct and conscious factors: (1) Take advantage of the speaker's grammatical features, such as various pronouns in a sentence (redundancies). (2) Benefit from "repetition, not necessarily exact repetition, but rephrasing and recasting. Sometimes this is marked by such phrases as —'I mean [...],' 'What I'm trying to say is [...]'; but we also often hear or read the same idea simply repeated in slightly different words" (Abbott 64).

h. **Maximize the senses:** Use all senses, according to Dueñas González and her colleagues; and if aware of the senses to which one gives preference, work on sharpening the weaker ones:

> It is important to point out that all of the senses, not just hearing, enter into the processing of spoken messages. Aural, visual, olfactory, tactile, and gustatory cues all play a role in memory, although the first three predominate. Moreover, individuals focus on different sensory stimuli, depending on their aptitudes. This is particularly true of visual and auditory perception; some people are "visualizers," and some are "verbalizers."[8]

i. **Eliminate external interferences:** It is worthwhile repeating here that one should block out factors external to the interpretation act, such as what people are wearing, next-door sounds, or a pretty scene outside the window. One word missed may cause a serious and even grievous error.

INADEQUATE TRAINING. It is a commonplace that interpreters do not usually receive (adequate) training before beginning to provide services. A major inadequacy can afflict both native English speakers (ironical and not acceptable) and non-native speakers of English (unfortunate but still unacceptable) who display embarrassing lapses that occur to understanding of words, memory, ability to predict, and speed of recognition:

(iii) We are very much more likely to come across stretches of language which we do not understand at all. We have then either to devise ways of working out their meaning from context or to train ourselves to ignore what we cannot understand....

(iv) As we are much less familiar with the FL it is more difficult for us to anticipate and predict and we cannot select with the same degree of confidence [....] Thus more processing time is taken up. [...]

(v) Our STM for FL material is likely to be much less efficient [Abbott 63].

NECESSARY INTERRUPTIONS IN CI. Although mentioned earlier, and the subject of a full discussion in Chapter 14 (subsection "Interrupting long testimony"), interruption merits attention here. Notwithstanding rapid and effective note-taking and memory skills, intervention is sometimes necessary. The key questions are when, why, and how to interrupt in CI?

**When:**
1. Try to wait for a natural pause at the end of a response.
2. Stop the speaker if the situation has become hopeless.

**Why:**
3. To stop any speaker if he has not understood an idea in the preceding testimony.

**How:**
4. Always preface the interruption to the presiding officer with "Interpreter speaking."
5. Always explain the reasons briefly (e.g., slurring at the end of a sentence; too long an answer). Request that the presiding officer advise or remind the witness to speak clearly.
6. To minimize interruptions, prepare the scene by trying the following: (a) Ensure that the "rules of the game" are stated at the beginning of the event. Insist on this, realizing that some attorneys do not want this for personal reasons. (b) Have the witness speak in parts. Use hand and/or visual gestures to make the point.

UNDESIRABLE INTERRUPTIONS AND RISK. Difficulties with court interpreting take place when a witness speaks too rapidly, does not enunciate clearly, slurs (especially at the end of sentences), will not stop responding, and uses a combination of Spanish and English ("Spanglish") with a horrible accent, all of which lead to not being able to decipher what the witness is saying. ("Spanglish" is discussed at length in Chapter 15, section C, "Code-Switching Patterns of Bilinguals.") Although these verbal glitches become extremely annoying and can motivate an interruption, it is still prudent for the interpreter to cope with the difficulties and avoid interrupting a witness:

> The length of the utterance the interpreter must remember varies from a simple "yes" or "no" response to a rambling, disjointed answer from a witness to a long, complex question from an attorney. A competent interpreter is able to process and interpret forty to sixty words of question-and-answer testimony without having to interrupt the speaker. In fact, the Federal Court Interpreter Certification Program regards this ability as a minimal performance standard in CI [...] [Dueñas González et al. 395–6].

Furthermore, under the following conditions, it is inadvisable to interrupt the witness orally:

a. Do not begin to provide a consecutive interpretation while the witness is still speaking.
b. Do not interrupt and address the witness to ask for a repetition.

Experience — especially with less-educated witnesses (who are in the majority) — dictates that any of these actions will fluster them and be counterproductive. They will not understand that one is only asking them to speak in parts or to repeat something already said. Furthermore, witnesses will give a different response than the one for which you interrupted by using different words, instead of clarifying and then completing the original response, or they will simply stop speaking, leaving the response truncated.

## D. Simultaneous Interpreting (SI)

LEGAL REASONS FOR SI. In general, one usually employs SI from English to the other language. With both CI and SI, the legislature and the courts have ruled their use to protect the rights of the limited-English proficient person. To ensure those rights, the LEP individual has to hear everything that is said, be it in the courtroom or in a deposition, and to know what other witnesses are saying. This includes objections by attorneys and the outcomes, as well as what the judge says to a jury, including instructions. In the words of Alicia Edwards:

> With simultaneous interpretation the defendant can hear every word that the judge, the attorneys, and witnesses are saying, to follow the case and aid in his own defense. For example, when an FBI witness holds up a bloody jacket and says: "This was Juan's jacket," the defendant, Luis, hearing this through the interpreter, can tap his lawyer on the shoulder and say: "No, that is wrong, that was my jacket," and indeed, it does show the cut corresponding to the stab that Luis himself had received in the struggle.[9]

**SI, ROUTINE DURING A TRIAL.** Virginia Benmanan sums up the parts of a trial where SI is routine:

> [...] attorneys' opening and closing statements; discussions between the attorneys and the judge and the attorney's examination of English-speaking witnesses; the judge's instruction to the jury; legal arguments; and expert witness testimony covering a wide range of specialized fields and highly technical terminology.[10]

**SI AND PARALLEL PROCESSING.** It is useful, when talking about understanding simultaneous interpreting, to make an analogy with the parallel processing that derives from computer engineering and finds an analogy in the brain-mind. Any analogy, by definition, is only partial and approximate. The comparison is that thoughts can skip easily and quickly from one sentence or idea to another, and then to another, which leads at the same time to a parallel voicing of the thoughts. The flow does not end, because before one finishes uttering the thought, another is being generated inside the brain-mind. The function of the brain-mind in this stream of consciousness takes on added significance and difficulty when that seat of consciousness and thought is, in addition, required to move from one language to another with almost the same amount of clarity, celerity, and facility.

**TIME LAG OR *DÉCALAGE*.** But the analogy breaks down rapidly. The movement from one language to another, unlike the nanosecond speed and accuracy in computer parallel processing, necessitates a time lag that does not ensure clarity or accuracy. In CI, the time lag between a statement and the interpretation is very noticeable. In contrast, in simultaneous interpreting (SI), a gap, however minimal, exists. The interpreter passes the message to the TL at practically the same time as it is uttered by the SL. Although brief, the time lag between the two actions, namely hearing the utterance(s) and providing the translation, is critical. Linguists use the term in French and refer to this lag as *décalage*. Simultaneous interpretation is by definition simultaneous because it appears to be so. But the *décalage* does really exist, stresses Nancy Frishberg, and matters greatly.[11]

**EVS ACCOUNTS FOR THE TIME LAG.** According to De Jongh, the so-called Ear-Voice Span (EVS) "is the time between a message reaches the ear and the moment it is reproduced in the target language." She adds and clarifies:

> The interpreter must group a certain amount of material before beginning to interpret, the amount varying with the position in the sentence of certain key words such as the verb. However, because of limitations in short-term memory capacity, an interpreter cannot afford to lag too far behind the source-language speaker. [...] [T]he interpreter characteristically lags behind the speaker by two or three seconds. [...] [T]he interpreter makes use of his own chunking as well as the segmentation produced by the speaker [De Jongh 47–8].

The first step in SI is, then, to discriminate rapidly what one hears, make sense of the content, do something with it, and speak. David and Margareta Bowen calculate that this should take between two or three seconds, that the "recognition speed [...], not [...] typing or dictating speed [...], should come out at [...] a minimum of 120 spoken words a minute."[12]

**Delays within the time lag.** It can prove very challenging to keep up with the speaker while trying to grasp quickly the entire message. Therefore, Lederer points to frequent "delays within the time lag," so to speak. We keep up, catch up, fall behind again, yet must always render appropriately everything:

> [T]here are times when interpretation follows fluently upon the speaker's output with a delay of between 3 to 6 seconds. There are other times however when the interpreter pauses and lets the speaker get very much ahead of him. And there are still other times, usually following a pause in the interpreter's rendering when the flow of words coming out of his mouth increases to a very quick delivery. [...] I suggest that this pause was necessary for the interpreter to get the amount of information required for his understanding of the speaker's meaning.[13]

**No stops in SI.** Unlike in CI, in SI one cannot interrupt the speaker for clarification or dictionary verification. It is not only that the time lag is the only permissible hiatus, the definition of SI would be subverted by stopping. This means, also, that the interpreter cannot look up an unfamiliar word or phrase in a dictionary, however uncertain of the meaning or particular use of a word or expression. Until one develops enough experience, difficulties and embarrassments arise. The constant problem is that while trying to decipher what was said for faithful and accurate transmission in the TL, the forthcoming new utterance has to be deciphered rapidly for accuracy, and so on:

> If the interpreter begins processing the SL message before receiving enough contextual information, the interpreter may misunderstand the meaning (call up the wrong schema). Then the interpreter must waste time backtracking to begin again, falling further and further behind the speaker. The experienced interpreter is able to lag behind the speaker just enough to obtain sufficient information for accurate processing without falling so far behind that retaining the SL message in memory is impossible [Dueñas González et al. 363].

In *Fundamentals*, coauthors Dueñas González, Vásquez, and Mikkelson, quoting Wilss (1978), summarize the objective and subjective factors that account for the permissible time lag:

a. Objectively: the nature of the SL text and the relations of equivalence between the SL and TL;
b. Subjectively: the interpreter's knowledge and familiarity with the situation and speaker, fatigue, and simply individual preference;
c. "Syntactic anticipation": [prediction] plays a key role in determining the amount of *décalage* [366].

**An appropriate SI.** The objective within SI, continues Lederer, is to make the language appear natural. Although not mentioned in the following description, a good SI tries to maintain and replicate the register of the SL:

> The elements of a good simultaneous interpretation include the following: the target language rendition sounds effortless; the interpreter's voice sounds pleasant and inspires confidence; the interpretation does not sound like a "word-for-word" translation; and the interpretation is complete. The innuendos, inflections, nuances, as well as the style and register of the original speaker must be maintained (Lederer 51).

**Queuing's benefits.** Queuing, or lagging behind, is a technique that can prove most helpful in SI to keep up with the speaker:

This term refers to the technique of lagging behind in the processing of information during heavy load periods (messages densely packed with information and delivered at a rapid speed) and catching up during periods when the rate of delivery is slower and the content of the message is not as dense. [David] Gerver discusses the hypothesis that interpreters take advantage of pauses in the speaker's delivery to catch up, thus compensating for the so-called heavy load periods [...] [Lederer 367].

## A BIT OF HISTORY

After World War II, technological developments and the faster pace of life made SI both possible and necessary: the development of electronic equipment enabled one audience to hear an original speaker while another audience listened to the interpretation on a closed-circuit system [...] the technique was originally introduced by court interpreters during the Nuremburg trials conducted after World War II (Gonzalez et al. 359, quoting Ramler 1988).

**SWITCHING FROM CI TO SI.** When involved in CI, sometimes one needs to switch to SI. This can happen as an automatic, nonconscious decision to implement when the witness just keeps on speaking. A failure to switch to the SI mode right away prevents retaining the minimum necessary verbal communication. This switch can provoke curious looks, but if it proves necessary, then interrupt at an appropriate time. Say, "Interpreter speaking," or "Your honor, the interpreter requests...," and point out the problem; the judge can remind the witness to speak in parts. This is effective at hearings when the witness has become very emotional, cries, finds it difficult to speak. At these points, a recess is in order so that the witness can gather thoughts and calm down from an over-emotional experience. (This topic is also discussed in Chapter 14, "Playacting and Power Relationships in the Courtroom," subsection "Interrupting long testimony.")

**SMALL-TEAM SI.** According to James Nolan, who served as Deputy Director of the Interpretation, Meetings, and Publishing Division of the U.N., "simultaneous interpreters normally work in teams of two per booth, taking turns in shifts of about 30 minutes each for a maximum of about three hours at a time, which has been found to be the maximum average time during which the necessary concentration and accuracy can be sustained. [...] In certain situations (e.g., in a meeting where one language largely predominates), a single team of three people, [called in French] the 'petite équipe,' will work both ways, rather than two booths of two people each" (Nolan 4). SI can be as stressful as that of the job of an air-traffic controller, according to Nolan, therefore interpreters' associations have ruled that "simultaneous interpreters are usually required to cover a maximum of seven three-hour meetings per week, except during peak periods" (Nolan 7).

**TWO VIEWS ON SI.** "Listen" to how SI, complex and demanding, affects two interpreters. First De Jongh:

> The speaker speaks, and you are speaking too. If memory plays little part, neither does the personal element in the reconstruction of speech. Your sentence must, of necessity, follow the pattern of those which the speaker has pronounced [....] [T]he original sentence may suddenly be turned in such a way that your translation of its end cannot be easily reconciled with your translation of its start. [...] Listening intently, translating half unconsciously, consciously intervening to redress the forms and balances of syntax, touching up, putting in fillers [...] [De Jongh 46].

Coauthor Sibirsky actually enjoys SI even more than CI, and concurs with many other interpreters in finding SI easier than CI, despite appearing to be more difficult. How does one reach this point of satisfaction? This can be achieved by studying, training, and practicing.

## E. Whispered SI, or Chuchotage, in Diplomacy

In the absence of equipment during a conference, another variant of SI comes into play, called "whispered SI," or *chuchotage* in French. Frishberg describes the procedure as appropriate "when one or a small number of people speak one language, which is not the language the group is using. An interpreter will whisper the translation for the benefit of this individual or small group" (20). Who has not seen on TV or in photos a prime minister, shah, sheik, president, or ambassador being personally whispered to, *sotto voce*, in his own language by an interpreter standing or sitting behind or to one side?

*Chuchotage*, carried out by Russian interpreters, came into play at two historic international conferences involving the U.S. and the Soviet Union on the subject of nuclear weapons. From 11 to 28 July 1945, at the Potsdam (Germany) Conference, Harry S Truman and Winston Churchill (replaced 28 July by Clement Attlee) met with Joseph Stalin to discuss Germany's surrender and future and the war with Japan just weeks before the U.S. dropped an atomic bomb on Hiroshima. Truman, alone, without his interpreter, approached Stalin and said to the Soviet leader's interpreter, Vladimir N. Pavlov, that the U.S. had "a new weapon of unusual destructive force." Thus, the interpreter, even before Stalin, was the first Russian to learn officially of the device. He then whispered that startling news to his wily boss, who feigned indifference, but in his mind was already preparing an official investigation and penetration of the secret. Forty-one years later (11–16 October 1986), Ronald Reagan met with Mikhail Gorbachev at Reykjavik, Iceland, to discuss the Strategic Defense Initiative and the reduction of armaments. Pavel R. Palazhchenko, like Pavlov, was the first Russian to learn of the U.S. plans on nuclear disarmament before transmitting them. Interpreters, then, play an initial and pivotal, but apolitical role, in conveying correct whispered messages to the political and policy-making leaders.

Gamal Helal, senior diplomatic Arabic interpreter of the U.S. State Department, accompanied Condoleezza Rice to Middle East meetings. Journalist David Samuels witnessed Helal whisper to Secretary Rice in English the nuanced Arabic of Mahmoud Abbas, president of the Palestinian Authority. Helal, says Samuels, would turn to Abbas "quietly" to confirm whether Rice understood their (i.e., Abbas's and Helal's) Arabic: "[Abbas,] says Helal, quietly [would] ask me if what he understood in English was correct or not. Because every nuance makes a difference."[14] Imagine Helal whispering in an instant to Secretary Rice the proper nuanced meaning of Abbas's Arabic *inshallah* ("God willing"), "which in general usage can be the equivalent of 'We'll look into it,' [but] can also mean that the speaker will rely on God's will to make something happen."

Helal's opinions on interpretation and translation corroborate the main themes in this book. Bilingual dictionary renderings of a word or phrase can be self-limiting and fossilized. Spoken language, for its part, is multidimensional, part of a changing culture and a fluid situation. Samuels, extrapolating from Helal, affirms that "English words may exist in Arabic-language dictionaries, but the universe of concepts that determines their meaning is different." Helal's core view of interpretation stems from the thought that "logic is local [...] not universal." Helal concludes with the following sage comment: "[Proper interpreting] depends on so many variables, and you will not be able to get the right message unless you are familiar with everything — the body language, with the way the phrase is being said. [...] [W]ords without meanings, [he concludes,] are meaningless."

## F. Interpreters as Scapegoats

Morry Sofer comments on how an interpreter's whisperings to a king or commander turn him into a scapegoat when negotiations fail with a foreign leader. The interpreter is blamed for the failings of others when correct information provided is construed as deceptive or error laden. Sofer conjectures, in agreement with other language specialists, that prior to writing, tribes and nations had developed dialects and even languages, and that those with a special talent for learning various dialects and/or languages interpreted for the various groups. This was not always a felicitous decision:

> They played a vital role in both trade and in the affairs of state. Quite often, they became confidants of the ruler, and enjoyed special privileges. There was, however, a downside to the life of the interpreter. Since the interpreter was often at the center of important events, taking part in crucial negotiations and decisions, if things went wrong, if a deal failed, or, worse yet, a battle was lost, the interpreter was often used as a scapegoat.[15]

Even words "with meaning" and the proper cultural inflections in Arabic — or Spanish, or Russian — can have unintended problems in diplomatic interpreting. Consider the downside of whispered translation, where the interpreter becomes the "fall-guy," when, despite having translated faithfully the words, ideas, and culture of the diplomat, they later cause embarrassment to the source. This gaffe surfaced in the interview of Iraqi Prime Minister Nouri al-Maliki to the German magazine *Der Spiegel* regarding al-Maliki's and Democratic presidential nominee Senator Barack Obama's coinciding timetable for American troop withdrawal. The State Department and the Republican White House objected because they had not cleared the statement. Another objection had to do with U.S. election politics. According to Jeffrey Goldberg, writing in *The Atlantic*, "[T]he statement buttressed [Democratic candidate] Obama and damaged [Republican candidate John] McCain."[16] In diplomatic relations gone awry, the interpreter, not the prime minister, nor the shah, nor the president, becomes the scapegoat for a perfect rendition that turns out to be politically incorrect.

Beginning on 11 September 2001, the Departments of Defense and State and other agencies and contractors launched intensified and complex operations with the peoples, languages, cultures, and idiosyncrasies of governments, tribes, and ethnicities in turbulent Iraq, Afghanistan, Pakistan, and other Middle Eastern countries. In Iraq, with the invasion that started 3 March 2003, the U.S. government and the prime and subcontractors required the services of thousands of interpreters and translators. Since then, not only have life and limb for the interpreters and translators been in constant danger, but they have also been mistrusted by their employers and been blamed for operations and communications gone awry.

Nowhere is the precarious situation more vividly illustrated than in George Packer's essay, "Betrayed: The Iraqis Who Trusted America the Most," which he later turned into a play titled *Betrayed*. The 90-minute drama vivifies the essay's theme regarding how Iraqis who lent their undivided services and loyalties as "terps" to U.S. government agencies and contractors became distrusted, then trapped and estranged in a no-man's land between disdainful employers and rival Sunni and Shia militias who considered them traitors, or *alaasa*, i.e., "lookouts/informers."[17] Even the "new [Iraqi] government" brought to power by Americans, according to Packer, "distrusted and despised [the interpreters]."

Packer underlines the gifts and skills that the interpreters brought to the table for Americans unskilled in Arabic and in Middle Eastern cultures: "But what the Iraqis had to offer went beyond linguistic ability: each of them was, potentially, a cultural adviser, an intelligence officer, a policy analyst." Despite the advantages, few officials of the U.S. government agencies, while availing themselves of these services, would defend the Iraqi professionals from harm or injustice. At one point, the U.S. agencies replaced many Iraqis with Jordanians, who were believed to be more trustworthy, thus alienating the "terps" further from their own people and from a chance to earn a living.

In a stunning reversal of policy that finally recognized the interpreters' contributions and the need to protect them, despite the dangers and the alienation, Congress agreed to a "tenfold increase in special visas for Iraqi and Afghan translators and interpreters, whose work with U.S. military personnel and diplomatic officials makes them targets for terrorist violence."[18] As George Packer points out, this official concession was carried out by the State Department belatedly, grudgingly, and haltingly only after former U.S. military and civilians from Iraq campaigned for a redress to the newspapers and to Congress. Although the DoD's Defense Advanced Research Projects Agency (DARPA) has recently produced a portable device to voice translate Arabic to English and vice-versa, no happy ending awaits the scapegoated human interpreters and translators in Iraq. *The New York Times* reports that "more than 2,000 have already taken advantage of [the] fast-track visa program." An Iraqi "terp" declares, "I can never live in Iraq again. [...] I am a dead man in Iraq, I have no future in Iraq. All sides hate the 'terps,' even the Iraqi government side because they blame us for all the humiliations they got from American soldiers, and we had to translate for them."[19]

# G. Conference Interpreting (ConfI)

CONFERENCE INTERPRETING IN ACTION. This variant of SI, sometimes labeled "seminar or mono-logic interpreting," when practiced in training classes and mediations, is widely used in small and large conferences, including some in which speakers of more than two languages participate. In a court or social services setting, this mode benefits the LEP, who can have the advantage of hearing what is transpiring without causing interference to others in attendance; for their part, the attendees benefit by not having to spend a lot of time accommodating to the needs of the LEP.

Conference interpreting occurs on a regular basis in medium-sized settings (e.g., the annual Americas Conference in Miami), and large settings (the ongoing United Nations and the Organization of American States). At the U.N., interpreters who have trained for years at the demanding University of Geneva language schools perform their tasks in enclosed, soundproof glass booths, surrounded by high-tech equipment, while wearing earphones and talking into a microphone. The electronic arrangement at the United Nations, where the official languages are English, French, Spanish, Russian, Arabic, and Mandarin Chinese, allows representatives of 130 foreign governments to speak in the General Assembly in their native tongue and have the speech translated simultaneously into one of the official languages through earphones wired to the seats of the guests or delegates. This procedure uses concentrated and organized high-tech procedures to achieve economies of scale in the rapid transmission and communication of thousands of messages to thousands of users.

In conference interpreting, interpreters with extraordinary linguistic skills have been known to embellish and correct the SL in their TL version, and, if necessary, make the original statements more understandable. This cannot and should not happen in the courtroom. *Fundamentals*, by Dueñas González et al., notes that it is surprising to learn that in conference interpreting there is flexibility allowed to respond to the difficulty in achieving a perfectly equivalent translation in that mode without omissions because of the speed maintained by the speakers; sometimes there is also permission to provide a more polished rendition than the original SL version:

> [C]onference interpreters may often deliberately improve a speaker's delivery and condense the TL rendition of an original source message (Seleskovitch, 1978a, 1978b; Weber, 1984). They polish usage and syntax; edit faulty logic and predication; omit repetition, hedges, hesitations, and false starts; illuminate the subject for the listener; and make speakers sound more articulate and lucid than they sound in their own language. [...] Relaying the conceptual message in conference interpretation is sufficient [...] [Dueñas González et al. 27].

**PERSONAL NOTES ON CONFI.** Coauthor Sibirsky has interpreted in a glass-enclosed area in a private firm providing technical assistance to agencies abroad and interpreted in the SI fashion by way of a conference call. In his experience, he had to remind participants at both ends to let him interpret everything to enable everyone to understand. He marveled at having to bring order out of chaos among fifteen persons with different speaking styles and voices, and having to understand quickly every one of them.

Sibirsky offers these recommendations: It is important that the facilitator announce the interpretation service so that nobody will find it strange to find participants "talking in a loud voice." Furthermore, the interpreter must make special arrangements for the LEP participants and guests. Using the foreign language, ask that LEP participants sit in a confined area, together with the other LEP persons, as far away as possible from the other participants to diminish interference. A facilitator who does this in English will not help the LEP too much. Finally, ensure that all LEP participants have ample opportunity to be heard in the Q&A and in the commentaries.

**REGARDING EQUIPMENT.** Sibirsky reports, further, that having had to interpret when the equipment malfunctioned, despite preparation and testing, a Plan B is required to provide for delays, postponements, alternate equipment at a moment's notice, or translating without the equipment. The interpreter in charge is responsible for quality assurance. To underline its importance, De Jongh devotes a whole paragraph to the details of testing equipment, keeping the microphone on, having back-up equipment, controlling the volume button, and maintaining the "proper distance from the microphone (De Jongh 51).

Sibirsky's experience is relevant in describing equipment used during conference interpreting for an insurance company that had brought in salespersons from Argentina to explain both insurance policies and company policy and procedures to improve sales techniques. He says that it is very advisable to get the participants used to the equipment and then ascertain that it is working properly.

# H. Sight Translation (ST)

**DEFINITIONS AND USAGE.** The term "sight translation" denotes the oral and on-the-spot translation of documents interpreters are often asked to make during a proceeding. This happens most often in the judicial and legal administrative systems where one encounters the following documents:

- The plea-bargain agreement, conditions of release, a stay-away order, a civil-protection order, a pre-sentence report, letters in aid of sentencing, indictment, and parts of jury instruction.
- A deposition (especially of parts of an interrogatory).
- Reports at a quasi-governmental agency.
- A Treatment Plan for a client at the State Department of Children and Families (DCF).
- A large document in Spanish brought by a claimant at a Social Security Office of Hearings and Appeals. Prior to the client's appearance before the hearing board — usually without a lawyer — the document summarizing that person's status needs to be understood and reviewed by the board.

Owing to tight time requirements, one can only summarize. It is well to ask for time to gain familiarity with the document with the hope of avoiding errors or delays while translating aloud and also to get used to the document's register in order to try to replicate it verbally. Difficult or illegible handwriting presents additional problems.

An interpreter who is asked to translate a written document orally has the option of deciding whether to do so if directly hired. However, one working for a state court needs to indicate that the request has to be made to the central office. A person subcontracted by an interpretation agency probably needs to indicate that that company's policy requires prior notification and permission to handle written translations separately from the interpretations. If the document is short and by translating it relations are improved, discretion may dictate complying with the request as a part of interpretation; this also avoids "making waves."

**COMPARING ST TO SI.** Finally, ST bears comparison to SI because both require speed, which forces one to use the same predictive prowess as in SI, and also to apply simultaneously reading and comprehension skills:

> The most difficult aspect of sight translation is that the SL text is on paper, and it is therefore much easier to be constrained by the structure of the original. The interpreter must avoid being "hypnotized by the words," as Seleskovitch (1978a) emphasizes, concentrating instead on the underlying meaning:[...] the interpreter must abandon the external structure of the SL message and penetrate to the underlying meaning [Dueñas González et al. 407].

So vital is reading comprehension to the task of the court interpreter that the written portion of the Federal Court Interpreter Certification Examination (FCICE) includes a section (p. 16) that measures this skill. The coauthors of *Fundamentals* explain the reason for this part of the exam:

> Reading comprehension questions assess the examiner's ability to read keenly, to analyze a written passage from a variety of perspectives, including his or her understanding of not only explicit material but also of assumptions underlying such materials and its implications. The length of the written passage creates a substantial context that enables the reader to examine a variety of relationships within the passage [...] [Dueñas González et al. 402].

For further details on reading and translation skills, the reader is referred to Chapter 7, "Training, Testing, and Certification."

# I. Guidelines for Improving Performance

1. **Overall sense and meaning.** It is important to look for sense meaning, not for a verbatim, word-for-word translation:

   > [Y]et many novices fail to include this fundamental element in their attempts to render an SI of a message. They focus on finding word-for-word equivalents rather than penetrating the message to find the underlying meaning [...] [Dueñas González et al. 363].

2. **Chunk units of meaning.** The key is to look for units of meaning, chunks, segments; break up the phrases into meaningful, abstract parts, as discussed earlier:

   > Lederer (1978), in her discussion of units of meaning, emphasizes that until the speaker has completed a thought, the interpreter is unable to process the words for comprehension. Only after "synthesizing" the meaning of a string of words can the interpreter associate them with previous cognitive experiences or recollections, leading to a "merging into sense" (p. 330) [....]

   > Units of meaning have little to do with words per se; they are abstract ideas into which the interpreter reduces the SL message [Dueñas González et al. 364].

3. **Levels of predictability.** Anticipate, if possible, upcoming processes and outcomes based on body actions and utterances. A clever interpreter utilizes adequate vocabulary in order to bring into play knowledge and mastery of human thinking and expression. Use schemas or scripts to try to predict what is going to be said next. Being able to predict events based on experience will forestall difficult situations and will improve an interpretation event for all concerned.

   > Predictions are "guesstimates," or informed speculations about what is to occur, based on knowledge of the world, of the language and culture, and of the subject matter. The efficiency of information processing increases as a function of the interpreter's ability to predict the outcome of partially stated messages [....] The professional training of the interpreter undoubtedly helps greatly to progressively reduce the extent of this rate by decreasing the novelty of that which is heard [...] [Dueñas González et al. 364–5].

4. **Self-training.** And we need to train ourselves, learn techniques to help us concentrate our listening more efficiently and to increase our capacity to retain linguistic terms, and especially sense or content, with "relevant meaning."

5. **Self-monitoring.** Try to hear yourself and correct "on the spot," without dwelling too long because you may miss the incoming, new context.

# CHAPTER 12

# Verbal and Nonverbal Equivalencies in the Courtroom

## A. Searching for Verbal Equivalency

Everybody here knows, declares Maurice Pergnier, that the interpreter forgets the words he has heard in one language immediately after he has heard them and that he cannot be said to translate these words as such into the "target language." Yet he translates, that is, he says in a different language what he has heard in another language. He transfers not the words but the meaning of the message, thus demonstrating that to translate a message and to find *equivalences* between words of two languages are not one and the same thing.[1]

In essence, the whole interpretation and translation effort herein described, whether carried out in a courtroom, an attorney's office, a doctor's clinic, or in a library, has one "universal" goal, i.e., to render a faithful and accurate rendition from the original SL to the TL. The title *Language into Language* is not a catchphrase, but the aim and requirement of interpretation and translation. In interpretation, the objective is to achieve at minimum two levels of "language," i.e., verbal and nonverbal simultaneously, both equivalent in the TL to the SL message. The interpreter must achieve the "conservation" and equivalency, extracting the details of the content. Nonetheless, the truth hidden behind the exigency is that at best one cannot achieve a fully equivalent interpretation. What we try to achieve is a not "too dissimilar" interpretation.

A big exception resides, as discussed in Chapter 11, "Modes of Interpreting and Translation," with United Nations conference interpreters who have the license, skill, and distance from the speaker—which also assures anonymity—to embellish and improve on what the diplomats at the U.N. express without distorting the intent.

*"A FAITHFUL ECHO"* OR EQUIVALENCY. The often-quoted Elena De Jongh coined the following felicitous expression: "[...] interpreters should aspire to live up to the label of a 'faithful echo.'"[3] To accomplish this, the interpreter needs to bring several capabilities and pieces of information to the interpretation event to be able to "be on top" of the material to be decoded and re-encoded:

1. Mastery of language.
2. Familiarity with the subject of the event.
3. Familiarity with the antecedents of the event.
4. An understanding of the meaning underlying the words being used.

5. Understanding of the nonverbal language to ease comprehension of the message.
6. Finally, knowledge and experience to handle successfully the intangibles of intent and esoteric implicit meanings.

**EQUIVALENCE: MAXIMIZE SAMENESSES OR MINIMIZE DISSIMILARITIES?** This is the fundamental question. Listen to Sándor Hervey et al. as they try to find the right balance:

> SL speakers' responses to the ST are never likely to be replicated exactly by effects on members of a different culture. The notion of cross-cultural "sameness" of psychological effect is a hopeless ideal. [...] At best, a good TT [TL] produces a carefully fabricated approximation to some of the manifest properties of the ST. This means that a sound attitude to translation methodology should avoid an absolutist attempt at *maximizing sameness* in things that are crucially different (ST and TT), in favour of a relativist attempt at *minimizing relevant dissimilarities* between things that are clearly understood to be different. Once the latter approach is accepted, there is no objection to using the term "*equivalence*" as a shorthand for "not dissimilar in certain relevant respects."[2]

The underlying premise in securing a "faithful echo," of course, is that the interpreter needs to be bilingual and bicultural — to the extent possible — and the "interpretation strategy" should be to replicate in TL culture the SL culture. Next, in order to be a "faithful echo" of the LEP, the interpreter will reflect through the equivalent rendition the level of the LEP's literacy, education, and accompanying associated cultural traits. In a way, interpreting is a playing out of the role of trying to understand where the speaker is coming from, to be able to figure out very quickly what he or she is actually saying and meaning. The interpreter, then, has to know quite a bit about many aspects of the world and have good analytical skills. The sticking point is that if the interpreter does not possess the required knowledge and skills to offer a "faithful echo" in a particular situation, he needs to excuse himself and then proceed to obtain them.

The interpreter represents the witness. When before a jury or in a deposition, the listeners do not simply observe the witness, they receive a message about the witness from the rendering of the interpretation. The interpreter, according to Susan Berk-Seligson, must always be aware that a misinterpretation, not merely of words, but also of gestures and tone can provide an erroneous image of the witness:

> The fact that the interpreter stands alongside the witness at the witness stand, in full view of the court, and utters her English interpretations to a room that is silent but for her voice, draws to her own rendition of the testimony as much attention as is paid to the witness's, if not more, since his is incomprehensible to the average juror.[4]

The interpreter is a special kind of bridge. The interpreter becomes the questioner and the respondent.

**LATINATE LEGAL TERMS.** U.S. attorneys and judges, by training and by the nature of the profession, employ purposefully phrases and terminology that come from Latin and its derivatives, making legal language obscure except to the initiated. Common to the U.S. legal profession are the following Latin phrases with their equivalents:

*Nolle prosequi.* I shall stop the process.
*Nolo contendere.* No contest.
*Obiter dictum.* A judge's opinion uttered beyond the terms of the case.
*Res ipsa loquitur.* The thing speaks for itself.
*Stare decisis.* Observe or respect the precedents.

And the list goes on. The ambitious reader can consult James Nolan's *Interpretation: Techniques and Exercises,* where he lists alphabetically (A to V) 214 Latin terms that might be useful in a courtroom: A (*reductio ab absurdo* [*sic, ad absurdum*], "a reduction to the absurd"); V (*vox populi*, "the voice of the people").[5] Disguised Latin derivatives in English would include terms like "reciprocity," "adjudicate," and "probate." An interpreter in a U.S. court who sought equivalents or translations in Spanish to the Latin terms would have recourse to *West's Spanish-English-Spanish Law Dictionary*, which clearly defines *nolle prosequi* and many other Latin terms in Spanish.[6]

It is clear from the preceding that legal terminology, whether written or oral, has little relationship with colloquial English. This is not accidental; the apparent aim of the judges and lawyers consists of obfuscating the language and increasing the linguistic distance, so as to enhance the authority and control of the legal professionals over plaintiffs, defendants and witnesses, according to Nancy Bonvillain in her section on "Legal Settings."[7]

If the legal language is intentionally obscure for average Americans, imagine how much more difficult it is for persons with limited English ability, whether from a foreign country, or with limited U.S. schooling, or those with schooling but no legal experience. For his part, what chance does the courtroom interpreter have — lacking legal training — of understanding such esoterica and of successfully transmitting arcane terminology to an LEP? David Mellinkoff, who did an exhaustive study of the language used by the legal system, nails down the point that Latinate language used in the courtroom divides the attorneys and judges from the accused and the accuser, and by extension, the interpreters from the clients for whom they are to provide full disclosure.

Mellinkoff asks: "At what point does the language of the law lose contact with the common speech? What are the hallmarks of the language of the law? The elements overlap. They are intertwined. They affect each other. The composite is a specialized tongue that distinguishes lawyer and non-lawyer."[8] The following is a partial list from Mellinkoff of the chief characteristics of the language of the law:

1. Frequent use of common words with uncommon meanings (Section 9).
2. Frequent use of Old English and Middle English words once in common use, but now rare (Section 10).
3. Frequent use of Latin words and phrases (Section 11).
4. Use of Old French and Anglo-Norman words which have not been taken into the general vocabulary (Section 12).
5. Use of terms of art (Section 13).
6. Use of argot (Section 14).
7. Frequent use of formal words (Section 15).
8. Deliberate use of words and expressions with flexible meanings (Section 16).
9. Attempts at extreme precision of expression (Section 17).
10. Mannerisms associated with professional expression are separately considered.

It is incumbent upon an interpreter, therefore, to make extensive preparations to learn the special legal terminology in two languages before appearing in a courtroom. With regard to Latin-derived legal terms familiar to the interpreter, the irony — cautions Roseann Dueñas González and her colleagues — is that it is not for the interpreter to define to the witness or defendant the meaning of them; they should be rendered in the original language: "If the interpreter were to define terms, this practice might be viewed as improperly giving legal advice or practicing law."[9] The attorney will know from nonresponsive answers or a request for rephrasing by the LEP witness that the term is not being understood. What is most alarming is that the interpreter should not trespass the boundary of rendering an equivalent translation and enter into an explanation of a foreign term because he becomes liable to a charge of an illegal act.

In addition, the interpreter must be sensitive to the educational and intellectual imbalance. To demonstrate the effect of legalisms, consider a few typical examples. One occurs when an attorney, wanting to have a statement or question discarded and replaced, will say "strike that" or "withdraw that." Common sense dictates that these phrases will not be understood in literal translation by an undereducated witness unless rephrased or paraphrased. It falls to the interpreter to render the phrase or legal terms in an acceptable synonym, or to use several words for an equivalent but easy-to-understand translation. Again, matter-of-fact legal terms can create confusion in the LEP. When the administrative judge "offers representation"—a phrase derived from Latin—the helpful interpreter, instead of translating it literally as *brinda representación,* would better serve the undereducated witness by paraphrasing it as "that means you can have an attorney."

Attorneys, heavily influenced by their profession, often use language that is not necessarily appropriate to a situation. For example, to instruct a witness in a deposition "to use words rather than gestures," lawyers usually ask the witness to "speak aloud," a phrase that an English-dominant witness understands as needing to raise one's voice. If the lawyer had been aware of the translation to Spanish (*hablar en voz alta*), he would not have said that. A sensitive interpreter, correcting the attorney, would give the adequate nuance of "speak aloud" to the LEP as "always use words." This technique saves the attorney from embarrassment and even misunderstanding. Attorneys capable of comprehending some Spanish repay the clarification with a visual gesture of appreciation. In addition, if the interpreter is not familiar with the legal term and wants to make certain that he is repeating it correctly, he can add, "Interpreter speaking," and ask for clarification. In addition to references in the text, the "Authors and Works Cited" section points to West's bilingual legal dictionary and to glossaries by Holly Mikkelson and Alexander Rainof.

COURTROOM "RULES OF THE GAME." The following rules, suggested earlier, will enable the interpreter to carry out a faithful equivalency. Before starting a courtroom process, to help ensure a successful event, apprise those unfamiliar with the interpretation act—(administrative) judge and attorneys, doctors, and others—of the "rules of the game." Ask that the witness be advised to proceed slowly, part by part, rather than providing long answers. This procedure guards against the interpreter forgetting something. The witness must only answer in the native language. Furthermore, the witness needs to first wait until the interpreter translates the entire question into the TL before answering. (A full discussion of the rules is in Chapter 14, "Playacting and Power Relationships in the Courtroom," subsection "Interrupting long testimony.")

EXAMPLES OF EQUIVALENCY. Berk-Seligson's comments focus more and more closely on what is meant by "equivalency." She provides an example when the interpreter attempts to render the SL concept in the TL, but not a verbatim, word-by-word translation:

> For instance, in English, there are countless "two-word verbs," or what are sometimes called "verb plus particle" constructions (such as "put on" [...] "turn over"). The equivalent of these in Spanish more often than not would be a single verb [*Intersection* 1095].

Because words can have connotations, the interpreter must take care not to make a mistake on the nuance of a word. The interpreter must repeat everything the client says as heard, even if the answer is given wholly or partly in English. Those in positions of authority — judges, attorneys — can instruct the witness to use the TL language.

Every interpreter with undereducated persons for clients has to decide what is actually meant by the witness in order to render an equivalent meaning in TL. In a recent situation, a 22-year-old who was seriously hurt in two vehicle accidents formulated his ideas in his primary language, Spanish. His mastery of Spanish vocabulary was terribly deficient, so he was continuously looking for words in that language that he could not come up with, code-switching then to English, called "Spanglish." The point of this discussion involves his expression, "*No lo puedo tomar*" (Anglicism for "I cannot take it"), referring to the pain he constantly felt in several parts of his body. The problem was that he meant the equivalent of "tolerate"; "*tomar*" ("take" in English) does not extend to "tolerate" with the meaning of endure or withstand. One explanation is that he confused *tomar* ("take") with *llevar,* also meaning "take," but with the added nuances of "take away," "bear," "carry." Thus he might have expressed his inability to "take it" as *No lo puedo llevar.* More to the point, which the witness did not know or could not call to mind, would have been the usual Spanish for "bear the pain," *No lo puedo aguantar* or *soportar.* This interpreter quickly decided to interpret *tomar* as "bear" and immediately signaled "Interpreter speaking" and explained not merely the word but the semantics, adding that the witness had just used Spanglish, and meant "take" in the sense of "tolerate" or "bear" metaphorically, but not "take" in the literal sense of pick up or hold something. It turned out that this distinction was very meaningful in the hearing and worthy of praise. (For a full discussion of "Spanglish" and code-switching, see Chapter 15, "Implications of Bilingualism.")

**Seeking equivalent language.** Attorneys often tell the witness, "I will now ask a series of questions about your work history," or "tell me about your work history." The less sophisticated Spanish speakers often do not understand the common term in Spanish for "work history" (literally, *su historia de trabajo*), although they may understand "health history" (*historial de salud*) in Spanish. The attorney's job is to figure out whether he is on the right track from the witness's response, but if this translation still does not elicit proper answers from the witness after several repetitions, the interpreter may feel bound ethically to clarify by saying, "Interpreter speaking," and add: "It appears that the witness does not understand the usual term for 'work history' in Spanish, and I will have to use another, such as *antecedentes laborales,* translated as 'work background.'"

**Nonresponsive or strange answers.** When the questioned provides a nonresponsive answer or a nonsensical one, the interpreter can "say" with the eyes and a slight, unobtrusive shrugging of the shoulders that will not embarrass the LEP or upset the LEP's attorney, that "this is what the witness said. If you want to, pursue the idea with more questions." In this way, the interpreter is not deviating from the provision of an equivalent translation and is simultaneously alerting to the fact that the interpreter asked an equivalent question. Many less-educated witnesses use unusual, substandard, or metaphorical combinations of words, or invent a new word reminiscent of other words with a different meaning. For example, how does one interpret or translate quickly and accurately *los huesos estrellan* ("the [my] bones crash" or "the [my] bones creak")? The important thing is to say, "Interpreter speaking," and then state the facts, followed by an explanation of what the witness may have meant by the misspoken or unusual phrase or neologism.

At times a witness will provide a wrong number, for example, "the problem occurred in

1906," instead of "2006." This may simply be a slip of the tongue, or may be caused by heavy sedation because of mental health problems or chronic pain. The interpreter, echoing faithfully, must repeat the number provided by the witness. In settings in which a modicum of flexibility is allowed or in which the actors other than the witness have worked with the interpreter before and mutual professional respect has been gained, the interpreter may discreetly signal visually or with a shrug or movement of the shoulders that it is not the interpreter who has committed a *faux pas*.

There are times when a witness will give unusual meanings to words. For example, some use the word *pie* ("foot") to also mean *pierna* ("leg"). We suggest that if the witness pointed to the leg, the interpreter should say: "Interpreter speaking. I believe the witness pointed to her left leg." And if the witness does not point, the interpreter can clarify with: "Some Spanish speakers use the word *pie* ('foot') to also mean *pierna* ('leg'). It appears to the interpreter that the witness meant 'leg.'" The attorneys usually express appreciation for the explanations and then corroborate (or not, as they wish) what was said through new questions. This adds to the respect for one's professionalism and competence.

**DOUBLE/DOUBTFUL MEANINGS OF FOREIGN WORDS.** Very often an interpreter faces an awkward situation because it is not clear which meaning is intended or understood by a witness. The interpreter should not confuse the issue by providing the various possible meanings simultaneously. Instead, the interpreter should say, "Interpreter speaking," and indicate that the witness used a word that in Mexico, for example, can mean either of two types of vehicles, which gives the questioner the opportunity, if it is desirable, to probe further.

It is not unusual, either, for a witness to use a foreign-language word that is new to the interpreter or at least the nuance given to it by the witness. The interpreter should interject in the usual way and explain the difficulty and ask for help in having the meaning clarified. The interpreter should not ask the witness to repeat the word or for a definition. It may happen that a judge will ask the interpreter to address the witness directly to receive the clarification. In this case, the interpreter should report back, not by saying, "He says" or "She says," which are anathema to the court reporters, but by saying, "Interpreter Speaking," and then providing the responses of the witness. The interpreters are not to engage in a long dialog with the witnesses and need restrict themselves to the issue at hand to not bias the line of questioning or the witness's responses. (A full discussion of "He says," "She Says," is in Chapter 14, "Playacting and Power Relationships in the Courtroom.")

**PORTUGUESE EQUIVALENTS.** At one trial, a Brazilian witness answered yes or no questions in the affirmative with the term *acho*, which literally means "I find" (implying "I find it to be so," or "I believe it so"). The interpreter realized that the witness was answering affirmatively, and translated it as "yes." To remove any doubt and to get it on the record, the first time the witness uttered the word, the interpreter interrupted properly and explained the above. Whenever the witness answered "*acho*" in the future the interpreter simply said "yes."

The Portuguese *saudade*, loosely defined as "homesickness" or "nostalgia," exemplifies a term with charged and unique meanings for which an equivalent is difficult to find. A native from Lisboa or Rio de Janeiro living in the U.S. who employs the term feels sadness mixed with excitement toward the homeland, with its family ties, music, language, and food. The same nostalgia or *saudade* might be difficult to transmit to a Chicagoan in Paris, but one can come close if a Parisian mentioned to him the Chicago Bears or the Chicago Bulls. Words transmit emotions and sentiments. The question is to find the right word for the appropriate person at the proper time.

INTRA-LINGUAL, INTER-LINGUAL EQUIVALENTS. Given that many intra-lingual expressions are similar, that many linguistic paths can be taken to reach inter-lingual equivalents, and that many concepts (e.g., the Portuguese *saudade*) are marginally translatable from culture to culture, and given that time is of the essence, the simultaneous and consecutive interpreters have to problem-solve quickly and employ various interpretation techniques. In the following Spanish dialog, focus on Person B's comment and choose two variations from among several modalities in English:

PERSON A: "Se encuentran esas cualidades en Picasso."

PERSON B: "En efecto, pensaba en Picasso."

(In an oral TT, the *en efecto* would probably be rendered, not with the connective "indeed," but by voice stress and intonation)

PERSON A: You often get those qualities in Picasso.

PERSON B: I was *thinking* of Picasso.

[...] or by intonation and sequential focus:

PERSON A: You often get that in Picasso.

PERSON B: It was Picasso I had in mind [Hervey et al. 77].

GENDER DENOTATION IN SPANISH/ENGLISH. In Spanish, but not in English, arbitrary convention deriving from the Latin language classifies all nouns and their corresponding adjectives into masculine or feminine. In both languages, of course, references to male and female individuals or animals are, *ipso facto*, masculine or feminine. With respect to inanimate nouns, Spanish retains the masculine/feminine distinction, again deriving from either Latin or Greek. Generally speaking, in Spanish inanimate nouns that end in "a" are feminine, those that end in "o" are masculine. Notable exceptions are derivatives from Greek that end in "ma" or "pa," such as, respectively, *problema* and *mapa*, which are considered masculine. The singular definite articles — *el* for masculine and *la* for feminine are clues to the nouns' gender. Where one word, such as *papa*, can have two or more meanings, the masculine definite article (*el*) and stress distinguish between the Pope/father (*el Papa/el papá*). Context alone, rather than stress, sets apart the two meanings of *la papa* when used with the feminine definite article: "The hot baby bottle" and "the hot potato," both represented in Spanish by *la papa caliente,* would be clear according to the social context.

With regard to subject pronouns (I/*yo*, he/*él*, she/*ella*, you/*Usted, Ustedes*, they/*ellos, ellas,* we/*nosotros*), the determining factor is that in English a subject pronoun before or after a verb is obligatory every time to identify a male or a female. In Spanish, once gender and number are determined, the subject pronoun does not have to be repeated; the exception occurs when the person first mentioned changes, or there is a gender change, then a clarifying subject noun or pronoun is required.

If necessary, the court should be made aware of these grammatical distinctions. The interpreter can say, "In Spanish, the nouns denote gender; therefore we know that the witness actually meant by *la prima* "the female cousin." This is done for the sake of accuracy and because the interpreter does not know if the information is of factual interest to the attorney(s), (administrative) judge, mediators/investigators of the Commission on Human Rights and Opportunities or a social worker investigating a referral of negligence or abuse of a child. In the following example by Gerardo Vázquez-Ayora that deals with gender identification vis-à-vis a subject pronoun, the interpreter would be advised to seek a simple, direct, and unedited translation strategy to achieve equivalency:

ENGLISH: She is reading.

SPANISH: Ella está leyendo [*or* Está leyendo].[10]

Going from English to Spanish carries one set of problems, the reverse also has its complications. One has to determine swiftly whether in going from English to Spanish or Spanish to English a simple translation applies. It is important to know the gender if it is the first time the person is mentioned, and whether the limited-English-speaking witness, does not know or remember, e.g., the name of a clinic and of a doctor. In going from Spanish to English, when a gender is mentioned by an article and noun, e.g., *el doctor* or *la doctora*, a wise interpreter interjects appropriately and adds, "In Spanish we specify gender to determine whether a male or female doctor is involved. In this case it is a female doctor." This clarification has proved of significant help to medical practitioners and potential witnesses.

**REARRANGING GENDER.** With regard to answers that do not match the gender of the questioner, where, for example, the witness says, "Yes, sir," to the male interpreter, whereas the deposing attorney is female, the interpreter should say, "Yes, sir," for the sake of equivalency. Only the attorney can correct or not correct the witness. The attorney for the witness is obligated to rectify this awkward and highly laughable situation.

**"COURT" IN SPANISH.** The dictionary words for courthouse in Spanish are *tribunal* and *palacio de justicia*; in Puerto Rico *tribunal* is used by the courts themselves. Most Spanish speakers in Connecticut and elsewhere, nonetheless, tend to use the word *la corte*. It is recommended that *la corte* be used in oral translation, and that both be used in written translation, with one of them appearing once within parentheses, e.g., *corte* (*tribunal*), to ensure that everyone can understand what the English word means in Spanish.

**LIMITED FORGETFULNESS.** The interpreter should overcome embarrassment and make it known if the meaning of a word escapes memory. Once, when very fatigued, an interpreter could not find the Spanish word for "brush," and the word for "pencil" got lost in cerebral heaven. He explained politely what was happening and asked for a brief recess. Within 60 seconds the common words came back and the deposition went on normally again.

**SIGNALS, SIZE, DISTANCE, SOUNDS, AND CURRENCY.** With regard to these cases, the interpreter should only reproduce the words used by the witness and let the questioners handle the understanding of the physical information the witness is attempting to provide. Do not reproduce signals or movements indicating distances or size because it is impossible to reproduce them with assured precision. According to De Jongh, "sounds (e.g., mouthing a whistle) should not be reproduced; it is sufficient to state, 'The witness has just whistled'" (40). Refrain from converting measurements of the metric system to yards and feet, centigrade or Celsius to Fahrenheit. This also applies to foreign currencies. The interpreter needs to reproduce exactly what was said. It is up to the interrogator to try to obtain equivalent measurements from a witness.

**THIRD-PARTY STATEMENTS AND REQUESTS.** Often witnesses do not understand that the interpreter is the intermediary, not the principal questioner, and so refer to the attorney/questioner as a third party. If the witness says, "tell him that...," and "ask her that...," the interpreter should translate these and like phrases verbatim without editing them. The parties involved may become confused, however, and the transcript of the proceedings will be unclear if this third-person style is used. To avoid confusion, however, the interpreter should make the following request to the judge: "Interpreter speaking. Your Honor, would the Court please instruct counsel and the witness to address each other directly rather than use the third person?" A similar request should be made to the attorney in a deposition. There are attorneys who find it extremely difficult to avoid using the third person, which can become terribly uncomfortable for the interpreter, who is forced to constantly repeat the request. At times the attorney becomes exasperated and "orders" the interpreter to ask the question in the third person. The interpreter may then oblige the attorney to desist, objecting for the record in the presence of the other attorney. Such behavior is preferable to abandoning the deposition after the fact. For a variant see Chapter 14, subsection "Interpreter speaking: 'He says,' 'She says.'"

EQUIVALENTS FOR SLANG AND OBSCENE LANGUAGE. Interpreters must be prepared to translate slang and obscenities. The interpreter's ethics, religion, upbringing, or other influences should not be a barrier. The interpreters must not be embarrassed by what they need to translate. Judges, as well as attorneys and other pertinent actors, will often also have to repeat the offensive words and are certainly accustomed to their usage in their settings. If a witness is verbally rude to a judge or to an attorney in a deposition, so be it. The interpreters must transfer the abrasive comments into the TL, without fear that anybody will consider the interpreter personally offensive. For that matter, the vulgarity may depend for its effect and also the degree of its effect on the knowledge of the culture in which the vulgarity is used. Depending on the slang word or expression, the interpreter can provide an equivalent translation or say it in the TL and spell it for the sake of the court reporter. In this case, the questioner can pursue the meaning of the word or expression directly with the witness or request the interpreter to provide a definition and/or explanation of it.

The interpreter may also feel sympathy for a witness and consider that certain rude, vulgar, or offensive statements being made by the latter are going to hurt the witness's case. But the interpreter must remain an impartial bridge and continue to provide an equivalent interpretation. The interpreter must remember that it is up to the witness's representative to defend the witness and take appropriate action if it is called for and available.

REPRODUCING BELLIGERENT IDIOLECT. The interpreter must make all efforts to reproduce the language or speech pattern of an individual, e.g., an idiolect, even if it means copying the gruff nonverbal and verbal — or other manifestations of that person's personality. As an example, one Social Security claimant with handicaps was in such chronic pain that it made him impatient, abrupt, and seemingly ill-tempered. Through efforts to calm him down and to represent him adequately, he showed that he was not normally belligerent, but could not help his behavior and was not aware of the damaging and false impression it left. It is not known whether the administrative judge thought well or ill of him; one could only hope that the judge was able to — through the equivalent rendition — appreciate the actual personality of a claimant conflicted by constant pain.

TRANSMITTING ANGER. Often interpreters do not know how to handle the anger expressed by a speaker. The transmission of anger usually entails raising one's voice and giving it a rough edge. The personality of some of the interpreters may make it difficult for them to impersonate a person who speaks angrily. Nonetheless, room has to be provided for the interpretation of anger. Attorneys may use it as a tool to provoke a witness, or to intimidate a witness, or to convince a jury. Witnesses may become exasperated and respond with anger. It is not to anyone's benefit to provide a perfect replica in the TL of the anger expressed in the SL. It is very difficult to imitate the intensity of anger, and really unnecessary because, it bears repeating, the tone used by the interpreter will remind the listeners—be they judge, jury, attorneys—of the anger being transmitted by the SL speaker which they have just experienced. An additional, secondary factor is indeed that interpreting can strain one's voice and the imitation of loud anger may therefore affect it adversely.

Should the interpreter "interpret" anger fully? To what extent should an interpreter be expected to replicate emotions such as anger, whether real or simulated? How much is the interpreter expected to act out to achieve equivalency? No unanimity exists on this matter. There are interpreters who object to the acting part and/or are afraid of its effect on their vocal chords. Experience advises not to imitate the anger fully but to give an attenuated version in register and tone. The listeners, including jury members if it is a trial, will be able to associate the interpreter's register and tone with the shrill one of the witness as well as the latter's body language, including facial and other gestures. The interpreter is an actor, but should not and need not be totally equivalent in exaggerated or harmful circumstances. This is a special case in which it suffices to provide what the listeners need for them to formulate a correct equivalency.

## B. Strategies for Finding Equivalencies

Following are descriptions and examples of the most typical techniques used to interpret from one language to another. It is of great help to remember these techniques in order to be able to apply them "on the run," because no "official time out" is provided during the interpretation act. The interpreter will find that, in time, it will become gradually easier to select the best technique when it presents itself.

TRANSPOSITION AND INTERFERENCE. Transposition refers to different scenarios. One is described by James Nolan (*Interpretation* 217) as "looking for an approximate equivalent" in the target language for an event or story that originated in the source language. Vázquez-Ayora (*Traductología* 122), for his part, applies transposition to word order and the parts of speech that usually vary in their positioning between languages. Interpreters and translators have to be alert, as professional speakers of languages, for those who, through interference, allow uncalled for transposition to happen, and not to make the mistake themselves. A newly arriving LEP can easily substitute the word order and syntax of the dominant language, not realizing that he or she is rendering the correctness of his native language. Using Vázquez-Ayora's example:

SPANISH: "*Tiene los ojos azules.*" (This is customary and correct Spanish.)

ENGLISH: "She has blue eyes." (This transposition provides a clear English translation. A garbled message can occur through interference and when the learner does not transpose properly and pursues doggedly the original language's syntax and grammar, to wit, "She has the eyes blues.")

A longer, but possible, reach in grammar and word order from the original Spanish is "She is blue eyed." A newcomer to English and Spanish from Latin America, or a neophyte interpreter, might be challenged by the word order and syntactic transpositions and say, whimsically, in correct grammar but unintelligible prose: *Ella está azulada de los ojos*; or *Ella tiene los ojos azulados.*

An English-speaking student of Spanish would do well to use *Roget's Thesaurus* and a serious bilingual dictionary to decipher the dual meanings of the English "to think much of him" and compare that with "to think much about him."

ENGLISH: I did not think much of him.

SPANISH: No *he pensado mucho en él* [Vázquez-Ayora 262].

The Spanish version actually means "I have not thought about him very much." The correct Spanish version would be *Tenía mala opinión de él* (I had a low opinion of him) [Dueñas González et al. 311].

The use of a literal translation strategy means that the real meaning of "to think much of somebody" is lost.

Who knows how often, though, one has to come up with linguistically different wording to achieve sense or meaning equivalency. This is typical interpretation translation strategy. For example, many attorneys begin a deposition with:

ENGLISH: And how are you today?

And you quickly decide that you need different but equivalent wording:

SPANISH: ¿Y cómo le va hoy?

Or another phrase:

ENGLISH: It is raining [like] cats and dogs.

SPANISH: Está lloviendo a cántaros.

**PARAPHRASING.** Often one faces the dilemma of deciding whether to add a couple of words to make what is implicit in the SL language, because of its constructions, explicit in the TL, and therefore readily understandable to the listeners. This strategy to render an equivalent rendition is called explicitness or paraphrase, and is very typical. For example:

ENGLISH: To knock a place flat.

SPANISH: *Derrumbarlo todo hasta dejarlo aplanado* [Vázquez-Ayora 358].

The difference in the grammatical rules of two languages can also force the interpreter to say: "Interpreter speaking. Because of the difference between the two grammars, the witness meant 'yes' when she said 'no.'" The deposing attorney, for example, may simply accept this intervention by the interpreter or, for the sake of complete clarity in the transcript, change the wording of the question to avoid the grammatical problem and elicit a clear response as it is translated into English. An example of the confusing answer follows:

ENGLISH: You didn't know the speed limit for that stretch of U.S. 1, isn't it true?

SPANISH: *Sí [Yes]*.

**ADAPTATION.** There is also the adaptation technique, which indeed derives from significant cultural differences between groups:

The example cited by Nida and Rayburn (1982) of "God forgives" being translated into "God doesn't hang up jawbones" in New Guinea illustrates this technique. [...] When terms of a high cultural content are used, sometimes it is preferable not to translate them at all [Dueñas González et al. 312].

The interpreter may also choose to repeat the term used in the SL when an equivalent translation cannot be found.

**Compensation.** And then comes one of the most interesting and challenging situations. How do you render into another language cultural patterns that do not exist in the TL, such as the use of the common familiar forms of "you" in the Romance Languages, e.g., Spanish *tú* and *vosotros*? Since "thou" and "thou all" are archaic and do not make sense, use the strategy of compensation, or adding words that come close to an equivalent translation, in the example from Roseann Dueñas González and her coauthors Victoria Vásquez and Holly Mikkelson:

> This means taking an element of the SL message and conveying it in a different form or at a different level of communication. For example, if a witness is testifying in Spanish and uses the familiar second-person pronoun *tú* to emphasize informality, *Mi patron me dijo, "tú vete para allá," muy despectivamente, y eso me ofendió*, the interpreter can compensate for the lack of a familiar pronoun in English by saying, "My boss said to me, '**Hey you**, get over there,' very rudely, and that offended me" [314].

A caveat: although *tú* is usually used among friends and family, it was not used in a friendly or family way in the preceding quote.

**Amplification.** Very often, given cultural differences between nations, and technological developments in one area of the world that have to be described elsewhere, for instance, we at times cannot identify equivalent words or terms and need to find a way to interpret the utterance. The solution is usually the strategy of amplification, of using as many words as is necessary to convey an equivalent meaning:

English: They charged $2,000 for overhead.

Spanish: *Cobraron $2,000 por concepto de gastos generales* [Vázquez-Ayora 358].

## C. Equivalencies via Grammar or Linguistics

**Compression and its limitations.** Taylor observes, in the preparation of this section, that the opposite of amplification, or compression, comes into play where it takes fewer words to be able to provide a translation:

English: The committee has failed to act.

Spanish: *La comisión no actuó* (The committee did not act.) [Vázquez-Ayora 362].

In this instance, though, Taylor must disagree reluctantly with Vázquez-Ayora's shortened rendering, although on almost all other points he is very much on target. In compressing, the translation did not assign to the mentioned committee its due blame, but restricted the meaning to merely "not acting." Nor did the translation remain faithful to the original verb's traditionally labeled present perfect (*viz.*, "has failed"), but rendered it in what grammarians call the preterite ("failed"/*actuó*). A more faithful translation — which covers both failure to act and the required verbal aspect — would have been *La comisión ha dejado de actuar*. This translation is as long as the original, showing that compression for its own sake, for all its benefits of impact and economy of space, loses value when it abandons the nuances of the original text.

How would the translator and/or interpreter render in Spanish the following two more complex, compressed conversational phrases which are difficult for Latinos and others: "Long time, no see"; "J'eet jet?" The uncompressed version of the first might be the understandable *Hace tiempo que no nos vemos,* or *Tanto tiempo sin vernos.* The second compressed phrase is more puzzling — albeit more comical — and derives from sound-distorting Brooklynese, where the uncompressed version would be: "Have you eaten yet?" The closest translation to Spanish with a compression or contraction might be: *¿Comite ya?*

Vázquez-Ayora's *explication de texte* of his preceding example leads to the following commentary that should be and could be of prime interest to interpreters and translators, many of whom were/are trained in Spanish and other languages using traditional methodologies. First, look at a bit of background. The traditional methodologies of present-day Spanish grammar derived from the illustrious philosophers and academicians of the nineteenth century who influenced generations of teachers and students during the first half of the twentieth century. Of prime importance was the Venezuelan polymath Andrés Bello, not merely known as Simón Bolívar's tutor, but starting in 1829, when he was invited to Chile to revamp the educational system, as the author of a series of tomes on legal matters, education, metrics, and grammar.[11] Following in Bello's intellectual footsteps was the American professor, Marathon Montrose Ramsey, whose seminal contribution, *A Text-Book on Modern Spanish Grammar* (1894), affected U.S. textbook writers, teachers, and students for fifty years.[12]

Ramsey's ideas, especially on prepositions, contrastive analysis, verbs, time, and tense, were refuted in the sixties and seventies by studies on modern linguistics by various professors, notably William E. Bull and Robert P. Stockwell from UCLA, and Dwight L. Bolinger from Harvard.[13] Dr. Bull, using ample raw data from multiple sources, showed that Ramsey's and others' applications of time/tense to verbs, using terms like the present, past, and future, did not correspond to usage and reality. For Bull and other linguists the traditional present tense becomes the Moment of Speaking or Prime Axis of Orientation, the axis from which all events — past, present, and future — spring.

In keeping with Bull's presentation, the previously mentioned present perfect tense in Vázquez-Ayora's examples, is re-wired and oriented as a Retrospective Action completed at the Moment of Speaking, while the preterite becomes a Retrospective Action started or completed prior to the Moment of Speaking. In the new linguistics, "tense" is abandoned and replaced by the term "aspects of the verb," which emphasize the verbs' event-related, simultaneous or sequential "aspects," rather than their "time/tense" functions. "Time" no longer inheres to verbs, but belongs to the surrounding "adverbs of time." The new methodology, championed by Bull, Stockwell, Bolinger, and others, improved upon and replaced the concepts of Bello and Ramsey.

In a practical sense, while LEPs or ambassadors may know nothing of grammar and linguistics, they do know what happened to them and in what order the events took place, which lies at the heart of the Prime Axis of Orientation's Moment of Speaking — the "now," according to Bull and other applied linguists, from which they derived retrospective or projected events, which precede, are simultaneous, or are posterior. Bull and others discarded "tense," "present," "past," and "future." It is up to the interpreters and translators to learn to employ linguistics in their thinking and oral and written expressions because it impinges directly on how they must shape and sequence events heard or read for fidelity to the original language and culture.

## D. Nonverbal Equivalencies or Gestures

"Words, words, words," Hamlet's sardonic response to Polonius's question about what the Prince of Denmark is reading, are central to the issues concerning human beings, and especially key to interpreters and translators and their respective tasks and audiences. These professionals define themselves and their clients with their words. Actions, because they are not structured by a 26-letter alphabet, have less value, but nonetheless they are important. The great debate is whether "actions speak louder than words." "Sticks and stones may break my bones, but words cannot harm me," learned from childhood to ward off and shut out invective from parents and taunting from bullies, may soothe the savage beast within us temporarily, but as we grow older those old tapes from childhood may play back in our brain to cause psychic harm.

Nonverbal gestures — like smiles and laughs, smirks and scowls, a relieved face and a finger pointing to a pained limb — transmit their own messages, i.e., smiles indicate a judge's admiration; a victorious attorney pumps the air with his fist; a guilty victim's pained face and a troubled immigrant's sobs. The preceding form part of the kinetic collage from the human comedy that readers have seen played out in this book time after time. They are gestures — voluntary and involuntary, practiced and spontaneous — silent subsets of the verbal equivalencies that inform human brain activity instead of words.

According to the introduction by Adam Kendon, the editor of the academic journal *GESTURE*, the term and title refer to phenomena with "fuzzy boundaries." However "fuzzy," the term provides some insights into what interpreters encounter:

> Thus the movements of the body, especially the hands and arms, that are so often integrated with spoken expression, the use of manual and facial actions to convey something without speech, or the manual and facial actions of sign languages, are all recognized as a part of "gesture," broadly conceived, whereas expressions such as laughing and crying, blushing, and the like are less likely to be so considered, unless they are feigned or enacted.[14]

Gesture, as a source of ample, ongoing investigation, belongs to "different disciplines, including linguistics, anthropology, cognitive psychology, sociology, communication studies, and semiotics, as well as, more recently, informatics." Surely, it belongs, also, to interpretation as theater, elements that have a conjoined base in this book. American Sign Language does not play a significant role in this book, yet ASL plays a major role in language and interpretation because it codifies gesturing for the hearing and voice impaired. Indeed, ASL was the forerunner of the "relationship between language and thought in the gesturing and signing of the deaf and of savages" (Kendon 2).

**Culturally dictated gestures.** Gestures can be affirming or very disruptive and even insulting. Take the example of looking at another person, especially a person with authority, directly in the eye. In the dominant U.S. culture, that act could be taken as a sign of courage, defiance, or an admission of guilt. Individuals in non–Western, non–Anglo cultures, when facing a medical doctor, a professional, such as a judge or an attorney, would consider it prudent to not face them directly. It is a sign of challenge and disrespect, and should be avoided.

> It should never be assumed that gestures have the same meaning in two different cultures. In fact, certain gestures significantly differ in meaning from country to country. In Brazil, for example, the

Anglo-American "OK" sign, with forefinger and thumb touching and the other fingers extended, is considered obscene [De Jongh 58].

GESTURES/NONVERBAL EQUIVALENCIES AND THE COURT REPORTER. Gesturing, however important, does not hold validity with respect to the court reporter. No matter how eloquent, undecipherable, or violent the body action of a witness, the interpreter cannot convey that meaning to the court reporter for transcription. For the sake of recording testimony by the court reporter, the witness, the attorneys, and judges need to use words, not nods or shrugs, nor use gestures, nor make untranslatable utterances. When a witness, as part of a verbal response, points to something, for example, the left shoulder or sections of the room when estimating distances, the interpreter intervenes in the usual way and clarifies to the court by saying, "I believe the witness pointed to her left shoulder." With regard to a witness who lacks formal education and tries to describe the passing of time, the interpreter may indicate to a deposing attorney that educational and cultural factors may make the witness more aware of time elapsing than of the distance covered. For example, a person who was in an automobile accident may respond more readily to how long an action took place rather than to the distance the car moved from point A to point B before the accident. Naturally, this needs to be done off the record, during breaks, or after a deposition has ended, making it clear that the interpreter is not making the suggestion as an interpreter *per se,* but merely voicing an opinion based on experience.

INTERPRETER'S USE OF GESTURES. Is the interpreter to replicate gestures, which are a part of nonverbal communication? The interpreter is an actor, but to what extent does that require kinesics, histrionics, and theatrics? When trying to provide an equivalent register and tone, for example, should one attempt to replicate gestures of anger? This was discussed above. In the first place, the interpreter needs to "read" and understand gestures properly in their cultural context:

> For example, twirling the index finger around the ear, a gesture used in the United States by Anglophone Americans to mean "crazy," is used in the Netherlands to indicate someone is wanted on the phone [De Jongh 58–9].

Will the interpreter know that the use of the tip of the thumb pressed to the forefinger in a circle means OK in the U.S., but to a European or Latin American it may indicate an obscenity? What should the interpreter make of that?

Some interpreters, on the other hand, see some validity in facilitating the process through interpreting gestures. The interpreter's use of gestures to aid the person being questioned in the understanding of the questions, especially a person with limited vocabulary and cognitive skills development, so they say, can speed up and elucidate the questioning process. The use of the hands by the interpreter to help transfer the question to TL can help immeasurably if the words and actions refer to a specific physical action that both parties understand. For example, in conjunction with a question, using both hands to indicate beginning and ending points when asking how long an experience lasted, such as the distance from the beginning of a car movement until the point of collision, will often help the witness understand the point being asked.

Often in the course of a courtroom procedure unrecorded signals, rather than words, facilitate meaning. Interpreters make eye contact with the other players, signal with their eyes, raise an eyelid, shrug a shoulder, and blink to confirm, deny, question, elicit a pause, or show surprise. An interpreter's hand gestures or body language do not substitute for "Interpreter speaking" to object to something, but they do draw the attention of judges and attorneys. When practiced judiciously, they can be useful.

These nonverbal equivalencies require further study. One can feel sure that the increasing attention dedicated to gestures by, among many others, the Gesture Focus Group at Stony Brook University and by David McNeill in his book *Language and Gesture*, will lead to beneficial results for the field of interpretation.[15]

# CHAPTER 13

# Settings and Procedures in Legal and Social Venues

## A. Existential Aspects of Interpretation

"Existential" in this case does not refer to the philosophical movements guided by Jean-Paul Sartre and André Gide in France after World War II, but to the more prosaic dictionary definitions regarding existing in time and space. Interpretation takes place within circumscribed times and places, with specific and differing protagonists — which will be discussed in great detail in this chapter — but not to the exclusion of intangible behavioral drives, linguistic singularities, and cultural ramifications.

## B. Factors That Affect the Settings

As a preamble to the settings, it might be appropriate to look at the external, environmental factors that affect the processes. Although the following passage from Bruce Anderson refers to the conference interpretation mode, it can readily apply to the various modes discussed fully in this chapter: "[W]e refer to such things as whether or not the interpreter is physically isolated from those from and to whom he is interpreting, the noise level, and the like."[1]

Instead of launching directly into the settings, interpreters and translators may benefit from a preparatory rhetorical Q&A approach regarding the settings and one's tolerance and coping abilities for inconveniences that beset most freelance interpreters and translators. Review the following nine exogenous factors and their questions. The responses can show a person's great flexibility or the limits of patience to uncomfortable venues. Choose an answer from among the four to determine a reaction to the process and outcome:

a. NONE, *or*
b. MINIMUM, *or*
c. MAXIMUM, *or*
d. APPEARANCE OF AFFECTING THE PROCESS AND OUTCOME

1. Does a small, cramped space with inadequate ventilation or air conditioning have an impact on the interpreter, on others, and on their decisions?
2. Does a comfortable place have an impact on all concerned and their decisions?

3. Would the availability of water and/or coffee and how much (freely or only upon request), or who gets to drink (nobody, somebody, or everybody) affect an interpreter?
4. Are fatigue factors relevant to you, inasmuch as some interpretation events are lengthy without a break, or one is available upon request?
5. Can hostile or indifferent emotional attitudes of judges, attorneys, and court reporters to the interpreter and to each other affect the event?
6. Does negative cultural stereotyping on the part of doctors and attorneys to LEPs influence interpreting and decision-making?
7. Most times, court reporters remain semi-visible, inaudible, and inscrutable. Infrequently they break their stony silence by interrupting with loud and abrupt questions like: "What was that? What did she say?" Does their silence or loud questionings have an effect?
8. Would you be affected by the pseudo-interpreters of foreign languages in court or doctors' offices (attorneys, nurses) who inject their limited knowledge, thus adding to the confusion and frustration of the client or patient?
9. And how does a well-educated, nicely dressed, and composed interpreter conduct himself/herself with an often undereducated, poorly dressed, and agitated LEP, the center of the interpretation act?

Such are some of the external questions and components of various settings that affect the interpretation event, for better or worse. They fall beyond the reach and control of the interpreter, who, nevertheless, must cope with some or all of them. The reader is cordially invited to test his flexibility against some of these difficult external factors to determine coping factors. Apply the four standards given at the beginning of this exercise.

MULTIPLE AND VARIED SETTINGS. Interpretation services occur in numerous places, some of which will surprise even the most astute professional. This chapter lists and describes the most common sites and mentions a few of the more uncommon ones. The interpreter just starting out will benefit greatly from these examples and can acquire basic, practical information on how to serve varying constituencies. Notice how the requirements can differ from setting to setting. Coauthor Sibirsky has prepared this unique platform that describes interpretation settings that transcend lawyers' offices and courtrooms, the sites that frequently appear in most other books in this genre.

Once familiarized with the varied settings, preparation will be much easier and surprises will be fewer and less severe. This preparation also includes mastery of the appropriate vocabulary, awareness of the actors involved, and adaptation to each setting. Good communication skills require any interpreter to question the actors in advance on how best to conduct the service; the answers to that question will obviate being told derisively that the interpreter "should know" or "should have known" how to perform his business.

## C. Classification of the Settings

To organize the reader for the settings, note the classification of the various interpretation settings and the three modes primarily used in them: Consecutive or **CI**, Simultaneous or **SI**, and Sight Translation or **ST**. The typical procedures and whether the interpretation needs to be faithfully rendered or interpreted can be summarized as Faithfully Rendered/Interpreted (**FR/FI**), a Summary (**SummI**), or a Paraphrase (**ParI/PI**). The latter depends on the role that is envisioned for the interpreter. Bear in mind that living subjects interact within inert settings.

A reminder: It is impossible to illustrate all the settings. Three specific kinds of court cases and depositions defy classification: (1) one that involves representation rights of an American business granted to an individual in another country; (2) a deposition that deals with a traffic accident and injuries; (3) falls that resulted in injuries whether in a parking lot or inside a supermarket.

The table that follows reproduces the codes for the three modes, their two types within modes, and two equivalency levels. Below that sits a second table that lists the basic framework of each setting.

## Codes, Acronyms, and Abbreviations

**Three Modes:** Consecutive (CI); Simultaneous (SI); Sight Translation (ST)
**Two Types within Modes:** Conference (CONF); Whispered (WhispI)
**Two Equivalency Levels:** Faithfully Rendered/Interpreted (FR/FI);
Summary (SummI)/Paraphrase (ParI or PI)

## Framework for Each Setting

1. Setting
2. Physical arrangement
3. Participants
4. Placement of participants
5. Procedures
6. Mode
7. Observations

**CHARACTERISTICS OF THE SETTINGS.** The settings are classified alphabetically, below, into **Nine Subject Areas** and **38 Interpretation Settings** according to their most salient characteristics. One can imagine many more settings than these. Readers can utilize the framework to facilitate proceeding to the settings most relevant to their own situations.

## Directory of Subject Areas and Settings

| Nine Subject Areas | 38 Interpretation Settings |
|---|---|
| A. Agency Investigations | 1–2 |
| B. Education Matters | 3–5 |
| C. Health Issues | 6–11 |
| D. Home Visits | 12–14 |
| E. Juvenile Cases | 15–17 |
| F. Legal Actions | 18–30 |
| G. Mediations | 31 |
| H. Meetings | 32–36 |
| I. Telephone Conferences | 37–38 |

## (A) Agency Investigations

**[1.] AGENCY INVESTIGATION—TYPE OF HEARING**

1. *Setting:* **Commission on Human Rights and Opportunities (CHRO)**
2. *Physical arrangement:* People gather in a conference room.

3. *Participants*: A CHRO investigator, claimants, representatives of accused company, attorney for the latter, and the interpreter.
4. *Placement of participants*: Around a table, with the interpreter next to the limited-English-proficient claimant and/or witness.
5. *Procedures*: A CHRO investigator facilitates the meeting and asks all the questions. Everybody else must ask their questions through the CHRO investigator. Interruptions are allowed at times. After all the evidence is in, the investigator attempts to mediate an agreement between the parties by meeting with them separately and together and, if this proves futile, announces that a decision will be mailed to all the parties.
6. *Mode*: CI–FI, and SI–WhispI when the LEP person is only listening to what others are saying to each other.
7. *Observations*: Advance notice is given if the session is to be lengthy. The interpreter will probably need to explain how his services could be used to advantage and the appropriate "rules of the game."

## [2.] AGENCY INVESTIGATION—TYPE OF HEARING

1. *Setting*: **National Labor Relations Board**
2. *Physical arrangement*: A courtroom scenario that includes a bench for the judge, a stand for the witness, and desks and chairs for the attorneys.
3. *Participants*: As in a courtroom, an (administrative) judge, reporter, claimant, attorneys for both sides, witnesses, security, and the interpreter.
4. *Placement of participants*: The judge's bench is front and center; to the side are the witness stand and jury boxes. Facing the bench are two separate tables for the opposing council, the plaintiff or prosecutor, and the accused along with other personnel. Up front sit the court reporter, a clerk, marshals, and other needed ancillary staff. In the rear sit observers, witnesses, members of media, and the interpreter who waits to be called.
5. *Procedures*: Same as in a courtroom.
6. *Mode*: CI–FI.
7. *Observations*: The procedure is analogous to that of the courtroom. The judge who knows the interpreter and respects the quality of his work may ask him to direct words to the witness. Although flattering, this procedure goes against protocol. It is best to obey the judge instead of advising him to make the statement directly, which will be interpreted.

## (B) Education Matters

## [3.] EDUCATION—PARENT/TEACHER MEETINGS

1. *Setting*: **Parent / Teacher Meetings**
2. *Physical arrangement*: Classroom-type arrangement.
3. *Participants*: Groups of parents and individual teachers.
4. *Placement of participants*: Informally standing or sitting in a classroom
5. *Procedures*: The interpreter and the LEP parent(s) go from classroom to classroom as per a programmed schedule, or the interpreter is called upon as needed.
6. *Mode*: SI or CI–FI
7. *Observations*: The interpreter may need to ask the teacher to speak in parts to permit the interpretation, or may have to explain that proper placement of participants is needed to provide SI without auditory interference with the teacher and other parents.

## [4.] EDUCATION—PUPIL PLACEMENT TEAM (PPT) MEETINGS

1. *Setting*: **PPT Meetings**
2. *Physical arrangement*: A conference room.

3. *Participants*: Teachers, counselors, evaluators, and parent(s).
4. *Placement of participants*: Around a table.
5. *Procedures*: An update on the child's progress and the results of any evaluations are provided as well as teacher/counselor/evaluator's recommendations. During the ensuing discussion, an Individualized Educational Plan (IEP) is developed, modified, or created provisionally for the following school year. The IEP is developed or modified if the child is a late transfer.
6. *Mode*: CI and SI–FI.
7. *Observations*: The session is best served if the interpreter reviews the "rules of the game" with participants to avoid a situation in which the parent will only be listening at times and will require SI.

## [5.] EDUCATION—SPEECH AND LANGUAGE EVALUATION

1. *Setting*: **Speech and Language Evaluation**
2. *Physical arrangement*: A speech pathology room for the assessment of children.
3. *Participants*: Speech and Language Evaluator, the child, and the interpreter.
4. *Placement of participants*: Usually the Evaluator and the child sit facing each other, while the interpreter sits next to the child.
5. *Procedures*: The specialist uses, typically, a standardized test and illustrations.
6. *Mode*: CI–FI. After the interpreter discusses the test with the specialist, it may be necessary to change the register to accommodate cultural differences and to adapt to a child's register.
7. *Observations*: The interpreter needs to appear empathetic, someone the child will accept positively. The cultural tidbits that the specialist may ask for are given off the record.

## (C) Health Issues

## [6.] HEALTH—BLOOD DRIVES

1. *Setting*: **Red Cross Blood Drives**
2. *Physical arrangement*: Red Cross office or other facility with a large room.
3. *Participants*: Red Cross staff and volunteers
4. *Placement of participants*: In different areas: Waiting area, information and form-filling area, and blood-giving area.
5. *Procedures*: Red Cross staff prepares the donors for their contributions.
6. *Mode*: CI–FI and at times informal presentation of information, such as directions to the waiting area.
7. *Observations*: These meetings can last several hours; the interpreter waits to be called and may not be needed at the blood-giving stage.

## [7.] HEALTH—HOME THERAPY

1. *Setting*: **Home Therapy**
2. *Physical arrangement*: In a home; depends on the therapy and the accommodations that can be made.
3. *Participants*: Therapist, child, parent(s) or grandparent(s), perhaps another relative or relatives, interpreter.
4. *Placement of participants*: Same as physical arrangement (No. 2 preceding).
5. *Procedures*: Therapy takes place. The interpreter attends to the adults and, if needed, to the child/youth.
6. *Mode*: CI–FI.
7. *Observations*: To facilitate the therapy, the settings can be quite informal to gain the sympathy of the child/youth and the adults. The therapist may ask the interpreter to provide useful cultural data to best serve the relatives of the child/youth, with the proviso that the inter-

preter's comments are off the record. A personal side note: Once a week for several months, interpreter Sibirsky assisted a vision therapist attending to a legally blind three-year-old, which resulted in improvements.

## [8.] HEALTH—MEDICAL DOCTOR

1. *Setting*: **Doctor's Office**
2. *Physical arrangement*: Waiting room, registration window, examination room, X-ray room, and other offices.
3. *Participants*: Patient, doctor, medical office staff, and interpreter; perhaps an insurance company nurse attends who processes claims for the insurer.
4. *Placement of participants*: Everything depends on the nature of the examination and the equipment to be used. The doctor sits or stands; the witness usually sits; the interpreter tries to find a convenient place—standing or sitting—from which to observe and be observed.
5. *Procedures*: When they ask the interpreter to begin, he relays the verbal exchange in the third person ("s/he says"). If formality prevails, and the interpreter acts as a "faithful echo" of the other participants, the latter may feel uncomfortable. Over time, they will probably adjust to the interpreter's style.
6. *Mode*: Consecutive.
7. *Observations*: Experience dictates that caution is the key word. The interpreter needs to perform professionally and to protect himself. The professional aspect may require arriving 15 minutes before the appointment time to anticipate that the patient will also arrive early and be ushered promptly into the examination room; early arrival avoids the uncomfortable situation of barging in during a medical examination. If, in the examination room, a female patient has to disrobe, the LEP and the male interpreter may suffer embarrassment; avoid this if possible for self-protection. Arriving early also permits translating verbally the basic information forms and the confidentiality statement, which the patient has to sign.

   The self-protection aspect also involves getting paid for the extra 15 minutes. This requires updating the start time (unless the total does not exceed the 2-hour minimum) and having the doctor or staff sign and verify the timesheet. Check whether the office will validate parking.

   If a medical insurance company or the Worker's Compensation Office requires the visitation, the interpreter will not usually have an advanced idea about the doctors involved or the procedures, and may not be able to prepare specialized vocabulary. The possibilities abound: A primary medicine doctor asks a series of questions; he may perform a painful physical exam, which may be disagreeable for the interpreter; he orders X-rays. An orthopedist may order physical therapy exercises. A chiropractor may order a vocational rehabilitation type of evaluation. For each of these, the interpreter requires special vocabulary.

## [9.] HEALTH—PHYSICAL EVALUATIONS

1. *Setting*: **Physical Rehabilitation Evaluation**
2. *Physical arrangement*: Takes place, very often, in a large, specially equipped therapy treatment room of a medical center associated with related medical specialists.
3. *Participants*: Therapist/evaluator, client, and the interpreter.
4. *Placement of participants*: Based on particular action requested by the evaluator of the client.
5. *Procedures*: The evaluator gives instructions and/or explains condition, status, and purpose of action.
6. *Mode*: The evaluator is usually not familiar with the interpretation services and simply wants the client to understand perfectly well what s/he or the client is saying. As usual, the preferable mode is CI–FI, and if the client says something that is not a response to a question or a request for comments or questions, the interpreter should say, "Interpreter speaking," and then state the client's SL comment in TL.

7. *Observations*: Most often, this is a Worker's Compensation or car insurance case. Once again, the interpreter who has rapport with the therapist can provide, if asked and extra-officially, a cultural perspective. It is possible that the patient may have severe disfigurement and pain as well as resulting depression, which can affect a sensitive interpreter.

## [10.] HEALTH—PHYSICAL THERAPY

1. *Setting*: **Physical Therapy**
2. *Physical arrangement*: Large therapy room with specialized equipment within a medical center; one associated with a related medical specialist.
3. *Participants*: Therapist, client, and interpreter.
4. *Placement of participants*: This depends on the particular exercise or application.
5. *Procedures*: The therapist gives instructions and/or explains condition and status and purpose of application or exercise.
6. *Mode*: The therapist is usually not familiar with the interpretation services, but the goal is to simply get the client to understand perfectly well what is being said. CI–FI is appropriate. If the client says something that is not a response to a question or a request for comments or questions, the interpreter adds, "Interpreter speaking," and then states the client's SL comment in TL.
7. *Observations*: Most often, this is a Worker's Compensation or car insurance case. As in Setting 9, good rapport with the therapist permits, if asked, extra-official cultural tidbits. Again, severe disfigurement, pain, and depression may beset the patient and can affect the interpreter.

## [11.] HEALTH—PSYCHOLOGICAL OR PSYCHIATRIC EVALUATION

1. *Setting*: **Psychological or Psychiatric Evaluation**
2. *Physical arrangement*: A professional office.
3. *Participants*: Present are the psychologist or psychiatrist, the client, and the interpreter.
4. *Placement of participants*: The usual arrangement is that the professional sits behind a desk; the client and the interpreter sit next to each other facing the professional.
5. *Procedures*: The psychologist or psychiatrist explains the case to the interpreter and then asks the client to come in. The professional asks questions and the client responds.
6. *Mode*: CI–FI. It may be necessary to discuss many times with the professional the phrasing used by the client, so that both may agree on phrasing the question at a register closer to the client's level of education.
7. *Observations*: A medical insurance company or the courts ordinarily request the evaluation. If the client should be a felon (e.g., an accused rapist), and should the psychologist ask the interpreter for cultural comments, it would be prudent to refrain from giving them; indicate that the questions exceed the interpreter's role.

## (D) Home Visits

## [12.] HOME VISITS—INVESTIGATIONS

1. *Setting*: **Home Investigations**
2. *Physical arrangement*: Persons gather at the home of the person being investigated; at times they meet at the office of an investigator or an attorney.
3. *Participants*: Investigator, the person being investigated, possibly witnesses, and the interpreter.
4. *Placement of participants*: If the meeting takes place in a private home, participants can sit at a dining-room table or other informal setting. If in an attorney's office, participants sit around a table.

5. *Procedures*: The investigator conducts a taped interview, with the knowledge and permission of the person interviewed.
6. *Mode*: CI–FI.
7. *Observations*: In a meeting involving car accidents and alleged car thefts, the interpreter may be asked to translate the witness's answers to the investigator's questions. The witness reads them, takes the oath, and then signs the statement, which the investigator then notarizes. The following incident is rare, but possible: A zealous investigator may ask the interpreter to perform extra-legal or unethical activity — like repeating a client's confidential comments. Avoid this.

## [13.] HOME VISITS — STATE DEPARTMENT OF CHILDREN AND FAMILIES (DCF) HOME INVESTIGATIONS

1. *Setting*: **Home Investigation**
2. *Physical arrangement*: Participants gather in a house or an apartment in, most often, an impoverished urban setting.
3. *Participants*: DCF investigator, family member(s), typically a mother and a child (providing the child is not in school). Others in attendance could be children, relatives, neighbors, and/or friends.
4. *Placement of participants*: People sit around a living room or kitchen table. The investigator will probably want to see the child's or children's bedroom(s) and the bathroom.
5. *Procedures*: The investigator explains the purpose of the visit and asks a lot of questions. He then tells the parent(s) what the next step(s) will be, and the role of the parent(s).
6. *Mode*: The examiners are flexible and only want to get an answer to their questions and a feeling about the client. CI–FI is most appropriate in providing the register and tone that will be helpful to the examiner.
7. *Observations*: This investigation usually starts as the result of a referral or tip to the DCF Hotline. A referral would emanate from a school counselor, social worker, or a teacher; a tip would come from an anonymous caller. Most probably, the information is that an altercation or domestic violence took place in which a child suffered bruises.

   A cultural sidelight that is discussed in another chapter: Undereducated Latin Americans, in disciplining their children, are conditioned culturally to using physical punishment without fear of interference from the authorities. Well-educated people in finely furnished apartments in nice neighborhoods can also inflict child abuse. Whatever the source, in the United States, child abuse is an equal-opportunity crime and punishment.

   Two ways to get to the residence: The interpreter may meet the investigator at the DCF office, and both will ride in a state vehicle. This mode offers an opportunity to air the case. Or the interpreter travels by himself to a poor neighborhood where he finds, unsurprisingly, a bleak apartment devoid of furniture. At the residence of the person being investigated, he learns that the abused child lives with a grandparent who lacks formal schooling. Interpreting takes place under difficult conditions.

## [14.] HOME VISITS — SOCIAL WORKER

1. *Setting*: **State Department of Children and Families (DCF) — Home Visit**
2. *Physical arrangement*: A house or, usually, an apartment in (usually) an impoverished urban setting.
3. *Participants*: In addition to the interpreter, a DCF social worker, family member(s) (usually the mother), and the child, if not in school. Sometimes other children, relatives and neighbors and/or friends are present.
4. *Placement of participants*: People gather informally in a living room on couches and chairs, or in the kitchen around a table. The social worker will probably want to see the child or children's bedroom and the bathroom.

5. *Procedures*: The social worker, in accordance with the family's treatment plan, makes announced and/or unannounced home visits. They are scheduled weekly, biweekly, or monthly. The status of the case is reviewed as well as new developments, compliance with services and actions recommended, and how the children are behaving at home and at school.

6. *Mode*: The examiners are flexible and only want to get an answer to their questions and a feeling about the client and what is happening. CI–FI is the proper mode in providing the register and tone that will be most helpful to the examiner.

7. *Observations*: Because most of the detailed observations in Setting 13 apply here, refer to them to reduce redundancies. In summary, a tip or referral is made to the DCF Hotline from an anonymous caller or from a professional close to the minor who has noted bruises. In Connecticut, most times the cases involve undereducated parents from a Latin American country who discipline children physically for moral infractions, talking back, or taking drugs. DCF labels the situation as a child or youth "Uncared for," or victim of "Physical or Emotional Negligence."

   Grandparents often raise children abused or abandoned by parents. Since child abuse cuts across all social strata, the neighborhood and living quarters could be substandard or very comfortable.

   Travel arrangements are similar: Meet at a DCF office and travel together in a state car with an investigator or travel to the site alone.

## (E) Juvenile Cases

### [15.] JUVENILE CASES—RESIDENTIAL FACILITIES—CASE CONFERENCES

1. *Setting*: **Juvenile (Non-Legal) Facility: Residential — Case Conference**
2. *Physical arrangement*: Conference room of the administrator's office.
3. *Participants*: Attending are the child or youth's immediate family, including siblings; facility staff, among others, the cottage representative, teacher, psychologist, facility director, DCF case social worker, the therapist, and the interpreter. One usually interprets for the parent(s) of the youth; the youth is usually bilingual, but with low fluency in Spanish.
4. *Placement of participants*: The usual informal arrangement sometimes leaves the interpreter wondering where to sit, although the preferred spot is next to the child/youth's parent(s). In case many English-speaking relatives are present, out of courtesy the interpreter might ask where they would like him to sit.
5. *Procedures*: The official participants converse with the child's relatives at length and then call for the child or youth to join them.
6. *Mode*: Owing to general lack of familiarity by the participants of the modes and styles within the interpretation process, it would be advisable to discuss them. CI–FI will probably provide the best service possible to the relatives of the child/youth and to the professionals.
7. *Observations*: If the interpreter is willing, he can listen to confidential family matters. If asked to do so by the therapist, he can provide insights — always unofficially — to succeeding therapists. A good job will be helpful to all concerned and could also mean reflecting in the TL in a sympathetic, intelligent, and equivalent manner what was said in the SL.

### [16.] JUVENILE CASES—RESIDENTIAL FACILITIES

1. *Setting*: **Juvenile (Non Legal) Facility — Residential**
2. *Physical arrangement*: Cottages, administration building, school grounds. The buildings range from an old jail to a very new welcoming edifice. Security levels also vary, from minimum security — thus making escape a very real possibility — to medium security, making evasion more improbable.

3. *Participants*: Family therapy sessions with parent(s), child or youth, and sometimes other siblings. One usually interprets for the parent(s) of the youth; the latter is usually bilingual, with low fluency in Spanish.

4. *Placement of participants*: The facility determines whether one is in a conference room, one designed for therapy sessions, or the therapist's office. Experience indicates that most therapists do not have a preference about where the interpreter sits because they do not know how best to use interpreting services.

5. *Procedures*: The therapist engages in dialogue with the relatives of the child or youth for much of the session and then calls for the child or youth to join them.

6. *Mode*: If possible, the interpreter will benefit greatly from discussing with the therapist, in advance, the styles and modes of the process. CI–FI will provide the best service possible to the relatives of the child/youth and to the therapist.

7. *Observations*: Most of the observations in Setting 15 apply here also. The interpreter can play a significant role when and if the family and the child/youth feel that they can be open about very confidential and intimate personal and family matters to a stranger for a long period of time. As in Setting 15, the interpreter can assist a therapist, provided that the help is unofficial, requested, and confidential. A positive personal reflection: A good job of reflecting in the TL a sympathetic, intelligent, and reflective sensitivity to the family's or child's plight will create goodwill to all concerned.

### [17.] JUVENILE CASES—RESIDENTIAL FACILITIES—TEMPORARY RESIDENTIAL

1. *Setting*: **Juvenile (Non-Legal) Facility — Temporary Residential**
2. *Physical arrangement*: Large building, with two or more floors.
3. *Participants*: Staff, guards, and troubled youths from dysfunctional families.
4. *Placement of participants*: People meet in all areas: bedrooms, eating area, kitchen, living room, computer, electronic games, T.V.; minister on Sundays; trips in agency van; staff who serve as guards.
5. *Procedures*: Interpreter waits to be called.
6. *Mode*: CI–FI or SummI
7. *Observations*: In contrast with the possible shared confidences with families and children in Settings 15 and 16, here one must avoid personal engagement with youths who display varying symptoms of deteriorating mental health and/or antisocial behavior.

    Expect the staff to be gruff and unwelcoming. Troubled youths can leave this facility any time they please because the staff cannot restrict or confine them, which leads to many AWOL situations and high recidivism rates. In this very unsettling assignment, patience and caution by the interpreter are required; because of the long delays, reading material or a computer help pass the time.

## (F) Legal Actions

### [18.] LEGAL—ATTORNEY AND INCARCERATED CLIENT INTERVIEW

1. *Setting*: **Correctional Center**
2. *Physical arrangement*: An enclosed, small cubicle, just enough for the attorney and the interpreter to sit in, with a thick glass partition separating them from the prisoner.
3. *Participants*: Attorney, prisoner, and the interpreter.
4. *Placement of participants*: Same as "physical arrangement" (No. 2 preceding).
5. *Procedures*: Experience dictates that drugs are involved; the attorney carefully presents the options available to the accused and recommends that the inmate accept the prosecutor's offer.
6. *Mode*: CI–FI.

7. *Observations*: In a correctional facility security is high; caution is warranted. The interpreter will surrender all personal belongings, including a driver's license, coat, cell phone, and computer. Because guards enforce a time limit on the session, come to the point and be brief.

## [19.] LEGAL—COURTHOUSES

1. *Setting*: **Civil Court Cases**
2. *Physical arrangement*: Practically the same as in criminal courthouses but with fewer ancillary participants.
3. *Participants*: The same as in criminal courthouses but with fewer ancillary participants.
4. *Placement of participants*: The same as in criminal courthouses.
5. *Procedures*: The same as in criminal courthouses but with fewer ancillary participants.
6. *Mode*: CI and SI–FI.
7. *Observations*: In divorce cases, one may interpret for both parties or, if another professional has been engaged, for one party.

## [20.] LEGAL—COURTHOUSE

1. *Setting*: **Courthouses, Criminal — Courtroom**
2. *Physical arrangements*: The judge's bench is front and center; to the side are the witness stand and jury boxes. Facing the bench are two separate tables for the opposing council, the plaintiff or prosecutor, and the accused along with other personnel. Up front sit the court reporter, a clerk, marshals, and other needed ancillary staff. In the rear sit observers, witnesses, members of media, and the interpreter who waits to be called.
3. *Participants*: This is explained in "physical arrangements," preceding.
4. *Placement of participants*: Some additional comments are in order. The court reporter and the clerk sit below the judge, but next to and on either side of him. The marshals are situated where they can best provide protection as the circumstance dictates. One marshal usually stands to one side awaiting the judge's instructions. When interpreting, the interpreter stands (or sits) to one side of the testifying person, making sure the jury, if there is one, can see the testifying person clearly and completely.
5. *Procedures*: Complete details are contained elsewhere in this book.
6. *Mode*: CI and SI–FI are frequent, and sometimes ST is provided.
7. *Observations*: Other chapters of *Language into Language* devote special sections and chapters to this matter. Two useful reminders are in order, among many discussed in greater detail elsewhere. Does the judge permit the interpreters to read what they want, or does he limit them to reading material pertinent to the case or to reading, e.g., bilingual glossaries? Secondly, a judge confident of the interpreter's abilities may instruct him or her to relay a statement to the person testifying. The interpreter should carry this out, instead of telling the judge to use the first person. The instruction to the witness, to wit: "The judge has asked me to tell you the following, etc."

## [21.] LEGAL—COURTHOUSES

1. *Setting*: **Courthouses, Criminal — Non-Courtroom**
2. *Physical arrangement*: Among the innumerable variations: a lockup, holding tank, probation office, public defender's or prosecutor's office, traffic infraction room, bail office, courthouse hallway, fingerprinting room, or polygraph examination room. The precise settings could include parole, probation, bond and family relations offices, jails, halfway houses, and others.
3. *Participants*: Staff in (No. 2) preceding, alleged perpetrators and defendants found guilty, witnesses, relatives, attorneys, and ancillary staff, specialists, and interpreters.
4. *Placement of participants*: Varies greatly, making it impossible to describe precisely.

5. *Procedures*: Among the following five actions picked at random, all involve interpreters: a) At a bail hearing, the interpreter needs information to relay to the bailee; b) For a pre-sentencing report by a probation officer, the interpreter gathers personal data; c) For a polygraph exam, the interpreter needs special instructions; d) With regard to hundreds of traffic violators, the interpreter awaits the prosecutor's instructions; e) Public defenders or private attorneys stand in hallways where they ask the interpreter to inform a relative of a defendant of the happenings.
6. *Mode*: Insist on CI, occasionally SI and ST.
7. *Observations*: In a courthouse, the interpreter — who is an officer of the court — is under scrutiny. To continue meriting respect, interpreters should adhere to the "rules of the game" by displaying professionalism. Insist on the appropriate modes; do not exchange comments on cases with anybody; arrive on time and properly dressed; remain modest, i.e., "invisible." Stay alert to not miss a thing. Always expect the unexpected.

## [22.] LEGAL—DEPOSITIONS IN AN ATTORNEY'S OFFICE

1. *Setting*: **Depositions**
2. *Physical arrangement*: Persons gather at an attorney's office in the conference room or in his office (sometimes the attorney's residence). Comfort levels depend on the size of the room, the temperature, and availability of space for the interpreter to put his belongings.
3. *Participants*: Present, usually, are two or three attorneys (for the plaintiff and the defendant), a witness or two, court reporter, and the interpreter.
4. *Placement of participants*: Participants gather around a conference table. The court reporter, usually a female, sits at one end, and the interpreter or the witness to one side. The deposing attorney sits opposite the witness being deposed. The witness's attorney sits on the same side of the table as the witness. If other witnesses are present, they await their turn — if the attorneys allow them access. They sit to a side and participate except when being deposed.
5. *Procedures*: The court reporter, after administering the oath, first to the interpreter and then to the witness, may ask the interpreter to ascertain the spelling of the complete [especially foreign] name and address of the witness. The deposing attorney reviews the rules of the deposition and questions the witness. From this moment on, the action can take many twists and turns. One course of action occurs when the opposing attorney objects to a question asked, or to a line of questioning, or to the form of a question, which is followed by a polemic of varying duration. At this point, the deposing attorney may insist on the correctness of the action, in which case the opposing attorney states an objection for the record. Or it may be that the deposing attorney will rephrase the question.
6. *Mode*: Consecutive.
7. *Observations*: The interpreter should, as soon as possible, ask the court reporter which person she prefers at her side, the witness or the interpreter; this pays respect to the court reporter's prerogatives. It is not necessary to repeat here ample material found in another chapter regarding deposition hearings, with special reference to personal comforts, the oath, the "rules of the game," and the use of legalese.

## [23.] LEGAL—DEPOSITION—PREPARATION

1. *Setting*: **Pre-Deposition — Preparation**
2. *Physical arrangement*: Depositions take place in an attorney's office or conference room.
3. *Participants*: Present are the attorney, client, and the interpreter.
4. *Placement of participants*: An informal arrangement on chairs or around a table is suitable.
5. *Procedures*: The attorney instructs the interpreter on the procedures of the upcoming deposition by first describing the participants. The attorney proceeds to the three "hows": how it is done, how to behave, and how to answer and not answer questions. The interpreter helps

clarify the SL–TL process and, if pertinent, offers "how" advice similar to that of the attorney, or reinforces it with the attorney's approval.

6. *Mode*: CI–FI.
7. *Observations*: Explaining in advance the procedures will lead to a more relaxed and profitable session. The attorney and the client understand that during the deposition process the interpreter will be impartial and objective. During the deposition preparation, the interpreter can provide — if asked — important and ethical service beyond his official capacity.

## [24.] LEGAL — EXAMINER — CLAIMANT INTERVIEW

1. *Setting*: **Social Security Administration — Examiner's Level**
2. *Physical arrangement*: Those affected gather in a regional office. The examiner borrows a small office or a cubicle with just a desk and space for two or three chairs.
3. *Participants*: Examiner, interpreter, and claimant or claimant's parent (usually the mother). An aside: Most often, female parents appear who lack a formal education but need the services of an interpreter.
4. *Placement of participants*: They sit across from the desk the examiner is using.
5. *Procedures*: The examiner asks questions and writes the answers on an official questionnaire.
6. *Mode*: CI–FI provides the register and tone that will be most helpful to the examiner.
7. *Observations*: The examiners are flexible and practical. They prefer answers to direct questions to get a feeling about the examinee. These examinations are for persons who allege handicaps severe enough to meet Social Security guidelines for benefits for the handicapped, or need a periodic re-examination per regulations, or are appealing a decision rejecting their petition. An interpreter who develops good rapport with the examiner can provide, unofficially and when asked, useful cultural information.

## [25.] LEGAL — FORENSIC INTERVIEWS

1. *Setting*: **Forensic Interview**
2. *Physical arrangement*: The room has a two-way mirror, a small round table, and chairs. The setting might take place in a community agency with specialized services to women.
3. *Participants*: Forensic interviewer, a child between 5 and 14 years of age, other officials, and the interpreter.
4. *Placement of participants*: A round table permits visual communication and use of paper and crayons.
5. *Procedures*: Statutes mandate that DCF and police conduct joint investigations of sex abuse when a minor is the alleged victim. Video and sound taping is used, which becomes part of police evidence. During an interview, a forensic interviewer asks questions of a child or youth and gives that person explanations and instructions, or he may request that the child draw with the crayons certain actions or persons.
6. *Mode*: CI–FI
7. *Observations*: The case reviewers are the forensic interviewer, the policeman who filed a report, a psychologist, perhaps a school counselor, and the parent(s) of the child. The persons involved discuss strategies on how to interview the child based on age, behavior since the incident, and on the child's personality and educational performance. The interpreter cannot use a notepad during the interview; he receives oral instructions. The interpreter asks the interviewer "to speak in parts." If necessary, part of the interview is repeated. After the interview, the child/youth leaves the room while the officials review the case.

If the interpreter is flexible his role could be positive during and after the interview. After the interview, the officials review the case with the interpreter's input. A caveat: During this delicate session, only an interpreter who is knowledgeable about these matters should ask questions or take part, otherwise serious problems can ensue that nullify the interview. These interviews are extremely sensitive. This requires the interpreter to act in a manner that will convince the interviewee and the parent that the extremely confidential events under review can be discussed openly.

A personal and positive sidelight: Interpreter Sibirsky, who claims a lot of experience with the type of interaction involved, has often asked questions that elicit helpful and relaxed responses. During an interview, a 14-year-old girl understood the purpose of the questioning and answered in parts, which enabled him to go into TL with ease.

## [26.] Legal—Hearings

1. *Setting*: **Social Security Administration — Offices of Hearings and Appeals**
2. *Physical arrangement*: In a hearing room, a judge sits on a platform behind a podium. On either side of a rectangular table for the claimant sit the interpreter and the claimant's attorney or representative (if there is one). The facilitator, who records everything, sits to one side, usually to the left (facing the judge) and as close to the judge's stand as possible to be able to exchange documents with the jurists. Specialists may participate as well. If the hearing room is small, expect the facilitator to pass to the participants the few, shared microphones.
3. *Participants*: Present are the administrative judge, claimant, attorney or representative, facilitator, possibly a specialist at the request of the judge (orthopedist, psychologist, vocational rehabilitation, etc.), and the interpreter. If the claimant is a minor, the judge may or may not want the claimant present. The claimant can have relatives or friends present for emotional support, but they need to sit in back and remain silent. The relatives can also serve as witnesses, in which case they will need to remain in the waiting room until called.
4. *Placement of participants*: See number 2 above.
5. *Procedures*: Appeals/Claims for benefits for handicaps.
6. *Mode*: Consecutive is preferred; however, simultaneous if the judge wants the claimant to know what is being said when the claimant is not actively participating.
7. *Observations*: Administrative judges usually are not aware of how the professional role of the interpreter can help facilitate the proceedings. Many times these judges voice their preferences to the interpreter, which usually happens when objecting to what the interpreter has done. Judges have individual styles; some want everything interpreted to the claimant; most only want direct questions and answers interpreted. Judges, however, have a legal agenda and know what they are trying to ascertain. It is therefore important to let the witness answer directly the judge's questions on the ability of the claimant to speak English, and only translate the judge's questions into the TL when it is clear that the claimant will not answer the question directly. The judges are also very careful not to engage in any conversation about the case after the hearing is completed, either with the interpreter or anyone else present, even though both the judge and the interpreter might be interested in commenting on certain compellingly interesting events.

## [27.] Legal—Juvenile courts

1. *Setting*: **Juvenile Courts**
2. *Physical arrangement*: As described above, in Sections 20 and 21, regarding criminal courthouses.
3. *Participants*: Similar to criminal courthouses, but with fewer ancillary participants and more children/youth and attorneys for them.
4. *Placement of participants*: As described earlier (Sections 20, 21), in "Criminal courthouses."
5. *Procedures*: See Sections 20, 21, preceding, "Criminal courthouses."
6. *Mode*: CI and SI–FI. SI is expected for parent(s) and/or other LEP relatives.
7. *Observations*: Courtrooms can be very highly "ritualized." In this likelihood, the interpreter is expected to be knowledgeable of the protocols and procedures. He assumes a risk if he has no prior training in these matters or knowledge of the workings of a particular court. At

minimum, it would be wise, before the proceedings start, to ask pertinent personnel what to expect and when and how to treat the proceedings.

## [28.] LEGAL—PROBATE COURT—MENTAL HEALTH CASES

1. *Setting*: **Mental Health—Probate Court**
2. *Physical arrangement*: A large room adapted to serve as a conference room.
3. *Participants*: Involved are the probate judge, the judge's assistant, a patient accompanied by an attorney who represents the patient's interests, medical professionals, interpreter, and security personnel.
4. *Placement of participants*: Fifteen or more persons sit around a long, rectangular table. The probate judge sits at one end. The patient sits to a side and the interpreter is adjacent.
5. *Procedures*: In Connecticut, every year a judge reviews each case of a confined mental health patient. The probate judge decides whether to continue the confinement or to try another arrangement, such as a halfway house.
6. *Mode*: CI–FI if the patient is asked a question or to comment; SI–WhispI to enable the client to hear what is being said when the patient is not participating directly.
7. *Observations*: This can be one of those heart-wrenching experiences. Most of the patients will end up dying in the institution because they are incapable of fending for themselves and/or are dangerous to others. Very often, the patient does not respond or is incoherent. The responses usually show that the patient has a severe mental illness. Usually, a medical specialist/psychiatrist will give a report on the latest interview of the client and furnish a recommendation of the patient's placement for the following year. Then the other professionals will render their opinions; the patient's attorney will probably ask questions of the medical specialist/psychiatrist. The judge will render a decision on the patient's future placement.

   A chilling personal aside from Sibirsky: A soft-spoken interpreter can achieve responses by making the patient feel safe and/or more at ease. This backfired somewhat. Having calmed a woman to respond to my questions during interpretation, she convinced me that she had knifed to death her unfaithful husband in their bed. I found out later that her story was a figment of her deranged imagination.

## [29.] LEGAL—TYPE OF HEARING—MISBEHAVING ATTORNEY CASES

1. *Setting*: **Misfeasance by an Attorney**
2. *Physical arrangement*: Conference room in a law office.
3. *Participants*: Grouped together are the mediation/arbitration attorney, complainant, complainant's attorney, accused's attorney, and the interpreter.
4. *Placement of participants*: The presiding attorney sits at the head of the table.
5. *Procedures*: Similar to a courtroom or deposition, but much more informal, and with an air of familiarity among the attorneys present.
6. *Mode*: CI and SI–FI and probably some ST.
7. *Observations*: In this proceeding, a limited-English-speaking complainant accuses an attorney of unethical and/or inept services and demands reimbursement of funds, or not to have to pay for services.

## [30.] LEGAL—TYPE OF HEARING—WORKER'S COMPENSATION

1. *Setting*: **Workers' Compensation Board**
2. *Physical arrangement*: The design is similar to that of a courtroom: a bench for the judge, a stand for the witness, and desks and chairs for the attorneys.
3. *Participants*: As in a courtroom: an (administrative) judge, court reporter, attorneys for the parties, the claimant, and the interpreter.
4. *Placement of participants*: See preceding sections on the courtroom.
5. *Procedures*: Similar to those in a courtroom.

6. *Mode*: CI–FI.
7. *Observations*: Same as in the courtroom scenarios. In addition, if the judge respects the interpreter's quality, he may ask him to address the witness. This goes against the interpreter's protocols, but one is better off obeying instead of telling the judge that s/he should make the statement directly, which will be interpreted as disobedience to a judge's order.

## (G) Mediations

### [31.] MEDIATIONS

1. *Setting*: **Mediations**
2. *Physical arrangement*: Conference room.
3. *Participants*: The mediator meets with the parties in conflict and their legal representatives; included is the interpreter.
4. *Placement of participants*: All sit around a table. The interpreter sits next to the limited-English-proficient party.
5. *Procedures*: A mediator facilitates the meeting. Interruptions are allowed. After all the evidence is reviewed, the investigator will try to mediate an agreement between the parties by meeting separately and together with them.
6. *Mode*: CI–FI, and SI–WhispI when the LEP person is only listening to what others are saying to each other.
7. *Observations*: One can expect lengthy sessions. The interpreter should explain the best use of his skills and the appropriate "rules of the game." Any cultural clarifications by the interpreter should be deemed as personal and unofficial.

## (H) Meetings

### [32.] MEETINGS—ADMINISTRATIVE CASE REVIEWS (ACR)

1. *Setting*: **State Department of Children and Families (DCF)**
2. *Physical arrangement*: Conference room in a regional DCF office.
3. *Participants*: Usually the case social worker, the case social worker's supervisor, and the parent (usually the mother, but sometimes both parents). At times one service provider may also be present.
4. *Placement of participants*: All sit around a table. The interpreter who needs to interact with two persons should sit between them or across from them.
5. *Procedures*: The social worker supervisor runs the meeting and fills out a special form in which the supervisor records the discussion points of the Annual Plan Review, including changes participants may have recommended. The first protocol is to sight-translate the initial draft sections. A problem can arise if the DCF staff forgets to explain to the parent(s) that signing the form does not mean that they agree, partially or totally, with its contents. An attentive interpreter can serve the interests of both parties if he asks permission of the DCF staff to explain the form to the parents in their native language, not in his official capacity but on a personal basis. This personal procedure validates the parents' legal rights and has the added advantage of gaining their confidence, which can lead them to sign the form. At the conclusion, everybody present signs an official attendance form.
6. *Mode*: CI–FI and ST–FI.
7. *Observations*: The interpreter renders all the SLs and may have to remind participants of this several times. The parents, who usually lack a formal education, may have problems related to substance abuse, drugs, domestic violence, mental health and/or other issues. An inter-

preter can feel the sadness of the parents who are told that DCF will request the courts to abrogate their parental rights.

## [33.] MEETINGS—COMMUNITY MEETINGS

1. *Setting*: **Community Meetings — Formal**
2. Physical arrangement: A table or platform for panelists who face the many citizens who crowd the hall or auditorium.
3. *Participants*: One can expect community members and leaders and representatives of pertinent state and local agencies.
4. *Placement of participants*: Panelists and the public face each other.
5. *Procedures*: Plans, progress reports, guidelines or other documents, often in draft form, are distributed and explained orally; reactions are elicited.
6. *Mode*: CI or SI–FI.
7. *Observations*: The interpreter should ensure agreement in advance of the meeting or hearing on the mode to be used and that the speakers will be informed to speak in parts and of the reasons why. Some meetings are for the hearing-impaired and their LEP parents or other relatives. Other meetings focus on attracting volunteers and future foster parents.

## [34.] MEETINGS—COMMUNITY MEETINGS—INFORMATIONAL

1. *Setting*: **Community Meetings — Informational**
2. *Physical arrangement*: In a large hall, community residents gather to discuss issues.
3. *Participants*: Community members and leaders gather with representatives of pertinent state and local agencies.
4. *Placement of participants*: Presenters sit at a table or simply stand facing the public.
5. *Procedures*: Bulletins, pamphlets, and brochures are passed out to attendees on, for example, car safety seats.
6. *Mode*: CI or SI–FI.
7. *Observations*: The interpreter should ensure agreement in advance of the meeting or hearing on the mode to be used. He must inform the speakers to speak in parts and of the reasons for that. Some meetings are for the hearing impaired and LEP parents or other relatives.

## [35.] MEETINGS—CONFERENCE INTERPRETING

1. *Setting*: **Conference Interpreting**
2. *Physical arrangement*: The venue can be a university auditorium, hotel conference room, or boardroom adequate to accommodate the expected audience.
3. *Participants*: Presenters and an interested audience face each other. The interpreter may be at the main table, to one side, or in an interpretation booth.
4. *Placement of participants*: The presenters sit at a table on a platform in front of the audience.
5. *Procedures*: The interpreter and the LEP members of the audience may require special translating equipment.
6. *Mode*: SI–FI.
7. *Observations*: The goal is to convey information at workshops, lectures, training meetings, and telephone call conferences for technical assistance. The "rules of the game" should be explained to the audience so that everyone understands what is taking place. Facilitators should ask in advance in the LEP's language whether members of the audience require headphones or other devices.

## [36.] MEETINGS—PUBLIC HOUSING

1 . *Setting*: **Public Housing**
2. *Physical arrangement*: A Public Housing Project community meeting room serves as a forum.

3. *Participants*: Representatives of a financing/construction private company under contract with the federal government, representative of the landlord(s), tenants, and interpreter.
4. *Placement of participants*: Informal, with tenants facing officials.
5. *Procedures*: If the meeting is an initial one, a presentation on the purpose is expected; if a followup meeting, then an update is expected. In both types, a Q&A period usually takes place.
6. *Mode*: CI–FI and at times ST of information.
7. *Observations*: The usual topics are renovations, repairs, and temporary or permanent evacuations. The interpreter may be able to offer unofficial cultural tidbits, if asked, to the presenters.

## (I) Telephone Conferences

### [37.] TELEPHONE—CONFERENCE CALLS

1. *Setting*: **State Department of Children and Families (DCF)**
2. *Physical arrangement*: The DCF office communicates by phone with a parent or grandparent at home.
3. *Participants*: A DCF counselor or therapist, the parent or grandparent of the child/youth, and the interpreter link up.
4. *Placement of participants*: The interpreter is at a phone extension in a living room or kitchen. The parent or grandparent is at home. The child/youth is located in a custodial facility.
5. *Procedures*: The interpreter travels to a home, at the request of DCF, to interpret a phone conversation between a parent or grandparent and a therapist (or counselor). They communicate with a child or grandchild at a residential or correctional facility, mental health institution, or drug treatment center.
6. *Mode*: CI–FI, but the interpreter also places the call and tries to have the counselor or therapist located.
7. *Observations*: At the request of DCF, the interpreter drives directly to the LEP person's home, where the two parties place the call. Despite the confirmed place and time, in a high percentage of cases the counselor or therapist is not available. This leaves the parent or grandparent very disappointed.

### [38.] TELEPHONE—INTERNATIONAL BUSINESS CONFERENCE CALLS

1. *Setting*: **Negotiations**
2. *Physical arrangement*: A conference call takes place to a company abroad.
3. *Participants*: A three-way call takes place among an agent in the U.S., representatives of a company abroad, and the interpreter.
4. *Placement of participants*: The agent and the interpreter are at a desk talking with a representative abroad.
5. *Procedures*: The U.S. interpreter's first step is to identify himself to the representatives abroad who may have their own bilingual interpreter and set the agenda for the conversation.
6. *Mode*: CI, SummI and PI, and possibly ST. The modes and styles will vary according to conditions, i.e., summarize, paraphrase, or CI interpret. Be prepared to perform ST, for example, of a contract's clauses for approval or suggested changes by the party on the other line.
7. *Observations*: If the negotiations deal with, for example, an athlete's contract to play a sport for a foreign team, a lot of SummI and PI may take place. The difficulties are that the participants abroad may confer among themselves for a long time and change thoughts in midstream. To forestall delays, it helps to ask both sides to agree to the "rules of the game,"

explaining carefully that this will permit CI more readily and therefore make it easier for both parties.

In summary, this chapter on settings, their logistics, their subject matter, and their participants offer for the interpreter and translator an overview of what to expect and how to perform in multiple official and quasi-official surroundings with a variety of people, places, and circumstances.

## CHAPTER 14

# Playacting and Power Relationships in the Courtroom

## A. Interpreters as Actors

INTERPRETATION: A COMPLEX PROCESS. Many persons, actions, processes, and phenomena are involved in the complexity of interpretation. The cognitive, linguistic, and cultural dimensions — multivariate and intricate — become further complicated by singular interactions in the performance of interpreting. One receives a message, analyzes and understands it, and while doing so, in a flash (or so it appears), produces an equivalent version and delivers it verbally. Hardly has one uttered that, when one processes a new response in another language and again produces another seemingly simultaneous, or near simultaneous (or consecutive), equivalent rendition, of this response. All of this takes place in a particular setting with other corresponding participants. To put this process in a dynamic perspective, what comes to mind is the metaphor of the interpreter/intervener/actor in a courtroom/stage play, surrounded by other actors — i.e., judges, lawyers, court reporters — enacting and interpreting their corresponding roles.

INTERPRETATION AND ACTING. The interpretation act, in almost every setting in which it is carried out, is analogous to a play on a stage. Myriad activities take place, carried out by various protagonists/antagonists who may vary in number depending on the setting and the particular case, but who have an impact in differing degrees on the interpretation act. For that matter, while they implement the characteristic behaviors dictated by our present human makeup, all the actors anticipate and predict, use verbal and nonverbal communication, infer in their statements and are continuously "interpreting," in William M. O'Barr's view, what they hear and sense in the play of life and on the stage or setting in which circumstances have placed them:

> But this is not the only kind of interpretation that occurs in court. In testifying, witnesses interpret. They report recollections, and in doing so interpret the past. Lawyers interpret at critical points in the trial: Opening remarks and summations are interpretations — suggested interpretations lawyers hope will be accepted by the decision makers. The jury also interprets in rendering its verdict. It decides and announces publicly which version, or suggested interpretation, it accepts.[1]

The other actors assess the interpreter and judge him/her on the basis of present or previous experience, or of whether they think he/she will or will not benefit their self-interest in the case at hand. Owing to the critical role the interpreter plays in being capable of influencing decisions through excellent, adequate, or deficient interpretation, the other actors can subtly sense, adds Richard W. Brislin, the coercive power of the interpreter.[2] These points are the bases of this chapter, and later on the interpreter's power and activities shall receive greater scrutiny.

Before proceeding to the other protagonists, a key question comes up: If the interpretation act resembles a play with actors, is the interpreter a principal actor or a stand-in? Interpreter/author Alicia Edwards describes a courtroom — although any venue will do — as a stage in which a play ensues.[3] In contrast with the coauthors, Edwards disparages the idea that the interpreter forms part of the regular cast. This is very puzzling given her experience. Edwards twists and turns to make this assertion, but neither she nor anybody else familiar with the interpretation process can exclude interpreters as "actors" — a noun derived, in effect, from a fifteenth-century equivalent of "doers." Everybody concerned interacts, observes, participates and "does" or "plays" a part. The interpreter's role of intervener — "a third party in a legal proceeding," according to Webster's — among one or more other actors involves two languages and two cultures. This specially equipped professional has to pursue either a pre-learned script — from academic training or experience — very quickly or adapt to a rapidly unfolding unwritten script for which he has to determine the meaning of two languages with their cultures, gestures, nuances, and errors. In an instant, the interpreter/intervener has to decide whether or not to mimic the witness's hand signals for an estimated distance, time, or dimension and/or to act out the varying registers, tones, and styles of attorneys, witnesses, doctors, patients, and social workers. It is clear that this acting part — Edwards's view notwithstanding — is no less important, and sometimes more so, than that of the other cast members.

INTERPRETER'S INVISIBILITY IN DOUBT. It is illusory to demand that the interpreter be an invisible agent, as many trainers and administrators in the judicial system think. Throughout this book, the reader finds multiple reasons for interpreter intervention beyond simply rendering one language into another language. The analysis provided as well as the examples furnished attest to the fact that injustices occur when the interpreter is held — in the courts, at depositions, and in other settings — to a unitary task. By merely being present and offering verbal and nonverbal interpretation of what the LEP states, the interpreter may feel under the obligation to reproduce gestures and emotions, and this in a measured and professionally calibrated manner. To consider the interpreter invisible presents dangers to the court and to justice by underestimating this important role. In his official and legal capacity, he can, wittingly or unwittingly, falsify the rendition of comments to the LEP and, vice versa, that of the LEP's testimony to the court's actors. Invisibility would mitigate against the practice of this difficult art form.

INTERPRETER'S VISIBILITY. The interpreter's courtroom role is legally sanctioned, thus unavoidable, and plainly visible under professional conditions of ethics and accuracy. In the exercise of that visibility, asserts Brislin, the interpreter has the obligation to interrupt the event to intervene and to point out a misunderstanding (*Contributions*, 209). It is a prerogative to interrupt a proceeding and explain to attorneys, (administrative) judges, medical doctors, and others that, because of the difference in the grammars and cultures of Spanish and English, a "no" in one person can mean "yes" in another. The interpreter, who may realize better than anybody else that an LEP has neither the experience nor the vocabulary to understand a term like "impairment deterioration rate," can impart this to the authorities, and even determine whether the deposing attorney or medical doctor is trying to manipulate the witness's ignorance or simply does not understand the LEP individual's problem and, if concluding the latter, and can offer the appropriate explanation. These examples, of course, illustrate a powerful and helping role that supports visibility and goes against the notion by some of total and permanent invisibility. (Visibility and invisibility were first touched on in Chapter 11, "Modes of Interpretation and Translation.")

The interpreter who perceives a palpable, tangible injustice unnoticed by others — because it takes place in a foreign language via a foreign culture — is in a dilemma. If the Code of Ethics and some judges require one to be "invisible" and merely a "faithful echo," then the interpreter is in a double bind. At what point should or could an interpreter remain unobtrusive and still stay faithful to ethics? Of course, if asked about personal matters beyond one's professional role, an interpreter can step out of the official role and offer a personal opinion in as respectful a manner as possible. An interpreter — in a hallway, or eating with a judge or attorney, or when asked unofficially — can voice an opinion. In his unofficial capacity, the interpreter can earn credentials and bona fides, thus gaining the respect of the other pertinent actors. Notwithstanding the Code and certain members of the judiciary, the interpreter in his official capacity has to walk a thin line. But he does not operate in a vacuum. Interpretation requires a cast of players.

## B. Roles of the Other Players

OTHER ACTORS. Having described characteristic experiences of interpreters, the goal now is to single out significant accompanying actors in the drama played out on the stage of the various settings in which interpreting takes place and to provide information and suggest techniques and roles to those actors and to the interpreters who are characters in the same play. A range of witnesses could be considered actors, e.g., forensic experts, those skilled in English, the plaintiff, and the defendant. Also counted among the actors are claimants who have requested social security benefits because of a handicap; included is a fired worker lodging a complaint with the Commission on Human Rights and Opportunities (CHRO) who accuses the employer of discrimination based on, for example, the ousted employee's national origin. Other actors in the courtroom involve, obviously, an administrative judge, attorneys, the court reporter, and the security staff. The ensuing discussion will illustrate the parts they play and the actions they take with regard to the interpreter and his or her activities.

(ADMINISTRATIVE) JUDGES AND THE INTERPRETER. Judges, in the course of business, listen intently to the interpreter to attempt to ensure that every word in the official script is rendered and that no editing takes place. This attentiveness is more acute if the judge is not familiar with the interpreter. If the judge should develop a direct relationship with him or her, he can instruct that person to relate a message to the LEP witness. Although this goes against protocol, the interpreter cannot question a judge's prerogative, and, using discretion, must comply rather than asking the judge to speak directly to the witness. A judge, if he is so moved, can show pleasure at a professional translation and smile, or he can smirk at a less than adequate one. Nor are attorneys and witnesses immune from a judge's displeasure. If they, too, deviate from the legal script or display erroneous or clumsy behavior, they can be the target of a judge, who, in effect, controls all activity in the courtroom drama.

**JUDGES AND COURTROOM DECORUM.** Courtroom protocol requires the interpreter to stand up to answer or ask a question of a judge. One addresses the magistrate by saying, "Your Honor" or "Judge, if it (should) please the court," or most often, "Interpreter speaking." One never walks in front of the judge or stands between the attorney's table and the bench. This does not indicate belittlement because even attorneys have to ask permission to approach the judge, avoiding, except by invitation, that sacred zone. An interpreter cannot leave a courtroom until officially excused by the judge or the clerk, or until court has adjourned. It is important to find out in advance whether a judge objects to reading material unrelated to the legal profession or the case at hand.

Other interpreters, court marshals, and the court calendar can be good guides to proper decorum. The clerk of the court or marshal should be apprised of the interpreter's location; talk with an official before going to the bathroom. Courtesy as well as prudence dictate silencing the cell phone during official business; an irritated judge might impound the instrument should it ring during a proceeding. The court calendar holds a wealth of information, such as presiding judges, case names and numbers, code violations, and other data.

**ATTORNEY-INTERPRETER INTERACTION IN INFORMAL SETTINGS.** A good interpreter benefits the attorney and his client's and the LEP witness's testimony if he can interview early on both client and witness in their native language informally outside the courthouse. In a courtroom or sitting for a deposition, a higher and more inflexible set of rules and conduct prevails than in informal settings, making it even more imperative that the interpreter have a chance to prepare for the case by advance meetings with the attorneys.

A good interpreter, furthermore, in an informal setting would be more successful in gaining trust from the attorneys to permit explaining to them that it is unnecessary to speak to their clients using an overly simple or very slow level of English. In its place, the interpreter would suggest using an appropriate register that reflected the attorney's style and would be reassuringly understandable to the claimant. Attorneys, in this instance, are able to achieve a better understanding of their clients' description of their injuries and illnesses and their reactions to their adverse life circumstances.

**ATTORNEY-INTERPRETER COMMUNICATION LEVELS.** Prior to the start of a trial or deposition, the interpreter may question the attorneys how they prefer the voice level, high or low, with regard to the witness and the other actors. Experience dictates that most attorneys have not wanted a high voice level, fearful that it might confuse and unnerve the witness. The attorneys, not the interpreters, determine the level of communication with or education of a witness. Interpreters must try to be as clear as possible in their speech and, employing proper register, choose words in the TL at an equivalent level to those in the SL; that is, if the witnesses or patients are not well educated the TL must reflect that level of comprehension.

Attorneys and (administrative) judges often ask: "Do you understand or speak any English?" The interpreter should wait a reasonable amount of time to give the witness a chance to respond. The interpreter can engage in eye contact with the attorney or (administrative) judge to help determine if the witness has been allowed enough time to process the question and to indicate whether he or she understood it and will respond without waiting for the translation of the question. The interpreter should use this technique only when certain that the attorney or (administrative) judge prefers it.

It is up to the attorney in a deposition to solve problems, not the interpreter. Nor do the interpreter and the witness engage in conversation. Should the interpreter need to have the witness repeat a statement because of inaudibility, the interpreter always states to the attorney/deposer, "Interpreter speaking, I could not hear well what the witness said."

**ATTORNEYS' OBJECTIONS.** Wait for the attorneys' joint decision (or court's ruling) on an objection before translating the answer. If the objection is sustained, give no answer. If the objection is overruled, one may give the answer. If, because of prolonged argument during an objection, the interpreter does not remember either a question or an answer, the obligation is to ask to have it repeated or read from the record.

**ATTORNEYS' MISTAKES AND THE INTERPRETER'S ASSISTANCE.** At times, a questioner, usually an attorney at a deposition, will be bored and/or tired, and will ask questions absent-mindedly and inadvertently leave out of the question something important or give a wrong date. If the interpreter feels comfortable with all the participating attorneys and fairly comfortable with the particular attorney's reactions, the interpreter can say, "Interpreter speaking," and proceed to add a clarification that will alert the attorney to the oversight and thus cause him to rephrase the question properly. For example, when an attorney, half-asleep, albeit with open eyes, asks, "Do you have any questions?" and then forgets to complete the question, the interpreter, if familiar with the good nature of the attorney — having worked with him in the past — can interject with "Interpreter speaking. Do you mean 'of the accused'?" This impromptu interjection allows the attorney to get his bearings by saying, "Withdrawn! Let me rephrase."

**ATTORNEYS WHO REJECT INTERPRETERS.** Some attorneys prefer not to use interpreters, either because they think the witness will give a better impression answering in English or are doubtful that the interpretation services will be adequate. But an interpreter can signal, when appropriate, if he thinks the witness needs a part-time or full-time interpreter. The appropriate moment depends upon the setting. An eye signal to an administrative judge, or mediator, or hearing officer for whom the interpreter has provided services before and with whom there is excellent professional rapport and respect will let that person know whether the interpreter thinks the witness needs assistance. The interpreter, of course, does not make the decision. And in settings that are more flexible than courtrooms, where legislation requires an interpreter, the decision can be that the witness can hear questions and answer them in English and, when uncertain, can ask that they be interpreted. Interestingly enough, when this procedure is used, the witness, upon finding out that the interpreter is adequate and helpful, more often than not ends up using the service fully.

**INTERPRETERS EMPOWER ATTORNEYS.** Attorneys with foreign-speaking clients get a competitive edge at trial by hiring an interpreter, according to the expert opinion of Marilyn R. Frankenthaler.[4] She recommends to attorneys who lack bilingual and bicultural staff to take into consideration the importance of contracting personnel to advise a particular LEP client on cultural and linguistic factors that could be relevant at trial. Furthermore, the attorneys who do not have an interpreter available may not understand the client's responses and also fail, therefore, to follow up to gain more insight into the case's significant factors.

**MISUNDERSTANDINGS BETWEEN ATTORNEYS AND INTERPRETERS.** If an attorney has contested an interpreter's version, either because the attorney has misunderstood the interpretation or has twisted it to benefit his client, then the interpreter has the professional obligation to speak out. It takes courage and self-assurance to act properly when a reaction might incur scolding, intimidation, or retaliation. The interpreter says, "Interpreter speaking," and provides a professional, brief, and clear response. "Say it like it is" even when asked not to, advises Nancy Frishberg in a play on words.

Occasions may arise when comments are said for the record that an attorney may ask the interpreter not to reproduce. The interpreter is obligated by the interpreter's Code of Ethics to provide the information to the LEP. For the same reason, when an attorney objects before a judge or in a deposition, the interpreter is to render the entire exchange. Frishberg, an excellent author on interpreting for the hearing impaired, has put it very well:

> The classic dilemma for the interpreter has been what to do when one party in the interaction (especially one in authority) says, "Now don't interpret this [...]." This situation is one of the most awkward; the interpreter needs to communicate that everything heard and seen will be translated, and at the same time has an obligation to maintain the dignity of the communication setting. Even when the interpreter has begun the interaction with a brief introduction to how to proceed using an interpreter and what can be expected, the dilemma may still come up.[5]

(For additional perspectives, see below section C, "Varieties of Power," subsection "Incomplete rendering of message.")

LENGTH/COMPLEXITY OF ATTORNEYS' QUESTIONS. Not all attorneys' questions are short and readily understandable. But rules exist that apply in theory to the attorneys. They must be sure to not load the questions in ways that make them overly difficult for the interpreter to capture their sense and register. Cooperating attorneys can make their questions short and enunciate them at a speed that is not cumbersome for the interpreter. When an attorney asks an awkward or ambiguous question, the interpreter says, "Interpreter speaking," and indicates that the question needs rephrasing.

ATTORNEYS SEEK AN ALLY. Opposing attorneys are constantly involved in adversarial moves to gain the upper hand. In this game, some lawyers resort to the device of trying to win the support of the court-appointed neutral interpreter. They may employ, for example, very lengthy, repetitive, and banal-seeming questioning by the opposing attorney as an excuse to communicate with the interpreter through the use of body language, including the eyes, to indicate and/or seek sympathy. The interpreter must avoid this trap and not acknowledge either attorney's attempts at seduction. One obvious reason to avoid this is that any attention that favors one attorney over the other, however subtle or unintended, could be noticed by one attorney and impugned as bias towards the other attorney or the witness.

INTERRUPTING LONG TESTIMONY. This point was covered in Chapter 11, "Modes of Interpretation and Translation," as part of a discussion of the techniques and pitfalls of consecutive interpretation (CI) and simultaneous interpretation (SI). The present perspective repeats some of the previous material, but now underscores the obligations and powers of the interpreter vis-à-vis court officers and witnesses. Interpreters should make sure the attorneys have reviewed the rules of the interpretation act with the witnesses in advance of trials and depositions. A basic rule involves the need for the LEP person not to speak at length in consecutive interpretation (CI). Doing so makes it very difficult for the interpreter to be able to capture the entire SL utterance, including the register, and to be able to render fully and accurately the TL. Difficulties arise when an attorney begins a deposition before the interpreter can review the rules with the attorney. Should this happen, interrupt the attorney immediately and request that the "rules of the game" are (re)explained fully to the witness. The interpreter must make eye contact with the person in charge (judge in a court, or doctor in an exam), so that the latter will interrupt the witness or claimant to remind that person of the importance of brevity, and, if necessary, ask the attorney to repeat the question or the witness to reinitiate the response.

Some witnesses find it extremely difficult to comply with the request to slow down, pause, or speak in parts. The reasons can include personality, habits, sociocultural traits, uncontrollable nervousness, or mental health problems. The interpreter's obligation is to use a strategy that will achieve the needed result without disturbing testimony, or that will make this type of witness forget something or mistakenly omit it because of the interpreter's interruption. The interpreter can, by means of a friendly eye message and/or a hand gesture, get a witness to stop in order to allow the translation to proceed. From then on, the witness answers in parts without getting frustrated and does not shorten or forget sections of the intended response. The same friendly hand gesture can send a visual message to let the witness know that she or he can resume answering the questions. To set up the proper pattern, the interpreter should request the speaker to utter one or two sentences and then stop to enable the interpreter to translate. If the interpreter had established good rapport with the witness beforehand and continued it during the question-answer phase, the witness is bound to understand and comply with the interpreter's requests.

As a last resort, in those instances where fearful and nervous speakers lose their train of thought if interrupted, or who simply cannot speak in parts, or who are incoherent in their logic, the interpreter can switch from CI to simultaneous mode (SI). In extreme cases, one may need to ask the court for help. Interpreters, despite the challenges, must overcome the speakers' difficulties via personal coaxing, court assistance, using CI with enhanced memorization aids, or by switching to SI.

A WITNESS'S INTERJECTIONS. When a witness indicates a desire to ask a question, add to a response, or state something different, at an opportune moment the interpreter can say, "Interpreter speaking," and indicate that the witness wants to speak. The interpreter should first signal to the witness not to address the interpreter. Similarly, if during a proceeding the witness asks the interpreter about the action the witness should take, the interpreter says, "Interpreter speaking," and relays what the witness stated to the proper authority.

A WITNESS QUESTIONS THE INTERPRETER. If the witness requests information off the record, the interpreter should indicate that the answer would go beyond the scope of his responsibilities and indicate the type of office or professional that may provide an answer or help. The interpreter must make it clear that "office advice" is not permissible for ethical reasons and because the interpreter can make a serious mistake giving advice that pertains to a different specialized field.

AVOID FAVORITISM TO COURT PERSONNEL. Court personnel sometimes address the interpreter as "Mr. Interpreter" or "Madame Interpreter." These titles may seem simply to be part of court protocol or to be expressions of courtesy, but, under certain circumstances, they can also be viewed as trying to curry favor with the interpreter if the personnel are involved directly or tangentially with the testimony or witnesses. In addition, marshals and other court staff, who exercise considerable sway within their setting, can also exhibit attitudes of favoritism or passive power. The interpreter needs to understand and get used to this particular culture. It is not advisable to allow behavior from or to the minor players to lessen professional standards of impartiality by showing affection or by playing favorites.

COURT REPORTER OR HEARING MONITOR. As a professional courtesy and as a demonstration that the interpreter understands the role, importance, and special needs of a court reporter, he can ask that officer—immediately after the latter has completed setting up the equipment—where best to sit, because the court reporter or hearing monitor needs to hear and understand the interpreter clearly. The interpreter, working in partnership with, and for the sake of, the court reporter, would do well to spell out foreign names of persons, places, or objects. Because the court reporter usually administers the oath, be sure the oath is in keeping with the interpreter's faith. Ask the court reporter, before the deposition goes on record, whether she or he knows the words for the oath and provide assistance if necessary. The interpreter who does all of the above will gain a grateful, respectful, and powerful ally. Court reporters often complain about having worked with untrained interpreters who do not perform as recommended above and who consequently create problems with those officers' duties as guardians of the transcript. (For important comments on the transcript, go to the subsection that follows and to the one on page 181, "Avoid 'He says,' 'She says.'")

ENGLISH, THE COURT REPORTER, AND THE TRANSCRIPT. The court reporter, affirms Elena De Jongh, has the obligation of recording only the interpreted English-language version. Does it seem an irony or a diminishment of the claimants' voiced experiences and the interpreters' that the foreign language—which is the key, original testimony—has no standing in a deposition or courtroom?

> When interpreting in the consecutive mode, court interpreters must be able to "go into" two languages [....] It is critical to realize that *it is the interpreted version of the testimony and not the witness's original source language utterances which become part of the official court record.*[6]

It is a fact that however well the interpreter understands and speaks the foreign language, that language, understood by the interpreter and emitted by the witness or claimant, does not become part of the official record via a court reporter or stenographer. From another perspective, the laws protect the LEP by providing an interpreter, which ensures two-way communication and affords full disclosure, but the foreign language and its speaker, with their cultural and linguistic idiosyncrasies, are not transcribed, videotaped, or tape recorded. Only English, through the interpreter's perspective, provides the cultural and linguistic "bridge" to the official record. This is the major reason that the onus falls on the interpreter to do the best that his personality and training allow, in an ethical way, to represent both the linguistic and cultural reality of the witness or claimant.

From the perspective of a literary critic or anthropologist, the preceding matter might be focused in different terms. The foreign language that describes an event can be likened to a palimpsest over which English is recorded and viewed—i.e., translated and/or transliterated—by the bilingual interpreter. In this action, the court reporter plays a passive role. He/she copies the English version from the interpreter (notwithstanding that the direct events witnessed or participated in by a foreigner), employs native language and implants filtered experiences from a foreign culture. The court reporter's perception of the filtered version is recorded in English, right or wrong, understood or misunderstood.

## C. Varieties of Power

THE LIMITED POWER OF UNIQUENESS. Interpreters can be powerful actors, under the right circumstances *primus inter pares*, if for no other reason than that in the courtroom they are usually the only ones who are fluent in the second language, the language in which the other actors (judge, attorney, victim, claimant, defendant, plaintiff, witness) have a stake. It is rare that any other person present has the ability to monitor the accuracy and faithfulness of the testimony and interpretation. Notwithstanding this uniqueness, interpreters are not immune from scrutiny nor do they enjoy impunity, which was made very clear in Chapter 5, "Professional Standards," when discussing NAJIT's Code of Ethics.

LAWS AND VOWS OF SECRECY GRANT POWER. Beyond the language capability, the overwhelming power of the interpreter, especially in a legal setting, derives principally from the statutes that mandate a presence in situations where an individual of limited-English capacity merits full disclosure and protection of the laws. In business settings, the interpreter/translator is powerful because he is sworn to secrecy and paid to protect the vested interests of corporations. In political/military settings, the contracted or employed interpreter, who has gone through a vetting process, is entrusted to convey but never reveal the nuances of government officials who mediate between peace and armed conflict.

MANAGING POWER. The interpreter's power can be very helpful in settings in which flexibility prevails and when respect exists for the interpreter's knowledge, experience, and sincerity. The best example occurs when the interpreter is allowed to add questions, present opinions, and so on, with the agreement of all concerned that the interpreter is tendering a personal opinion. These settings can include examiners' meetings with claimants for social security benefits for the handicapped when an undereducated LEP claimant is asked for symptoms of illness, or in an interview of a four-year-old who alleges sexual abuse and the interpreter and the interviewer exchange ideas on the presentation and formulation of questions. The interpreter can employ cultural and linguistic knowledge and also act in a manner the child will accept because the interpreter is present, participates, and appears to the child to be a caring adult who is asking some questions.

ORGANIZE FOR POWER: DICTIONARIES, NOTE-TAKING. Indispensable before any proceeding starts, but especially an encounter with witnesses, lawyers, and judges, is a well-presented organizational framework. Organize in advance with a general and legal bilingual dictionary, bilingual glossaries, writing and recording instruments, computer, and notepads. Should the situation require verification of a term, the interpreter would excuse himself appropriately and indicate the need to consult a dictionary. Most present would agree that it is better to delay the proceeding for a short while to define or translate precisely terms like "past-due benefits," which can mean "accumulated," or the term "contingency fee."

Notepads, especially those with hard backs, are most useful for note-taking, especially during the consecutive mode. And speaking of taking notes, according to James Nolan and others, interpreters need a code system, a shorthand mnemonic device, to jot down reminders of facts, dates, titles, addresses, and lists of medications.[7] Besides facilitating recollecting ideas, the code system is indispensable should the interpreter's notebook go astray and fall into the wrong hands. A personal code protects the interpreter from an intrusive finder, who will never be able to decipher names, dates, proceedings, and results. But the main reason for taking notes is that the entire knowledge one can accumulate and note on the language and settings will enhance organization and effectiveness.

EMPOWERING THE CLIENT. An interpreter's role can begin quite early in a proceeding. For example, an attorney can ask for help to prepare a client (witness) for a deposition (deponent) or a trial (defendant) in a courthouse or in his office. A preparatory, unofficial meeting with a client whom the interpreter is helping to guide through a deposition, or with a client who is waiting for a hearing to commence, or to see a doctor, permits a familiarity with the client's sophistication. While it is best not to prejudge the ability of any witness, the odds are that a large number display a lack of formal schooling, which results in a very limited vocabulary and poorly developed cognitive skills.

In these cases, the interpreter can take the initiative and ask the LEP witness for the basic requirements of name, address, country of origin, family matters, and level of education. The preliminary conversation will elicit the accent, speech defects, idiolect, and speech style. This then forecloses the possibility of a problem of not understanding the witness's response because of an unusual accent during the deposition itself.

The familiarity also helps the parties to relax. An attorney who was interviewed for this book complimented Sibirsky with, "You give them a sense of comfort." An interpreter who displays a calm demeanor is often automatically reassuring to many claimants who face a stressful situation. On the other hand, beware the comfort level that can tend at times to lull the witnesses into blurting out information about which they were not asked, or go beyond "yes" or "no" answers, providing information that the attorney of the other party or the administrative judge can use against their claims.

But beyond the preliminary questions and answers, the conversation also prepares the client for the play on center stage, i.e., in a courthouse or in an administrative office where many elements are at risk. To this end, the interpreter counsels on the following:

- Explains the proceeding in the client's dominant language.
- Explains the importance of understanding and of asking for a repetition if one is not certain of the meaning of a question.
- Explains what is meant by being responsive to a question.
- Advises to speak in parts and not to answer in haste nor to worry about a doubt.
- Suggests how to combat nervousness.

LANGUAGE ABILITY INVITES CONFIDENCE. Clients, witnesses, defendants, and deponents born in Puerto Rico, South or Central America, or Mexico might harbor doubts that a U.S.-born interpreter would be capable of understanding Spanish. The suspicion — well-founded until dispelled — of native Spanish speakers is that an American interpreter cannot perform as a native speaker of Spanish and, therefore, cannot defend their interests. Reassurance, then, is vitally important. If an introductory meeting is possible, the interpreter can establish rapport with the aforesaid, assuring them of the language and cultural competence of the interpreter, thus gaining that person's confidence.

Professional interpreters usually handle high-frequency foreign words and phrases, but the question of regionalisms raises many questions among foreigners. No Spanish-speaking interpreter can manage or memorize the Spanish regionalisms, euphemisms, or slang of eighteen Caribbean and Central and South American countries. To ameliorate the problem, at the introductory conversation, a wise interpreter learns about the client's regionalisms. This will permit the interpreter to inform himself and the court or administrator of new or unusual regionalisms and help the interrogator to prepare for the need to rephrase questions or to find some other ways to get clarification.

EXPERT-WITNESS POWER AND IMPARTIALITY. The interpreter may be asked to serve as an expert witness for a law office or medical insurance company. The Code of Ethics prevails in these situations. This means that impartiality and strict adherence to what one can assert truthfully and factually should prevail no matter who is paying the bill. Under some conditions, the interpreter might be serving two masters. As one example, he might have to delineate between interpretation issues as distinct from language fluency matters. If he deals with language fluency, then he is no longer functioning as an interpreter, but as an academic or grammarian.

## D. Power Misplaced

MISINTERPRETING THE WITNESSES. Some examples of interpreter errors turn out adversely for witnesses. They exemplify the negative side of the interpreter's power. Sibirsky shares examples obtained from an excellent Vietnamese-English interpreter who preferred anonymity:

> Example 1: In Vietnamese, a tonal language, the same word can mean "my girl" or "my daughter." While the latter inflection carries an affectionate tone, the interpreter translated it as "my girl," against the meaning of the witness, resulting in a harmful outcome.

> Example 2: A Vietnamese witness who was highly educated, while the interpreter was not, used the wrong register. The witness carefully stated that he was expressing an opinion, not a certainty, but the interpreter missed that and the prosecutor took advantage of it:
>
> WITNESS: "I would like to tell you, as I see it, it is a cup."
>
> INTERPRETER: "It *is* a cup." [Emphasis by interpreter]
>
> PROSECUTOR: "How do you know it was a cup?"

> Example 3: An undereducated, but very moral, witness, was accused of sexual harassment because he hugged a child. When asked if he loved his daughter, the following ensued:
>
> WITNESS: "My culture showing affectionate to children very rare."
>
> INTERPRETER: "We don't show love to children."

The result: The witness who was interpreted as being callous and uncaring in a very sensitive situation was found guilty and went to jail.

Reference has been made to the influence that the tone of voice lends to the credibility of a witness before a jury. David Crystal focuses on the fact that the tone can leave the jury thinking that the witness is or is not credible, is or is not bright and discerning, and is or is not guilty.[8] The interpreter should be able — even though it is very challenging — to reproduce equivalently the witness's style. The interpreter — wittingly or unwittingly — possesses the power to misrepresent the witness's personality and thus become an agent of a mistaken decision.

A poor performance or misrepresentation by an interpreter may reduce the credibility of the witness or lead to a wrong decision. If the interpreter is not attentive to the avoidance of errors, the mistaken impression can be well-nigh unavoidable in all the protagonists who are viewing the interpretation event. While speed in interpreting is essential, that very speed may lead to overlooking and miscalculating, for example, the fear in an LEP person's tone or facial expression, which can be extremely important in a psychiatric exam or a hearing on a claim for handicap benefits.

CONUNDRUM OF A LYING WITNESS. It is impossible, during the interpreting process, to ascertain whether the witness or defendant is lying. But suppose that the interpreter translates a statement from a witness that he knows is a lie because of information gleaned from a prior assignment. The interpreter could be in a double bind. Should the testimony prove to be perjury, can the interpreter be accused of aiding or abetting false testimony? Sibirsky advises not acting on impulse or out of exaggerated ethics to report the situation. Interpret exactly what the witness says. The interpreter's area of responsibility does not include learning and determining the facts.

MEASURING AND REPORTING FEAR AND LYING. If an interpreter felt that a client displayed fear or was lying during a preliminary interview, during a deposition, or on the witness stand, how would he validate the intuition or feeling and to whom could he report the feelings? On the witness stand or during a deposition, intervention would not be plausible or ethical. During a preliminary talk, the interpreter could inquire about a witness's fears with the purpose of allaying them. If asked, and if it helps to shed light in a psychiatric exam, the interpreter may report the fear as a sensation but not as a medical certainty. During a preliminary session, an interpreter may subtly question a client's veracity. But sensing fear in an LEP is different from sensing a lie; the latter involves questions and testimony that only lawyers, judges, and juries can determine. The more important question remains, to wit, whether palpable or measurable by any means, does the interpreter's area of responsibility extend to reporting fear and lying?

Daniel Goleman offers two scientific solutions for determining fear and lying. Unfortunately, interpreters cannot apply either to the profession. But they are interesting for philosophical purposes. Regarding fear, Goleman reports that "the amygdala [in the brain] spots signs of fear in someone's face with remarkable speed, picking it up in a glimpse as quick as 33 milliseconds, and in some people even in a mere 17 milliseconds [...] so fast that the conscious mind remains oblivious to that perception."[9] With respect to lying, he indicates that the liar usually responds about two-tenths of a second later than a person being frank, because the liar has to compose words and facial gestures more carefully (Goleman 23–4). Goleman's explanations shed light on the physiology of fear and lying, but do not help an interpreter untrained in physiology in transmitting data to doctors or attorneys.

DISTORTING A WITNESS'S TESTIMONY. Interpreters involved with the five most used languages are less prone to distort a witness's testimony than those involved in obscure languages. The reason is that interpreters of esoteric languages, or those less prevalent in a state, are often insufficiently trained and are less likely to be challenged. This occurs less often now — nationally — than when the studies by Susan Berk-Seligson and her colleagues were done on what they called powerful *versus* powerless testimony and narrative as opposed to fragmented testimony. (For an interesting comment, see subsection "Politeness as powerlessness," Chapter 16, "Cultures and Languages in Play.") But Sibirsky has witnessed the types of distortions described below in Connecticut state courts:

> [C]ourt interpreters tend to lengthen witness testimony [...and] convert "fragmented" speech style into a more "narrative" style of speech [....] introduction of elements associated with yet another speech style, known as "powerless" speech, which stands in juxtaposition to a testimony style that is considered to be "powerful" [...,] the interpreter will be shown to create one sort of impression of the witness, while the witness in his native language conveys another.[10]

AVOID "HE SAYS," "SHE SAYS." This bears emphasis because it is one of the most common errors committed by interpreters. It is also easily remediated. The error and ensuing confusion arise when, at a trial or deposition, an interpreter interrupts to state something and prefaces the statement by referring to the witness as "He says [...]" or "She says [...]." The court reporter is forced to record "He says" or "She says." This can render an important part of the transcript useless, because when read, the indefinite antecedent will not be clear. One lawyer expressed that an interpreter repeatedly had forced the attorneys to interrupt the deposition because of a lack of knowledge of interpretation practices. The repeated use of "he says" or "she says" had made the transcript contentious and useless. As a result, the two parties were not able to reach agreement, causing them to go to trial. The solution is an easy one, but requires attention. Whenever an interpreter has to interrupt questioning to state something, the comment is prefaced by "Interpreter speaking," and followed by a specific mention of the person involved, such as "The witness said," or "Would the attorney please advise the witness to." Unless a rare setting calls for "he says" or "she says," avoid them in the courts, in depositions, and during quasi-judicial settings and hearings.

MISCALCULATING MEANING, REGISTER, AND TONE. There are as many ways to be clear as there are to be imprecise. Lack of precision could cover gross violations of meaning, such as substituting "three feet" for "three meters," to details such as switching "this" for "that." Again, a translation that does not reflect a register accurately will provide a distorted image of the SL questioner or of the LEP person, according to Alicia Edwards's excellent examples:

> Register has to do with the level of language, its degree of formality, elegance, or lack thereof [....] If a witness says *El señor venía hacia mí* [the gentleman was coming toward me], he did not say "the guy," in which case it would have been *el tipo*, or *el cara*. [...] Various registers might include the legal, the deliberately obscure, the academic, scientific, elegant, cultured, polite, low rent, vulgar, and deliberately offensive. The interpreter needs to be able to identify the position of a given word in the register or spectrum of language [Edwards 92–3].

There are times when interpreters err in not reflecting the tone and style of the witness or use a different tone of voice. On other occasions, the interpreter may not mask his negative emotions and may appear angry in addressing the witness, rendering the impression that the interpreter does not believe the witness.

SEEKING HELP FOR MISUNDERSTOOD SPEECH. Witnesses may be difficult to understand because of what they say or how they say it. To avoid serious distortions, the interpreter must not guess at the word, nor can he be reticent about having to seek help. The heavy accent of many LEP witnesses impedes interpreters from understanding names, places, and addresses. The proper reaction is, "Interpreter speaking. I was not able to decipher the term." Sometimes attorneys or administrative judges will assist, if they can, by pronouncing the difficult term correctly and spelling it if necessary for the record. The last recourse, though, when nobody else can provide the information, is for the interpreter to hand a notepad and pen to the witness and, using body language, inquire whether the witness can write it out. Spell out letter-by-letter what the witness wrote, even though misspelled. Offer, "Interpreter speaking," and hand the spelled word or words to the court reporter or monitor for transcription.

VOICE AND ACCENT IDENTIFICATION. An interpreter — however skillful and well traveled — would be making a gross error using such talents to identify the country, accent, and origin of recorded voices and conversations of suspected violators of the law. Edwards provides good advice on what to do in these cases, which is to indicate in a careful, professional way that interpreters are neither trained nor obligated to identify a voice or an accent from other countries:

Some attorneys or police may want you to listen to a tape and tell them whose voice is being heard. Because we were not there, it is best to indicate (male voice) $MV_1$, or $MV_2$, *etc.*, on the transcription and translation. Among voices, when one or more people converse, one may hold a belief as to which voice ($MV_1$, or $MV_2$) is speaking on a particular section of a tape. But who was really there we do not know. If anyone is to identify a voice, it is the case agent involved, not the interpreter.[16]

On the same basis, interpreters ought not to voice an official opinion on a witness's place of birth based on an accent. More than likely, witnesses have lived in several countries, which results in influences on their accent. As evidence, consider that persons from two neighboring countries sound alike (Argentineans and Uruguayans); or those raised in a border area may have acquired the accent of the neighboring country. Natives of the same country who live in different areas display different accents, e.g., those in the highlands of Bogotá, Colombia, speak differently from those in coastal Cali and Medellín. Oddly enough, coastal residents from different Latin American countries have commonalities in speech. Socioeconomic and educational disparities can affect the language of persons from the same city. Although interpreters may feel flattered to be sought out as experts in these matters, prudence dictates not serving as a specialist in accent identification. Any comment provided should be given as a personal, unofficial opinion.

AN OPPOSING INTERPRETER'S ERROR. If there are opposing attorneys, there are also rival interpreters. At an important deposition, one battery of attorneys may contract an interpreter to crosscheck the accuracy of the opponents' interpreter with the purpose of using its own person to undertake the interrogation. In the event that one interpreter believes that a rival has made an error of substance, the most discreet procedure is to ask for permission for everybody concerned to approach the bench to discuss the matter. Sibirsky provides personal and distasteful experience based on two separate incidents. In both instances, the opposing interpreters made substantial errors. However unpleasant it is to dispute a colleague's version, the overriding principle is allegiance to one's client and to the truth. Although this conduct is warranted and ethical, and serves justice, incidents that involve contravening another interpreter, rather than bringing satisfaction, leave a bitter taste.

BIASED STATEMENTS BY PROFESSIONALS. Disputing an interpreter is one thing; it is quite another to comment or protest when a high-level professional makes statements that seem erroneous or biased. This occurred with a doctor who harbored serious prejudices. He voiced a certain religious persuasion and displayed a negative attitude towards those who did not share his religious beliefs. He expressed disdain for LEPs because of their low economic status. This specialist was hired to review the medical files of claimants and to provide an analysis and recommendations to administrative judges. In keeping with his disdain, he considered LEPs unworthy or unqualified for medical benefits, but could not state this officially. Instead, he put this negativity into practice by rejecting LEPs' claims when presented with less than perfectly constructed medical documents. Perfect records and analyses may prove difficult, if not impossible, because overworked and constantly rotating doctors in clinics for the poor or emergency rooms with large caseloads are not able to write detailed charts or diagnoses. The proper procedure for a bona fide, impartial specialist would be to ask that a new evaluation be done that supplied the missing or doubtful data.

As if the preceding were not bad enough, this medical specialist called into question the English language proficiency of one claimant, the domain really of the interpreter. In this matter and others, his abrupt and irresponsible statements were completely unmerited. He pursued injustice in serving LEPs, in not respecting differences of opinion, in negating religions not his own, and in disparaging the reputations of overworked doctors. The interpreter refrained from complaining about this specialist to higher authority. The truth is that the interpreter cannot readily report a doctor's biases and quirks. Only the judges or attorneys, who learn of a professional's prejudices from other sources, can take appropriate action to inquire into this type of damaging activity.

**BIAS, OBJECTIVITY, AND SELF-SCRUTINY.** Carl H. Weaver emphasizes that the interpreter needs to look in the mirror for self-analysis to detect biases that may hamper objectivity. It is not an easy task to "know thyself." If the source of the bias can be found, the interpreter needs to develop strategies to overcome it. This is difficult, because not all biases can be resolved by analyzing one's formative experiences. Humans are also creatures of genetic codes and are not conscious of the DNA determinants for attitudes and biases:

> Everyone is biased — toward honesty or dishonesty, hard work or laziness [...] and everything else man ever has contact with. Every concept we have has an emotional component in it; that is, we see it as unpleasant or pleasant. You can, by introspecting a little, see that this is true of you too. You can also probably find some concepts that contain both like and dislike; in this case, we say you are ambivalent.[11]

(For more perspectives, see Chapter 16, "Cultures and Language in Play," subsection "Interpreter vis-à-vis the dominant language.")

**INCOMPLETE RENDERING OF MESSAGE.** The emphasis has been on interpreter attentiveness, concentration, and zero omissions. It is worthwhile emphasizing that very sharp attorneys are listening to the testimony. Some attorneys may capture key words in the SL or recognize cognates. They may point out that the interpreter has not provided a complete interpretation. The interpreter who omits part of a question or response can damage a case.

If a misunderstanding occurs in the source language, the error will undoubtedly come out incorrectly in the target language. Depending on the context, a word may have opposite meanings. An attorney says: "When we were here last week, we pled [...]"; the unfinished utterance may cause the interpreter to blurt out "pled guilty." The plea, surprisingly, is "innocent." The interpreter who guesses at the meaning of a word out of context does so at personal risk.

**IMPERMISSIBLE ADDITIONS/OMISSIONS.** In observance of the doctrine of the "faithful echo," it is worthwhile restating that an omission or addition by the interpreter will easily be taken to mean a distortion by the witness, with a corresponding loss of credibility to the witness. In keeping with this, the interpreter is not to add words to either the witness's or the questioner's utterances in order to make a question or answer clearer unless and until receiving permission to do so. Note the following two impermissible additions or clarifications:

ATTORNEY: Which month?

INTERPRETER: *¿Cuál mes, más o menos?* [Which month, more or less?]

Or:

WITNESS: *No.*

INTERPRETER: No, I can't remember.

The interpreter is trying to help, but is distorting the speaker's utterances and is modifying the register. An interesting occurrence for the interpreter takes place when the attorney at a deposition does not ask a question well, leaving out an important part. Instead of asking, "Are there any stairs to get to the apartment?" he asks instead, "Are there any stairs?" The interpreter must leave it to the opposing attorney to object because of the lack of sufficient specificity and not add what is obviously missing. The exception to adding words occurs when a prior understanding exists with an examiner or investigator. Or, preferably, one can ask the questioner if a part should be added.

Novice interpreters, especially, could benefit from the following illustrations of statements and questions that cannot be altered, especially so when the interpreter may not be sensitive to the hidden strategies used by interrogators to elicit information. Adding or editing can also misinterpret the personality and credibility of an LEP person, especially a person accused of violating the law. Berk-Seligson's comment below is sagacious, and her example illustrates how what seem to be minor distortions (additions or omissions) can have unintended negative effects:

> ATTORNEY: Of what country are you a citizen?
> INTERPRETER: ¿De qué país es usted ciudadano?
> WITNESS: México.
> INTERPRETER: *I am a citizen of* Mexico.

The impression that this conveys is one of perhaps pride and surely hypercorrectness. The witness did not give this ample answer, nor would the response be typical of an English speaker [Berk-Seligson, *Intersection* 1110–1].

There is no exaggerating the importance of precision in interpretation or translation. The following example, also from Berk-Seligson, illustrates the difference caused by seemingly unimportant additions that an inexperienced interpreter may insert thinking that greater precision is achieved. The illustration shows the difference between what is said in the SL and how this is made emphatic in the TL:

> Thus, if one were to answer in the affirmative the question, "Did he have a beard at that time?" one would most typically say, "Yes, he did." [...] For one to answer, "Yes, he did have a beard," is to place special emphasis on the fact that he did. [...] This kind of interpreter-induced lengthening results in an impression of greater certainty: the witness's interpreted testimony in English is far more sure-sounding than is his own Spanish testimony [Berk-Seligson, *Intersection* 1108–10].

**HESITATION WORDS, HEDGES, AND FILLERS.** Spanish, like English, often contains hesitation words, hedges, fillers, particles, and taglines. Before beginning a sentence, a Spanish speaker might use one of two common hesitation fillers: *bien* ("well," "so," "right"), and *éste* (a demonstrative pronoun meaning "this," but the equivalent in English of "um"). Neither one adds substance, but does buy the hesitant or inarticulate speaker time to express a full utterance. State them if they occur, but if not, the interpreter should control his knowledge of Spanish and not add *bien* or *éste* unless it forms part of the SL. Doing so could distort the image of the speaker.

Many Spanish speakers customarily employ a question as filler, i.e., they repeat a question before responding to it. Is the latter an unwarranted redundancy, or is it, as experience shows, a phenomenon caused by a nonconscious helpful desire to ensure that the interpreter understands the message, or to give the interpreter extra time to decipher the present and future SL and its equivalency in the TL? (Berk-Seligson 1111).

Interpreters may find that they are nonconsciously repeating certain words, such as "yes" and its synonyms (e.g., "of course"), after already having interpreted what the LEP person had said with the word "naturally." Avoid the interpretation technique of repeating what one has said because it may distort the picture of the speaker. If the LEP speakers do not complete a sentence, the interpreter needs to leave the phrase truncated.

It is even possible to consider the client's body language and gestures of frustration, such as arm waving or rubbing one's forehead, as message-bearing fillers or hesitations. The interpreter may be tempted to reproduce the physical communication, but is not required to do so. The other actors have been privy to these displays of frustration and may make of them what they want. The nonverbal gesture, already discussed in Chapter 12, may add visual theatricality and emphasis, but the court reporter cannot transcribe it in the record.

**WILLINGNESS TO ADMIT ERRORS.** The nature of the profession results in mistakes. When an attorney points out an interpreter's error, whether inadvertent or not, the interpreter should own up to it in a professional way, again with the proper preamble, and then admit, "The interpreter committed an error," or "The interpreter misspoke." However much mistakes cause embarrassment, the greater embarrassment comes from refusing to come to terms with them. The absolution and catharsis derive from saying, "Interpreter speaking," and confessing the error or the omission. In a courtroom, the other actors will know whether it is necessary to question a witness again. Since most of the interpreting process is nonconscious, the interpreter may become aware of the error or omission some time after the occurrence. In this case, the interpreter should wait for an opportune moment in which to bring up the matter and should not decide whether the error or correction is relevant. This is a question to be decided by judges and attorneys in a courtroom, and diplomats and military officers in their respective settings.

## E. The Power of Excellence and Modesty

Interpreters and translators are prone to misfortune because of elements within their control that cause damage, such as fatigue, distraction, lack of preparation and information, and indifference. On the other hand, court interpreters, especially, can be part of incidents that go awry from elements beyond their control, such as LEPs' cultural and linguistic difficulties, legal and judicial constraints, lawyers' overzealousness, and limitations placed on them by the Code of Ethics. The readers have glimpsed the preceding negatives and many more in the course of this and prior chapters.

The abiding power, nevertheless, of the courtroom interpreter consists of persevering and overcoming the alluded to negativities in their grasp. They can also blunt or attenuate the power of the elements that are seemingly beyond their control. These, too, have been referred to many times. For example, the judges and district attorneys rule the roost, but they can be persuaded to soften or alter their opinions by solid and temperate reasoning from interpreters at the proper time, place, and manner. Those who know the foreign language and culture can explain to them the cultural climate that may have given rise to misunderstandings, misdemeanors, and even felony charges.

But interpreters, as officers of the court, sworn to uphold the law and to abide by the Code of Ethics, can exert power and influence in subtle ways. Their shields are laws that permit them to operate in government and social agencies despite English-only laws; education, intelligence, discretion, and due diligence bolster their presence; they uphold impartiality, confidentiality, and the truth; and they protect LEPs from legal, bureaucratic, and medical obfuscation.

Their strong offensive weapons are their voices and the ability to transfer correct messages with precision and speed from a language unknown to the other actors in judicial, legal, and administrative settings. And in other venues, such as in business, diplomacy, and military, the process and outcome are the same. All the previously mentioned have to take the word of the impartial interpreter/translator.

The preceding are some defensive and offensive weapons. One could also mention a concealed weapon, modesty. To cap off a job well done, the other actors may congratulate the interpreter for an excellent performance. The satisfaction comes when the interpreter/translator has exceeded professional expectations and can, without false modesty, exclaim after a compliment, in whatever language is in play, "Just doing my job!"

# CHAPTER 15

# Implications of Bilingualism

## A. *Defining Bilinguals and Bilingualism*

BILINGUALS. It goes without saying that bilingualism and its corollary biculturalism — whether minimally acceptable, properly functional, or ideally total — are the *sine qua non* to the profession of the interpreter and translator. Who can deny, states Taylor in the preparation of this chapter, their importance? Who can deny also that it takes time, money, effort, opportunity, incentive, and organization to achieve a professional level of linguistic and cultural ability? If to be monolingual requires years of continual proximity to the language urgings and clarifications from family, friends, teachers, and peers — undergoing trials and errors to define sounds with clarity and to use syntax with logic — imagine the difficulties with learning a second or third language.

DEFINING BILINGUALISM. As with most things of an abstract nature, it is difficult to define bilingualism, and controversy prevails about what it takes to truly achieve it or approximate it. To begin with, the native language (A) and the second language (B) have to be at least close to their respective mother tongues in actual fluency to be able to achieve what is usually thought of as "true bilingualism." By mother tongue is meant the language acquired directly as a child at home and in one's surroundings. Persons who as a child move to a different environment have two mother tongues, either simultaneously or sequentially. One points easily to millions of children of immigrants all around the world who pick up a second language in the foreign country. Some researchers, like Christopher Thiery, believe that a learner of a second language can never equate the intimate familiarity afforded by the imprint of a native language:

> It is in the mother tongue that any speaker can detect a phrase that is wrong, even if it is apparently grammatically correct. It is in one's mother tongue that one can recognize garbled phrases over a faulty loud-speaker, merely by their outline, just like a face can be recognized by a glimpse even from an unusual angle. The adult second-language learner never achieves such an instructive, creative relationship with his second language, and the reason may be that his painstaking performance has not been built on the appropriate linguistic competence, but on cognitive structures established for another language, his mother tongue.[1]

Thiery's definition of bilingualism appears realistic and practical, especially given the impossibility of ascertaining through valid and reliable testing the mastery of facility in a language, of accurate and spontaneous use of its verbal and nonverbal components, including appropriate idioms and gestures. It is worthwhile to highlight his definition: "A true bilingual is someone who is taken to be one of themselves by the members of two different linguistic communities, at roughly the same social and cultural level" (147).

As author David Sacks observes, a narrow window of opportunity beckons for becoming bilingual, however imperfect, as a child. Sacks comments on learning a second language as a child: The "first year or two of life represents a golden chance to become bilingual, which [linguist Kenji Hakuta] terms a 'simultaneous bilingual.' [...] After about age two, if you learn a new language, you will probably fail to imitate perfectly those sounds you are not used to. The brain is by then shutting down that department. You will speak the new tongue probably in a foreign accent, however slight," termed a "sequential bilingual."[2]

**BILINGUALISM IS WIDESPREAD.** If that second-language advantage is not achieved at childhood, how, then, have people been speaking more than one language for centuries? There is no shortage of bilinguals. The 2005 U.S. Census reports that 35 million live in households where a language other than English is spoken. From another perspective, 12.5 percent of families speak at home a language other than English. Indeed, the linguist David Crystal claims that three-fourths of humanity speaks two or more languages and that no nation is entirely monolingual.

---

## BILINGUALISM SPREADS TO CATS

Once upon a time there was a house mouse in his hole. Being bored and hungry, he decided to take care of the problems by going out to get a snack. But wait, he thought, What about the cat that he sensed was meowing and sniffing about? Cautious but clever, the mouse put his ears to the hole to sense the enemy. All he could hear was "Grr, Bow Wow." Sure signs, he inferred, that a dog was out there, but not his enemy. "I could easily outmaneuver a dog," he boasted as he stuck out his head. But it wasn't a dog that pounced on the house mouse. Licking his whiskers, a very clever feline bragged, "I knew that someday learning another language would come in handy."[3]

---

**LANGUAGES AND CULTURES.** Mastering two languages does not automatically guarantee mastering the cultures. Furthermore, the cultural differences between countries with the same national language, as is the case in Spanish America, put an even greater burden of responsibility on the interpreter. Cultures encompass patterns of behavior and of envisioning the world and life that languages need to express. Although bilingualism automatically carries cultural manifestations — because a language is influenced by its surrounding culture — yet its effect on the bilingual person may be tenuous and usually extremely nonconscious, based on where and how the person was raised. A wide range of possibilities exists from being monocultural, to bicultural, to multicultural. For a more in-depth range of perspectives, see Chapter 16, "Cultures and Languages in Play."

**TYPOLOGIES OF BILINGUALS.** Researchers have found it useful to create typologies of bilinguals. Joshua Fishman, in *Bilingual Education: Current Perspectives*, distinguishes between **élite** bilinguals and **folk** bilinguals, the difference being that the former choose deliberately, through schooling and travel, to learn and perfect a second language, while the latter form part of immigrant groups forced to cope as children or as adults with the dominant language of their new, perhaps hostile, environment.[4]

The Stanford University linguist Kenji Hakuta uses his own system of typology. Hakuta, besides having described "simultaneous" and "sequential" bilinguals (mentioned above), proceeds to other classifications. "Balanced" bilinguals, he asserts, can claim relative competence in two languages, while those new to the second language and culture are classified as "semi-lingual." Other terms and euphemisms in use for the latter are limited-English-proficient (LEP), English-language learners (ELL), second-language learners (SLL), and potentially English-proficient (PEP).[5]

## B. Bilingual Interpreters and Translators

EXPLORING THE FOLK *VS.* THE ÉLITE BILINGUAL. The inquiry, for the purposes of this investigation, should be that the professional requirements for an interpreter and translator not equate with the casual conversational and letter-writing skills of a tourist, or of a bilingual or multilingual trained in a language from birth and/or learned in school. Consider the following four scenarios: An American schoolteacher, using high school French, converses in a Paris restaurant. A Texan from Laredo negotiates his groceries in Tex-Mex across the border in Nuevo Laredo, Mexico. A Dutch-speaking citizen is cross-trained in French and German, because since childhood he has been sensitized to invasion. A Swiss speaks out of necessity the four languages of his country (Italian, German, French, and Romansh). All these persons display to a lesser or greater degree bilingualism or familiarity with a second or third tongue. But would you want their representation in court, or judging treaty language at a meeting of foreign ministers, or for them to be your language and cultural adviser while selling multi-million-dollar oil equipment to Saudi Arabia, or the professional translating your manuscript into another language? The answer is that the casual or folk bilingual person, even speaking two languages from childhood, cannot equate with the élite bilingual, trained as interpreter or translator.

A further shade of distinction arises between the interpreter who spoke Spanish at home and the interpreter who learned English at home but mastered Spanish through advanced studies, travel, and diligence. All things being equal, which of the two would be a better interpreter? Consider the reasoning and life experience of coauthor Sibirsky on this matter. Born in Uruguay, where he practiced Yiddish at home, Spanish in school and on the streets, and some English in school, Sibirsky emigrated at fourteen to New York to begin a new life — without his family. Armed with elementary school notions of English, all of a sudden, he had to practice English on the street, at a job, and at Boys High School, Brooklyn. With diligence, he overcame language difficulties, excelled in his studies, and merited an NYU scholarship, from which he graduated to earn a master's and doctorate. By dint of hard work, he became a bilingual university instructor and, in his later years, a certified interpreter and translator. His own education and experience convinced him that the difference between a native speaker of a foreign language and one who mastered it as an adult or as a second language could be minimal and really lacking consequence. His nuanced and self-effacing opinion is that some of the U.S.-born interpreters who studied Spanish with passion and devotion, who mastered its grammatical rules, conventions, variations, and vocabulary could, in many cases, far surpass that of the vast majority of the native-born, Spanish-speaking interpreters without training. Sibirsky's strong opinion: "I would rather have the former interpret for me; there is less probability of mistakes!"

LANGUAGE STORAGE AND RECALL AND RECOGNITION MEMORY. Another important consideration is that the two languages used by a bilingual person live together and act and interact within the person; they do not function separately. This long-term storage of the native language permits a person, without thinking about it, to count to ten or a hundred in the native language after many years in the adopted country. This explains why an interpreter whose native language is Spanish will automatically use the TL of the speaker's SL even when the speaker uses the SL that is supposed to be the TL. This co-mingling of languages demonstrates long-term memory storage in our schemas and experiences, nonverbally, enabling the mechanical switching of languages. Danica Seleskovitch claims that "there is a constant two-way flow whereby mental impulses are converted into language and language is reduced to mental impulses."[6] It is fascinating to realize that thoughts are neither verbal nor laid out in our brain in words. One may learn words and phrases from index cards and facilitate learning them by alphabetical arrangements, like a dictionary or by theme, but they exist in the brain as neurons or electrical impulses and are called up for use by recognition and/or recall memory.

INTERPRETER VIS-À-VIS THE DOMINANT LANGUAGE. Particularities of dominance in one language over another — for example, in an interpreter — can mean that the interpreter will do better in the dominant language because of greater facility in speaking, thinking, and understanding, but may encounter difficulty expressing an equivalent utterance in the second language. And a secondary effect may be bias toward the witness with the same dominant language as the interpreter. The interpreter often finds herself or himself immersed in the job for several hours. This can cause stress and mental fatigue, which in turn may cause the switching to, or favoring of, the dominant language. The interpreter can forget key phrases, may take longer to analyze, find relevant long-term and short-term memory and interpret the utterance, and find it difficult to encode and decode, all owing to mental fatigue. Fatigue, in Stanislav Dornic's view, can also cause language interference, in which case the dominant language usually begins to hold sway.[7]

All those who speak two or more languages have had different levels of experience in the various areas of human knowledge, especially those in the technological fields. It is common for bilingual persons to use the language in which one has greater mastery in particular areas of knowledge. For that matter, it is rare to find bilingual persons who are "equally fluent" in two languages. To state that a person is "truly bilingual" engenders a hyperbole, an exaggeration, because no one can master all the specialized vocabulary in all the multiple fields of human knowledge in one language, let alone two. Who can keep up with the linguistic changes caused by the exponential growth of science and technology, and be equally and thoroughly familiar with the oral and written conventions of the two languages? One linguist estimates that some 4,000 to 5,000 new words enter English each month owing to neologisms and borrowings from journalism, the military, foreign languages, medicine, computers, information technology, and science. The editors of the 2007 edition of *Merriam-Webster's Collegiate Dictionary* regret that space limitations permit printing only 10,000 new words at the expense of obsolete and archaic terms.

## C. Code-Switching Patterns of Bilinguals

CODE-SWITCHING, BILINGUALISM, AND BICULTURALISM. Interpreters have to be attuned to the ways in which foreign-language speakers, in this case *Hispanoparlantes*, make themselves understood when moving from their native language to unadorned English. In the process of doing so, the Spanish speakers in the U.S. interweave words, phrases, and idioms from English, the dominant language. This is called code-switching. A formal definition comes from Carl A. Grant and Gloria Ladson-Billings, who define code-switching as "the systematic shifting or alternation between languages in discourse among bilinguals sharing common language codes. The elements involved in code-switching retain their own meaning and adhere to the rules of pronunciation and grammar that govern the language of origin."[8] To refine the definition in basic linguistic terms, code-switching occurs among bilinguals of the same language pairs or codes.

It is fascinating to a listener to absorb how two persons use code-switching with utter facility, choosing spontaneously the most appropriate language for each separate sentence, or phrase, or expression as an exercise in bicultural sharing. As an illustration, listen to some Chicanos *charlando* in border talk: "*Me dio un* ride *pa'l pueblo*" (Sp./Eng./Sp.). Tune in to the vivid examples from Mexico specialist Gregory Rodríguez, a columnist for the *L. A. Times*, who describes the commercial and cultural Americanization of the northern industrial city of Monterrey, Mexico. Rodríguez captured the following expressions from middle-class Mexicans in an upscale neighborhood: "Particularly when discussing entertainment," he says, "[...] *Regios* (i.e., short for *regiomontanos*, citizens of Monterrey) like to pepper their Spanish with English. They'll talk about going to a '*lugar muy* nice' [Sp./Eng.], they'll say they're going to '*tomar un* break' [Sp./Eng.] or '*echar unos* drinks' [Sp./Eng.]."[9]

Code-switching or language-switching, according to linguists Suzette Haden Elgin and Elena De Jongh, enables the limited-in-proficiency in a language to adapt and adopt to be understood, a process with which interpreters have to be familiar. "Spanglish" or "Tex-Mex" are the popular names given to code-switching for Spanish/English speakers.

First Elgin:

> One of the most amazing things about the linguistic competence of speakers is their ability to move back and forth among languages, dialects, and registers, with ease, as demanded by the social situation or their own inner necessities. This skill is called *code-switching*. In the United States today, especially in academic and business situations, the ability to code-switch is clearly a survival skill.[10]

Now De Jongh:

> "Spanglish" may be defined as "a speech variety which is rich in the use of loan words and shows a certain degree of grammatical interference from English." It is characterized by the borrowing of words and phrases from one language (English) and incorporating them morphologically, phonologically and syntactically into another language (Spanish).[11]

More specifically, the switching can take various forms, according to David Crystal:

> A long narrative may switch from one language to the other. Sentences may alternate. A sentence may begin in one language, and finish in another. Phrases from both languages may succeed each other in apparently random order (though in fact grammatical constraints are frequently involved).[12]

The term "Chicanos" is emblematic of code-switching bilingualism for the purposes of biculturalism and group pride. The young men and women who crossed the Mexican border, and formed gangs and social groups in California and Texas to preserve national identity, took pride in calling themselves, by 1954, Chicanos. Carol Styles Carvajal, in *The Concise Oxford Spanish Dictionary*, indicates that "Chicanos" were defamed by "Americans of European descent" as unsavory. Over the past four decades, however, as Chicanos took on middle-class values and loosened their association with marginal social groups, the term became linked proudly to Chicano radio stations, music, literature, and university programs of study.

The etymology of Chicanos represents a simulated return to the quasi-original sound of the Mexicas tribes — as heard and spelled by Hernán Cortés and his followers in the early 16th century. The Spaniards detected a /sh/ sound in the Náhuatl word Mexicas, which, at that time existed in Castilian and was represented by the letter "x." In modern times, this has given rise to two Hispanicized alternate sounds, according to Webster's, "shi-'kä-(,)nos *also* me-chi-'kä-(,)nos." How did "Chicanos" come about? A logical explanation is that the Mexican-American youths, in their desire to hark back to their native tribal roots, the Mexicas, dropped the weak first syllable "Me," maintained the strong infix "chi," and added the group-forming suffix "canos," which resulted in the strong-sounding and group-identifying Chicanos.

Nancy Bonvillain, in *Language, Culture, and Communication: The Meaning of Messages*, dedicates a section of her excellent volume to analyzing code-switching in five languages: English, French, Hindi, Mohawk, and Spanish. Bonvillain talks about the many reasons for code-switching, some of which involve "social values" and prestige, "marking discourse boundaries," an "attention-getting device," "a dramatic device," "emphasis," "syntax" switching, and to "segment phrases" for elaboration. She sums up by offering that "code-switching is a complex process having many grammatical interactional functions." "Additionally," she says "switching requires communicative competence, learning how to use linguistic devices as emphatic, contrastive, and/or emotional signals."[13]

**OPPOSITION TO "SPANGLISH."** It is important to point out the negative comments about the terms "Spanglish" and "Tex-Mex." While they are the commonly used descriptors for the Spanish-English version of code-switching, the terms appear pejorative to some educators. The language researchers and educators who consider them negative cite two reasons:

First, they obstruct important educational and social objectives, such as realizing that it takes time — if ever — for the undereducated to transfer wholly from one language system to another.

Second, the terms defame the native language by creating a hybrid, hyphenated language and speaker, i.e., a truncated person with two truncated languages, longing to become, but never realizing, integration and wholeness, i.e., Spanish-American, Latin-American. These are the bifurcated in color of skin, appearance, ideas, and language. Despite the pejorative usage in some quarters, both terms persist in common parlance with a touch of humor, are found in dictionaries, and are used here as neutral descriptors.

# D. LEPs and Other Second-Language Learners

**MONOLINGUALISM *VS.* BILINGUALISM.** If learning to understand, speak, write, and read English well presents serious challenges for American preschoolers and students, imagine the difficulty for the newly-arrived immigrant. Crystal's summary of an American child's difficulties in "Learning English as a Mother Tongue" anticipates the hurdles an immigrant has to jump over: "control [17 to] 20 vowel [sounds] and 24 consonant [sounds]; absorb some 50,000 words; understand a thousand grammatical constructs; manipulate prosody; combine phrases for clarity; and, ironically, bend or break the previous rules."[14]

At this point, it would be useful to narrow the discussion to the limited-English-proficient (LEP) in an interpretation session, the typical witness, patient, claimant, or examinee. It is critical to keep in mind what they are experiencing, and when the occasion calls for it, to educate others to this. Gerry Abbott's studies reveal that they will, typically, evidence "symptoms" such as taking longer than normal, making more mistakes than the average, being misunderstood more often than others, finding it more difficult to anticipate and predict what the speaker is about to utter, and being less capable of using their short-term memory and even losing it.[15]

Indeed, educator Alice C. Omaggio urges empathy and understanding in how difficult it is to be learning another language, or at the very least, to be surrounded by it and to need to make oneself understood — let alone understanding others. Omaggio notes that obvious cues are missed, which hinders the process of association of experiences and memories and also even the otherwise typical span of retention of useful cues.[16] For the LEP, schema can be distorted because of the effect of the world view created by the influence of one's native cultural "interpretations" of reality on the experiences in the new cultural setting.

**BILINGUAL WITHOUT SOCIOECONOMIC SECURITY.** Being bilingual does not assure adequate cognitive development in both languages and cultures if the socioeconomic conditions that underlie them are substandard. Nor does the term "bilingual" provide a measurement of the fluency in the two languages involved. Those who have worked closely with LEP students know the devastating effect of both being bilingual but having low fluency in both languages. In the authors' experience as teachers of English to speakers of other languages (ESOL), we noted among some social classes the prevalence of low fluency in both languages in students who were bilingual. The typical accompaniment of social instability and economic poverty was, too often, a sad predictor of failure, of the lack of language sophistication that would permit adequate cognitive development. Unfortunately, many of the persons encountered in interpretation sessions fall within this category.

**BILINGUALISM SEEN AS AN IDEAL.** Bilingual education in U.S. public schools exists as an ideal, mostly, for American students who desire to dominate a foreign language. Regrettably, at the public-high-school level, many American students become discouraged from dominating a foreign language by the grammar-translation method, which produces pieces-and-parts *analysis* of the foreign language validated by fill-in exams, rather than the conversational method, which bases itself on a holistic, *synthesis* approach that results in producing intelligible and actionable sounds. More success has been achieved in bilingual education at the elementary school level, because learners aged six to ten — in the pre-analytical stage — more readily mimic, absorb, and retain meaningful or, even to begin with, meaningless sounds than the children twelve and above who, analyzing the language, blunt their learning by wanting to know "why."

**A SOUTH FLORIDA BILINGUAL EXPERIMENT.** While public elementary, middle, and high schools in South Florida are required, under the Florida Settlement Agreement with the Florida Commissioner of Education, to mainstream children from some sixty language groups to English, nine South Florida charter schools have embarked on training elementary- and middle-school children in foreign languages and cultures. Journalist Hannah Sampson reviews this small, successful countercurrent in bilingual, bicultural studies at the following schools: three Archimedean schools with 721 students who learn Greek; 600 students study Hebrew at the Ben Gamla Charter School in Hollywood; the Excelsior Academy of Hialeah teaches Spanish; the International School of Broward [County] in Hollywood instructs in French; French, Italian, and Spanish are imparted to 255 students at the International Studies Charter High School in Coral Gables. As part of this limited movement to prepare young people for a globalized, competitive community, Mandarin Chinese will be the basis of the curriculum, in 2009, for the Integrated Science and Asian Culture Academy in North Miami–Dade County. Judging from Sampson's report, students and teachers are enthused, and the schools themselves receive high marks on the Florida Comprehensive Assessment Test (FCAT). Florida International University Professor of Mathematics George A. Kafkoulis, who founded Archimedean, states, "The focus is to produce scientists and intellectuals of the next generation." And the children take well to the rigorous program of math, science, the humanities, and the languages. As a coda to this outline and in anticipation of the next subsection, note the astonishment of twelve-year-old Constance Thurmond at Archimedean who captures without understanding how the brain's mysterious operation facilitates the complex Greek-to-English translation process: She says: "It's interesting. [...] When you hear it in Greek, you sort of in your mind take it to English."[17]

The excitement for volunteering to learn a foreign language has crept upward, for one example among many, to Miami-Dade [Community] College (FL), where hundreds of self-selecting adult students realize the socioeconomic advantage of learning foreign languages for international jobs and are enrolling in sections of Spanish, Arabic, Chinese (Mandarin), Haitian Creole, Farsi, French, German, Japanese, Italian, Portuguese, and Russian. One lesson, among others to be learned, is that where the college curriculum imposes a foreign language, not all students will be eager or able to learn it. Where ability and self-interest coincide, the students will choose the foreign language and perform better. This self-motivation also leads business persons and travelers short of time but not of interest and funds who require a flexible schedule to elect the expensive Berlitz method and the prepared tapes and manuals from, for example, Paul Pimsleur and Rosetta Stone. For those dedicated to learn a language, but short of money and long on time, the lowest price for language lessons at the greatest convenience can be found by turning to Google on the Internet and typing in "foreign language courses."

## E. The Brain and Second-Language Learning

BILINGUALISM AND CREATIVITY. The bilingual person has access to a more ample menu to express thoughts and feelings. There are some things expressed better in one language than in other ones — often associated with culture:

> [In] attempting to convey an idea which has *not* found concise formulation in the language he is using will in fact be giving his audience some insight into the structure of the other society. Much can be learned by observing how people ask each other for the time in the street in London, Paris, or Dublin. Everything is different: choice of words, voice, posture, distance between speakers and so on [Thiery 151].

Taylor, in his article, "Bilingualism, the Brain, and Creativity" (in NAJIT's journal, *Proteus* [Spring 2010]), expands on the themes in this section and documents further that learners or speakers of another language improve the brain's ability to enhance cognitive and motor functions, which leads potentially to greater creativity.

BILINGUALISM AND THE BRAIN. In an article, "Bilingualism Strengthens America," Carlos Alberto Montaner reports that "the latest findings of psycholinguists seem to demonstrate that bilingualism stimulates the development of intelligence by substantially multiplying the neuronal connections in certain regions of the brain. Researchers who measure and compare the intelligence quotients of people who are monolingual and multilingual usually confirm that relation: the more languages the higher the IQ."[18]

Montaner, a philosopher/journalist but not a neuroscientist, echoes research studies by hundreds of professionals, like Ellen Bialystok of York University, who, with the aid of the Stroop Color and Word Test and "brain-imaging tools such as PET and fMRI scans," reveals that children who learn "two languages have a 'distinct [cognitive/motor] advantage'" over monolingual children.[19] The widely used Stroop Test, designed in 1935 by psychologist J. Ridley Stroop, has contributed to understanding and measuring bilingualism. The test challenges the brain's hemispheres to differentiate between the visualized color which belies and confounds the symbol it represents. For example, on a card Stroop wrote the word "red" in blue ink, thus confusing the reader and causing a time lag in identifying the word. Stroop's revelations led to further studies of the brain in bilinguals and monolinguals for interference, time lag, attention, and fatigue, which have resulted in statistical inferences that favor bilinguals for cognitive and motor abilities over monolinguals. Researchers have measured in detail, using Stroop, cohort groups of differing ages, education, low and high use of English, and other foreign languages. The researchers have documented that bilinguals perform better than monolinguals on a variety of skills.

Whereas psychologists use Stroop and other tests to measure the external capacities of monolinguals and bilinguals, thus inferring concentrations of brain power, it remains for the neurologists and neurosurgeons, utilizing brain-scanning and mapping devices — positron emission tomography (PET) and functional magnetic resonance imaging (fMRI) — to determine the role of the brain in language activity. How do the devices operate? The PET scan detects the presence and flow of colorized blood via radioactive tracers placed in a glucose solution and injected in the body and visible in the prefrontal lobes, the sites of major language activity. Unlike PET, which is invasive and produces dynamic images, fMRI utilizes a powerful magnetic field and radio waves to produce static images in smaller areas of the brain. The two devices in tandem have revolutionized research on the brain and its relationship with language.

PIONEERS OF BRAIN RESEARCH. The devices have validated, in part, the early pioneering work of French neurologist Pierre Paul Broca, who purported to have found the location of speech in the left frontal lobe (1861), the area named for him.[20] Following on Broca's discoveries, Carl Wernicke had another area of the brain named in his honor when he determined in the 1870s that the site of the vocal apparatus and speech lay in the primary motor cortex of the left frontal lobe. Other researchers discovered the neural connection that appeared to separate the two areas, called the *arcuate fasciculus*. University of Washington neurosurgeon George A. Ojemann expanded and updated Broca's and Wernicke's theories after extensive brain mapping by showing that some people have language capabilities in the right hemisphere and others in both. According to Ojemann, "when people are gifted bilinguals [...] the brain develops separate, tightly organized essential areas for naming in each language. The same must be true for all language-essential areas."

Broca's, Wernicke's and Ojemann's discoveries have been superseded by the research of

Antonio Damasio, professor of psychology and neurology at the University of Southern California. Damasio weighs in with his theory, also based on brain mapping. He proposes that, instead of language emanating from separate zones, "convergence zones" are at work pulling together sounds that make sense (phonemes) from one area, to join with learned logical syntactic units from another area, which also couple up with meaningful visual units (morphemes) from another brain area, which together merge into spoken and written language. (See Chapter 14, section "Power Misplaced," for Daniel Goleman's comments on the brain's amygdala, which detects fear in an instant.)

Based on external measurements (Stroop Tests, etc.) and on physiological, internal investigation (brain scanning and mapping) done by hundreds of psychologists, neuropsychologists, and neurosurgeons, it appears clear that those in training for learning a foreign language, or are already gifted in more than one language, enjoy cognitive and motor advantages over those who are monolingual and are prepared to remain that way. This is good news for interpreters, translators, linguists, and foreign language teachers.

## F. The Bilingual Education Act

> "The most certain test by which we judge whether a country is really free is the amount of security enjoyed by minorities."
> Lord [John E. E. Dalberg] Acton (1834–1902)

It is curious that the same Civil Rights Act (1964) that gave birth to the Federal Court Interpreters Act and its Amendments which require interpreters and translators to appear in the court system and before social service agencies to support clients and witnesses who are not capable in English also launched the Elementary and Secondary Education Act with its Title VII (1968, revised 1974, and subsequently), also known as the Bilingual Education Act (BEA). In 1971, Massachusetts took the lead among states with the mandatory Transitional Bilingual Education Act. And the landmark Lau *v.* Nichols (i.e., San Francisco Unified School District [414 U.S. 563 1974]) was adjudicated by the U.S. Supreme Court in favor of the Chinese appellant (and councilman of that city), who claimed that his daughter and 1,800 other non–English speaking Chinese students were being denied the equal protection of the laws by not having foreign language-speaking teachers transition them from their native languages to English.

> [T]here is no equality of treatment merely by providing students with the same facilities, textbooks, teachers, and curriculum; for students who do not understand English are effectively foreclosed from any meaningful education.[21]

In that same year, Congress followed up with the Equal Educational Opportunities Act, which codified the responsibilities of school boards "to take appropriate action to overcome language barriers that impede equal participation by its students in the instructional programs" (20 U.S.C. § 1703 [f]).

Also adjudicated, curiously enough, was "black English," or Ebonics, which the Ann Arbor, Michigan, School District dismissed as inferior English rather than as a protected "minority dialect of English." Judge C. W. Joiner found it "appropriate to require the defendant Board to take steps to help its teachers to recognize the home language system [...] and to use that knowledge as a way of helping the children to learn to read standard English." The case was Martin Luther King Junior Elementary School Children, et al., v. Ann Arbor School District (73 F. Supp. 1371 [E.D. Mich. 1979]). See James Crawford's comments on this matter and other legal issues: www.ourworld.compuserve.com/homepages/jwcrawford.

In an odd tautology, from that same liberal San Francisco environment which prompted Lau, of Lau v. Nichols, to sue the Unified School District's board and led to the BEA, there also emerged another person of Asian descent, the Canadian-born Nisei S. I. Hayakawa (1906–1992), the semanticist and author of, among others, *Language in Thought and Action*.[22] Hayakawa's fame or notoriety as president of San Francisco City College, where he personally intervened in quelling student demonstrations over the war in Vietnam, led to his election to the U.S. Senate (1976–1983). From that pulpit, the linguist-educational administrator-conservative politician demanded in 1981, against all odds, a constitutional amendment to make English the official language. It appears that not all linguists believe in linguistic pluralism. The Congress never accepted Hayakawa's demand, and he was not re-elected. After leaving the Senate, Hayakawa persisted in his quest and founded U.S. English (1983) to promote his cause. The idea is still in active debate, as the readers noted in Chapter 3, "Language and the Legal Systems," in the sections dedicated to English-only activities that affect interpreters and LEPs.

The jurisprudence in the 1960s changed the linguistic, social, and political landscape for immigrant school children and adults and palliated the linguistic imperialism that many claim existed in the U.S. But the English-only groups were held at bay temporarily. Over the years, conservative Congresses and presidents chipped away at the funding for the BEA, denying monies that promoted any meaningful form of bilingualism, and allocated funding for programs that promoted transitional, mainstreaming and workforce English.

As a teasing side note, it would be interesting to learn how many bilinguals resulted from the Bilingual Education Act, and further, how many, if any, became professional interpreters and translators. The BEA, despite its promising title, contributed little to bilingualism; indeed, the title was either a misnomer or a deception. Its true purpose was not to encourage immigrants to maintain the native language and learn English, nor to encourage Americans to learn a foreign language and thus bilingualism, but rather to mainstream foreign students to monolingual English as soon as possible so as to acculturate them for future employment. One can only conjecture how many bilinguals resulted from this Act, whose alleged mission was undermined by reduced Congressional funding and by the English-only laws and attitudes in 26 states.

## G. Political, Cultural, and Security Aspects

SECOND-LANGUAGE DEVELOPMENT: U.S. *vs.* CHINA. The U.S. pays a high price for having discouraged over the past thirty years second-language learning. The U.S., a vaunted leader in the global economy, requires multilingual specialists. But oddly, since the expiration of the National Defense Education Act in the late sixties, which had poured millions into second-language learning institutes to rival Russia's competitiveness in that area during the Cold War, conservative presidents supported by like-minded Congresses have not considered language learning a priority. China, in contrast, long isolated politically, technologically, and economically, is the awakening giant in foreign-language teaching, especially of English. Journalist Andrés Oppenheimer, in a conference at the University of Miami's Center for Hemispheric Policy (8 Feb. 2008), reported that on his trip to Beijing he learned that one institute of language learning has some 650,000 students in its English-language classes. What is more, students in China start English in the third grade. Although China has dispatched some forty teachers to the U.S. to teach Mandarin, can that match the fervor in China for the English language? If English no longer undermines the Chinese political system, why should learning Spanish, Chinese, Pashto, Dari, or Arabic damage America? Of course, the analogy with China is not symmetrical. China does not have — as does the U.S. — 44 million Hispanics living there, according to the 2007 U.S. Census Bureau; nor will China have 100 million, the projection for the U.S. in 2050.

BILINGUALISM AND XENOPHOBIA. Bilingualism, however prevalent and unstoppable in the U.S. and other countries, presents sociopolitical problems. Crystal, the eminent Welsh linguist, emphasizes that public controversy surrounds the presence of minority groups and their adherence to non-native languages (*Linguistics* 409). Montaner, in the previously cited article, "Bilingualism Strengthens America," recognizes that problems exist, but they can be solved in favor of America. Montaner goes on to chide Congressman Tom Tancredo (Republican, Colorado) for his anti–Spanish vitriol: "[Tancredo] best expresses the American fear of other languages. [He believes that] [...] the United States must avoid at all costs becoming bilingual or bicultural because that would weaken the American identity and sow the seeds of disunity and conflict." Tancredo's fears at the political level replicate at the academic level those of Samuel P. Huntington (1927–2008), first expressed in his *Foreign Affairs* article (1993), "The Clash of Civilizations," expanded in his famous book of the same name with the subtitle *The Remaking of World Order* (1996), and sharpened in 2004, in his controversial *Who Are We? The Challenges to America's National Identity.*[23] Their common predecessor appears to have been the conservative Republican California senator and semanticist, the late S. I. Hayakawa, discussed above. Tancredo, echoing Huntington and Hayakawa, expresses fears that large-scale Latino immigration could split the U.S. in two, culturally, politically, and linguistically. But Tancredo, emblematic of other English-only politicians, hides behind the national [dis]unity argument to foreshadow the concern that the Latin American émigrés in the exercise of their voting rights will create new constituencies and voting blocs that overturn traditional groups. Should bilingualism, or U.S. schoolchildren learning a second language, pit Republicans against Democrats, or should the question of learning a foreign language be framed as a matter of national security and economic survival in a globalizing world?

This hot-button issue divides along party lines. Before assuming the presidency in January 2009, Senator Barack Obama — then the Democratic presidential candidate — stated that the global economy made clear that the English-only advocates were causing great harm and confusion. Senator Obama went on to say:

> Now I agree that immigrants should learn English. [...] But understand this: Instead of worrying about whether immigrants can learn English — they'll learn English — you need to make sure your child can speak Spanish. You should be thinking about how can your child become bilingual? We should have every child speaking more than one language. [...] It's embarrassing when Europeans come over here, they all speak English, they speak French, they speak German. And then we go over to Europe, and all we say, "*Merci beaucoup.*" Right?[24]

In defense of Obama's line of thought, Crystal (*Cambridge Encyclopedia* 115) calls attention to a possible default position posited by the English Plus pressure group. Formed in 1987, the group encourages English "plus" one or more other languages, and even proposed — in opposition to Hayakawa's English Language Amendment — a "Cultural Rights Amendment" to ensure that "ethnic and linguistic diversity would be celebrated and used as a national resource rather than condemned and suppressed."

Following Obama's talk, journalist Andrés Oppenheimer reported the following adverse reaction: "Immediately, the anti-immigration camp went berserk. CNN's Lou Dobbs and other Hispanic-allergic cable television anchors claimed Obama was, in effect, calling on Americans to study Spanish — rather than any second language. The mere thought of more Americans speaking Spanish raised their nightly dose of agitation up a notch."[25] Obama, on the other hand, was advocating learning any second language; the Spanish language was one example among others. But learning Spanish has become a political metaphor for advocating undocumented immigration and colluding with the increasing Hispanic-American population, themes that seem to have ignited political partisanship.

This chapter concludes with the concept that the U.S. confronts shortages in teachers, students, interpreters, and translators in critical languages given, in part, the xenophobia that afflicts certain social and political elements in America. It is no surprise, then, to discover that government agencies and private corporations have come up short in finding and funding foreign language experts for jobs locally and internationally in embassies and consulates, the military, border patrols, police departments, translation departments, and security agencies. In his article, Oppenheimer cites a U.S. Department of Education report that "out of every 100 college credits taken by U.S. students in a given semester, only 8.6 are for studying a foreign language. [...] Although more students are studying foreign languages," according to the DoE report, "as a percentage of total college enrollments, the number of American students who take foreign languages has decreased since the 1970s." These figures reflect a trend that does not bode well for the U.S. in a security-conscious, globalized, competitive world.

# CHAPTER 16

# Cultures and Languages in Play

## A. *Cultural Possibilities*

Culture has been defined in many ways and from various perspectives. In keeping with the purposes of this book, the authors will propose definitions of culture which single out its importance, comprehensiveness, and continuity via the use of language as one of its prime vehicles. In general, culture encompasses the traditions and customs of a society as well as its artifacts, predominant worldviews, governmental structures and laws, and obviously its language or languages. It also includes objects crafted and transformed by humans, such as furniture, as distinct from the natural components, i.e., wood or metal. The style imposed on a wooden chair demonstrates human imagination and capacity to create as contrasted with the natural state of wood in a tree. We underscore that every human production, be it furniture or gestures, is a manifestation of culture at work. And when definitions refer to societies and communities one must understand that their size is irrelevant; two persons — a married couple, for example — can form a group that develops certain cultural behaviors that could represent their invented culture as distinct from that of others. Matt Ridley, a renowned English scientist, author, and chair of the International Centre for Life — who will be referred to often — adds a critical nuance to the definition of culture. He emphasizes the dramatic capacity of our species to retain and make use of its accumulated knowledge, and this on a shared, global basis, rather than because of the DNA singularities of the human race or even our individual cultural acts per se.[1]

---

*"The addition of language into human brains involved a revolution rather than an evolution of function."*

Joseph LeDoux[2]

---

**INTERTWINING OF LANGUAGE AND CULTURE.** Interplay between language and culture exists. The latter provides a framework to enable humans to order and make sense of reality, which is composed of myriad and disparate phenomena impinging upon humans simultaneously. Language, for its part, formulates, finds a way to express culture's interpretation of reality through the signs and symbols called words and gestures.

Two linked questions: What came first, societies and their cultural manifestations or language? How did they evolve? Perhaps culture blossomed before language, because language may presuppose first the existence of societies that, as they grow in complexity, develop languages extensively (Ridley 173). Yet, there is no exaggerating the revolutionary role language has come to play for human culture. Borrowing Ridley's concepts, one can say that the critical thinking skills that our thought patterns in the brain-mind permit, and the ready transmission of their products through culture and technology has exponentially accelerated human and societal development, avoiding the slower pace of evolutionary changes (Ridley 174).

Although it is generally assumed that technological transformations have nullified evolutionary changes in human beings, to the extent that there have not been any significant biologically dictated changes in our species in the last 10,000 years, two journalists, Randolph E. Schmid and Nicholas Wade, reporting independently of each other, indicate that this is not the case.[3] Nonetheless, the rollover of language growth is immeasurably more rapid than biological evolution. One can speculate that the development of prehistoric farming patterns led to the diminishment of hunting-gathering, thus leading to more stable communities: conclusion, the concomitant patterns of communal life spearheaded the exponential transformations in culture and the consequent need for the expansion of the role of languages. Science may not yet be able to determine with certainty when language started or its relation to the cultural manifestations at that early time. Peter J. Richerson and Robert Boyd aver that language and culture have been linked and have mutually influenced each other since their remote beginnings, thus characterizing all human societies, and both have evolved everywhere.[4]

Christine Kenneally, an expert on language and the brain, asserts that language may shape cognition, even to the extent that it has made our brain-mind infinitely more complex than that of other mammals. The cultural differences between peoples and their transmission through varying languages certainly give us the impression that "we think differently."[5] Avant garde scientists now believe that various parts of our brains have evolved in size in accordance with the amount of information processed in those areas. From that perspective, a corollary finding has been that a key to understanding the impact of evolution on the capabilities of the brain is not simply that it has grown significantly larger than in other species but rather that the human brain is larger relative to the human body. This implies that large areas of the brain are not used to input data through the senses that have been developed to process the evolved production of language. One result, then, is that humans have evolved characterized by the language capability, in effect to be language-speakers, with a brain and related cognitive processes shaped to produce language (Kenneally 252–3). Furthermore, humans can combine words, phrases, and sentences in myriad ways, what linguists term the (re)combinatorial potential or nature of language. If we add to that the capacity to generate multi-variate metaphors, there is no end to the ways language can express thoughts and emotions. Consider the depth of careful study that logical thinking can lead to, and the complex social patterns, and cultural and technological transformations that *Homo sapiens* has manifested.

**LANGUAGE IS TRANSMITTED CULTURALLY.** Humans possess the gift of languages. The brain-mind, with its genes and neural networks, generates the capacity that allows language to develop. Furthermore, there is not one abstract, ethereal language. Wherever humans exist particular languages are being used, generation after generation, learning and reproducing languages anew. In Geoffrey Leech's view, each language, innate in us as a capacity, develops by having individuals learn it and transmit it within societies, which is in part a social and cultural act.[6] Socioeconomic and other factors in each setting are cultural determinants that reveal how language is used. Language use is characterized by differences supposedly based on socioeconomic diversity and ethnic group identity and development within ethnic enclaves. The linguist David Crystal argues that certain groups try to have a standard language prevail, often from certain occupations and educational levels, and family standing while others insist on speaking a dialectical variation.[7]

John le Carré in *The Mission Song*—quoted earlier in Chapter 9—whose protagonist, Salvador Bruno, interpreted expertly in English, French, and three African dialects, describes masterfully the salient features of various languages and how they shape behavior by affecting our senses in consonance with their particular cultural features:

> A word here regarding the psychology of your multi-linguist. People who put on another European language, it is frequently observed, put on another personality with it. An Englishman breaking into German speaks more loudly. His mouth changes shape, his vocal cords open up, he abandons self-irony in favor of dominance. An Englishwoman dropping into French will soften herself and puff out her lips for pertness, while her male counterpart will veer towards the pompous. I expect to do the same. But your African languages do not impart these fine distinctions. They're functional and they're robust, even when the language of choice is colonial French. They're peasant languages made for straight talk and good shouting in argument, which Congolese people do a lot of. Subtleties and evasion are achieved less by verbal gymnastics than by a change of topic or, if you want to play safe, a proverb. Sometimes I'll be aware, as I hop from one language to another, that I have shifted my voice to the back of my throat to achieve the extra breath and husky tone required. Or I have a feeling, for instance when I am speaking Kinyarwanda, that I am juggling a hot stone between my teeth. But the larger truth is, from the moment I settle into my chair, I become what I render.[8]

CULTURE AND VERBAL AND NONVERBAL LANGUAGE. There is also a constant interplay between verbal and nonverbal language, and between rational, emotional, and culturally biased behavior. An example is the use of voice to express emotions, which is recognized within each culture. Characterized as emotive or expressive language, it is used to discharge stress (i.e., swear words) or manifest joy, often nonconsciously. The expressions are culturally identifiable, using the signs and symbols of particular languages and therefore cultures, which is, in essence, the role of semiotics.[9] The role of nonverbal language, then, makes culture and language inseparable. The more sophisticated our understanding and our knowledge, the more nuances we will discern that will help us comprehend much better what we are interpreting, what we get from the SL. Culture determines much of behavior by means of the nonverbal way to communicate. The latter combines with verbal expression colored by cultural determinants on how to react to certain particular events. Culture widens our perception when we use language, but culture manifests itself in particular through nonverbal language. It behooves us as interpreters and translators, for example, to analyze why we and others behave in certain ways dictated perhaps by native cultural patterns. The wider the experience a person has of several cultures, the easier it should be to figure out what a person of another culture is manifesting through behavior or is trying to bring across through words and body language. Languages are given personality by their cultures. Languages are replete with idioms, gestures, myriad variations, and imaginative richnesses that characterize each individual when compared to others, and also characterize each culture and make it distinct in some ways from all the other ones. From this perspective, languages are an integral part of cultures, which provide most of the material used to compose them.

CULTURE STRUCTURES TIME, DISTANCE, AND BEHAVIOR. Culture is everything that surrounds us and so much of what determines our behavior; for example, what appear to be simply individual traits, such as how we feel and handle time; how we establish appropriate space with others; what our priorities are with regard to spending time with family vis-à-vis spending time dedicated to work or making money. As Edward T. Hall presciently understood, much of this cultural tableau that distinguishes us is manifest in action, not only verbally, but also through appropriate behavior, which is the vehicle to manifest our feelings, as Hall has described it, "in our silent language" of nonverbal communication.[10] "Distance zones," what linguists call proxemics, are often clear markers of cultural differences between peoples of varying cultures. Linguist Crystal (*Linguistics* 6) points out what those of us interested in the Hispanic culture already know, that "Latin Americans, for example, prefer to stand much closer to each other during a conversation than do North Europeans." In a traditional caste system, such as in India, "the acceptable distance zones between the members of different castes can vary greatly — from less than 2 metres to over 20." Culture affects almost everything, from prenatal care to rituals for the dead (and the living), from ethical codes to guide our behavior to the words and gestures used to communicate. Culture affects all individuals' self-identity and their behavior, the various relationships and interactions of groups of people, patterns of predominance of the various thinking skills and/or prevalence of emotional conduct, the roles of males and females, how to raise and discipline children, the predominant visual, body language and gestures cues, and so on.

Note how le Carré, returning to *The Mission Song*, delineates the compartmented cultural behaviors along language fault lines:

> To provide factual accounts of ourselves we spoke English. For our lovemaking French. And for our dreams of Africa, how could we not return to the Congolese-flavoured Swahili of our childhoods with its playful mix of joy and innuendo? [le Carré 58].

## B. Culture and Interpretation

UNOFFICIAL INTERPRETATION OF CULTURE. Culture, then, permeates everything. Interpreters must be totally familiar with the cultural manifestations of non–English-speaking persons. This was the core thought of Arabist Gamal Helal, expert interpreter for Secretary of State Condoleeza Rice in her discussions with Mahmoud Abbas, president of the Palestinian Authority. (As reported by David Samuels, in Chapter 11, section E, "Whispered SI, or *Chuchotage*, in Diplomacy.") Gamal Helal, after translating Secretary Rice's words to President Abbas and his to her, turned to the president off the record, quietly, to explain the cultural ramifications of Abbas's Arabic and her English.

Gratifying moments present themselves in which the diplomatic and business interpreter has the amplitude to explain cultural differences to the parties involved, but carefully and quietly. It bears repeating at this juncture that the court interpreter is under tighter restrictions. He can, if requested — but unofficially — explain and interpret cultural practices and attitudes for an attorney, medical doctor, or therapist. Yet, he is under an obligation to make it clear that, in effect, the comments are exploratory; they have not compromised the official interpretation. In the same vein, the court interpreter may have to emphasize that he does not serve as an expert on cultural differences and voice and accent identification.

What are the limits? An interpreter can explain or underscore, if necessary, cultural norms, such as addressing a Spanish-speaking person by their last name rather than their first one, to avoid making the witness or patient feel patronized and deprived of respect and dignity. Also, the interpreter, if asked, can try to explain that the importance given to education, to the development of cognitive skills and to the use of reason rather than preference for emotionalism and commonsense perceptions, varies from culture to culture and from within societies and regions of (so-called) nations. By way of suggestion, an interpreter can also transmit respect through the tone of the voice and the style of the register.

R E-INTERPRETING CULTURAL FLUENCY. In summary, while the cultures of the persons for whom one is interpreting influence their behavior, including the way they formulate their questions and answers with words, tone, and body language, the interpreters have to "re-interpret" these elements to others using their cultural fluency into equivalent language, register, and tone. An instance where cultural fluency can influence decision-making can occur in the case of a visit to an LEP's home by an interpreter and an insurance investigator to settle a claim. The latter most probably wouldn't discern the client's level of education from the books and works of art — or lack of them — and therefore trustworthiness, which an experienced interpreter would perceive. That is a pity, because the difference in discernment of cultural tastes and idiosyncrasies may impinge upon the outcome of the claim. Whereas the interpreter has gleaned these idiosyncrasies vicariously from study and travel, the clients or claimants involved have acquired them from family members and from others, having been passed down in the oral tradition by imitation, generation after generation to be stored in the brain-mind (Richerson/Boyd 5). It stands to reason that the insurance investigator, in this instance, would be at a greater loss and have to depend on the interpreter to filter the client's cultural affect into a decision on the validity of the claim.

Developing experience and sophistication, and getting cultural training, enable the interpreter to discern more readily cultural differences, the legitimacy of cultural behaviors different from ours and forms of forwarding messages in ways strongly or subtly different from the acceptable ways in our particular culture. In other words, interpreters need to master at a minimum two languages and two cultures. It is critically important to learn how to conceptualize and verbalize experiences and gained knowledge, and to learn how to manifest them to play out roles using the script for the play correctly.

A NTICIPATING THE CULTURAL "DIFFERENCE." People in general and specialists, like interpreters, communicate not only through language, but also by responding or failing to respond to the cultural characteristics and expectations of others. In any personal contact situation, the behavior of the persons involved is influenced by their cultural background, their roles in a given situation, and the particular circumstances in which they find themselves. Marilyn R. Frankenthaler sums it up in this way: The more knowledgeable one becomes, the more one learns to anticipate cultural expectations, to wit:

a. the meanings each person assigns to verbal and nonverbal expressions;
b. what can create misconceptions and misunderstandings, like a witness's inability to think concretely and provide "yes" or "no" answers;
c. the cultural differences that can render a question or an answer incomprehensible to the listener; and
d. the perspective of every courtroom protagonist, e.g., attorneys for both parties, plaintiff, and defendant.[11]

E FFECT OF CULTURAL DIFFERENCES. Reactions derive from genetic imprints and from the cultural patterns learned at home and in society. An interpreter's reactions to an LEP or to a witness from a foreign country at depositions and trials can influence, positively and negatively, the interpreter's perspectives. As outlined in Renee Hansen's book, consider the devastating effects on all parties of one lawyer's attempts to win at the expense of cultural sensitivity:

The lawyer decided on the most dramatic piece of testimony available: to have the wife testify about seeing her brother tortured. This would be sure to win the case. On the third question, "Now tell us about what happened to your brother," the witness stopped speaking, covered her eyes, began to convulse, scream, vomit, swear and generally have a bad time.

The clever lawyer, smelling victory at hand, forgot to consider the extra stress on this shy Arab woman forced to tell this horrible story in public to strange men in English. The lawyer forgot that this stress might be so great as to stimulate or trigger an episode of post-traumatic stress disorder. The lawyer simply forgot to consider the cultural ramifications of the strategy chosen.[12]

Hansen continues with another tale. An experienced interpreter familiar with the "trials and tribulations" of immigrants everywhere will benefit from the following anecdote, which will evoke memories and provide an important message about the need to learn to detect cultural differences:

A young lawyer, fresh out of law school, got his first *pro bono* criminal case in the federal Court. [...] His client was a Nigerian from the Yoruba Tribe in Benin City charged with white collar fraud. The young lawyer brought his client into his office for the client interview. After 15 minutes he walked out and told his senior partner, "That client is a lying 'son of a gun.' He's not telling the truth. We can't represent him." The senior lawyer, who had some familiarity with the Yoruba culture [...] conducted a completely different type of initial client interview in which the truth was easily uncovered. You see, a polite Yoruba never answers a question directly. It is considered very, very rude. For centuries the Yoruba have relied on their pattern of story telling—they tell stories in circles and the circles get progressively smaller till they get to the point [Hansen 128–9].

**INFLUENTIAL CULTURAL DIFFERENCES.** The coauthors reiterate, but do not overstate, the stress and anguish that immigrants can feel in their new and so often drastically different cultural surroundings. Interpreter Sibirsky reports the devastating effect cultural differences can have on the lives of immigrants because of actions taken with unintended consequences. Once, a college-trained Ecuadorian woman who was babysitting another woman's four-year-old in a house with other immigrants, left the child alone to watch television in order to attend an important meeting. The mother was at work and the babysitter had planned to take the child with her. But the child knew that her father, estranged from her mother, was coming to pick her up and refused to go with the babysitter. In this case, the sitter decided to leave the child to watch TV—admonishing the child to stay put until her father showed up 15 minutes later—and left, against her better judgment in order not to miss the appointment. When the father arrived, he was shocked to see the child unattended. Using this as an excuse to harm the child's mother, he called the police, who called the Connecticut State Department of Children and Families (DCF). The outcome was that both women were threatened with police and court action that could result in jail time (which could also mean deportation).

In another interpreting assignment for a middle-class professional couple from Ecuador, the wife was accused of child abuse. Because the school staff had noticed a bruise on her five-year-old daughter, the staff referred her to DCF as the law requires. The result was a threat of removal of the child from the home if the parents did not take parenting and anger management classes. In Ecuador, this physical discipline would not have been a problem that brought in the police and other authorities, but in the U.S. the mores and state laws call for habits that immigrants are not aware of.

**CULTURE AND THE PHYSICIANS' POWER.** As with judges and attorneys (see Chapter 12, "Verbal and Nonverbal Equivalencies in the Courtroom," subsection "Latinate Legal Terms"), so too with doctors does a cult of esoteric language, backed by knowledge and power, enshrine them with control and authority. The sight of stethoscopes draped over white coats, prescription pads in hand, lead LEPs — and for that matter most patients in distress — to plead for pills and potions that palliate pain. A study of science and the medical profession by the German philosopher Jurgen Habermas lends itself to the conclusion that the doctors' technocratic background endows them with the right to exert authority in speech acts with patients who seek their assistance.[13] For most patients the doctors are divinities whose opinions cannot be called into question.

LEP individuals from Latin America are conditioned that medical doctors are experts who are worthy of respect. The patients do not look at the doctors directly. They do not acknowledge pain when asked for fear of offending, and for believing that prescient medical expertise would have located the point of pain without having the patient mention it. For example, in a medical office, the doctor can be touching the area around a wrist and expecting, because he requested it, that the witness will tell the doctor if it hurts upon touch. All too often, patients will feel terribly intense pain and not say a word or give any signal that they are afflicted. The physician, for his part, assumes the patient has no pain. An interpreter familiar with this cultural phenomenon can explain this idiosyncrasy to the doctors. The protocol is to ask for the doctor's permission to explain to the patients that they must follow his instructions and advise him through the interpreter regarding any pain. The interpreter, in turn, can then notify the practitioner. Invariably doctors have been grateful for this service. An added benefit is that it has helped them understand that interpretation entails cultural understanding as well as word-for-word translation.

INTERPRETER EXPLAINS CULTURAL MISPERCEPTIONS. In a revealing experience of cultural misperception, a claimant stated to an administrative judge that she spoke "very little" English and needed the interpreter. During the Q&A period, she seemed to belie her "very little" English tending at times to respond before the interpreter could transfer the question to the TL. This action puzzled the judge who drew two negative impressions. After the hearing, the judge expressed the belief that the witness had lied about her lack of English proficiency because she had answered some questions in English before they were rendered in Spanish. He believed this even though she replied only in Spanish. Again, appearances can be deceiving. The interpreter had to explain to the judge that the claimant was not lying. Her English capabilities were limited to understanding and speaking social niceties, and that she seemed to answer quickly — in Spanish — to avoid being labeled stupid. For one thing, she was thinking and processing two languages at once and slowly translating to herself (aloud) into Spanish and then verifying in limited English. Her prior sixth grade education in another country and her attaining a G.E.D. in the U.S. did not serve her well in this legal situation where languages were used quickly and to the point. The claimant, limited in English and not culturally sophisticated, never dreamt that her credibility on the stand could have been at stake. The judge learned the advantages and perils of interpreting for a claimant dominant in a foreign language. More importantly, this exemplified how injustices take place, due, on the one hand, to a well-meaning and ethical judge who lacks cultural understanding and to a claimant (or witness) who lacks the sophistication to decipher the misunderstanding that she is causing.

## C. Words Transmit and Distort Culture

CULTURE AFFECTS "REFERENTS" AND "REFERENDS." In order to understand the meaning that witnesses attach to a lexeme, or "referent," one must be familiar with the cultural context, or "referend" associated with that word. The cultural differences that affect on the LEP person include the differences in the content and *weltanschauung* ("a comprehensive conception or apprehension of the world especially from a specific standing," according to *Webster's*) guiding, for example, the LEP's and the interpreter's legal systems. If the interpreter is not fully familiar with the legal systems of those for whom he is interpreting, i.e., those of both the SL speaker and the TL listener, very serious omissions or misperceptions can take place. Referents such as "the police" and "justice" symbolize referends that conjure up well-founded distrust in the LEP person, which carry over to U.S. legal and judicial systems. Elena De Jongh alerts and sensitizes the reader to differing legal and police systems. If from a nation in which police shoot first and ask questions later, where justice favors wealth and cronyism, where no presumption of innocence exists, or worse still, where it is expected that judges will find the accused guilty no matter what valid arguments of innocence the defense may have, the LEP in America has reason to fear the authorities.[14]

Since culture and language are intertwined, a Spanish-English interpreter ignores at his risk not knowing of vocabulary peculiar to a particular subculture of Latin America. Culture permeates a simple word like "yes" (*sí*). A Spanish-speaking witness from certain regions will instead answer *ya,* or some other equivalent word. The subtext of certain words can be deceptive. Coauthor Taylor, during his 16 years in Panama, learned that *sí* can camouflage feelings of fear, mistrust, self-doubt, and unfulfilled commitments. A friendly carpenter responded to Taylor affirmatively, "*sí, seguro que sí,*" when asked to repair a door the following day at 4:00 P.M. The friendly carpenter never showed up, nor did he ever explain his absence or express regret. His cultural upbringing did not allow him to refuse; he just could not say, "No, I can't, I'm busy."

**BELITTLING EXPRESSIONS.** Once again, an interpreter may or may not want to explain certain cultural differences during breaks or after a proceeding ends. It is better to err on the side of caution, because the listener may feel belittled. For example, a mediator may have said to two claimants: "If you two want to speak alone, just say so to me." The mediator meant the question literally and without implicit offense, but the statement sounded insulting because the witnesses had been talking to each before the statement was made. A cautious interpreter could explain to the mediator during a break or at the end that the witnesses might have felt belittled, and that the mediator should have communicated the message differently.

**DEFERENTIAL *VS.* PATRONIZING ATTITUDES.** Very often witnesses, often undereducated but not always so, will use honorific titles or at least always employ the title equivalent to "Sir" or "Madam," either because of culture and upbringing or to make a favorable impression on interpreters or court officials. The reverse might also occur, in that interpreters may feel the need to add certain forms of address because the culture usually calls for them. In the former case, the interpreters should not wonder what the motivation of the witness is and object to what may appear to be a subservient attitude. In the latter case, it is wise to avoid the addition. In both cases, do not add or subtract, but remain a faithful echo. Similarly, the interpreter must not add or omit what may be patronizing words. If the TL language differentiates between polite and familiar forms of address (e.g., Spanish *Usted* and *tú*), and the SL does not, as is the case with English ("you"), the interpreter must use for adults the terms that show respect when addressing adults. The LEP may also feel offended and patronized if a judge, attorney, social worker, or doctor uses the LEP's first name without permission. This is a serious, culturally based difference. If the setting permits it and the interpreter feels comfortable doing so, the interpreter may make observations about the polite and impolite forms of address, but off the record, and emphasizing that the interpreter is trying to provide cultural information unofficially and not as an interpreter.

**Addressing an LEP to increase trust.** Most LEPs find it very distasteful and painful when social workers and doctors address them by their first name without asking permission. The professionals do not realize that this is a patronizing behavior from the perspective of the culture of the LEP, who, out of fear or respect, will not express disdain. When appropriate, an interpreter can point this out very gingerly, carefully, to the English-speaking persons, who have been invariably grateful to learn about this cultural difference. Interpreters, judges, and attorneys need to learn the forms of address that will not seem culturally and therefore personally patronizing to the LEP person. In addition, the proper forms of address increase the LEPs' trust and consequently their understanding and cooperation.

**Surnames for Spanish-speakers.** When the opportunity arises, the interpreter can explain to doctors, judges, attorneys, and other relevant officials the rules for last names in Spanish-speaking countries, including Puerto Rico. The placement is as follows: For a single person, the father's last name comes first, as the principal surname, followed by the mother's maiden name. This means that if the last names of either an unmarried male or single female claimant are, for example, José ***López García*** and Laura ***González Jiménez***, and only one last name will be used to identify the claimant, that surname should be López [the father's] for José and González [the father's] for Laura. If the single woman Laura González Jiménez marries Juan Pérez, she has two options depending on family circumstances. One, she can take the full surnames, Laura González de Pérez, which means Laura uses her father's family name González, followed by her husband's principal last name, which is Pérez. If Laura does not want to be *de*—"of" or "from" her husband—indicating property of or belonging to, she can use the more liberated surname to identify the relationship, i.e., Laura Pérez. Feminine liberation nowadays is such that married Latin-American women can maintain, for professional purposes, their own maiden names.

**Titles of address.** Most attorneys, judges, and social workers will be appreciative to learn about certain cultural differences during breaks or after a proceeding ends. But one needs to exercise great caution to avoid condescension or belittlement. The interpreter can explain, for example, that Spanish speakers may feel patronized and made to feel inferior when addressed by their first name rather than by a title in English like Sir/Mr. or Madam/Mrs. The witness should be addressed in translation as "*Señor*," "*Señora*," or "*Señorita*" (respectively, "Mr.," "Mrs.," and "Miss"). This protocol is also dependent on the age of the LEP. It may not be appropriate to address a child in the same way as an adult. An adult LEP who declares in advance that the formal name protocols are unnecessary, so long as everybody is treated with respect, can be addressed by his first name. If the interpreter feels professionally comfortable with those officials who did not address the LEP person properly, he may explain the matter to them and stress its importance, but only off the record. When practicing, the interpreter must simply limit himself to translating orally what the questioner has said. Because of the way the interpreter addressed the LEP when they first met, the latter will know that the interpreter "knows better" and is simply reproducing in TL what the person obviously unfamiliar with the culture of the LEP person has said. We should add that the use of the titles automatically also lends the proper formal tone to the proceeding.

**DATES.** In the Spanish-speaking world and the Anglo-language world, the dates line up differently: in Spanish, Date/Month/Year (i.e., 4 de julio de 2010); commonly in English, Month/Date/Year (July 4, 2010), or in some government offices, 4 July 2010. In Spanish, the months take lower case; the comma is omitted; and the preposition *del* *"of"* is used to show "part of" or "belonging to." In Puerto Rico, the U.S. sequence is followed, despite the protests of Puerto Rican nationalists who lament the U.S. procedure; they blame it on insufficient education. The interpreter in court is obligated to point out when single digits or the numbers 10, 11, or 12 denote the month and the date: "Interpreter speaking: The dates follow a different sequence in Spanish-speaking places than in the English-speaking ones." Nonetheless, often Spanish speakers use the English-language sequence, or it is unclear which sequence the witness used.

**COMMON-LAW MARRIAGES.** When a witness refers to a person to whom she or he is not legally married but lives with and has a caring relationship with — i.e., a common-law marriage not recognized in all states of the U.S. but prevalent in the entire world — one must know, in a cultural sense, whether to translate the word as husband or wife, or fiancé(e), or life companion, or partner, or simply as boy- or girlfriend. The many Latin Americans who have common-law marriages refer to themselves and their partners as *esposos/*"spouses," which they are in fact if not in law. It is very frustrating, during an interpretation, to have attorneys show surprise when they "discover" that a witness uses the word for husband in Spanish, *esposo* or *marido*, to refer to a common-law husband and not to a legally married spouse. Some attorneys ask disparaging questions about this matter, such as "Are you legally married?" or "You never married so and so?" Sometimes they even aggravate the situation with, "And you have children with so and so?" Through this harangue, the interpreter must simply translate orally when an attorney berates a witness by tone of voice and choice of words for living with someone else without being married. Sometimes the attorney wants this recorded in a deposition, perhaps to take credibility away from the witness down the road. It is doubtful that an attorney of experience would be surprised regarding this common practice among humans. A sensitive interpreter would explain this matter to them after the proceeding is over or during a break, running the risk of a negative reaction or alienation.

**PUERTO RICO AND PUERTO RICANS.** It is a commonplace that few U.S. attorneys know or respect the fact that Puerto Rico is a Commonwealth State of the United States and that Puerto Ricans, owing to the Jones Act of 1917, are therefore U.S. citizens. It follows, then, that it is incorrect and pejorative to slur these U.S. citizens by asking denigrating and racist questions, such as "When did you come to this country?" "When did you come to the United States?" "Are you a citizen of the United States?" and "Do you have dual citizenship?" The proper way for the attorney to phrase the question is by referring to "mainland U.S.A" (in Spanish, *Estados Unidos Continental*). There are Puerto Ricans who, understandably, are offended by some attorneys' questions. An interpreter may want to explain this matter after the deposition or other proceeding is over or during a break. Doing this runs the risk of a negative reaction. At any rate, the attorney's statements require a faithful translation, not an editorial.

**SUDDEN, ABRUPT END TO QUESTIONING.** It is disheartening that after two hours or more of bombarding a witness with questions, attorneys, or (administrative) judges, or medical doctors at times suddenly announce that the questioning and deposition or hearing is over. The abrupt termination that does not let the LEP know clearly that the event is over can be felt as disrespectful by the LEP. However, an attuned interpreter can inform the witness in a low voice — if desirable — that the deposition or hearing has been completed and what follows is off the record. The interpreter can soften the situation even further by indicating that the witness can now stop worrying and breathe more easily.

POLITENESS AS POWERLESSNESS. Susan Berk-Seligson points out that it is unfortunate that cultural differences in what is considered "polite" behavior often makes a false impression on an LEP unacquainted with the patterns of politeness of the dominant culture. That ignorance in an LEP witness, who equates politeness with innocence and trustworthiness, can even lead to travesties of justice:

> *Politeness.* [...] politeness is one of the features characteristic of powerless testimony style, and persons who use powerless speech on the witness stand tend to be evaluated more negatively than do persons who use the powerful style.[15]

SPEAKING ALL AT ONCE TO SAVE FACE. It is important for the interpreter to understand that in certain settings, especially community-related ones, situations will arise in which several persons are speaking simultaneously. The following are some examples among many taken from real incidents:

- Meetings of tenants in a public housing building about remodeling schedules and related matters.
- A meeting at a community-based non-profit organization on child car safety belts and seats.
- A visit to a doctor by a patient with a spouse, group, or family therapy sessions.
- State Department of Children and Families (DCF) annual reviews or home investigations.

At these and other meetings, people will interrupt each other a lot and talk at the same time as others. The interpreter, by speaking clearly, assertively, patiently, and with courtesy, will usually help the participants understand that they need to modify their behavior to carry on business. The interpreter can help the unaware sponsors of the meeting understand the legitimacy of the behavior of the participants by explaining that they are practicing a cultural pattern of sharing, socializing, and communing. Close attention to details and business are less important goals. To get the desired results and outcomes, it is very important not to embarrass the attendees. It might not be apparent, but many could have serious mental and physical health issues; they could be self-conscious about their limited education and physical appearance. By clear and forceful example, the interpreter can, in these situations, help the participants "save face" and the hosts achieve success. Parenthetically, this may help the interpreter in another way. When those receiving the professional services of the interpreter are satisfied, they may request the services of the same interpreter sometime in the future.

DOMINANT LANGUAGE BIAS. The interpreters need to be aware of the danger of somehow favoring members of their own dominant, native language and ethnic group or, if they are not native speakers of that language, of the members of their second language group. When this bias occurs, it may manifest itself as a nonconscious behavior. The interpreter must always try to be aware of the danger of the occurrence and ascertain it is not happening. It should also be pointed out that the interpreter should not be influenced by any personal cultural bias toward another ethnic group or sub-ethnic cultures within the personal ethnic identity of the interpreter when the witnesses evidence usages of words that are different or less sophisticated than those of the interpreter.

**AMOUNT OF SPANISH VIS-À-VIS ENGLISH.** Experience and studies indicate that it usually takes about a third more words in Spanish than English to express the same thought. Persons with some familiarity with Spanish will become suspicious of the interpreter (and perhaps for good reason) if the amount of language used by the interpreter is not consistently greater in Spanish; this applies to all languages.

**TIME, SPACE, AND CULTURE.** The interpreter may have to explain off the record to court officials the cultural or social implications of witnesses or claimants from other countries that arrive late or not at all to official hearings. Witnesses conditioned by their cultures may have a different conception of time and may arrive late for a hearing or fail to anticipate the travel time and distance for a hearing in case of traffic delays. Or the witness may treat time as an instrument at the mercy of (religious) fate and therefore decide at the last moment not to attend a hearing, giving no prior notification, leaving quite a few people waiting in vain at the hearing site. Or the witness procrastinates. Despite being given sufficient time to obtain an attorney from a Legal Aid Society, the witness or claimant delays calling or visiting the agency. Even if the agency agrees to take on the case, it has to notify the witness that there is not enough time available for its attorney to prepare for the hearing. If the claimant has exhausted the number of times to get a postponement of a hearing because of the lack of an attorney, the judge may be forced to hold the hearing with an unrepresented claimant *in absentia.*

This is a matter that the interpreter can discuss unofficially with (administrative) judges, attorneys, investigators, examiners and others to explain the possible cultural differences involved or the socioeconomic difficulties of the LEP individual (e.g., lack of travel money, fear of getting lost, or an inability to get a ride). Of course, during the interpretation event itself, the interpreter cannot give an opinion.

**LANGUAGE INSPIRES CONFIDENCE.** If the interpreter speaks thoughtfully, pronounces clearly, and uses a Spanish vocabulary common to the cultural group in question, the witness or claimant will readily understand and be grateful, having been relieved of a worrisome barrier. A gratifying experience takes place at the conclusion of an interpretation act when the LEP person is pleased with the interpretation and the rapport with the interpreter, and wants to show appreciation by shaking hands. All interpreters feel particularly gratified to have the witnesses' relatives come over at the end of a proceeding to offer thanks without any apprehensions. This gesture expresses in a meaningful way their gratitude for having experienced an appropriate relationship. This emotional reaction, derived from the interpreter's proper and sensitive use of a kindred language, generates cultural affinities that turn an adversarial situation into a win-win situation.

## D. Alternative Cultural Perspectives

The cultural chapter concludes with a brief section that suggests to readers further sources and musings on attitudes from various perspectives: historical, scientific, psychological, religious, humanistic, political, neurological, and evolutionary. The objective is to share a concern that the area of responsibility for practitioners in the fields of translation and interpretation not limit itself to details of modes, settings, courtroom procedures, dictionaries, and linguistics, but be as ample as time, energy, and curiosity permit.

Our species has created monumental architectural structures and labeled them "cultural," which exist because the imagination has endowed them with a physical and/or abstract intellectual existence, often divorced from their material existence, mostly the object of man's creative essence. If man deems them inanimate and no longer worthy of attention, they disappear for all practical purposes. Examples abound, and include empty churches, victims of population loss in decaying neighborhoods; Albert Speer fulfilled Hitler's dream of an imposing Reichstag, which was laid to waste by the Russians in 1945; a rusted Bethlehem steel mill in Pittsburgh remains a remnant of Andrew Carnegie's vision and tenacity. They were erected, flourished, developed a place in history, and then fell into desuetude. At the apogee of their constructs, humans are sometimes willing to sacrifice their lives for the inanimate objects and abstract concepts and what they symbolize because of their uniqueness (Ridley 341).

Consider the myths involved in defending prevailing cultural icons. Some zealous Christians, Jews, and Muslims vie for and might die for obtaining exclusive control over the Temple Mount in Jerusalem. Secret Service agents are trained to take the bullet to protect the president in the White House because he and it symbolize freedom and democracy. Although the U.S. Coast Guard protects the Statue of Liberty in New York harbor from terrorists because it has become a beacon and shelter to the "huddled masses," this sanctification was not always so. Recall that Bartholdi's gift to America in 1886 — now a cherished monument — survived, despite Congress's refusal to fund a base to erect it. But private groups had a special vision of France's contributions to America and were willing to pay for that vision. If it were not for that patriotic effort, the iron statue would have succumbed to the elements.

CUZCO, NAVEL OF THE WORLD. Human culture interprets the world almost invariably from a personal prism. Compare and contrast the Incas, discussed next and compared following that with the early Americans. For the Incas of Peru, Cuzco symbolized and meant "the navel of the world." Located seventy miles northwest of Cuzco sits Machu Picchu, that secret, sacred, terraced city in the remote Andes, where the royal family, priests, warriors, and the Virgins of the Sun resided between 1438 and 1471, under Emperor Pachacutec. From that aerie, Pachacutec directed an empire that ran from Ecuador through Peru, to Bolivia and central Chile. The Incas, to solidify their hegemony and maintain their uniqueness, compelled conquered tribes and peoples to uproot themselves, to move to Inca-controlled villages, and to assimilate to Incan cultural values, i.e., learn the Quechua language, submit to their Sun–God religion, offer tribute to the aristocracy, and adhere to Incan socio-economic structures. For reasons unknown, the Incas had abandoned that sacred refuge of the royalty a century before Francisco Pizarro and his soldiers, operating from Cuzco, dismembered the empire by turning half- brother chiefs Atahualpa and Huáscar against each other. Although Machu Picchu had been discovered and explored earlier by other outsiders, it took Yale archeologist Hiram Bingham and his team of scientists to reveal it to the North American world (24 July 1911). Unlike many other monuments in South and Central America abandoned by its original inhabitants for reasons of natural catastrophes, famine, war, or disease, Machu Picchu has been rescued from the jungle and isolation and remains a tourist attraction for millions of visitors who are awed by its construction and religious and astronomical reasons for being.

MANIFEST DESTINY. Americans, for their part, imbued with concepts of Puritanism and Protestantism, capitalistic entrepreneurship, rugged individualism, and Frederick Jackson Turner's ethos of Manifest Destiny ("from sea to shining sea"), developed their own myth that the U.S.A. represents centrality, universality, and invulnerability. Just as Cuzco was the navel of the Inca world, so too, analogously, Americans in the nineteenth century came to believe that other nations should orbit around it. This self-proclaimed national or religious uniqueness, this idea that "we are the chosen people"—while inspiring chauvinism at best and jingoism at worst—promotes discord between peoples.

**CULTURAL MISAPPREHENSIONS: "THE CHOSEN PEOPLE."** An example of this discord occurred among the leaders of the ancient Hebrews, who proclaimed themselves proudly "the chosen people of God." This title was resented by the early and later Christians, who felt it alienated them from the grace of God. That epithet and the blood libel of Christ-killers promoted a reaction against the Jews for centuries. According to Edward T. Hall, "When it becomes apparent to people of different countries that they do not understand one another, each tends to blame it on 'those foreigners,' on their stupidity, deceit, or craziness" (*Silent Language* 15). The xenophobia is promoted for reasons of national security and cultural compatibility. Harvard Professor Samuel P. Huntington (referenced in Chapter 15, "Implications of Bilingualism," and recently deceased) asserts that the present-day cultural divisions between and among Judeo-Christian and Islamic civilizations will be the source of ongoing armed conflict. Cultural assimilation will prove less viable, he holds, than forging alliances with similar and like-minded Western cultures and civilizations.[17]

**RHETORICAL QUESTION: IS THERE A UNIVERSAL CULTURE?** One response comes from Robert Wright, another from coauthor Sibirsky. Wright believes that knowledge and good sense can fight off our natural and genetically determined xenophobic tendencies. He supports this theory by an idealistic perspective of humans and humankind: "Our premise of cultural evolutionism is 'the psychic unity of humankind'—the idea that people everywhere are genetically endowed with the same mental equipment, that there is a universal human nature."[18]

Sibirsky, author of *¿Qué es la cultura?*, holds that culture is indeed universal because all humans and societies exhibit patterns and traits. He differs from Wright in two ways. The first is that no one individual can display universal cultural traits. For him, there is no cultural "Esperanto" because it is impossible to express this universality through universal particularities. Humans can only express individual cultural particularities: single and distinct behaviors with unique causal factors. These behaviors can only be glimpsed through each individual and societal prism. Second, he concludes from his premise that this is why cultural differences are ultimately unavoidable. Sibirsky extends his beliefs to the legal arena. These concepts hold true and deserve recognition in courtroom situations, where even interpreters trained in cultural distinctions, but most of all judges, attorneys, doctors, and social workers need to understand and apply this existential reality.

**CREATION STORIES OF CULTURES.** The preceding thoughts of Wright and Sibirsky beg the following question: How are humans created and with what characteristics are they endowed? Did an omniscient and transcendent God form a man-shape from clay and endow it with life with His breath, and then from that shaped life force create a feminine companion? Did humanoids take shape from God's doing or man's imagination and mind, or from the fusion of carbon, hydrogen, and oxygen? Scientists, poets, and religious folk hotly contest these ideas. Millions of fundamentalists in the U.S. consider the creation story in the Bible the inerrant word of God. The Mayans, in their creation story in the *Popol Vuh*, held literally that Hurakán (source of "hurricane") was the God-progenitor of a new civilization after a hurricane leveled everything in its path. Creation stories have found their way into modern writers. The Colombian Nobel Laureate Gabriel García Márquez in *Cien años de soledad* (*One Hundred Years of Solitude*) and the Cuban Alejo Carpentier in *Visión de América* (*Vision of America*) saw the importance of creation stories in the development of man's capacity to make myths:

> Al principio no fue el Verbo. Fue el Hacha. El hacha de Macunaima, cuyo filo de sílex — golpea que te golpea, taja que te taja — iba desprendiendo trozos de la corteza del Gran Árbol. A medida que caían al río, esos trozos de corteza se transformaban en animales [....] Y cada uno hizo escuchar su lenguaje, según su clan y según su manera. Entonces Macunaima, el más alto ser, dejó descansar el hacha y creó el hombre. El hombre empezó por dormirse profundamente. Cuando despertó, vio que la mujer yacía a su lado, y fue ley, desde entonces, que la mujer yazga al lado del hombre.[19]

> At the beginning it was not the Word. It was the Hatchet. The hatchet of Macunaima, whose silex blade — blow after blow, slice after slice — went on hacking off pieces of the bark of the Great Tree. Just the way that they fell into the river, those pieces of bark transformed themselves into animals[....] And each one made his language heard, according to his clan and according to his way. Then Macunaima, the highest being, lay the hatchet to rest and created man. Man began by falling into a deep sleep. Upon awakening, he saw that woman lay at his side, and the law held from that time forward that woman would lie by man's side *[Translation by Martin C. Taylor]*.

CULTURAL PARTICULARITIES. Let us look again at Wright's thoughts. People manifest similar cultural patterns everywhere, driven by the intertwined biological and cultural evolution of the human species, beginning with biological determinants (Wright 19). In recent times, it has also become more evident to neuroscientists that humans have evolved to interact socially. Despite differences of culture and language, despite physical separation, Daniel Goleman asserts, in *Social Intelligence*, that "we are wired to connect. Neuroscience has discovered that our brain's very design makes it *sociable*, inexorably drawn into an intimate brain-to-brain linkup whenever we engage with another person. That neural bridge lets us affect the brain — and so the body — of everyone we interact with, just as they do with us."[20]

Said another way, even if it is impossible to be close to several billion human beings, the neural systems of our brain relate and communicate with those of other human beings with whom we come into contact or that resonate within us even if we cannot communicate in the same language. It is fascinating, comments Adrienne Lehrer, to discern the several ways in which a universal cultural characteristic manifests itself in differing ways in the cultures of current human societies:

> These examples show that even a term like "father" is beset with difficulties if we take it as a semantic prime, because in some cultures the biological father may not be known, or if he is this fact must not be considered important. [...] Even the requirement that a father be male is not without exception. Among the Dahomey, if a woman wishes to be independent and head a compound, she must have control of the children who will eventually carry on the affairs of the compound. [...] [S]he "marries" another woman. The "husband" of this marriage selects a man to act for her to sire children [...].[21]

At the same time, most of our cultural traits are learned, acquired from our milieu, starting at home and encompassing school, street, clothing, styles, local accent, sexual behavior, and eating preferences. The sociocultural rules that govern humans — labeled "pragmatics" — antedate us, and as we grow, according to Richard Carrier, they reflect more and more the world outside the home where societies were first developed.[22]

We read about traditional misunderstandings about the exaggerated magnitude of the family's influence on the language of children; it is strong in the formative years, then wanes as they learn from peers in school and on the streets. Similarly, children of immigrants emulate the language of the parents and relatives then diverge from the dialect of their parents and other related immigrants. Richerson and Boyd confirm that children learn their primary language from their parents, but acquire a distinct idiolect and dialectical variation owing to the interaction and influence of their peers and role models outside the home (*Not by Genes Alone* 38).

CULTURE INVOLVES MEN AND BEASTS. Cultural traits reside in species other than humans. This is evident, for example, in male and female lions, with the latter hunting for food, caring for the cubs, and teaching them to survive, while the males share in the security of the pride. Richerson and Boyd (173) illustrate the point with monkeys: "Chimpanzee communities have norms and traditions (of sorts), and recognition of individuals, and mutually understood roles (of sorts) without language, and they also show some modest cultural transmission: traditions or 'technologies' for cracking nuts, fishing for termites, sponging water out of hard-to-reach sources."

HUMAN CULTURE IS UNIQUE. Nonetheless, the human being is distinct on earth. Humans can be certain of being drastically different from the other animals without being overly ethnocentric. Our species evolved in a manner that made possible the development of culture and social interaction. Using the features of their surrounding reality that were essential in their settings, humans aggregated into social groups that developed the distinct cultures illustrated in history, sociology, and anthropology books, and that can be experienced directly by travel. Cultures inhabit political, economic, and religious systems (Ridley 208). Long before René Déscartes posited doubt philosophically, humans had invented it as an essential development for survival; doubt and skepticism regarding the appearance of things and the trustworthiness of other humans took root through trial and error. Early humans learned prudence and perseverance; they survived hard times by mastering fire, seeking shelter, making clothing, conquering enemies, and by storing in advance food, water, and kindling. What propelled humans beyond the rudimentary cultures of other species was the ability to remember learned experiences, articulate them, and react to them appropriately. To that end and in that sense, states noted philosopher Daniel Dennett in *Freedom Evolves*, humans invented culture.[23]

NATURE *VS.* NURTURE AND THE PROFESSION. In addition to learning the basics of survival, the human species can learn through increasing cultural sophistication the benefits to survival of "altruism" and "reciprocity." Both concepts exist on a social level, but, according to Richard Dawkins's theories of the selfish gene, altruism and reciprocity form the basis of man's genetic components and reside in the DNA. As such, they permit and herald positive elements that benefit mankind.[24] Dawkins's theories should soften to a great degree Dennett's worrisome concepts about the "deleterious effect of the blind, mechanical genes," which he labels "genetic determinism" (Dennett 165–6).

Scientists and philosophers of science have now refined their thinking to appreciate the distinct role of the selfish genes and of the world beyond the genes, facilitated by social interaction and played out by culture, enhanced by the manifestations of social inventiveness and creative output. Studies on epigenesis aim to do away with genetic determinism. *Webster's* reduces it to the "development of a plant or animal from a spore or egg through a series of processes in which unorganized cell masses differentiate into organs and organ systems." When applied to societies, epigenesis refers to the forefront study of the impact of the environment on the genes. Daniel Goleman, in *Social Intelligence*, quotes Crabbe's definition: "Social epigenetics is part of the frontier in genomics. The new technical challenge involves factoring in the impact of environment on differences in gene expression. It's another blow against the naïve view of genetic determinism: that our experiences don't matter — that genes are all" (Goleman 151).

Ridley, for his part, does justice to the contribution of cultural anthropologist Franz Boas, which means, in essence, that the debate over the predominance of nature or nurture was misguided because there is a sequential type of relationship in which both work in tandem, with nurture, or culture, adding to nature what the latter could not provide (202). The quandary about the relationship between nature and nurture has taken on new meaning in our lifetime, stressing the growing influence of nature — which includes in this case science, technology, and cognitive psychology — over the determinism of our mechanical genes. Similarly, the development of the human brain-mind, a product of natural evolution, creates the inner makeup that enables the comprehension, critical reasoning skills, and social human interaction that have resulted in our evolving and unique cultural manifestations. Scientists have integrated the study of the physical nature of the human being with that of psychological behaviors and cognition. This integrated picture has permitted better choices for man. But it is not a one-way street; reciprocity prevails. The cultural factors are so powerful in human society that they, in turn, help determine our biological development and therefore the fate of our genes. Cultural factors affect which genes are favored by natural selection. Over the evolutionary long haul, culture has shaped our innate psychology as much as the other way around (Ridley 3–4). The expansion of choices afforded by culture also augments the perspectives and options on which interpreters and translators can base their intellectual and ethical principles.

# Chapter Notes

## Chapter 1

1. "Census Shows Immigration Slowdown," *The Miami Herald* (9 Sept. 2008): 4A.

## Chapter 2

1. For a thorough understanding of the enormity of the problem and the importance of international bilingual communicators, consult Jean Delisle and Judith Woodsworth, eds. and directors, *Translators Through History* (Amsterdam: John Benjamins, 1995), 263.

2. Several pages in Delisle and Woodsworth, *Translators*—148, 255–257, 260–263, and 303—trace the trajectory of translators and interpreters in the early Americas. George Bastin, in "Latin American Tradition," expands on this theme in Mona Baker and Gabriela Saldanha, eds., *Routledge Encyclopedia of Translation Studies*, 2nd ed. rev (London & New York: Taylor & Francis, 2009), 486–488. The quoted material fills in the coauthors' extensive knowledge of Spanish and Latin American history, i.e., the reconquest of the Iberian peninsula from the Muslims (788–1492), social, religious and political questions, and the voyages of Columbus and Cortés.

3. From Laura Esquivel's *Malinche* (New York: Washington Square Press, 2006). She presents an imaginary and stylized re-creation of Malinalli's life and legend.

4. See Genaro García's Spanish edition (Mexico: Porrúa, 1983). The Spanish title is translated as the *True History of the Conquest of New Spain*.

5. A. Mirandé and E. Enríquez, *La Chicana: The Mexican-American Woman* (Chicago, IL: University of Chicago Press, 1979), 24.

## Chapter 3

1. See "Report: Federal and Local Government Interpreter Certification Programs [...]," prepared by the Government of the District of Columbia's Office of Human Rights, Language Access Program (June 2005), 4. For the full text, go to the website of Cornell University's Law School, U.S. Code Collection, titled "In-terpreters in Courts of the United States," at www4.law.cornell.edu/uscode/28/1827.html.

2. See "Interpreters and Translators," *Encyclopedia of Careers and Vocational Guidance*, 13th ed., vol. 3 (New York: Ferguson, 2005), 804.

3. See "waiver," Bryan A. Garner, ed. *Black's Law Dictionary*. 8th ed (St. Paul, MN: Thomson-West, 2004).

4. "Waiver" in *West's Spanish-English/English-Spanish Law Dictionary*, ed. Raúl A. Gastazoro et al (St. Paul, MN: West Publishing, 1992), 739.

5. The text of the Negrón decision is found at http://onlineresources.wnylc.net/ph/ordocs/LARC and at www.United_States_ex_rel_Negron_v_NewYork_434F2d386(2dCir1970).

6. From Roseann Dueñas González, Victoria F. Vásquez, and Holly Mikkelson, *Fundamentals of Court Interpretation: Theory, Policy, and Practice* (Durham, NC: Carolina Academic Press, 1991), 50. Among the many comments on Negrón, see http://www.ourworld.compuserve.com/homepages/JCRAWFORD/negrón.htm.

7. See Virginia Benmaman's thorough review of the Negrón case and dozens of others that affect interpreters, "Interpreter Issues on Appeal," *Proteus*, IX.4 (Fall 2000). Online at http://najit.org/members-only/proteus/v9n4/benmaman_v9n4.htm.

8. See U.S. Congress, Executive Branch, *Civil Rights Forum*, 14.3 (Summer–Fall 2000), 1.

9. "Policy Brief 2," *Center for Child and Human Development*. Georgetown University (Winter 2000, 2003).

10. Among Crawford's many writings, see *Bilingual Education: History, Politics, Theory, and Practice*, 4th ed (New York: Bilingual Education Service, 1995); on the Internet: www.ourworld.compuserve.com/homepages/jwcrawford. In Crawford's "Language Rights," he reviews, among others, Gutiérrez v. Municipal Court (1988); Asian American Business Group v. Pomona (1989); Yñiguez v. Mofford (1990); Puerto Rican Organization for Political Action v. Knuper (1973); and Hernández v. New York (1991): http://ourworld.com puserve.com/homepages/JWCRAWFORD/RIGHTS. HTM. Consult the American Civil Liberty Union's postings at www.lectlaw.com/files/con09.htm.

11. For a more complete discussion, see two works:

D. E. Freeman and Y. S. Freeman, *Between Worlds: Access to Second Language Acquisition* (Portsmouth, NY: Heinemann, 1994); and R. Phillipson, *Linguistic Imperialism* (Oxford: Oxford University Press, 1992).

## Chapter 4

1. Bernard Hamel, a former classmate of coauthor Taylor at UCLA's Department of Spanish & Portuguese, founded a Spanish language bookstore in L.A. and wrote a fine text on cognates. On Spanish/English cognates, see "Authors and Works Cited" for texts by Hamel, Nash, and Prado.

2. Luis R. Marcos, "Effects of Interpreters on the Evaluation of Psychopathology in Non-English Speaking Patients," *American Journal of Psychiatry*, 136 (1979): 171.

3. Nancy Frishberg, *Interpreting: An Introduction* (Rockville, MD: RID Publications, 1986): 61.

4. Linda Haffner, "Cross-Cultural Medicine a Decade Later: Translation Is Not Enough. Interpreting in a Medical Setting," *The Western Journal of Medicine*, 157 (Sept. 1992): 257.

5. Alex Altman et al., "Briefing," *Time* (25 Aug. 2008): 15. Altman probably derived his figures from Congressional Budget Office, *Contractors' Support of U.S. Operations in Iraq* (GPO: Washington, DC, August 2008), 1, 9.

## Chapter 5

1. Nancy Frishberg, *Interpreting: An Introduction* (Rockville, MD: RID Publications, 1986), 61.

2. Danica Seleskovitch, *Interpreting for International Conferences: Problems of Language and Communication*. Trans. Stephanie Dailey and E. Norman McMillan (Washington, DC: Pen & Booth, 1978, rev. 1994), 28. Pen & Booth published a third edition, revised in 2001 and available at www.Amazon.com, or from Peter S. P. Lafferty, 237 W. Market St., Leesburg, VA 20176 (pen.booth@verizon.net). All rights reserved. The original text is *L'interprète dans les conférences internationales—problèmes de langage et de communication* (Paris: Minard, 1968). For information, contact Seleskovitch's colleague and literary executrix, Marianne Lederer (marlederer@wanadoo.fr).

3. Laurie Swabey and Pam Sherwood-Gabrielson, *Introduction to Interpreting: An Instructor's Manual* (Minneapolis, MN: Program in Translation and Interpreting, University of Minnesota Press, 1999), 93. Dr. Bruce Downing, program director at the University of Minnesota, reported a revised edition in Oct. 2008. We are appreciative of his comments, additions, and corrections.

4. Lesley Clark uses figures from the Inter-American Development Bank in "Migrants Expected to Send Less Money," *The Miami-Herald* (17 March 2009): A1, A11. Owing to the recession and layoffs of migrant workers, remittances to Mexico declined 20 percent from May 2008 to May 2009.

5. In Mel Thompson's *Ethics* (Chicago, IL: NTC/ Contemporary Publishing, 2000), 30. Meta-ethics, also labeled "analytic ethics," treats one of three branches of ethics, and asks, "What *is* goodness? How does one differentiate between what *is* good from what *is* bad?" Moira Inghilleri and Carol Maier wrote an esoteric article on "Ethics," unlinked to the great philosophers and impractical for practitioners, in Mona Baker and Gabriela Saldanha, *Routledge Encyclopedia of Translation Studies*, 2nd ed. (London & New York: Taylor & Francis, 2009), 100–104.

6. Read Camayd-Freixas's essay, "Interpreting after the Largest ICE Raid in U.S. History: A Personal Account," online at: http://graphics8.nytimes.com/packages/pdf/national/20080711IMMIG.pdf. His essay and the report to the House Subcommittee on Immigration, Citizenship, Refugees, Border Security and International Law (24 July 2008) appear at: http://judiciary/house.gov/hearings/pdf/Camanyd-Freixas080724.pdf. Julia Preston's comments on the essay, "An Interpreter Speaking Up for Migrants," *The New York Times* (11 July 2008) is at http://www.nytimes.com/2008/07/11/us/11immig.html. Certified interpreter Chris Durban talks about two cases of ethics regarding interpreters and the justice system in her column "The Onionskin," in "Interpreters and Immigration: Miscarriage of Justice?" *The ATA Chronicle*, XXXVII.10 (October 2008): 47–48.

7. In the Flores-Figueroa case, the U.S. Supreme Court ruled unanimously against the Department of Justice (DoJ). The Court declared that the DoJ intentionally misapplied the law when it callously overlooked the term "knowingly" with regard to *illiterate* immigrants accused of identity fraud in the use of wrong Social Security numbers. See Adam Liptak and Julia Preston, "Court Bars Identity-Theft Law as Tool in Immigration Cases," *The New York Times* (5 May 2009): A1, A15.

8. From *Encountering Naturalism: A Worldview and its Uses* (Somerville, MA: Center for Naturalism, 2007), 39, 41. Tom Clark graciously identified and clarified this quotation. For information on his not-for-profit Center for Naturalism, see http://www.naturalism.org/clark. Clark, in his phone conversation, differentiated between "naturalism" in literature (e.g., Emile Zola) and the aspect that he holds, which is human behavior beholden to scientific, provable, and empirical concepts.

9. In Michael S. Gazzaniga, *The Ethical Brain* (New York: Dana, 2005), 88.

## Chapter 6

1. Elena M. De Jongh, *An Introduction to Court Interpreting: Theory and Practice* (Lanham, MD: University Press of America, 1992), 114.

2. Daniel Goleman, *Social Intelligence: The New Science of Human Relationships* (New York: Bantam Dell, 2006), 269–270. Goleman's prior bestseller served as a prelude: *Emotional Intelligence* (New York: Bantam, 1995).

3. Mr. A. Samuel Adelo, a distinguished retired attorney and interpreter in Santa Fe, NM, is believed to be the author of "Ten Pointers on Physical Conditioning," the article on which this section is based. Mr. Adelo cannot find this article among his many writings,

nor can the authors locate a copy of the article to verify its origin. Mr. Adelo has written "Legal Translators and Translations" in *Case and Comment* (Nov.-Dec. 2005). Thanks go to interpreters Fabiano Cid, in Rio de Janeiro, managing director of "Ccaps," and to Steven M. Kahaner in New York for help in locating Mr. Adelo. See www.ccaps.net for the "Ccaps Newsletter" on interpretation and legal matters.

4. "Profession," Bryan A. Garner, ed., *Black's Law Dictionary*, 8th ed. (St. Paul, MN: Thomson-West, 2004).

5. Roseann Dueñas González, Victoria F. Vásquez, and Holly Mikkelson, *Fundamentals of Court Interpretation: Theory, Policy, and Practice* (Durham, NC: Carolina Academic Press, 1991), 473. Appreciation goes out to Professors Dueñas González, Vásquez, and Mikkelson for their cooperation.

6. Alicia B. Edwards, *The Practice of Court Interpreting* (Amsterdam: John Benjamins, 1995), 2.

7. From Gravier's "Preface," in Danica Seleskovitch, *Interpreting for International Conferences: Problems of Language and Communication* (Washington, DC: Pen & Booth, 1978, rev. 1994), v–vi. See Ch. 4, endnote 2, for comments on this text.

8. Carl H. Weaver, *Human Listening: Processes and Behavior* (New York: Bobbs-Merrill, 1972), 78.

## Chapter 7

1. See "Translation and Interpretation," *Degrees Offered by College and Subject*, v.3, 36th ed. (Farmington Hills, MI: Gale, Cengage, Macmillan Reference USA, 2009), 1578. The full reference is to William M. Park, *Translator and Interpreter Training in the US: A Survey*, rev. ed (Ossining, NY: ATA, 1990).

2. Mary Phelan, *The Interpreter's Resource* (Clevedon, Eng.: Multilingual Matters, 2001), 178–188.

3. California. California State Court. Office of the Judicial Council. "Judicial Rules for Court Interpreters," 3 ff. The authors are greatly indebted to the Judicial Council of California for permission to reprint these and the following comments from its website, www.courtinfo.ca.gov. The material is "reprinted courtesy of the Administrative Office of the Courts."

4. See the *Occupational Outlook Handbook*, U.S. Department of Labor, Bureau of Labor Statistics (Washington, DC: U.S. G.P.O., 2007), 267; consult, also, the website at www.bls.gov.

5. Bruce Downing, "Medical Interpreting: Progress toward Professionalism." *ATA Chronicle*, 9 (1997): 28. Dr. Downing is a leader in the medical interpretation field.

6. See Holly Mikkelson, "The Art of Working with Interpreters: A Manual for Health Care Professionals" and "Tips for Taking the Federal Oral Exam," both at www.acebo.com.

7. Serious researchers can find a thorough analysis of GSTI's programs and testing methods in David B. Sawyer, *Fundamental Aspects of Interpreter Education: Curriculum and Assessment* (Amsterdam: John Benjamins, 2004).

8. Nataly Kelly, "Interpreter Certification Programs in the U.S.," *ATA Chronicle*, XXXVI.1 (Jan. 2007): 31.

9. See "Report: Federal and Local Government Interpreter Certification Programs" (June 2005), District of Columbia, Government Office of Human Rights, Language Access Program.

10. Roseann Dueñas González, Victoria F. Vásquez, and Holly Mikkelson, *Fundamentals of Court Interpretation: Theory, Policy, and Practice* (Durham, NC: Carolina Academic Press, 1991), 193.

11. Elena M. De Jongh, *Introduction to Court Interpreting: Theory and Practice* (Lanham, MD: University Press of America, 1992), 130.

12. Jerry A. Fodor, *The Modularity of Mind: An Essay on Faculty Psychology* (Cambridge, MA: MIT Press, 1989), 61.

13. *The Interpreter's Edge: Generic Edition*. 4 vols. (Spreckels, CA: Acebo, 2005).

14. Alicia Betsy Edwards, *The Practice of Court Interpreting* (Amsterdam: John Benjamins, 1995), 4–5.

15. Morry Sofer, *The Translator's Handbook*, 5th ed., rev. (Rockville, MD: Schreiber, 2004).

16. Information Today, Inc., *LMP 2009*, vol. 2, 69th ed. (Medford, NJ: Information Today, Inc., 2009), 1731–1754.

17. Elizabeth Gamble Miller translated Ortega's series of essays from *La Nación*. They are included in Lawrence Venuti, ed., *The Translation Studies Reader* (London & New York: Routledge, 2000), 49–63. The quotation is from Anthony Pym, "The Spanish Tradition," in Mona Baker and Gabriela Saldanha, eds., *Routledge Encyclopedia of Translation Studies* (London & New York: Taylor & Francis/Routledge, 2009), 540.

## Chapter 8

1. "Interpreters and Translators," *Dictionary of Occupational Titles* (O*NET Definitions, Section 27–3091. 00), 1190–1193.

2. See an excellent review of the field, despite the outdated salaries, in the *Encyclopedia's* 13th ed., vol. 3 (New York: Ferguson, 2005), 799.

3. "Interpreters and Translators," *Occupational Outlook Handbook*. Department of Labor, Bureau of Labor Statistics (Washington, DC: U.S. G.P.O., 2007). See also www.bls.gov.

## Chapter 9

1. *Webster's Collegiate Dictionary* (New York: Random House, 1995). Also 10th ed. (Springfield, MA: Merriam-Webster, 2001).

2. Laurie Swabey and Pam Sherwood-Gabrielson, *Introduction to Interpreting: An Instructor's Manual* (Minneapolis, MN: Program in Translation and Interpreting, University of Minnesota Press, 1999), 23.

3. Danica Seleskovitch, *Interpreting for International Congresses: Problems of Language & Communication* (Washington, DC: Pen & Booth, 1978, rev. 1994), 2.

4. David Crystal, *How Language Works: How Babies Babble, Words Change Meaning, and Languages Live or Die* (New York: Overlook Press, 2005), 147–148.

5. M. A. Halliday, *Spoken and Written Language* (Oxford: Oxford University Press, 1985), 44.

6. Maurice Gravier, "Preface," in Danica Seleskovitch, *Interpreting for International Conferences: Problems of Language and Communication* (Washington, DC: Pen & Booth, 1978, rev. 1994), vi.

7. Kenneth S. Goodman and Frederick V. Gollasch, eds., *Language and Literacy: The Selected Writings of Kenneth S. Goodman. Vol. II, Reading: Language and the Classroom Teacher* (London: Routledge and Kegan Paul, 1982), 25.

8. Stanislav Dornic, "The Bilingual's Performance: Language Dominance," in D. Gerver and H. Wallace Sinaiko, eds. *Language, Interpretation, and Communication* (New York & London: Plenum, 1978), 267–268.

9. M. A. Halliday, A. McIntosh, and P. Stevens, *The Linguistic Sciences and Language Teaching* (London: Longmans, 1964), 92.

10. Morry Sofer, *The Translator's Handbook*, rev. 5th ed. (Rockville, MD: Schreiber, 2004), 52.

11. Eugene A. Nida and Charles R. Taber, *The Theory and Practice of Translation* (Leiden: E. J. Brill, 1974), 1–2.

12. See Joel Garreau's "Machines Lower Language Barriers," *The Miami-Herald* (24 May 2009): 27A. The mission of the American Association of Artificial Intelligence is at http://www.aaai.org. Further information is at AMTA, www.amtaweb.org; Free Online Translator, www.worldlingo.com; and Machine Translation Engine, www.foreignword.com.

13. Harold Somers, "Second-generation indirect systems," in Mona Baker, ed., *Routledge Encyclopedia of Translation Studies* (London & New York: Routledge, 1998, 2000), 140–149. See Ke Ping's amplification of the theme: "Machine Translation," in Baker, *Routledge Encyclopedia of Translation Studies*, 2nd rev. ed. (London & New York: Routledge, 2009), 162–169. The indispensable *Encyclopedia* has three parts: General [articles], History and Traditions, and Bibliography.

14. Jean Delisle, "Interpretive Approach," in Mona Baker, ed., *Routledge Encyclopedia of Translation Studies* (London & New York: Routledge, 1998, 2000), 113. The article derives from his *L'analyse du discours comme méthode de traduction* (Ottawa: Presses de l'Université d'Ottawa, 1980). The "interpretive approach," discussed at length in Chapter 10, is closely associated with Seleskovitch, Lederer, and the ESIT group (École Supérieure d'Interprètes et de Traducteurs).

15. John Le Carré, *The Mission Song* (New York: Little, Brown, 2006), 14.

16. Robert Ludlum, *The Ambler Warning* (New York: St. Martin's, 2005), 150. A UN interpreter is the central player in the action film *The Interpreter*, directed by Sydney Pollack. Nicole Kidman's character accidentally overhears a plot being hatched in the African language Ku, whereupon she is pursued by assassins who believe that she will reveal their secret.

17. See Ruth Evans, "Metaphor of Translation," in Mona Baker, ed., *Routledge Encyclopedia of Translation Studies* (London & New York: Routledge, 1998, 2000), 149.

18. Longfellow's translation, *Dante's Divine Comedy: Hell-Purgatory-Paradise*, illustrated by Gustave Doré (repr. Edison, NJ: Chartwell Books, 2008), 6. The Italian is taken from http://www.danteonline.it. Longfellow's grammatical inversion of "dark forest" to "forest dark" is analogous to the inversion of "red barn" to the paint color "barn red." Both take on new dimensions. Longfellow received the aid of Harvard scholar of Dante Charles Eliot Norton, who also published his own translation in thee volumes (1891–1893). No one translation of Dante satisfies everybody. As an illustration, dozens of different translations exist of the famous ominous inscription over the Gate of Hell: "*Lasciate ogne speranza voi ch'intrate.*" Norton, who translated Dante nine years after Longfellow did (1882), did not agree with his disciple's version. Longfellow wrote: "All hope abandon, ye who enter in!"

19. Taylor has written extensively on Gabriela Mistral, starting with *Gabriela Mistral's Religious Sensibility* (Berkeley & Los Angeles: University of California Press, 1964), translated as *Sensibilidad religiosa de Gabriela Mistral* (Madrid: Gredos, 1975). In 2008, in honor of a national exhibit of the Nobel Laureate's life and letters, the Biblioteca Nacional de Chile invited Dr. Taylor to give a lecture titled "*Una dedicatoria a Gabriela Mistral y a nosotros los amigos de ella*" (9 April 2008). In Chile, his writings on Mistral are listed in "*La trayectoria espiritual de Gabriela Mistral a la luz de 60 escritores,*" *Patrimonio Cultural. Gabriela Mistral: Edición Especial* (Verano 2008), 36–38.

20. See Walter Benjamin, "The Task of the Translator," in *Illuminations,* Hannah Arendt, ed (New York: Schocken, 1969), 71.

21. Professor Emeritus Eugenio Florit of Barnard College provided the dates and brief biographical sketch for this section in the online article "Miguel de Cervantes Saavedra": http://encarta.com/text_761563857_2/Cervantes.html. Cervantes (1547–1616) received his war wound during the Christian-directed naval operation against the Muslim Turks of the Ottoman Empire (7 Oct. 1571). The Battle of Lepanto was fought in what is now called the Sea of Corinth. The translation-resistant title *hidalgo* in the Anglicized version, "The Ingenious Hidalgo Don Quixote […]," refers to a mid-level nobleman who does not bear an aristocratic family tie adequate enough to enable him to ascend above a mid-station in the hierarchy of nobility. *Hidalgo* is a contraction of the demeaning and sardonic *hijo de algo*, and translates as "son of something." Samuel Putnam's translation offers a valuable biographical, historical, and literary overview: Samuel Putnam, *The Portable Cervantes* (New York: Penguin, 1951). Taylor's personal note: In a career-defining experience at N.Y.U., I studied *El Quijote* with Francisco García Lorca (brother of Federico García Lorca).

## Chapter 10

1. Danica Seleskovitch, *Interpreting for International Conferences: Problems of Language & Communication* (Washington, DC: Pen & Booth, 1978, rev. 1994), 43. Annex II (p. 154) lists five useful publications of the author from 1974 to 1977. International conference interpreter Seleskovitch (1921–2001), after taking a Ph.D. in 1974, "set up the first doctorate in translation studies at the University of Paris III–Sor-

bonne Nouvelle," according to her biography by Anne-Marie Widlund-Fantini, *Danica Seleskovitch, Interprète et Témoin du XXe. Siècle.* See an abstract at http://aiic.eu/ViewPage.cfm/page2655.

2. See David Crystal, *Linguistics* (London: Penguin Books, 1971), 267. Celebrated nationally for his 100 books, Crystal is also Honorary Professor of Linguistics at the University of Wales, Bangor.

3. Elena M. De Jongh, *Introduction to Court Interpreting: Theory and Practice* (Lanham, MD: University Press of America, 1992), 26.

4. See Franz Pöchhacker's "From Operation to Action: Process-Orientation in Interpreting Studies," *Meta: journal des traducteurs/Meta: Translators' Journal,* 50.2 (Avril 2005), 682–695. Consult p. 5 of www.erudit.org/revue/meta/v50n2011011ar.html; if unsuccessful, Google "Franz Pöchhacker." The original design derives from Danica Seleskovitch and Marianne Lederer's *Interpréter pour traduire* (Paris: Didier Erudition, 1984), 185. Readers will also find an excellent bibliography featuring studies in English, French, and German.

5. Etilvia Arjona, "Intercultural Communication and the Training of Interpreters at the Monterey Institute of Foreign Studies," in D. Gerver and H. Wallace Sinaiko, eds., *Language, Interpretation, and Communication* (New York & London: Plenum, 1978), 37–38. Springer Publications (The Netherlands, Germany, and New York) acquired Plenum Press.

6. Marianne Lederer, "Simultaneous Interpretation-Units of Meaning and Other Features," in D. Gerver and H. Wallace Sinaiko, eds., *Language, Interpretation and Communication* (New York & London: Plenum, 1978), 330–331.

7. Peter M. Milner, *Physiological Psychology* (New York: Holt, 1970), 427.

8. Camille Wortman, Elizabeth F. Loftus, and Mary E. Marshall, *Psychology* (New York: Knopf, 1988), 155.

9. David Bowen and Margareta Bowen, *Steps to Consecutive Interpretation* (Washington, DC: Park and Booth, 1984), 5–6. The Bowens, who taught at Georgetown, also edited *Interpreting: Yesterday, Today, and Tomorrow* (Binghamton, NY: SUNY University Press, 1990).

10. Elizabeth F. Loftus, *Memory: Surprising New Insights into How We Remember and Why We Forget* (Reading, MA: Addison-Wesley, 1980), 66.

11. Christopher Thiery, "True Bilingualism and Second-Language Learning," in D. Gerver and H. Wallace Sinaiko, eds., *Language, Interpretation and Communication* (New York & London: Plenum, 1978), 147.

## *Chapter 11*

1. Mary Phelan, *The Interpreter's Resource* (Clevedon, Eng.: Multilingual Matters, 2001), 6–18, refers to five types of interpretation not dealt with here: Bilateral or Liaison, Telephone, Television, Videoconference, and Wiretapping. Two sections on phone conferencing appear in Ch. 13, "Settings and Procedures in Legal and Social Venues," Section I, #37–38, "Telephone Conferences."

2. James Nolan, in *Interpretation: Techniques and Exercises* (Clevedon, Eng.: Multilingual Matters, 2005), 3. Nolan stresses relying heavily on memory. He is unaware that Professor Erik Camayd-Freixas is a spokesperson for a recent electronic device to aid memory. See Camayd-Freixas's "A Revolution in Consecutive Interpretation: Digital Voice Recorder-Assisted CI," *The ATA Chronicle,* XXXIV.3 ((March 2005): 40–46.

3. Elena M. De Jongh, *Introduction to Court Interpreting: Theory and Practice* (Lanham, MD: University Press of America, 1992), 38.

4. Carl H. Weaver, *Human Listening: Processes and Behavior* (New York: Bobbs-Merrill, 1972), 13.

5. From research by Barbara Mercer-Moser, "Simultaneous Interpretation: A Hypothetical Model and its Practical Application," in D. Gerver and H. Wallace Sinaiko, eds., *Language, Interpretation, and Communication* (New York & London: Plenum, 1978), 353.

6. Danica Seleskovitch, "Language and Cognition," in D. Gerver and H. Wallace Sinaiko, eds., *Language, Interpretation, and Communication* (New York & London: Plenum, 1978), 334.

7. Gerry Abbott, et al., *The Teaching of English as an International Language: A Practical Guide* (Glasgow: Collins, 1985), 62.

8. Roseann Dueñas González, Victoria F. Vásquez, and Holly Mikkelson, *Fundamentals of Court Interpretation: Theory, Policy, and Practice* (Durham, NC: Carolina Academic Press, 1991), 383.

9. Alicia Betsy Edwards, *The Practice of Court Reporting* (Amsterdam: John Benjamins, 1995), 13.

10. Virginia Benmaman, "Legal Interpreting by any Other Name Is Still Legal Interpreting," in *The Critical Link: Interpreters in the Community,* ed. Silvana E. Carr et al. (Amsterdam/Philadelphia: John Benjamins, 1997), 183.

11. Nancy Frishberg, *Interpreting: An Introduction* (Rockville, MD: Registry of Interpreters for the Deaf (RID), 1986), 20. An excellent introduction-summary of SI appears in Holly Mikkelson, *"The Interpreter's Edge,"* generic edition, "Simultaneous Interpretation." See http://www.acebo.com/egsim.html.

12. David Bowen and Margareta Bowen, *Steps to Consecutive Interpretation* (Washington, DC: Park and Booth, 1984), 19.

13. Marianne Lederer, "Simultaneous Interpretation-Units of Meaning and Other Features," in D. Gerver and H. Wallace Sinaiko, eds., *Language, Interpretation, and Communication* (New York & London: Plenum, 1978), 326.

14. The seminal article by Samuels on Middle East negotiations, "Grand Illusions," *The Atlantic* (June 2007): 72, displays clarity and sensitivity to the delicate nature of diplomatic interpretation, especially between Arabic-English languages and cultures. By the way, the term *"dragoman"* describes an official interpreter or tourist guide "chiefly of Arabic, Turkish, or Persian," according to *Webster's.*

15. Morry Sofer, *The Translator's Handbook,* 5th ed. rev. (Rockville, MD: Schreiber, 2004), 20.

16. Jeffrey Goldberg, in "The Wars of John McCain," *The Atlantic* (Oct. 2008): 42.

17. "Betrayed" appeared as an essay in *The New Yorker* (26 Mar. 2007) and was transformed to a stage

play in New York at the *Culture Project* (6 Feb. 2008). Coauthor Taylor viewed the taut drama at the GableStage Theater, Coral Gables, FL (31 Aug. 2008). The quotations derive from pages 3 and 9 of the online version of the essay at www.newyorker.com. For further comments on Iraq, see Chapter 4, section E, "Consequences of a Lack of Interpreters."

18. Anonymous report in *The Miami-Herald* (26 May 2007): 3A. Two juxtaposed reports in *Time* from the U.S. military regarding interpreters in Iraq ignite a conflict. The first report emanates from U.S. military spokesman Lt. Col. Steve Stover, who indicates that the Iraqi interpreters will no long wear ski masks because of "security improvements." Says Stover: "We are a professional army and professional units don't conceal their identity by wearing masks." The second report, from Staff Sergeant Jeremy Ziegler, defends the use of masks: "Why risk the lives of those who work with us?" *Reuters* reporter Erik De Castro inserts mortality figures, in "Briefing," *Time* (1 Dec. 2008): 18: "More than 300 Iraqi translators have been killed for working with U.S. troops." The controversy expands and elicits a response from Jiri Stejskal, president of the American Translators Association, who defends the utility and vulnerability of interpreters in a letter to Secretary of Defense Robert Gates: *The ATA Chronicle*, XXXVII.11 (Nov.-Dec. 2008): 11. Strict dependence on Iraqi interpreters for U.S. military and civilian personnel may soon lessen if an Arabic-English portable interpretation device proves successful. Previously discussed in Ch. 9, section G, "Machine Translators vs. Human Translators," DARPA (Defense Advanced Projects Research Agency) has produced a machine that converts spoken English to spoken Arabic and vice-versa, according to *Washington Post* reporter Joel Garreau, "Machines that Lower Language Barriers," *The Miami-Herald* (24 May 2009): 27A.

19. Alissa Rubin and Rod Nordland, "New Envoy Faces an Iraq of 2 Minds About U.S.," *The New York Times* (3 June 2009): A6, A10.

## Chapter 12

1. See Maurice Pergnier, "Language-Meaning and Message-Meaning: Towards a Sociolinguistic Approach to Translation," in D. Gerver and H. Wallace Sinaiko, eds., *Language, Interpretation and Communication* (New York & London: Plenum, 1978), 200.

2. Sándor Hervey, Ian Higgins, and Louise M. Haywood. *Thinking Spanish Translation* (New York: Routledge, 1995), 15–16. A debate took place in the 1990s about moving from "equivalence-based" to "norm-based" theoretical models of translation and interpretation. Without entering into this complex debate, we point to two starting points: John Kearns's "Strategies" and Mona Baker's "Norms," in Baker's *Routledge Encyclopedia of Translation Studies*. 2nd ed., rev. (London & New York: Taylor & Francis/Routledge, 2009), 282–285, 189–193.

3. Elena M. De Jongh, *Introduction to Court Interpreting: Theory and Practice* (Lanham, MD: University Press of America, 1992), 39.

4. Susan Berk-Seligson, "The Intersection of Testimony Styles in Interpreted Judicial Proceedings: Prag-

matic Alterations in Spanish Testimony," *Linguistics* 112 (1987): 1096.

5. James Nolan, *Interpretation: Techniques and Exercises* (Clevedon, Eng.: Multilingual Matters, 2005), 279–287.

6. Gerardo Solís, et al., eds. *Diccionario Legal: Español-Inglés/Inglés-Español*, (St. Paul, MN: West Group, 1992).

7. See Nancy Bonvillain, *Language, Culture, and Communication: The Meaning of Messages*, 4th ed. (Upper Saddle River, NJ: Prentice Hall, 2003), 391–398.

8. David Mellinkoff. *The Language of the Law* (Boston: Little, Brown, 1963), sections 9–17. Mellinkoff hammers the point of separable and confusing language: "Nothing serves better to mark the gulf between the language of the law and the common speech than a listing of common words that mean one thing to the eye or ear of the non-lawyer, and may mean something completely different to the lawyer. [...] The words are of day-to-day use in the practice: *action*, lawsuit; *alien*, transfer."

9. Roseann Dueñas González, Victoria F. Vásquez, and Holly Mikkelson, *Fundamentals of Court Interpretation: Theory, Policy, and Practice* (Durham, NC: Carolina Academic Press, 1991), 169.

10. Gerardo Vázquez-Ayora. *Introducción a la traductología* (Washington DC: Georgetown University Press, 1977), 257.

11. Andrés Bello, *Gramática de la lengua castellana destinada al uso de los americanos*. A reprint (Caracas: La Casa de Bello, 1995).

12. Revised by Robert K. Spaulding as *A Textbook of Modern Spanish* (New York: Holt, 1954).

13. William E. Bull, *Time, Tense, and the Verb: A Study in Theoretical and Applied Linguistics with Particular Attention to Spanish* (Berkeley & Los Angeles: University of California Press, 1968). Robert Stockwell et al. wrote, among other books, *The Grammatical Structures of English and Spanish* (Constructive Spanish Series) (Chicago: University of Chicago Press, 1965). Among Bolinger's voluminous writings is *Modern Spanish* (New York: Harcourt Brace, 1960, 1966).

14. Adam Kendon, ed., "Preamble," *Gesture*, I (Amsterdam: John Benjamins, 2001).

15. David McNeill, *Language and Gesture* (Chicago: University of Chicago Press, 2000).

## Chapter 13

1. R. Bruce Anderson, "Interpreter Roles and Interpretation Situations," in D. Gerver and H. Wallace Sinaiko, eds., *Language, Interpretation and Communication* (New York & London: Plenum, 1978), 219.

## Chapter 14

1. William M. O'Barr, *Linguistic Evidence: Language, Power and Strategy in the Courtroom* (New York: Academic Press, 1982), 97.

2. Richard W. Brislin, "Contributions to Cross-Cultural Orientation Programs and Power," in D.

Gerver and H. Wallace Sinaiko, eds., *Language, Interpretation, and Communication* (New York & London: Plenum, 1978), 209.

3. Alicia Betsy Edwards, *The Practice of Court Interpreting* (Amsterdam: John Benjamins, 1995), 19–20.

4. Marilyn R. Frankenthaler, comp., *Skills for Bilingual Legal Personnel* (Cincinnati, OH: South-Western, 1982), 2.

5. Nancy Frishberg, *Interpreting: An Introduction* (Rockville, MD: Registry of Interpreters for the Deaf [RID], 1986), 68.

6. Elena M. De Jongh, *Introduction to Court Interpreting: Theory and Practice* (Lanham, MD: University Press of America, 1992), 39.

7. Every interpreter needs a personalized note system. Extensive ideas for note-taking are available in the following texts: James Nolan, *Interpretation: Techniques and Exercises* (Clevedon, Eng.: St. Martin's, 2005), 294–298; Jean-François Rozan, *La prise de notes en interpretation consecutive* (Genève, Switz.: Librairie de l'Université de Genève; Géorg & Cie., 1970); Mary Phelan, *The Interpreter's Resource* (Clevedon, Eng.: Multilingual Matters, 2001), 9–12, 22; Danica Seleskovitch, *Langage, langues et mémoire; Etude de la prise de notes en interprétation* (Paris: Minard, 1975); Hana Laurenzo, "Note Taking for Consecutive Interpreting," *The ATA Chronicle*, XXXVII.10 (Oct. 2008): 24–28; Andrew Gillies, *Note-taking in Consecutive Interpreting* (Krakow, Pol.: Tertium, 2005).

8. David Crystal, *Linguistics* (London: Penguin, 1971), 288.

9. Daniel Goleman, *Social Intelligence: The New Science of Human Relationships* (New York: Bantam Books, 2006), 40.

10. Susan Berk-Seligson, "The Intersection of Testimony Styles in Interpreted Judicial Proceedings: Pragmatic Alterations in Spanish Testimony," *Linguistics* 112 (1987): 1088.

11. Carl H. Weaver, *Human Listening: Processes and Behavior* (New York: Bobbs-Merrill, 1972), 65.

## *Chapter 15*

1. Christopher Thiery, "True Bilingualism and Second-Language Learning," in D. Gerver and H. Wallace Sinaiko, eds., *Language, Interpretation and Communication* (New York & London: Plenum, 1978), 147, 151.

2. David Sacks in *Language Visible: Unraveling the Mystery of the Alphabet from A to Z* (New York: Broadway Books, 2003), 123.

3. Adapted from http://help.berber.com/forum22/11188-jokes-related-languages-translation.html. The Scottish poet Robert Burns (1759–1796) comes to mind. In his sympathetic poem, "To a [country] Mouse," he wrote that "the wee, sleekit cow'rin' tim'rous beastie, [...] with a] panic in" his "breastie," like the house mouse, stuck his head out at the wrong time. But this was no bilingual joke. Burns anguished over the death of the mouse from the farmer's plough, a symbolic victim of nature being uprooted in the name of urban development.

4. Joshua Fishman, "Bilingual Education: Current Perspectives," *The Social Science Perspective*, vol. I (Arlington, VA: Center for Applied Linguistics, 1977).

5. Kenji Hakuta, "Bilingualism," *Encyclopedia of Psychology*, Alan E. Kazdin, ed (Oxford: Oxford University Press), 411. Among Hakuta's writings, see C. Moran and K. Hakuta, "Bilingual Education: Broadening Research Perspectives," in J. Banks, ed., *Handbook of Multicultural Education* (New York: Macmillan, 1995); *The Mirror of Language: The Debate on Bilingualism* (New York: Basic Books, 1987).

6. Danica Seleskovitch, *Interpreting for International Conferences: Problems of Language and Communication* (Washington, DC: Pen & Booth, 1978; rev. ed. 1994) 99.

7. Stanislav Dornic, "The Bilingual's Performance: Language Dominance," in D. Gerver and H. Wallace Sinaiko, eds., *Language, Interpretation, and Communication* (New York & London: Plenum, 1978), 267.

8. See Carl A. Grant and Gloria Ladson-Billings, eds., *Dictionary of Multicultural Education* (Phoenix, AZ: ORYX, 1997), 44.

9. Gregory Rodríguez, "Where the South Meets the West," *The Miami-Herald* (15 Feb. 2008): 23A. Bill Cruz and Bill Teck, et al., compiled a humorous book of Spanglish: *The Official Spanglish Dictionary*, ill. David Le Batard (New York: Simon & Schuster, Fireside, 1998). More serious is Ilan Stavans, *Spanglish: The Making of a New American Language* (New York: HarperCollins, 2003). On "Spanglish" and "Chicanos," see Carol Styles Carvajal, et al., eds., *The Concise Oxford Spanish Dictionary*, 3rd ed. (Oxford: Oxford University Press, 2004).

10. Suzette Haden Elgin, *What Is Linguistics?* (Englewood Cliffs, NJ: Prentice Hall, 1979), 109.

11. Elena M. De Jongh, *Introduction to Court Interpreting: Theory and Practice* (Lanham, MD: University Press of America, 1992), 68–69.

12. David Crystal, *Linguistics* (London: Penguin, 1971), 414.

13. Nancy Bonvillain, *Language, Culture and Communication: The Meaning of Messages*, 4th ed. (Upper Saddle River, NJ: Prentice Hall, 2003), 355–360.

14. In David Crystal, *The Cambridge Encyclopedia of the English Language* (Cambridge: Cambridge University Press, 1995), 426.

15. Gerry Abbott et al., *The Teaching of English as an International Language: A Practical Guide* (Glasgow: Collins, 1985), 63.

16. Alice C. Omaggio, *Teaching Language in Context* (Boston: Heinle, 1986), 98.

17. Sampson reviews the efforts of charter schools in "Language of Choice," *The Miami-Herald* (20 Oct. 2008): 1B, 6B. The Florida Settlement Agreement involved LULAC and other plaintiffs. See a review at http://www.firm.edu/doc/omsle. Harvard Professor Nathan Glazer opposes no-work bilingual schools and defends multiculturalism and bilingualism in the curriculum of New York City's "minischools or alternative schools," which emphasize reading books and testing students about the culture, literature, and history of the Hispanic tradition. See his thoughtful speech, "Where is Multiculturalism Leading Us?" *Phi Delta Kappan*, 75.4 (Dec. 1993): 319–323. Also available electronically at *SIRS Researcher* (Fall 1997), 1–9.

18. Carlos Alberto Montaner, "Bilingualism Strengthens America." *The Miami-Herald* (17 June 2007): 19A.

19. Distinguished Professor Ellen Bialystok of York University (Toronto) wrote, among others, *Bilingualism in Development: Language, Literacy, and Cognition* (New York: Cambridge University Press, 2001). Judy Foreman provides a quick overview of the research for a general audience: "Bilingualism is Great for the Brain" (10 Sept. 2002), http://www.myhealthsense.com/F020910_bilingualism.html. Among the innumerable researchers on the brain and language, see C. M. MacLeod, "The Stroop Task: The 'Gold Standard' of Attentional Measures," *Journal of Experimental Psychology: General*, 121.1 (1992): 12–14. Note the complex article of Daniela Perani et al., "The Bilingual Brain: Proficiency and Age Acquisition of the Second Language," *Brain*, 121 (1998): 1841–1852.

20. Authors Tully, Barmeier, and Blakeslee provide elementary information on the history of brain research and computerized brain scanning: Elizabeth Tully, *The Forebrain* (Philadelphia: Chelsea House, 2005), 67–69; Jim Barmeier, *The Brain* (San Diego, CA: Lucent Books, 1996), 12, 52. Sandra Blakeslee, "Brain Yields New Clues on its Organization for Language," in Nicholas Wade, ed., *The Science Times Book of Language and Linguistics* (New York: Lyons Press, 2000), 135–137. Authors Damasio, Dickmann and Stanford-Blair provide advanced information: Antonio R. Damasio, *The Feeling of What Happens: Body and Emotion in the Making of Consciousness* (New York: Harcourt Brace, 1999), 13, 110, 111, 112, 329. Michael H. Dickmann and Nancy Stanford-Blair, *Connecting Leadership to the Brain* (Thousand Oaks, CA: Corwin Press, 2002), 21, 234.

21. For an outline review of legal actions at the state and federal levels regarding bilingual education, see Stefan Rosenzweig, "Language Rights," Center for Language Minority Education and Research (CLMER), California State University at Long Beach (Nov. 2005). His e-mail: Srosenzw@csulb.edu. His writings: http://www.clmer.csulb.edu/files/powerpoint/Language%20Rights(05).ppt#304,44,FL.Statute233.058(Repealed). Consult "Lau *v.* Nichols," *Encyclopedia of Bilingual Education*, Josué M. González, ed. (Los Angeles & London: Sage, 2008), 510–520.

22. S. I. Hayakawa, *Language in Thought and Action*, 5th ed. (New York: Harcourt Brace, 1990).

23. Samuel P. Huntington, "The Clash of Civilizations," *Foreign Affairs* (Summer 1993). Expanded as *The Clash of Civilizations and the Remaking of World Order* (New York: Simon & Schuster, 1996). In Huntington, *Who Are We? The Challenges to America's National Identity* (New York: Simon & Schuster, 2004), he berates American elites, "deconstructionists," and liberals who support Catholic, Spanish-speaking, and poverty-stricken immigrants who undermine a bedrock culture of Anglo-Protestant, English-speaking, and work-ethic-driven Americans. Unchecked Latino immigration, he warns, could "divide the United States into two peoples, two cultures, two languages." For another view, see Ch. 15, subsection "Xenophobia and culture." Very telling is Tom Tancredo's letter to Ida L. Castro, Chair, the Equal Employment Opportunity Commission (14 Dec. 1999), with an appendix to the *Amicus Curiae* brief of pro-English groups, et al., that challenge EEOC's discrimination claims against businesses that prohibit

non–English use in the workplace on the basis that section 602, Title VI, of the Civil Rights Act confused unjustly "a person's choice of language" with the "person's national origin." The Center for American Unity tells the complex story: http://www.cfau.org/sandoval/amicusmerits.html.

24. Andrés Oppenheimer, "The Oppenheimer Report," *The Miami-Herald* (8 July 2008): 19A. See Oppenheimer's chapter on China's dazzling and expanding crypto-capitalism in *Saving the Americans* (Mexico: Random House Mondadori, 2007). At the Americas Conference, in Miami (2–3 Oct. 2008), Mr. Oppenheimer personally approved attributed use of his comments for this book.

25. "The Oppenheimer Report," *The Miami-Herald* (17 July 2008): 10A.

## *Chapter 16*

1. Matt Ridley, *The Agile Gene: How Nature Turns on Nurture* (New York: HarperCollins, 2003), 201.

2. Joseph LeDoux, *Synaptic Self: How Our Brains Become Who We Are* (New York: Viking, 2002), 198.

3. Randolph E. Schmid, "Technology and Evolution." *The Hartford Courant* (11 Dec. 2007): A3; Nicholas Wade, "Evolutionary Theory of Right and Wrong," *The New York Times* (31 Oct. 2006); "Scientist Finds the Beginnings of Morality in Primate Behavior," *The New York Times* (3 March 2007): F3.

4. Peter J. Richerson and Robert Boyd, *Not by Genes Alone* (Chicago, IL: University of Chicago Press, 2005), 215–216.

5. Christine Kenneally, *The First Word: The Search for the Origins of Language* (New York: Viking, 2007), 106.

6. Geoffrey N. Leech, *Principles of Pragmatics*, 2nd ed. (London: Longmans, 1986), 49.

7. David Crystal, *Linguistics* (London: Penguin, 1971), 309.

8. John Le Carré, *The Mission Song* (New York: Little, Brown, 2006), 202–203.

9. On semiotics, the study of signs, the literature is vast and complex. A beginning text, notable for its clever instructional pictures, is Paul Cobley, Litza Jansz, and Richard Appignanesi, eds., *Introducing Semiotics* (Cambridge, Eng.: Totem Books, 1997), 4.

10. Edward T. Hall, *The Silent Language* (New York: Doubleday, 1959), 15.

11. Marilyn R. Frankenthaler, comp., *Skills for Bilingual Legal Personnel* (Cincinnati, OH: South-Western, 1982), 2.

12. Renee C. Hansen et al., "The Changing Face of America — How Will Demographic Trends Affect the Courts?" *Judicature*, 72.2 (1988): 128.

13. Jurgen Habermas, *Toward a Rational Society* (Boston: Beacon, 1970), 111. To add depth to this cultural dilemma, read Anne Fadiman's study of the Hmong from Laos in California. She quotes Dr. Dan Murphy, a resident physician, who captures the difficulties: "'The language barrier was the most obvious problem, but not the most important. The biggest problem was the cultural barrier. [...] [It is not only that the Hmong don't understand diabetes,] they don't have a

word for pancreas. They don't have an *idea* for pancreas.'" See Anne Fadiman, *The Spirit Catches You and You Fall Down: A Hmong Child, Her American Doctors, and the Collision of Two Cultures* (New York: Farrar, Straus and Giroux, 1997), 69. Distinguished Professor Virginia Benmaman pointed out this pertinent reference.

14. Elena M. De Jongh, *Introduction to Court Interpreting: Theory and Practice* (Lanham, MD: University Press of America, 1992), 62–63.

15. Susan Berk-Seligson, "The Intersection of Testimony Styles in Interpreted Judicial Proceedings: Pragmatic Alterations in Spanish Testimony," *Linguistics*, 112 (1987): 1112.

16. Alicia Betsy Edwards, *The Practice of Court Interpreting* (Amsterdam: John Benjamins, 1995), 146.

17. The schism is first expressed in Samuel P. Huntington, "The Clash of Civilizations," *Foreign Affairs* (Summer 1993), expanded in the book of almost the same name (1996), and intensified in *Who Are We? The Challenges to America's National Identity* (New York: Simon & Schuster, 2004). See Chapter 8, subsection "Bilingualism and xenophobia," for a longer discussion of Huntington's views on English-only and two languages and cultures in conflict.

18. Robert Wright, *Nonzero: The Logic of Human Destiny* (New York: First Vintage Books, 2000), 18–19.

19. Alejo Carpentier, *Visión de América* (Barcelona: Editorial Seix Barral, 1999), 39–41.

20. Daniel Goleman, *Social Intelligence: The New Science of Human Relationships* (New York: Bantam Books, 2006), 4.

21. Adrienne Lehrer, *Semantic Fields and Lexical Structure* (Amsterdam: North Holland Publishing, 1974), 170.

22. Richard Carrier, *Sense and Goodness Without God: A Defense of Metaphysical Naturalism* (New York: Authorhouse, 2005), 262. Among others, Carrier and Daniel Dennett are adherents of "naturalism." Thomas Clark directs the Center of Naturalism in Somerville, Mass. Clark and coauthor Sibirsky are friends who purport to share many of the philosophical concepts dealing with secular humanism, religion, nature vs. nurture, and gene theory.

23. Daniel C. Dennett, *Freedom Evolves* (New York: Penguin, 2003), 165.

24. Richard Dawkins, *Unweaving the Rainbow: Science, Delusion and the Appetite for Wonder* (Boston: Mariner Books, 2000). Dawkins, a distinguished professor at Oxford University, espouses secular humanism and wrote, among other works, *The God Delusion*. He has delved into the world of genomics and has posited the concept of the "selfish gene."

# Authors and Works Cited

Abbott, Gerry, et al. *The Teaching of English as an International Language: A Practical Guide*. Glasgow: Collins, 1985.

Adelo, A. Samuel. "Legal Translators and Translation." *Case and Comment*, Nov.-Dec. 1965.

Altman, Alex, et al. "Briefing." *Time*, 25 Aug. 2008, 15.

American Translators Association. *The ATA Chronicle*. The journal of the ATA.

Anderson, R. Bruce. "Interpreter Roles and Interpretation Situations." In D. Gerver and H. Wallace Sinaiko, eds. *Language, Interpretation, and Communication*. New York & London: Plenum, 1978.

Arjona, Etilvia. "Intercultural Communication and the Training of Interpreters at the Monterey Institute of Foreign Studies." In D. Gerver and H. Wallace Sinaiko, eds. *Language, Interpretation, and Communication*. New York & London: Plenum, 1978.

Baker, Mona. "Norms." *Routledge Encyclopedia of Translation Studies*. 2nd ed., rev. London & New York: Taylor & Francis/Routledge, 2009.

_____, and Kirsten Malmkjær, eds. *Routledge Encyclopedia of Translation Studies*. London & New York: Routledge, 1998, 2000.

Baker, Mona, and Gabriela Saldanha, eds. *Routledge Encyclopedia of Translation Studies*, 2nd ed. rev. London & New York: Taylor & Francis/Routledge, 2009.

Banks, J., ed. *Handbook of Multicultural Education*. New York: Macmillan, 1995.

Barmeier, Jim. *The Brain*. San Diego, CA: Lucent Books, 1996.

Bastin, George. "Latin American Tradition." In Mona Baker and Gabriela Saldanha, eds. *Routledge Encyclopedia of Translation Studies*, 2nd ed. rev. London & New York: Taylor & Francis/Routledge, 2009.

Bello, Andrés. *Gramática de la lengua castellana destinada al uso de los americanos*. A reprint. Caracas: La Casa de Bello, 1995.

Benjamin, Walter. "The Task of the Translator." In Hannah Arendt, ed. *Illuminations*. New York: Schocken, 1969.

Benmaman, Virginia. "Interpreter Issues on Appeal." *Proteus*. (Fall 2000): IX, 4. See *http://najit.org/members-only/proteus/v9n4/benmaman_v9n4.htm*.

Berk-Seligson, Susan. "The Intersection of Testimony Styles in Interpreted Judicial Proceedings: Pragmatic Alterations in Spanish Testimony." *Linguistics* 112 (1987): 1087–1125.

Bialystok, Ellen. *Bilingualism in Development: Language, Literacy, and Cognition*. New York: Cambridge University Press, 2001.

Blakeslee, Sandra. "Brain Yields New Clues on Its Organization for Language." In Nicholas Wade, ed. *The Science Times Book of Language and Linguistics*. New York: Lyons Publisher, 2000.

Bolinger, Dwight. *Modern Spanish*. New York: Harcourt Brace, 1960, rev. 1966.

_____, and Donald A. Sears. *Aspects of Language*, 3d ed. New York: Harcourt, 1981.

Bonvillain, Nancy. *Language, Culture and Communication: The Meaning of Messages*, 4th ed. Upper Saddle River, NJ: Pearson Education, 2003.

Bowen, David, and Margareta Bowen, eds. *Interpreting: Yesterday, Today, and Tomorrow*. Binghamton, NY: SUNY University Press, 1990.

_____. *Steps to Consecutive Interpretation*. Washington, DC: Park and Booth, 1984.

Brislin, Richard W. "Contributions to Cross-Cultural Orientation Programs and Power." In D. Gerver and H. Wallace Sinaiko, eds. *Language, Interpretation, and Communication*. New York & London: Plenum, 1978.

Bull, William E. *Time, Tense, and the Verb: A Study in Theoretical and Applied Linguistics with Particular Attention to Spanish*. Berkeley & Los Angeles: University of California Press, 1968.

California. California State Court. Office of the Judicial Council. "Judicial Rules for Court Interpreters."

_____. "Report: 'Exercises for Interpreters of all Languages'; 'Skills Enhancing Exercises.'" Rev. (Sept., Nov. 2006): 3, 60. *See www.courtinfo.ca.gov*.

Camayd-Freixas, Erik. "A Revolution in Consecutive Interpretation: Digital Voice Recorder–Assisted CI." *The ATA Chronicle*. XXXIV, 3 (March 2005): 40–46.

_____. "Interpreting after the Largest ICE Raid in US History: A Personal Account." *The New York Times*. See online report: *http://graphics8.nytimes.com/packages/pdf/national/20080711IMMIG.pdf*.

Carpentier, Alejo. *Visión de América*. Barcelona: Editorial Seix Barral, 1999.

Carrier, Richard. *Sense and Goodness Without God: A Defense of Metaphysical Naturalism*. New York: Authorhouse, 2005.

Carvajal, Carol Styles, et al., eds. *The Concise Oxford Spanish Dictionary*, 3rd ed. Oxford: Oxford University Press, 2004.

Clark, Lesley. "Migrants Expected to Send Less Money." *The Miami-Herald*, 17 March 2009, A1, A11.

Clark, Thomas W. *Encountering Naturalism: A Worldview and Its Uses*. Somerville, MA: Center for Naturalism, 2007.

Cobley, Paul, Litza Jansz, and Richard Appignanesi, ed. *Introducing Semiotics*. Cambridge, Eng.: Totem Books, 1997.

*The College Blue Book: Degrees Offered by College and Subject*. "Translation and Interpretation." V. 3, 36th ed. Farmington Hills, MI: Gale/Cengage/Macmillan Reference USA, 2009.

Crawford, James. *Bilingual Education: History, Politics, Theory, and Practice*, 4th ed. New York: Bilingual Education Service, 1995.

_____. "English-Only Laws." See *www.ourworld.compuserve.com/homepages/jwcrawford*.

Cruz, Bill, and Bill Teck, et al. *The Official Spanglish Dictionary*. New York: Simon & Schuster, Fireside, 1998.

Crystal, David. "Learning English as a Mother Tongue." *The Cambridge Encyclopedia of the English Language*. Cambridge: Cambridge University Press, 1995.

_____. *How Language Works: How Babies Babble, Words Change Meaning, and Languages Live or Die*. New York: Overlook Press, 2005.

_____. *Linguistics*. London: Penguin, 1971.

Damasio, Antonio. *The Feeling of What Happens: Body and Emotion in the Making of Consciousness*. New York: Harcourt, 1999.

Dawkins, Richard. *Blind Watchmaker*. New York: Norton, 1986.

_____. *Climbing Mount Improbable*. New York: Norton, 1996.

_____. *Unweaving the Rainbow: Science, Delusion and the Appetite for Wonder*. Boston: Mariner Books, 2000.

De Castro, Erik. "Briefing," *Time* (1 Dec. 2008): 18.

De Jongh, Elena M. *Introduction to Court Interpreting: Theory and Practice*. Lanham, MD: University Press of America, 1992.

Delisle, Jean, and Judith Woodsworth, eds. *Translators Through History*. Amsterdam: John Benjamins, 1995.

Dennett, Daniel C. *Freedom Evolves*. New York: Penguin, 2003.

Dickmann, Michael H., and Nancy Stanford-Blair. *Connecting Leadership to the Brain*. Thousand Oaks, CA: Corwin, 2002.

*Dictionary of Occupational Titles*. "Interpreters and Translators." (O*NET Definitions, Section 27–3091. 00): 1190–1193.

Diriker, Ebru. *De-/Re Contextualizing Conference Interpreting. Interpreters in the Ivory Tower*. Amsterdam: John Benjamins, 2004.

District of Columbia. Government Office of Human Rights, Language Access Program. "Report: Federal and Local Government Interpreter Certification Programs." (June 2005). See Cornell University's Law School, U.S. Code Collection, "Interpreters in Courts of the United States." See *www4.law.cornell.edu/uscode/28/1827.html*.

Dornic, Stanislav. "The Bilingual's Performance: Language Dominance." In D. Gerver and H. Wallace Sinaiko, eds. *Language, Interpretation, and Communication*. New York & London: Plenum, 1978.

Downing, Bruce. "Medical Interpreting: Progress toward Professionalism." *The ATA Chronicle* 9 (1997): 28–29, 41.

Dueñas González, Roseann, Victoria F. Vásquez, and Holly Mikkelson. *Fundamentals of Court Interpretation: Theory, Policy, and Practice*. Durham, NC: Carolina Academic Press, 1991.

Durban, Chris. "Interpreters and Immigration: Miscarriage of Justice?" *The ATA Chronicle*. XXXVII, 10 (October 2008): 47–48.

Edwards, Alicia Betsy. *The Practice of Court Interpreting*. Amsterdam: John Benjamins, 1995.

Elgin, Suzette Haden. *What Is Linguistics?* Englewood Cliffs, NJ: Prentice Hall, 1979.

"Interpreters and Translators." *Encyclopedia of Careers and Vocational Guidance*, 13th ed., v. 3. New York: Ferguson, 2005.

Esquivel, Laura. *Malinche*. New York: Washington Square Press, 2006.

Fadiman. Anne. *The Spirit Catches You and You Fall Down: A Hmong Child, Her American Doctors, and the Collision of Two Cultures*. New York: Farrar, Straus & Giroux, 1997.

Federal Court Interpreter Certification Program. "Examiner Handbook (Spanish/ English)." Rev. 22 March 2004. Sacramento, CA: Human Resource Services and Second Language Testing, 2004. See *www.cps.ca.gov/FCICE*, and e-book or Adobe Acrobat PDF file.

Festinger, Nancy. "Interpreting Legal Argument." *Proteus* (Fall 1992): 67–70.

Fishman, Joshua. "Bilingual Education: Current Perspectives." *The Social Science Perspective*, vol. I. Arlington, VA: Center for Applied Linguistics, 1977.

Florit, Eugenio, "Miguel Cervantes Saavedra." *Encarta Encyclopedia*. See *http://encarta.com/text_761563857_2/Cervantes.html*.

Fodor, Jerry A. *The Modularity of Mind: An Essay on Faculty Psychology*, 2nd ed. Cambridge, MA: MIT Press, 1989.

Foreman, Judy. "Bilingualism is Great for the Brain." (10 Sept. 2002). See *http://www.myhealthsense.com/F020910_bilingualism.html*.

Frankenthaler, Marilyn R., comp. *Skills for Bilingual Legal Personnel*. Cincinnati, OH: South-Western, 1982.

Freeman, D. E., and Y. S. Freeman. *Between Worlds: Access to Second Language Acquisition*. Portsmouth, NY: Heinemann, 1994.

Frishberg, Nancy. *Interpreting: An Introduction*. Rockville, MD: Registry of Interpreters for the Deaf (RID), 1986.

García, Genaro, ed. *Historia verdadera de la Conquista de la Nueva España*. Mexico: Editorial Porrúa, 1983.

Garner, Bryan A., ed. *Black's Law Dictionary*, 8th ed. St. Paul, MN: Thomson-West, 2004.

Garreau, Joel. "Machines that Lower Language Barriers." *The Miami-Herald*, 24 May 2009, 27A.

Gazzaniga, Michael S. *The Ethical Brain*. New York: Dana, 2005.

Georgetown University. Center for Child and Human Development. "Policy Brief 2" (Winter 2000).

Gerver, D., and H. Wallace Sinaiko, eds. *Language, Interpretation, and Communication.* New York & London: Plenum, 1978.

Gillies, Andrew. *Note-taking in Consecutive Interpreting.* Krakow, Poland: Tertium, 2005.

Glazer, Nathan. "Where is Multiculturalism Leading Us?" *Phi Delta Kappan,* 75:4 (Dec. 1993): 319–323. *See also* SIRS *Researcher* (Fall 1997): 1–9.

Goldberg, Jeffrey. "The Wars of John McCain." *The Atlantic* (Oct. 2008): 42.

Goleman, Daniel. *Social Intelligence: The New Science of Human Relationships.* New York: Bantam, 2006.

Goodman, Kenneth S., and Frederick V. Gollasch, eds. *Language and Literacy: The Selected Writings of Kenneth S. Goodman.* Vol. II. *Reading: Language and the Classroom Teacher.* London: Routledge & Kegan Paul, 1982.

González, Josué M., ed. *Encyclopedia of Bilingual Education.* Los Angeles & London: Sage, 2008.

Grant, Carl A., and Gloria Ladson-Billings, eds. *Dictionary of Multicultural Education.* Phoenix, AZ: ORYX, 1997.

Gravier, Maurice. "Preface." *Interpreting for International Conferences: Problems of Language and Communication.* Washington, DC: Pen and Booth, 1978. See Seleskovitch.

Gyatso, Tenzin. The Fourteenth Dalai Lama. "Our Faith in Science." *The New York Times* (12 Nov. 2005). See *www.dalilama.com/news.5.html.*

Habermas, Jurgen. *Toward a Rational Society.* Boston: Beacon, 1970.

Haffner, Linda. "Cross-Cultural Medicine a Decade Later: Translation Is Not Enough. Interpreting in a Medical Setting." *The Western Journal of Medicine,* 157 (Sept. 1992): 157, 255–259.

Hakuta, Kenji. "Bilingualism." In Alan E. Kazdin, ed. *Encyclopedia of Psychology.* Oxford: Oxford University Press. (See also Moran and Hakuta.)

_____. *The Mirror of Language: The Debate on Bilingualism.* New York: Basic Books, 1987.

Hall, Edward T. *The Silent Language.* New York: Doubleday, 1959.

Halliday, M. A. *Spoken and Written Language.* Oxford: Oxford University Press, 1985.

_____, A. McIntosh, and P. Stevens. *The Linguistic Sciences and Language Teaching.* London: Longmans, 1964.

Hamel, Bernard H. *Hamel's Comprehensive Bilingual Dictionary of Spanish False Cognates.* Los Angeles, CA: Bilingual Book Press, 1998.

Hansen, Renee C., et al. "The Changing Face of America—How Will Demographic Trends Affect the Courts?" *Judicature* 72–2 (1988): 125–132.

Hayakawa, S. I. *Language in Thought and Action,* 5th ed. New York: Harcourt, 1990.

Hervey, Sándor, Ian Higgins, and Louise M. Haywood. *Thinking Spanish Translation.* New York: Routledge, 1995.

Hickey, Leo, ed. *The Pragmatics of Translation.* Clevedon, Eng.: Multilingual Matters, 1998.

Huntington, Samuel P. "The Clash of Civilizations." *Foreign Affairs* (Summer 1993).

_____. *The Clash of Civilizations and the Remaking of World Order.* New York: Simon & Schuster, 1996.

_____. *Who Are We? The Challenges to America's National Identity.* New York: Simon & Schuster, 2004.

Information Today, Inc. *Literary Market Place (LMP 2009),* vol. 2, 69th ed. Medford, NJ: Information Today, Inc., 2009.

Inghilleri, Moira, and Carol Maier. "Ethics." In Mona Baker and Gabriela Saldanha, eds. 2nd ed. rev. *Routledge Encyclopedia of Translation Studies.* London & New York: Taylor & Francis/Routledge, 2009.

International Association of Conference Interpreters (AIIC). "Bibliography on Interpretation." Geneva, Switz.: AIIC, 2008. See *http://www.aiic.net/viewpage.cfm.*

Interpreter Standards Advisory Committee. "Bridging the Language Gap: How to Meet the Need for Interpreters in Minnesota." St. Paul, MN: University of Minnesota Press, November 1998.

Kearns, John. "Strategies." *Routledge Encyclopedia of Translation Studies.* 2nd ed., rev. (London & N. Y.: Taylor & Francis/Routledge, 2009): 282–285.

Kelly, Nataly. "Interpreter Certification Programs in the U.S." *The ATA Chronicle.* XXXVI, 1 (January 2007): 31.

_____. "Telephone Interpreting in Health Care Settings: Some Commonly Asked Questions." *ATA Chronicle* (June 2007): 18–21.

_____, Darci Graves, and Rocío Txabarriaga. "Culturally Capable Translations: The Essential Role of Culture in Translation Quality Processes." *The ATA Chronicle* (March 2007).

Kendon, Adam, ed. "Preamble." *Gesture,* I, 1 (2001): 1. Amsterdam: John Benjamins, 2001.

Kenneally, Christine. *The First Word: The Search for the Origins of Language.* New York: Viking, 2007.

Laurenzo, Hana. "Note Taking for Consecutive Interpreting." *The ATA Chronicle,* XXXVII, 10 (Oct. 2008): 24–28.

Le Carré, John. *The Mission Song.* New York: Little, Brown, 2006.

Lederer, Marianne. "Simultaneous Interpretation—Units of Meaning and Other Features." In D. Gerver and H. Wallace Sinaiko, eds. *Language, Interpretation, and Communication.* New York & London: Plenum, 1978.

LeDoux, Joseph. *Synaptic Self: How Our Brains Become Who We Are.* New York: Viking, 2002.

Leech, Geoffrey N. *Principles of Pragmatics,* 2nd ed. London: Longmans, 1986

Lehrer, Adrienne. *Semantic Fields and Lexical Structure.* Amsterdam: North Holland Publishing, 1974.

Liptak, Adam, and Julia Preston, "Court Bars Identity-Theft Law as Tool in Immigration Cases," *The New York Times* (5 May 2009): A1, A15.

Loftus, Elizabeth F. *Memory: Surprising New Insights into How We Remember and Why We Forget.* Reading, MA: Addison-Wesley, 1980. See also Wortman, Camille.

Longfellow, Henry Wadsworth, trans. *Dante's Divine Comedy: Hell-Purgatory-Paradise.* Gustave Doré, illus. Edison, NJ: Chartwell Books, 2008.

Ludlum, Robert. *The Ambler Warning.* New York: St. Martin's, 2005.

MacLeod, C. M. "The Stroop Task: The 'Gold Standard' of Attentional Measures." *Journal of Experimental Psychology: General* 121 (1) (1992): 12–14.

Marcos, Luis R. "Effects of Interpreters on the Evaluation of Psychopathology in Non-English Speaking Patients." *American Journal of Psychiatry*, 136–2 (1979): 171–174.

McNeill, David. *Language and Gesture*. Chicago: University of Chicago Press, 2000.

Mellinkoff, David. *The Language of the Law*. Boston: Little, Brown, 1963.

Mercer-Moser, Barbara. "Simultaneous Interpretation: A Hypothetical Model and Its Practical Application." In D. Gerver and H. Wallace Sinaiko, eds. *Language, Interpretation, and Communication*. New York & London: Plenum, 1978.

Mikkelson, Holly. "The Art of Working with Interpreters: A Manual for Health Care Professionals." See www.acebo.com for Mikkelson's other writings.

_____. *The Interpreter's Companion*. Spreckels, CA: ACEBO, 2006.

_____. *The Interpreter's Edge*. 4 volumes. Spreckels, CA: ACEBO, 2005.

_____. "Tips for Taking the Federal Oral Exam." See *www.acebo.com*.

Milner, Peter M. *Physiological Psychology*. New York: Holt, 1970.

Mirandé, A., and E. Enríquez. *La Chicana: The Mexican-American Woman*. Chicago, IL: University of Chicago Press, 1979.

Montaner, Carlos Alberto. "Bilingualism Strengthens America." *The Miami-Herald* (17 June 2007): 19A.

Moran, C., and K. Hakuta. In J. Banks, ed. "Bilingual Education: Broadening Research Perspectives." *Handbook of Multicultural Education*. New York: Macmillan, 1995.

Nash, Rose. *NTC's Dictionary of Spanish Cognates: Thematically Organized*. Lincolnwood, IL: NTC Publishing, 1997.

National Association of Judiciary Interpreters and Translators. "Direct Speech in Legal Settings." NAJIT Position Paper. *Proteus* (10 July 2004).

_____. *Proteus*. The journal of NAJIT.

Nida, Eugene A. *Toward a Science of Translating with Special Reference to Principles and Procedures Involved in Bible Translating*. Leiden, Holland: E. J. Brill, 1964.

_____, and Charles R. Taber. *The Theory and Practice of Translation*. Leiden, Holland: E. J. Brill, 1974.

Nolan, James. *Interpretation: Techniques and Exercises*. Clevedon, Eng.: Multilingual Matters, 2005.

O'Barr, William M. *Linguistic Evidence: Language, Power, and Strategy in the Courtroom*. New York: Academic, 1982.

_____, and John M. Conley. "Subtleties of Speech Can Tilt the Scales of Justice [...] When a Juror Watches a Lawyer." *Barrister* 3 (Summer 1976): 8–11, 33.

*Occupational Outlook Handbook*. See U.S. Department of Labor.

Omaggio, Alice C. *Teaching Language in Context*. Boston: Heinle, 1986.

Oppenheimer, Andrés. *Saving the Americas*. Mexico: Random House Mondadori, 2007.

_____. "The Oppenheimer Report." *The Miami-Herald* (8 July 2008): 19A.

_____. "The Oppenheimer Report." *The Miami-Herald* (17 July 2008): 10A.

Packer, George. "Betrayed: The Iraqis Who Trusted America the Most." *The New Yorker* (26 Mar. 2007): 3, 9. Online version: *www.newyorker.com*.

_____. *Betrayed*. The Culture Project. New York City (6 Feb. 2008); GableStage Theater. Coral Gables, FL (31 Aug. 2008).

Park, William M. *Translator and Interpreter Training in the US: A Survey*, rev. ed. Ossining, NY: ATA, 1990.

Perani, Daniela, et al. "The Bilingual Brain: Proficiency and Age Acquisition of the Second Language." *Brain*, 121 (1998): 1841–1852.

Pergnier, Maurice. "Language-Meaning and Message-Meaning: Towards a Sociolinguistic Approach to Translation." In D. Gerver and H. Wallace Sinaiko, eds. *Language, Interpretation, and Communication*. New York & London: Plenum, 1978.

Phelan, Mary. *The Interpreter's Resource*. Clevedon, Eng.: Multilingual Matters, 2001.

Phillipson, R. *Linguistic Imperialism*. Oxford: Oxford University Press, 1992.

Pöchhacker, Franz. "From Operation to Action: Process-Orientation in Interpreting Studies." *Meta: journal des traducteurs/Meta: Translators' Journal*, 50:2 (April 2005): 682–695. See *www.erudit.org/revue/meta/v50n201101lar.html*, p. 5.

Prado, Marcial. *Diccionario de falsos amigos*. Madrid: Gredos, 2001.

Preston, Julia. "An Interpreter Speaking Up for Migrants." *The New York Times* (11 July 2008). See *http://www.nytimes.com/2008/07/11/us/11immig.html*.

Putnam, Samuel, trans., ed. *The Portable Cervantes*. New York: Penguin, 1951.

Rainof, Alexander. *Translation English into Spanish: Methodology and Exercises—Teachers' Version*. Santa Monica, CA: A-Lexis Publications, 1996.

Richerson, Peter J., and Robert Boyd. *Not by Genes Alone*. Chicago, IL: University of Chicago Press, 2005.

Ridley, Matt. *The Agile Gene: How Nature Turns on Nurture*. New York: HarperCollins, 2003.

_____. *Francis Crick: Discoverer of the Genetic Code*. New York: Atlas Books, 2006.

Rodríguez, Gregory. "Where the South Meets the West." *The Miami-Herald* (15 Feb. 2008), 23A.

Rosenzweig, Stefan. "Language Rights." Center for Language Minority Education and Research. California State University at Long Beach. (Nov. 2005). See *http://www.clmer.csulb.edu/files/powerpoint/Language%20Rights(05).ppt#304,44, FL.Statute233.058* (Repealed).

Rozan, Jean-François. *La prise de notes en interpretation consécutive*. Genève, Switzerland: Librairie de l'Université de Genève, Géorg & Cie., 1970.

Rubin, Alissa, and Rod Nordland. "New Envoy Faces an Iraq of 2 Minds About U.S." *The New York Times* (3 June 2009): A6, A10.

Sacks, David. *Letter Perfect: The Marvelous History of our Alphabet from A to Z*. (Also titled *Language Visible: Unraveling the Mystery of the Alphabet from A to Z*.) New York: Broadway Books, 2003.

Sager, Juan C. *Language Engineering and Translation*. Amsterdam: John Benjamins, 1994.

Sampson, Hannah. "Language of Choice." *The Miami-Herald*, 20 Oct. 2008, 1B, 6B.

Samuels, David. "Grand Illusions." *The Atlantic* (June 2007): 72.

Samuelsson-Brown, Geoffrey. *A Practical Guide for Translators*, 4th rev. ed. Clevedon, Eng.: Multilingual Matters, 2004.

Sawyer, David B. *Fundamental Aspects of Interpreter Education: Curriculum and Assessment*. Amsterdam: John Benjamins, 2004.

Schmid, Randolph E. "Technology and Evolution." *Hartford Courant* (11 Dec. 2007): A3.

Seleskovitch, Danica. *L'interprète dans les conférences internationales: problèmes de langage et de communication*. Paris: Minard, 1968.

_____. Trans., Dailey, Stephanie, and E. Norman McMillan. *Interpreting for International Conferences: Problems of Language and Communication*. Washington, DC: Pen & Booth, 1978, rev. 1994, 2001.

_____. *Langage, Langues et Mémoire; Etude de la prise de notes en interprétation*. Paris: Minard, 1975.

_____. "Language and Cognition." In D. Gerver and H. Wallace Sinaiko, eds. *Language, Interpretation, and Communication*. New York & London: Plenum, 1978.

_____. *Systematic Approach to Teaching Interpretation*. Trans., Jacolyn Harmer. Rockville, MD: Registry of Interpreters for the Deaf (RID), 1989.

Sofer, Morry. *The Translator's Handbook*, 5th ed., rev. Rockville, MD: Schreiber, 2004.

Solís, Gerardo, et al. *West's Spanish-English/English-Spanish Law Dictionary*. St. Paul, MN: West Group, 1992.

Spaulding, Robert K. *A Textbook of Modern Spanish*. New York: Holt, 1954. Revision of Marathon Montrose Ramsey. *A Text-book on Modern Spanish Grammar*. 1894.

Stavans, Ilan. *Spanglish: The Making of a New American Language*. New York: HarperCollins, 2003.

Stockwell, Robert, et al. *The Grammatical Structures of English and Spanish*. Constructive Spanish Series. Chicago: University of Chicago Press, 1965.

Swabey, Laurie, and Pam Sherwood-Gabrielson. *Introduction to Interpreting: An Instructor's Manual*, 2nd ed. Minneapolis, MN: Program in Translation and Interpreting, University of Minnesota Press, 1999, 2008.

Taylor, Martin C. "Bilingulism, the Brain, and Creativity." *Proteus*. (Spring 2010).

_____. *Sensibilidad religiosa de Gabriela Mistral*. Madrid: Gredos, 1975.

_____. "La trayectoria espiritual de Gabriela Mistral a la luz de 60 escritores." *Patrimonio Cultural*. Santiago, Chile: Dirección de Bibliotecas, Archivos y Museos, 2008.

Thiery, Christopher. "True Bilingualism and Second-Language Learning." In D. Gerver and H. Wallace Sinaiko, eds. *Language, Interpretation, and Communication*. New York & London: Plenum, 1978.

Thompson, Mel. *Ethics*. Chicago, IL: NTC/Contemporary Publishing, 2000.

Tully, Elizabeth. *The Forebrain*. Philadelphia: Chelsea House, 2006.

United States. Congress. Civil Rights Act, 1964. Title VI, Section 601.

_____. "Contractors' Support of U.S. Operations in Iraq." GPO: Washington, D.C., August 2008. See *www.cbo.gov/ftpdocs/96xx/doc9688/08–12–Iraqcontractors.pdf*.

_____. Court Interpreters Act, 1978. Public Law 95–539. Title 18, § 1827(d) 1–2. 28 October 1978.

_____. Court Interpreters Act, 1988. Public Law 100–702, # 709. Amendments (18 U.S.C.), Subsection k.

United States Executive Branch. Department of Labor. Bureau of Labor Statistics. *Occupational Outlook Handbook*. "Interpreters and Translators." Washington, DC: U.S. Government Printing Office, 2007. See also *www.bls.gov*.

_____. Clinton, William J. Executive Order 13166, reinforces Title VI, Civil Rights Act. (11 Aug. 2000). *See Civil Rights Forum*. "Improving Access to Federal Services for the Limited English Proficient." Vol. 14:3 (Summer-Fall 2001): 1.

_____. Carter, James Earl (*Jimmy*). Court Interpreter's Act. October 29, 1978.

United Sates Judicial Branch. "Court Interpreter's Improvement Act Report." Washington, DC: U.S. Government Printing Office, 1988.

Vázquez-Ayora, Gerardo. *Introducción a la Traductología*. Washington, DC: Georgetown University Press, 1977.

Virginia Supreme Court. Judicial Planning Department. "General Information on Foreign Language Interpreters and Spanish Language Interpreter Certification in Virginia's Courts." Richmond, VA: Judicial Council of Virginia, 2006. See *http://www.courts.state.va.us/interpreters/usage.html*.

_____. "Voluntary Certification Process for Spanish Language Interpreters Serving Virginia Courts." See *http://courts.state.va.us/fli_spanish_cert.html*.

Wade, Nicholas. "Evolutionary Theory of Right and Wrong." *The New York Times* (31 Oct. 2006).

_____. "Scientist Finds the Beginnings of Morality in Primate Behavior." *The New York Times* (3 March 2007): F3.

_____, ed. *The Science Times Book of Language and Linguistics*. New York: Lyons Press, 2000.

Weaver, Carl H. *Human Listening: Processes and Behavior*. New York: Bobbs-Merrill, 1972.

*Webster's Collegiate Dictionary*. New York: Random House, 1995. Also 10th ed. Springfield, MA: Merriam-Webster, 2001.

Widlung-Fantini, Anne. *Danica Seleskovitch*. Paris: Age D'Homme, 2000.

Wisconsin Supreme Court. Office of Court Operations. "The Wisconsin Court Interpreters Handbook: A Guide for Judges, Court Commissioners, Attorneys, Interpreters, and Other Court Users." Madison, WI: Director of State Courts Office. See www.wicourts.gov/circuit/courtinterpreter2005.

Wortman, Camille, Elizabeth F. Loftus, and Mary E. Marshall. *Psychology*. New York: Knopf, 1988.

Wright, Robert. *Nonzero: The Logic of Human Destiny*. New York: First Vintage, 2000.

# Suggested Readings

Akmajian, Adrian, Richard A. Demers, and Robert M. Harnish. *Linguistics: An Introduction to Language and Communication.* Cambridge: MIT Press, 1984.

Almeida, F. M., and S. Zahler, eds. *Manual for Superior Court Interpreters.* Los Angeles, CA: Los Angeles Superior Court, 1981.

Appiah, Kwame Anthony. *Experiments in Ethics.* Cambridge: Harvard University Press, 2008.

Atwater, Eastwood. *"I Hear You": Listening Skills to Make You a Better Manager.* New York: Prentice Hall, 1981.

Ausubel, David P., Joseph D. Novak, and Helen Hanesian. *Educational Psychology: A Cognitive View.* New York: Holt, 1978.

Benmaman, Virginia. "Legal Interpreting: An Emerging Profession." *The Modern Language Journal,* 76:IV (1992).

_____, Norma C. Connolly, and Scott Robert Loos. *Bilingual Dictionary of Criminal Justice Terms* (English/Spanish). Binghamton, NY: Gould, 1991.

Bever, Thomas G. "The Cognitive Basis for Linguistic Structures." In John R. Hayes, ed. *Cognition and the Development of Language.* New York: Wiley, 1970.

Birdwhistell, Ray L. *Kinesics and Context: Essays on Body Motion Communication.* Philadelphia: University of Pennsylvania Press, 1970.

Bransford, John D., and Jeffery J. Franks. "The Abstraction of Linguistic Ideas." *Cognitive Psychology* 2–4 (1971): 331–350.

Cataldo, Bernard F., et al. *Introduction to Law and the Legal Process.* New York: Wiley, 1980.

Chaffee, John. *The Thinker's Way: 8 Steps to a Richer Life.* Boston: Little, Brown, 1998.

Congrat-Butler, Stefan, ed., comp. *Translation and Translators: An International Directory and Guide.* New York: Bowker, 1979.

Davies, Paul. "Taking Science on Faith." *The New York Times* (24 Nov. 2007).

Dean, Cornelia. "Scientific Savvy? In U.S., Not Much." *The New York Times* (30 Aug. 2005).

Deutscher, Guy. *The Unfolding of Language: An Evolutionary Tour of Mankind's Greatest Invention.* New York: Holt, 2005.

Dreifus, Claudia. "How Culture Pushed Us to the Top of the Food Chain." *The New York Times* (10 May 2005).

Edelman, Gerald M., and Giulio Tononi. *A Universe of Consciousness: How Matter Becomes Imagination.* New York: Basic Books, 2002.

Erickson, Bonnie, et al. "Speech Style and Impression Formation in a Court Setting: The Effects of 'Powerful' and 'Powerless' Speech." *Journal of Experimental Social Psychology,* 14 (3) (1978): 266–279.

Falk, Julia S. *Linguistics and Language: A Survey of Basic Concepts and Implications.* New York: Wiley, 1978.

Fasold, Ralph. *The Sociolinguistics of Society.* Oxford: Basil Blackwell, 1984.

Figliulo, James R. "Breaking the Language Barrier." *Litigation,* 10–2 (1984): 32–33, 62–63.

Fiske, Susan T., and Shelley E. Taylor. *Social Cognition.* New York: McGraw-Hill, 1991.

Framer, Isabel. "Interpreters as Officers of the Court: Scope and Limitations of Practice." *NAJIT. Proteus,* XIV: 2 (Summer 2005).

Gambier, Yves, Daniel Gile, and Christopher Taylor, eds. *Conference Interpreting: Current Trends in Research.* Amsterdam: John Benjamins, 1995.

Gile, David. *Basic Concepts for Interpreter and Translator Training.* Amsterdam: John Benjamins, 1995.

Grosjean, F. *Life with Two Languages: An Introduction to Bilingualism.* Cambridge, MA: Harvard University Press, 1982.

Gurowitz, E. M. *The Molecular Basis of Memory.* New York: Prentice Hall, 1969.

Haidt, Jonathan. *The Happiness Hypothesis: Finding Modern Truth in Ancient Wisdom.* New York: Basic Books, 2006.

Hammond, Deanna, ed. *Professional Issues for Translators and Interpreters.* Amsterdam: John Benjamins, 1995.

Hauser, Marc D. *Moral Minds: How Nature Designed Our Universal Sense of Right and Wrong.* New York: HarperCollins, 2006.

Hayes, John R., ed. *Cognition and the Development of Language.* New York: Wiley, 1970.

Hirst, William, Ulric Neisser, and Elizabeth Spelke. "Divided Attention: People Can Learn to Do Complicated Things at Once and Neither Activity Has to Suffer." *Human Nature* 1–6 (1978–1979): 54–61.

Howe, Michael J. A. "Using Students' Notes to Examine the Role of the Individual Learner in Acquiring Meaningful Subject Matter." *Journal of Educational Research,* 64:2 (October 1970): 61–63.

Huriash, Lisa J. "Interpreters Will Have Remote Access: Technology Allows Translators to Work Away from Courtroom." Sun-Sentinel (18 January 2010) 3B.

Jones, Rodney R., Charles M. Sevilla, and Gerald F. Uelmen. *Disorderly Conduct: Verbatim Excerpts from Actual Cases*. New York: Norton, 1987.

Joos, Martin. *The Five Clocks*. Bloomington: Indiana University Press, 1967.

Kaplan, Steven M. *Wiley's English-Spanish, Spanish-English Business Dictionary*. New York: Wiley, 1996.

Kelly, L. G. *The True Interpreter*. New York: St. Martin's, 1979.

Kihlstrom, John F. "The Cognitive Unconscious." *Science* 237 (1987): 1445–1452.

Kolb, Bryan, and Ian Q. Whishaw. *Fundamentals of Human Neuropsychology*. New York: W. H. Freeman, 1985.

Krashen, Stephen D. *Principles and Practice in Second Language Acquisition*. Oxford: Pergamon, 1982.

Krawutschke, Peter W. "The Proposed ATA Program Accreditation." Translation Excellence: Assessment, Achievement, Maintenance. American Translators Association Scholarly Monograph Series, ed., Marilyn Gaddis Rose. Binghamton, NY: SUNY Center at Binghamton, vol. 1, 1987.

Krawutschke, Peter, ed. *Translator and Interpreter Training and Foreign Language Pedagogy*. Binghamton, NY: SUNY University Press, 1989.

Kurzweil, Ray. *The Singularity Is Near*. New York: Viking, 2005.

Labov, William. *Sociolinguistic Patterns*. Philadelphia: University of Pennsylvania Press, 1972.

Lambert, Sylvie, and Barbara Moser-Mercer. *Bridging the Gap: Empirical Research in Simultaneous Interpretation*. Amsterdam: John Benjamins, 1994.

Le Ny, Jean-François. "Psychosemantics and Simultaneous Interpretation." In D. Gerver and H. Wallace Sinaiko, eds. *Language, Interpretation, and Communication*. New York & London: Plenum, 1978.

Levitin, Daniel J. *This Is Your Brain on Music: The Science of a Human Obsession*. New York: Dutton, 2006.

Lind, Allan E., et al. "Social Attributions and Conversation Style in Trial Testimony." *Journal of Personality and Social Psychology*, 36:12 (1978): 1558–1567.

López Guix, Juan Gabriel, and Jacqueline Minett Wilkinson. *Manual de traducción*. Barcelona: Editorial Gedisa, 1997.

Marslen-Wilson, William D. "Linguistic Structure and Speech Shadowing at Very Short Latencies." *Nature* 244 (1973): 522–523.

McCroskey, James C., and R. Samuel Mehrley. "Effects of Disorganization and Nonfluency on Attitude Change and Source Credibility." *Speech Monographs*, 36:1 (1969): 13–21.

Namy, Claude. "Reflections on the Training of Simultaneous Interpreters: A Metalinguistic Approach." In D. Gerver and H. Wallace Sinaiko, eds. *Language, Interpretation, and Communication*. New York & London: Plenum, 1978.

Newington, Veronica, Pam Sherwood-Gabrielson, and Laurie Swabey. *Consecutive Interpreting: An Instructor's Manual*. Minneapolis, MN: Program in Translation and Interpreting, University of Minnesota Press, 2008.

Ornstein, Robert, and Richard F. Thompson. *The Amazing Brain*. Boston: Houghton, 1984.

Pei, Mario. *Invitation to Linguistics: A Basic Introduction to the Science of Language*. Garden City, NY: Doubleday, 1965.

Pinker, Steven. *Blank Slate: The Modern Denial of Human Nature*. New York: Viking, 2002.

_____. *How the Mind Works*. New York: Norton, 1997.

_____. "Sniffing Out the Gay Gene." *The New York Times* (17 May 2005).

_____. *Words and Rules: The Ingredients of Language*. New York: Basic Books, 1999.

_____, and Paul Bloom. "Natural Language and Natural Selection." *Behavioral and Brain Sciences*, 13 (1990): 707–784.

Rawls, John. *Law of Peoples*. Cambridge: Harvard University Press, 1999.

_____. *Theory of Justice*. Cambridge: Harvard University Press, 1971.

Richards, Jack C. "Listening Comprehension: Approach, Design, Procedure." *Tesol Quarterly*, 17–2 (June 1983): 219–240.

Robinson, Douglas. *Who Translates? Translation Subjectivities beyond Reason*. Albany, NY: SUNY University Press, 2001.

Romero, Simon. "In Babel of Tongues, Suriname Seeks Itself." *The New York Times*, 23 Mar. 2008, 10.

Sales, Bruce Dennis. *The Trial Process*. New York: Plenum, 1981.

Schank, Roger C., and Robert P. Abelson. *Scripts, Plans, Goals and Understanding*. Hillsdale, NJ: Lawrence Erlbaum, 1977.

Schlesinger, Arthur, Jr. "Forgetting Reinhold Niebuhr." *New York Times Review of Books*, 18 Sept. 2005.

Seco, Manuel. *Diccionario Glosario de dudas y dificultades de la lengua española*. Madrid: Espasa-Calpe, 1986.

Shubin, Neil. "Birds Do It. Bees Do It. Dragons Don't Need To." *The New York Times*, 24 Feb. 2007.

_____. *Your Inner Fish: A Journey into the 3.5-Billion-Year History of the Human Body*. New York: Pantheon, 2008.

Stecconi, Ubaldo. "Semiotics." In Mona Baker and Gabriela Saldanha, eds. *Routledge Encyclopedia of Translation Studies*. London & New York: Taylor & Francis/Routledge, 2009.

Sukhodrev, Viktor. "A Quiet Middleman for Presidents and Comrades." *The New York Times* (1 October 2005).

Uhlenbeck, F. M. "On the Distinction between Linguistics and Pragmatics." In D. Gerver and H. Wallace Sinaiko, eds. *Language, Interpretation, and Communication*. New York & London: Plenum, 1978.

Wilson, E. O. *Consilience*. New York: Vintage, 1998.

Wilss, Wolfram. "Syntactic Anticipation in German-English Simultaneous Interpreting." In D. Gerver and H. Wallace Sinaiko, eds. *Language, Interpretation, and Communication*. New York & London: Plenum, 1978.

# Index